P9-DZA-018

BUILDING
FOR A
LIFETIME

BUILDING FOR A LIFETIME

THE DESIGN AND CONSTRUCTION OF FULLY ACCESSIBLE HOMES

Margaret Wylde, Adrian Baron-Robbins and Sam Clark

The Taunton Press

Back-cover photos:
Whirlpool Corporation (left),
Kevin Ireton (right).

Taunton
BOOKS & VIDEOS
for fellow enthusiasts

First printing: January 1994
Printed in the United States of America

A FINE HOMEBUILDING Book

FINE HOMEBUILDING® is a trademark of The Taunton Press,
Inc., registered in the U.S. Patent and Trademark Office.

The Taunton Press, 63 South Main Street, Box 5506,
Newtown, CT 06470-5506

Library of Congress Cataloging-in Publication Data

Wylde, Margaret A.
    Building for a lifetime : The design and construction
of fully accessible homes / Margaret Wylde, Adrian
Baron-Robbins and Sam Clark.
        p.   cm.
    "A Fine Homebuilding book" — T.p. verso.
    Includes bibliographical references and index.
    ISBN 1-56158-036-8
    1. House construction.   2. Physically handicapped
— Dwellings.   I. Baron-Robbins, Adrian.   II. Clark,
Sam. Title.
690 '.8 — dc20   93-20764
                                        CIP

ACKNOWLEDGMENTS

The authors would like to express their gratitude to the following:

the National Institute for Disability Rehabilitation and Research for its generous support of the research grant that led to much of the learning incorporated in this book;

the Institute for Technology Development, especially the Advanced Living Systems Division, for its patience and support;

the Mississippi Department of Rehabilitation Services, for providing a building to house our research environments.

Also deserving of thanks are the people who contributed in various ways to the book. Many companies generously donated products for our research environments, including: American Standard, Broan Manufacturing Co., CDI Wholesale Cabinet Supplies, Ferno-Ille, Gemini Distributors, HEWI, Honeywell, Hood Manufacturing Co., KitchenAid, LIFESPEC Cabinet Systems, LUWA Corporation, Meridian Mattress Factory, Milliken & Company, Moen Group, Pierce-Etheridge Furniture Group, Preso-Matic Lock Company, The Rose Hill Company, Sherwin-Williams Company, Waltec Sinkware and Whirlpool Corporation.

People who supplied us with photographs, ideas and inspiration include Karen Seeger and Michael Birnbaum; Randy and Gloria LaBay; David Palmer, David Scheckman and Barney Carlson of Iron Bridge Woodworkers and Builders; plumbers John Stead and Bill St. Cyr; Chryss Jones of the Vermont Center for Independent Living; Bob Weber of Weber Accessibility Systems; Susan Behar, ASID; Arthur Shuster, Inc.; Engelbrect and Griffin, Architects; Backen Arrigoni & Ross; University of Wisconsin-Stout Department of Industrial Design; Vocational Rehabilitation Services Division of South Carolina; the Design Coalition; Max Jacobson of Jacobson, Silverstein and Winslow, Architects; Della Davidson, Wobble and Sara Davidson; Wilbert and Mildred Ellis; Irene Getchell; and William Moore and family.

We would also like to thank the many people who have served as research subjects in our studies, as well as our editors, Jeff Beneke, who first imagined this project and worked tirelessly to make it happen, and Ruth Dobsevage, who worked cheerfully and meticulously to chase the final details of compiling the book.

CONTENTS

INTRODUCTION

This book is about building houses that will meet the needs of people throughout their lives. Building for a lifetime means designing and constructing living environments that conform with the needs and abilities of the occupants at any age. Despite the vast technological changes that surround us, we have yet to witness much innovation in the construction of our houses to support the variations in human abilities that are inevitable among people of different ages, genders and sizes. Houses are built to shelter humans, but their construction is guided by designs and dimensions that often demonstrate ignorance of actual human abilities, and are more likely to be determined by the convenience of manufacturers, shippers, designers and builders.

We intend this book to be a complete guide to building living environments, both interior and exterior spaces, for people of differing abilities. For years we have been part of a large group of people studying and advocating a change in the way we approach the design and construction of the built environment. This movement has assumed a number of terms and descriptions: accessible, barrier-free, universal design, inclusive design, aging in place, building for a lifetime. Some may quibble over the appropriateness of these terms, but we use them interchangeably. Whatever the terminology, our fundamental goal remains the same: houses that people can use fully throughout their lives.

This book is needed because there is no single, comprehensive source of information on accessible design for the designer, builder and home owner. The sources that are available tend to be limited in scope and to focus exclusively on the needs of wheelchair users, while ignoring other variations in human abilities and forms. And, given changing demographics and family structure, the costs of continuing to build as we have in the past are prohibitive. Too often, design professionals allow the built environment to define the capabilities of the resident. We prefer to reverse this approach: architecture should be defined by human needs and abilities.

This book is needed because building design standards do not address the design needs of more than one-third of our population. A revolution in building design standards is long overdue. Recent legislation, especially the Americans with Disabilities Act of 1990, has brought much-needed attention to the rights of all persons to enjoy equal access to places of work, leisure and recreation. But these standards focus on public places and work environments, and they offer minimal recommendations, not optimal ones. Further, they tend to foster the lingering image of disability as something different or unusual. We suggest, however, that humans do not fit neatly into categories of "abled" or "disabled." Rather, the scope of human abilities is a continuum, and an ever-changing one at that.

An elderly person with disabilities resulting from a stroke who is living in a thoughtfully designed environment can be more "abled" than a young injured athlete temporarily confined to a wheelchair who is living in a traditionally designed house.

Barrier-free design standards have been evolving for more than 30 years and have maintained a consistent focus on individuals who use wheelchairs. While these recommendations are good and needed, they fall short of meeting the needs of 98% of the more than 43 million people with a disability. Only about 3% of the "disabled" population uses a wheelchair (LaPlante, Hendershot and Moss, 1992), and all have a wide variation in their capabilities. Some benefit from wheelchair-accessible design, some don't.

We are accustomed to adapting ourselves to the built environment rather than adapting the built environment to meet our needs. The building and its contents have been considered immutable, and anyone unable to conform to the prevailing conditions must be impaired or disabled. You are disabled if you are unable to climb the steps, open the door, switch on the light, cook a meal or take a bath independently. But by eliminating the stairs, widening the doors, relocating the light switches and changing the layout and types of fixtures in the kitchen and bathroom, your disability can be made to vanish. Disabling environments are often the cause of "disabled" individuals. It is time for us to realize that it is much easier to alter the built environment than it is to change the human form. This book asks the reader to focus on the plasticity of function; to consider how the environment can be adapted to serve the many differences among people.

It is costly to continue to create living environments that work for only part of the population, part of the time. Converging social and demographic changes make it imperative that we overhaul our design and construction standards. Many people are living much longer than in the past but, because of a declining birthrate, there are fewer young people to care for them. And women, the traditional family service providers, are increasingly employed outside of the home. Further, the cost of providing private care is skyrocketing. In 1900, only 4% of the American population was over the age of 65, and there was an abundance of younger people in the extended family to care for them. Today, approximately 12% of the population is over 65, and that number is rising quickly. Having to provide care for someone who can no longer function independently can require changing jobs, moving and tremendous financial sacrifice.

The inability to function independently can take many forms. If you can no longer climb the stairs to the second floor of your house, you effectively lose half of your living environment. If you can no longer climb a ladder or get around in your yard to perform basic maintenance on the house, you have to pay someone else to do the work, and you feel inadequate. If you lose the ability to use the toilet or bathe independently, you lose much of your personal privacy. If you can no longer retrieve items from hard-to-reach shelves, you become dependent on others — or do without.

Faced with these dilemmas, many people are forced against their wishes to sell their homes and move to an environment more compatible with their abilities. Others cannot afford to sell and move, to remodel or to hire help. They become virtual prisoners in a home full of barriers. Many in this group steadily reduce the amount of the house that they use. They stop climbing the stairs, put a commode chair next to the bed because the bathroom is too far away, and get a small toaster oven because they can no longer reach or operate the controls on their stove. The garden and orchard are neglected, the books gather dust on inaccessible bookshelves, the sunken living room is too difficult to reach.

Most builders, architects, home buyers and home owners misunderstand the concept of universal design, assuming that it applies only to people with disabilities. At the same time, very few people consider themselves disabled. We once asked a man who had both legs amputated if he considered himself disabled. "No," he replied. "I am an accountant." He defined himself not by the fact that he could not walk and was severely limited by his environment, but by the work he could do. His work, his life, did not require legs. He did not see himself as different from others.

People with significant limitations caused by arthritis, muscular dystrophy, accidents and illnesses do not see themselves as disabled. Yet few people do not at one time or another, temporarily or permanently, become disabled by their living environment. The built environment, and the products that go in it, should be designed to accommodate people who have limited capacity, rather than under the assumption that everyone operates at full capacity.

Everyone appreciates good design. In our research studies we have observed people ranging in age from 15 to over 90 and people ranging in ability from no limitations to multiple limitations. The design flaws that stopped (i.e., "disabled") those with reduced capacity are the same design flaws that those without disabling conditions find inconvenient, troublesome, uncomfortable, dumb or "cheap." Conversely, improvements that make products or environments more user-friendly for those with limitations are also appreciated by able-bodied people.

Accessibility is not the same thing as having one accessible entrance, one accessible bathroom and one accessible bedroom in each house. That attitude constitutes what we call the "ghetto approach" to accessibility. An accessible house, a true lifespan house, opens all the rooms of the house to everyone, regardless of abilities.

The revolution in building design must encourage, compel and reward the designer who helps to create a universal, inclusive environment. Builders and developers must begin to see the

Limitations in L.E.A.D. 2010 Research Subjects

Difficulties in performing common movements limit a person's ability to function in the home. At right is a list of limitations of L.E.A.D. 2010 research subjects in descending order, from the most common and most limiting to the least common and least limiting in the residential environment.

1. Overall strength
2. Bending, stooping and kneeling
3. Walking
4. Standing
5. Maintaining balance
6. Using the hands to grasp
7. Coordinating movements (for example, muscles working together to walk, climb stairs or tie shoelaces)
8. Sitting
9. Using hands to move objects
10. Seeing
11. Moving the head right to left and up and down
12. Hearing

importance and necessity of creating buildings that serve people of all ages and abilities and to adopt universal design as the rule rather than the exception.

The Research Behind This Book

Much of the information in this book represents the results of research studies conducted at the Institute for Technology Development in Oxford, Mississipppi. We have studied and measured the abilities of people of all ages, but have concentrated on individuals with diminished capacity.

In 1986 the Institute for Technology Development received a grant from the National Institute for Disability Rehabilitation and Research to study and develop design criteria and performance standards for barrier-free environments. In addition to collecting and organizing information from previous research studies, the Institute built two 940-sq. ft. "study environments." These full-scale living laboratories were constructed to compare new ideas on product design and architecture with recent barrier-free standards (ANSI 117.1-1986). The study environments were constructed using conventional materials and techniques and looked like a regular house except that instead of ceilings they had catwalks overhead where researchers could stand to observe and record the motions of the research subjects.

The project was called L.E.A.D. 2010, which stands for the Laboratory for Efficient and Accessible Design for the year 2010 (the year that the first baby boomers will turn 65 years of age). The purpose of the project was to evaluate how well different people negotiated various living environments and what they thought of various products and architectural features.

Some limitations were common to nearly all of the participants in the study. The sidebar above lists the limitations of the participants in descending order from those causing the greatest difficulty to the greatest number of subjects to those causing less difficulty to fewer subjects.

The research subjects in this study were people between the ages of 18 and 88 who lived in the community. The 71 subjects were fairly evenly distributed across the age range, and 60% were women. More than 80% had graduated from high school, and 40% had at least some college education.

Tasks Performed by L.E.A.D. 2010 Research Subjects

Each of the 71 participants in the L.E.A.D. 2010 study performed the 17 routines listed below in two different barrier-free environments. Performance was monitored and evaluated by the researchers.

1. Enter the front door and move to the kitchen carrying a paper grocery sack loaded with one 2-liter bottle filled with water, one 5-lb. sack of flour and two rolls of paper towels.

2. Move from the entry door to the coat closet and put a coat on a hanger located on a clothes rod.

3. Move from lying down on the bed in the bedroom to the bathroom.

4. Load "dirty" clothes into the washing machine, add detergent, set the controls, unload weighted bags that simulated wet clothes from the machine.

5. Load wet clothes into the clothes dryer, set the controls, remove dry clothes from the dryer.

6. Get into, adjust the drain and faucet, and exit a bathing system called the Comfort Bath.

7. Get into and adjust the faucet and hand-held spray of a 36-in. by 36-in. shower with an 18-in. seat.

8. Get into, adjust the drain and faucet, and exit a conventional bathtub that had grab bars mounted according to ANSI 117.1 standards and an 18-in. seat built at the foot of the tub.

9. Wash hands, adjust faucets and drain controls at the lavatory.

10. Get onto a toilet with grab bars placed according to ANSI recommendations, reach for and retrieve a few sheets of toilet paper, and get off.

11. Retrieve a #2 can from the lowest shelf of the base cabinets, the highest reachable shelf of the base cabinets and the highest shelf of the wall cabinets.

12. Load and unload dishes, manipulate the faucets and drain at a sink. This task was completed three times, with the sink height adjusted to 28 in., 32 in. and 36 in.

13. Simulate a cooking activity, such as retrieving a carton of milk and egg carton from the refrigerator, getting a 1-qt. dish from the cupboard and a spoon from the silverware drawer and moving the dish from the counter to the stove or microwave.

14. Move two place settings (dinnerware, glass, cup, saucer and silverware) from the kitchen to the dining table in the adjacent dining area.

15. Open and close right-hinged and left-hinged entry doors, a sliding glass door, a bifold door, a sliding closet door, a double-leaf door and a pocket door.

16. Load the dishwasher with "dirty" dishes from the kitchen sink.

17. Simulate the use of the cooktop and microwave ovens by placing a cookware dish and adjusting the controls.

Each research subject spent almost six hours at the research site and was evaluated while completing a series of tasks in each of the environments. The goal was to assess the length of time needed to complete a series of tasks and to identify specific problems for virtually every task that would be completed in a home. The entire study was videotaped. The sidebar above lists the tasks that each subject was asked to perform.

The participants represented a diverse array of abilities, from those with no limitations to those who were unable to move from their motorized wheelchair without assistance. Sixteen (22.5%) of the participants did not use any assistive or prosthetic device, 26 (36.6%) used some device other than a wheelchair and 25 (35.2%) used a wheelchair more than 75% of the time.

The causes or conditions that impaired abilities among the

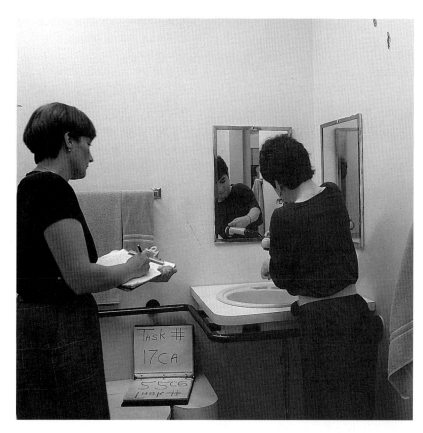

The L.E.A.D. 2010 research studied how individuals with a wide variety of abilities interact with their living environment. At left, a person with osteoarthritis is evaluated on the use of an ergonomically designed kitchen faucet, which replaced a traditional bathroom faucet. Below left, the subject is evaluated on how high she can reach the kitchen cabinets while holding a dish with both hands. In some studies, data points were captured by means of a camera lens connected to a computer. The camera was sensitive to infrared lights that were mounted on the subject, as shown below. (Photos: Institute for Technology Development.)

subjects included amputation of lower extremities (10 participants), paraplegia (8), multiple sclerosis (7), arthritis (6), polio or post-polio syndrome (6), cerebral palsy (3), ataxia (2), osteogenesis imperfecta (2), low-back pain (2), spina bifida (2) and stroke (2). The following conditions afflicted one each of the subjects: multiple injuries sustained in an automobile accident, weakness, blindness, congestive heart failure, dystonia, fractured femur and ligament, Guillain-Barré syndrome, hip dislocation, hydrocephalus, injured right arm, congenital deformation of the left knee, myotonic dystrophy, dead nerves in legs, osteomyelitis and quadriplegia.

The amount of information obtained from this study was enormous, but some of the lessons learned are relatively simple. The most significant lesson was that the designed environment is a major impediment to many of the participants. What many could accomplish in a few seconds or a single trip from one room to another required minutes and many trips for others. In most instances, the barrier could be readily identified, and therefore easily eliminated through better design.

Two key points emerged from our study of human factors (ergonomics). First, age alone is not a good indicator of a person's ability to use a product or negotiate an environment. Second, there is no clear distinction between able-bodied and disabled. Humans represent a continuum of abilities, not a dichotomy of abled and disabled.

Organization of the Book

The book is organized into five sections. The first section provides background information for designing and building residential environments for a lifetime. It includes discussions of the differences and abilities of people, the problems with present-day architectural and product design and tips for managing a construction project involving accessible design. The second section describes inclusive, universal design for the exterior components of the living environment (site, exterior surfaces, entryways, pathways and landscaping). The third section examines the design and new construction of the interior areas of the house. The fourth section deals with remodeling an existing environment. The fifth section discusses inclusive design for multi-family housing facilities and describes regulations and design specifics for the site and common areas.

Where appropriate, chapters end with a resource list of services and product manufacturers described in the chapter. A comprehensive bibliography at the end of the book cites source material and other publications pertinent to the material in each chapter.

About the Authors

The authors of this book represent diverse backgrounds and experiences.

Margaret Wylde is vice-president and director of the Advanced Living Systems Division of the Institute for Technology Development in Oxford, Mississippi. She spends most of her time doing human-factor and market research to define the abilities, needs and wants of people. She has evaluated thousands of people with differing abilities to define how the built and product environments can be made more user-friendly.

Adrian Baron-Robbins, who conceived most of the architectural designs and drawings in the book, is an architect with the Advanced Living Systems Division of the Institute for Technology Development in Oxford, Mississippi. For more than seven years he has been involved in research and design projects aimed at creating universally accessible homes and senior housing.

Sam Clark, who wrote Chapter 3 and reviewed much of the manuscript, has been a designer/builder for more than 25 years in Cambridge, Massachusetts, and in Vermont. He is the author of *Designing and Building Your Own House Your Own Way* and *The Motion-Minded Kitchen,* both published by Houghton Mifflin. From 1987 to 1992, he was involved with Goddard College in Plainfield, Vermont, working on a facilities study, renovations and grant programs and directing the work program. He works as a volunteer, board member and fundraising chair for the Central Vermont Habitat for Humanity. In 1991 he founded The Buildings Group in Plainfield, Vermont, a company that specializes in accessible design, affordable housing and facilities planning.

PART ONE

REDEFINING THE BUILT ENVIRONMENT

Our environment today is an eccentrically tailored cloak which enfolds all — but fits few. It binds here and chafes there, impairing the circulation and causing widespread irritation. The seams are frayed. Threadbare patches need reweaving, stains need removing.... Our environment urgently needs restyling, mending, sprucing up.
— National Association of Home Builders, 1965

CHAPTER ONE
A SURVEY
OF HUMAN
ABILITIES

More people can potentially benefit from accessible design than from conventional design. We estimate that at one time or another, 90% of us will be disabled by conventional building design. With our rapidly aging population, greater numbers of people are confronting the limitations of the environment in which they live.

Many more people than those who fit the legal definition of "disabled" are disabled by their environment. Legally, disabled people are those who are limited in performing work or limited in participating in specific major activities. Thus, we need to remember that the published numbers of people with disabilities are just the tip of the iceberg. There

Upper and Lower Reach Ranges For Men and Women of Average Height

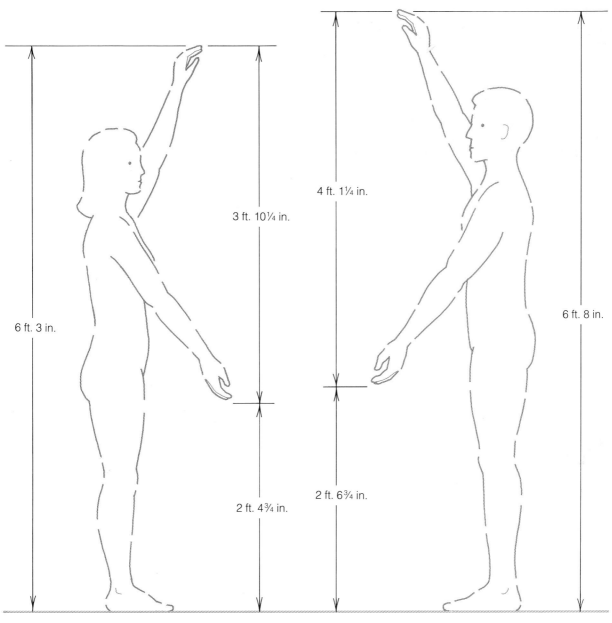

50th-percentile female

50th-percentile male

*The reaching height of the average male is 6 ft. 8 in., which is
5 in. higher than the reaching height of the average female. The
lower reach range while standing erect differs by only 2 in.
(2 ft. 6¾ in. for males, 2 ft. 4¾ in. for females). Much architectural
and product design strives to satisfy the midpoint between these
averages, a compromise that favors taller people, since almost
everyone can reach lower without assistance, but a shorter
person needs a stepstool or a ladder to reach higher.*

Functional Limitation Status
Persons 15 years and over by gender and age (numbers in thousands)

	Total	People with mild, moderate or severe functional limitations		People with severe functional limitations	
		Number	Percent	Number	Percent
Total males and females 15 and over	180,987	37,304	20.6	13,537	7.5
Males 15 to 64 years	75,551	9,487	12.6	2,315	3.1
Males 65 years and over	10,785	5,773	53.5	2,347	21.8
Males: total 15 and over	86,336	15,260	17.7	4,662	5.4
Females 15 to 64 years	79,014	12,352	15.6	3,682	4.7
Females 65 years and over	15,637	9,692	62.0	5,192	33.2
Females: total 15 and over	94,651	22,044	23.3	8,874	9.4

Source: U.S. Bureau of the Census, 1984 Survey of Income and Program Participation.

are many people who have difficulty interacting with the built environment who may not have been counted as having a disability.

A look at our coworkers at the Institute for Technology Development bears out the statistics. Of the nine full-time employees in our immediate office group, five currently spend significant amounts of time helping their parents (not to mention their grandparents) cope with their environments. One is building a new house with an upper floor intended for his mother-in-law, who is unable to live by herself because she becomes confused quite easily and forgets to take her medications. A chair lift is being installed to connect the two floors. This same employee's father, who is also incapable of living by himself, is being cared for by the employee's brother, who is retired.

The mother of another employee recently had surgery on both knees. She has gradually progressed over the past few months from walking with a walker to walking with a cane. The mother of another employee recently sold her house and moved in with him. She is in good health, but has retinitis pigmentosa, a condition that severely limits her vision. She is unable to see well enough to drive or to function very well outside of her home.

The father of another employee recently passed away. He had been injured in an automobile accident a few years ago and had been pretty much confined to their home because he used a wheelchair and was unable to get out of the house into the car. During his last few months (he had developed cancer), he was confined to his bed.

Another father has moved in with the brother of one of our colleagues. Dad has been in and out of the hospital over the years with a foot infection, which cost him a succession of toes and eventually the entire foot. He also has severe visual problems and is almost deaf (a hearing aid has been of little assistance). The family members spend considerable time attempting to communicate with him in the apartment they had to add on to their house.

The examples cited are by no means unusual. This chapter will explore the range of human abilities and limitations with the intention of enabling builders, designers and home owners to begin creating living environments that are more user friendly.

Much of the data in this chapter comes from a major research study completed during the 1980s. The National Institute on Aging has published information about the chronic conditions, disabilities and other aspects of health and social behavior among older residents of several communities in the United States (Cornoni-Huntley et al., 1986).

There are three categories of human abilities that are used in daily living: physical, sensory and cognitive. Physical abilities are influenced by size, strength, range of motion, manual dexterity and mobility. Sensory abilities used to monitor the home are vision, hearing, smell and touch. Cognitive abilities involve the brainwork needed to function within the home, such as understanding and remembering.

As shown in the chart on the facing page, 37.3 million people in the United States (21% of the population aged 15 and older) have sensory, physical or cognitive disabilities. These are the people who cannot work or who encounter serious problems participating in daily activities.

Homes are supposed to be safe havens, the shelters against the storm. But they are also the scenes of many fatal accidents, especially for the very young and very old. A house is safe for its occupants when its demands don't exceed their capacities. Safe, convenient and easy-to-use homes are built to accommodate differences over the lifespan.

Builders and architects who wish to be prepared for the 21st century must understand and be capable of building for the full range of human abilities. The aging of our population, combined with the activism of recent decades that helped bring us the Americans with Disabilities Act in 1990, have made people much more aware of the impact of building design on their lifestyles and personal independence. Increasingly, consumers will expect the residence to "fit" their physical, sensory and cognitive abilities.

PHYSICAL ABILITIES

Physical limitations affect many more people than those who use wheelchairs, walkers and crutches. Many people have significant problems with their living environments due to their size (height or width), lower back pain, fatigue or pain in their joints.

Sizes and standards   Height standards used as a reference in building and product design have been developed by adding the height of a large man to the height of a small woman and dividing the result by two. This formula yields an "average height" of 67.8 in. (5 ft. 8 in.). Unfortunately, this dimension is too high or too short for more than half of the population. It is more than 3 in. taller than the average woman and just 2 in. shorter than the average male.

The practice of attempting to accommodate all people through this kind of averaging is based on the logical, but faulty, assumption that building to the middle height will accommodate taller and shorter people equally. However, tall individuals don't need assistance from an external device to reach downward, bend, stoop or lower themselves, whereas short people cannot increase their reach (or height) above its limits without using a ladder, stepstool or other device. Building to a midpoint between the tallest male and shortest female prevents more than half of the females and all of the juveniles from using high cabinets, shelves, lights and other high items.

As shown in the drawing on p. 9, the highest comfortable reach for the average man is about 80 in., slightly more than 5 in. higher than the average woman. Conversely, the comfortable low reach while standing erect is 30.8 in. for males, while for women it is 28.7 in. Clearly there is less difference for low reach (2.1 in.) than for the high reach. Again, taller people are capable of reaching lower without assistance, while shorter people are required to climb on a stepstool, or chair or other convenient device to access areas beyond their reach.

Strength   Overall strength may be affected by gender, physical condition, health, age and posture. In our research we have found that people rank loss of strength as their most limiting and most pervasive problem. Loss of strength affects many routine activities. Hand strength is required when pinching or gripping a faucet, turning a door knob, opening a heavy door, carrying laundry or walking across the room. Muscle is required to lift the corner of a mattress when making the bed, to pull a loaded drawer from a cabinet, to operate a sliding glass door and to push a plug into a wall receptacle. Endurance and stamina are taxed when working in the kitchen, carrying items into or out of the house and taking care of many household chores.

Architectural and product design can affect the amount of strength required to complete a task. For example, pushing a plug into the wall is almost effortless when the outlet is easy to reach, especially if the person merely holds the electrical plug and pushes forward, using the weight of the body to help. Conversely, pushing a plug into a wall socket behind

Grip Strength

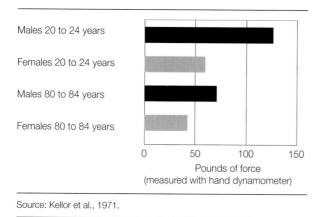

Males 20 to 24 years

Females 20 to 24 years

Males 80 to 84 years

Females 80 to 84 years

0   50   100   150

Pounds of force
(measured with hand dynamometer)

Source: Kellor et al., 1971.

the couch requires the person to perform a deep knee bend, to have a firm grasp on the plug with just the fingers and to exert sufficient force with the arm and hand in an awkward position. For some people this task is impossible, for others it is an awkward nuisance.

Grip strength is often considered an indicator of the overall strength of an individual. The grip strength of males and females is about equal from birth until about puberty, when males get a lot stronger and stay that way. On average, the grip strength of women is less than half that of men. At about age 40, the grip strength of both men and women begins to decline. The chart above shows the relative differences in grip strength among young and old men and women.

Another way to look at strength is to ask people what chores they can and cannot do. This sort of information bears on home design, especially on the amount and type of upkeep a home will require. As shown in the top chart on the facing page, almost 25% of the men between the ages of 65 and 70 cannot do heavy work such as shoveling snow, or washing windows, floors and walls. More than 60% of the men and 70% of the women over the age of 85 cannot perform heavy housework.

Range of motion Range of motion varies among individuals depending on their size, physical fitness, illnesses or injury. Range of motion encompasses bending, stooping, kneeling and reaching. People who

have a limited ability to bend at the waist or kneel are likely to encounter difficulties retrieving items from the floor, cleaning a bathtub or toilet, using the lower shelves in the kitchen, making beds and doing the laundry, among other things. People who have limited shoulder movement have trouble reaching items above their head.

Range of motion determines how we are able to use the space around us. A short person has a smaller range of motion than a tall person. Frequently, range of motion becomes restricted as we become older because of stiff joints, reduced physical agility, hip or knee problems, balance problems, low blood pressure and so on. As one of our research subjects, an active 85-year-old woman, told us, "Honey, when you get to be 85 you do not bend, you do not kneel, neither do you squat …"

Planning a lifespan house means planning an operating environment that takes into consideration differences in height, mobility and movement. As the middle chart on the facing page shows, more than 9% of the men and 15% of the women between the ages of 65 and 69 and almost 17% of the men and 30% of women 85 and older have some difficulty raising their arms above their shoulders. The limitation of reaching only to shoulder level reduces the upper reach range to about 53 in., even though a person's height may suggest a reach of 77 in.

Besides reaching above shoulder height, most homes demand access to the space just above the floor. As the bottom chart on the facing page shows, more than 30% of the men and 40% of the women between the ages of 65 and 69 have some difficulty stooping and crouching, while more than 40% of the men and 60% of the women 85 and older report difficulty stooping and crouching.

Manual dexterity Most houses demand good manual dexterity, which includes fine fingering movements such as gripping, grasping, turning, twisting or rotating items. Many people with small hands find it hard to grasp and turn large knobs or controls. Traditional doorknobs require good manual dexterity; to open a door, you have to grasp the doorknob with your hand, rotate the wrist and at the same time push or pull the weight of the door.

Opening cabinets and drawers, locking and unlocking doors and windows, adjusting thermostats,

Heavy Housework
Percentage of people who cannot do heavy housework such as shoveling snow and washing windows, walls and floors

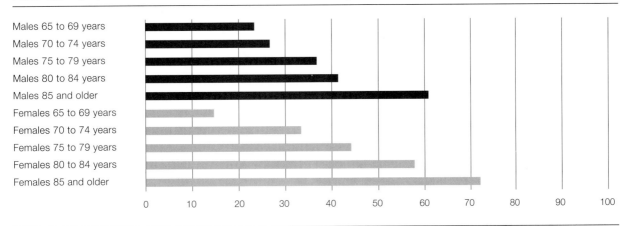

Range of Motion (Arms)
Percentage of people who have difficulty lifting their arms above their shoulders

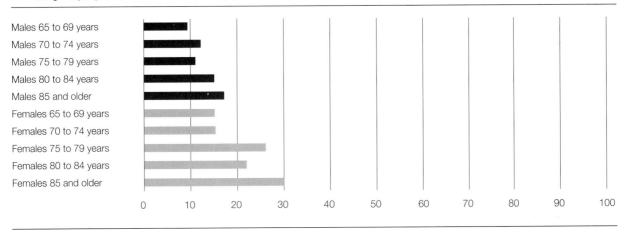

Range of Motion (Legs)
Percentage of people who have difficulty stooping and crouching

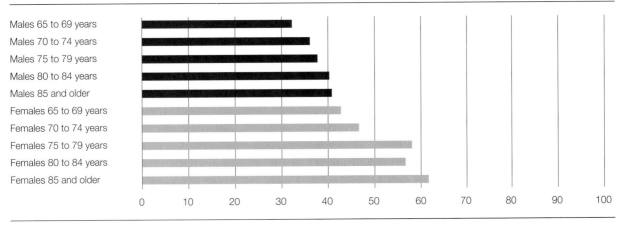

Source: Cornoni-Huntley et al., 1986.

Designing and building to abstract standards of human abilities force many people to confront barriers that needn't exist. These photos demonstrate some common demands that challenge many people: bending and reaching, pinching and pulling, gripping and twisting, standing on a stool and reaching, reaching across hot burners, and climbing stairs.

plugging and unplugging electrical cords, turning faucets on and off, opening and closing drains and turning cooktop burners on and off all demand fingers that are nimble and reasonably strong. The well-designed home, a house built for the lifespan, would minimize the use of objects that require fine fingering and would be outfitted with hardware and products designed for ease of use.

Movement The major movements performed in a home include getting from one place to another (walking or otherwise), standing in place, sitting and rising, lying down and getting up, going up and

down stairs and moving objects from one place to another. These movements require coordination among muscle groups and the ability to maintain balance.

Before designing a house with stairs, consider that more than 5% of the men and nearly 10% of the women between the ages of 65 and 69 and almost 20% of the men and about 33% of the women over the age of 85 years cannot climb stairs (see the chart on p. 16). (These are not people living in nursing homes, but people living in the community.)

People move about their homes in various ways, including walking, walking with assistance, wheeling (using a wheelchair or other wheeled de-

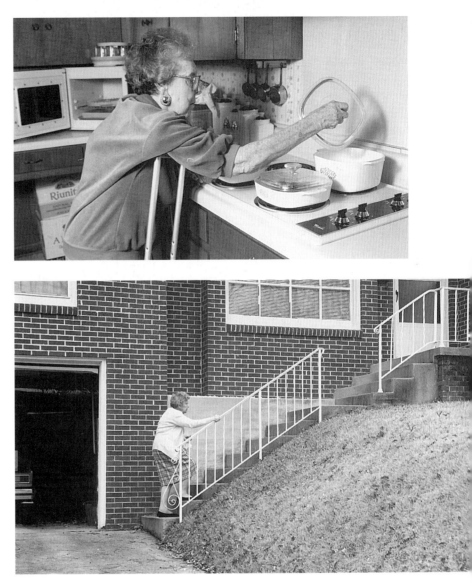

vice) and wheeling with assistance. Many who have difficulty getting about do not require the assistance of another person or a device. They may be limited in the distances they can walk, they may have to stay on one floor of the home because they cannot get up and down the stairs or they may be restricted to indoors. Other people have to use an assistive device such as a walker, cane, crutch, braces or artificial limb. Those with artificial limbs often do not encounter too many obstacles in the environment until they remove the limb before retiring or bathing.

Using a walker, cane or crutch occupies the user's hands and arms. People who use these devices require clear paths to items that are easy to reach. Many must relinquish the stability the cane or walker provides them in order to reach an electrical outlet placed close to the floor. Others find that they can use their walker to get everywhere in their living environment except the bathroom, where the door is too narrow.

Walkers come in a variety of sizes, shapes and forms. They may be equipped with small wheels. Newer wheeled walkers have large wheels, hand-operated brakes, baskets, trays, seats and a various accessories that add convenience and mobility to the device. The newer four-wheeled walkers, although

Movement
Percentage of people who say they cannot climb stairs

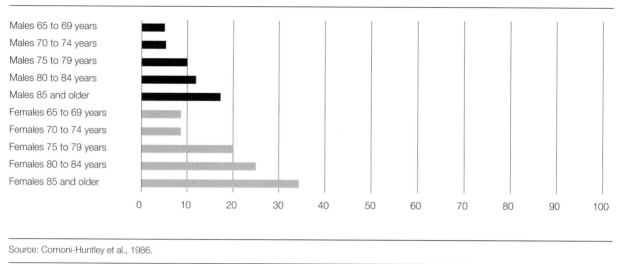

Males 65 to 69 years	
Males 70 to 74 years	
Males 75 to 79 years	
Males 80 to 84 years	
Males 85 and older	
Females 65 to 69 years	
Females 70 to 74 years	
Females 75 to 79 years	
Females 80 to 84 years	
Females 85 and older	

Source: Cornoni-Huntley et al., 1986.

they are designed for indoor use, are much better on rough terrain than the traditional walker.

Canes also are available in a variety of forms. While the walking stick used to be a fashion accessory, today it is considered an assistive device for individuals who have difficulty walking because of a problem with their feet or legs, lack of strength or balance. The traditional cane has a single leg with a variety of handle styles. Quad and tripod canes have multiple legs and are used by people who need a sturdy base when walking.

Crutches are often used on a temporary basis by people who are recovering from a fracture, sprain or surgical procedure. Some people use them on a permanent basis.

Users of canes, crutches or walkers should be considered one-handed. If they are to maintain their balance or stand erect, they usually must have one hand on the assistive device. This leaves only one hand free for opening doors, carrying items, operating the faucet set, and similar tasks.

Wheeled mobility Wheeled mobility, which has been the basis for many accessibility standards in the past, is undergoing a real transformation. First, many wheelchairs are becoming smaller, lighter in weight and less obtrusive. Many wheelchair users who have good upper-body strength need a chair only to get about — all they need is a good set of wheels and some comfortable seating. For these people, the high-sided, tall-backed chair with push handles can be replaced by a lightweight, flexible wheelchair that can easily fit under and through spaces that are inaccessible to larger, bulkier chairs.

Wheelchairs today are available that raise the user to a standing position. Not everyone who uses a wheelchair can use one with a standing aid, but many can. The primary problem some wheelchair riders have had with environments is that many spaces were beyond reach. The standing-aid wheelchair puts these spaces within reach.

The traditional wheelchair is about 42 in. long, 25 in. wide, 36 in. to 40 in. to the height of the push handles and up to 29 in. to the top of the armrest. When you add clearance for the user's toes, elbows, arms and hands that protrude beyond the wheelchair, the effective footprint of the chair becomes 48 in. long and 30 in. wide.

Three-wheeled scooters are becoming more popular. These devices have been created for both indoor and outdoor use. They present some greater challenges indoors because they are larger than a traditional wheelchair.

SENSORY ABILITIES

There are five primary human senses: vision, hearing, smell, touch and taste. Of these, only taste is not a factor in the design of a house.

Vision Many people who are blind or who have low vision become adept in many environments. Nonetheless, vision is important for safe and accurate performance of many household chores and is often adversely affected by the design of the home. Vision changes dramatically throughout the lifetime, and it can be corrected by assistive devices, medical procedures and improvement in lighting. But changes in vision are often gradual, and may go unnoticed or uncorrected.

Many homes have grossly inadequate lighting, particularly for older adults and for individuals who don't see well. Lighting in the home is often an afterthought, underbudgeted and ultimately incorrect. Careful consideration and better design of household lighting may go a long way in improving the overall ambience of a home, reducing the prospects of injury and aiding in the performance of daily activities.

At age 50, the retina receives about half of the light that it did in juvenile years. We experience a steadily decreasing ability to focus (power of accommodation), a steadily decreasing ability to adapt to changes in light level (dark adaptation) and a steadily decreasing resistance to glare.

Hearing Hearing is our 24-hour monitoring system. Even when asleep, our ears keep operating. Our sense of hearing tells us when the heater kicks on, when someone is at the door, when the telephone rings or when the smoke alarm goes off. A fairly mild hearing loss makes most of these sounds difficult to hear by themselves, and almost impossible to hear when there is competing background noise.

Although more than 25 million Americans have some degree of hearing loss (MarkeTrak, 1993), few of us are aware of hearing problems. We usually can't tell by looking that someone is having difficulty hearing. In fact, people who have hearing problems (especially those who are attempting to hide their problem by not wearing a hearing aid) are often thought to be a little "off," commenting inappropriately or nodding their head during a conversation that they can't hear. In other words, hearing problems are often hidden disabilities. More than 30% of the population over the age of 65 has difficulty hearing, and more than half of those over the age of 80 are hearing impaired (National Center for Health Statistics, 1990).

Hearing problems are not the same for all sounds. In general, people with hearing problems can hear sounds with low pitches rather well. These are the sounds of noise—the hum of motors, the loud bass on the stereo system, the lawn mower, the hair dryer and the washing machine. Many individuals who are hearing impaired have the greatest difficulty hearing high-frequency sounds. These are the important sounds of life. In fact, most of the speech sounds that help us discriminate among words (such as "fit," "hit," "sit" and "bit") are high-pitched sounds.

Planning an appropriate acoustical environment in the home means considering the sources of noise and wanted sound and determining how these sources may be isolated or enhanced. Basic principles of acoustics and a realization that most rooms have multiple uses both need to be considered. After all, a bedroom is not only a place to sleep and change clothes, but may also be a practice hall for a budding rock musician.

Smell The sense of smell is an important monitoring device. In many instances, smell is the first sense to be alerted to the presence of smoke, fire, gas and toxic fumes. Seven times as many people over the age of 65, as compared to those between the ages of 45 and 64, die every year in residential fires. Many die because they couldn't smell the smoke. Building a house for people who can't smell means planning an immediate escape route from each bedroom; specifying smoke detectors that detect smoke, gas and fire; and planning the warning and alerting system.

As we grow older our ability to detect and identify odors declines dramatically. As the top chart on p. 18 shows, the sense of smell begins its decline shortly after puberty. Research shows that a 65-year-old has about 10% of the capacity of a 15-year-old to discriminate among odors.

Smell
Decline in ability to discriminate among common odors as a function of age

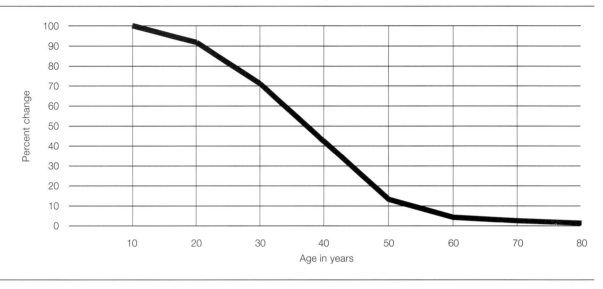

Touch
Decline in touch sensitivity as a function of age

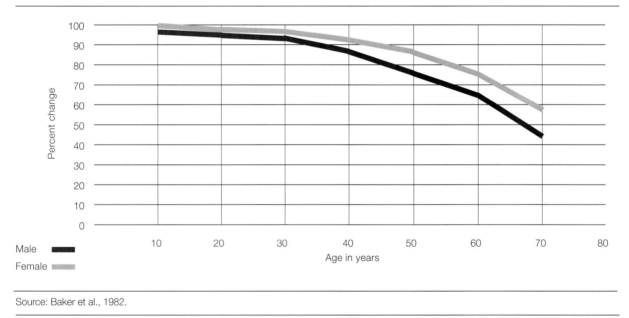

Male

Female

Source: Baker et al., 1982.

Touch   The sense of touch includes the sensation of cold and hot, the ability to orient oneself with respect to the environment (proprioception) and the ability to detect pressure. The receptors in our skin tell us if we are touching something, where it is in relation-

ship to our body, how much of our body is in contact with it and how firmly we are touching it and whether it is hot or cold.

The sense of touch warns us if something is sharp or too hot. It also helps us maintain our balance. When the sense of touch is disturbed, as it often becomes with advanced age, we are at risk for burns and falls.

The bottom chart on the facing page shows a general representation of the changes in the sense of touch over the lifespan. While touch is a sense that we rarely consider in planning a living environment, it should be kept in mind. Water heaters, mixer valves and other systems to protect the user from temperature extremes should be used routinely.

Balance and coordination   Balance and coordination are maintained through the sensory systems of vision, the vestibular system (which maintains equilibrium) and proprioception. (We use the term "sensory systems" to describe the process of neural communication from the sense organ to the brain centers and the communication among the brain centers.) We are best able to stay erect, walk steadily and right ourselves on a moving boat or bus if all three systems are functioning appropriately. We can even do well if only two of the three are working. If only one is working, however, we're in trouble. Many falls and injuries occur at night in the dark because the visual clues and sometimes also the proprioceptive cues aren't available.

COGNITIVE ABILITIES

We rarely stop to think. Our brains are so well programmed that we can usually function within our households without having to think about what we are doing — until, that is, we are learning to use a new product, or we've misplaced an item or we're somewhat disoriented because it is dark or we're a little groggy. Basic cognition is knowing. Underlying our knowledge of a particular moment in time — our knowledge of negotiating in our living environment — is a series of steps. We perform these steps without really being aware that we are.

First, we detect the elements of a situation. Then, we perceive the functions and comprehend the process. If cooking something in the oven, we turn the oven on by seeing (detecting) the presence of the controls. We perceive that the knobs on the oven are the devices for operating it. We comprehend their function and their relationship to heating the oven. We reach a hand forward, detect the control and grasp it. We turn the control in the direction necessary to increase the temperature in the oven. Our eyes send the stimuli to our brain to interpret the numbers on the control, while our brain comprehends its function. The action is accomplished with little thought or attention.

The effect of aging on cognition is the subject of significant debate. Despite adages like, "You can't teach an old dog new tricks," there is overwhelming evidence that we continue to learn and increase our knowledge throughout life. Aging does affect reaction time and the number of external stimuli that we can process at one time. Our ability to think does not change, but our ability to sort out competing inputs and to perceive the stimuli in our environment does.

As we become older we are also more susceptible to illnesses that affect cognitive abilities, such as Alzheimer's disease. A recent research report showed that 10% of the population over the age of 65 has Alzheimer's disease (Evans, 1989). Alzheimer's disease has taught us of the need to design and build houses that are "adultproof" as well as childproof. Building houses with the child's safety in mind is relatively simple, but an adult with dementia (particularly the early stages of dementia) presents a much bigger challenge. We can't just put potentially dangerous items higher — the afflicted person may be the tallest person in the household. The safe house of the future will need to have systems in place that will protect the occupants whether they are small or tall, young or old.

CHAPTER TWO
ARCHITECTURE AND PRODUCT DESIGN

We don't begrudge the animals their custom-designed environments in the zoo. The animals are, after all, captive. But we are distressed by the seeming lack of a concerted effort to develop a suitable living environment for human existence, because many humans, too, become captives in their own homes. When the demands of the built environment exceed their capacities, humans are confined to or excluded from rooms, homes and much of their communities. To provide for human needs, builders and designers must work together to ensure that the entire living environment — both the building itself and the products in the home — meet people's basic needs, in addition to structural integrity and affordability.

Electronic Controls

Well-designed products have controls that don't require fine fingering to operate. These electronic controls are shown in descending order, from easiest (1) to most difficult (7).

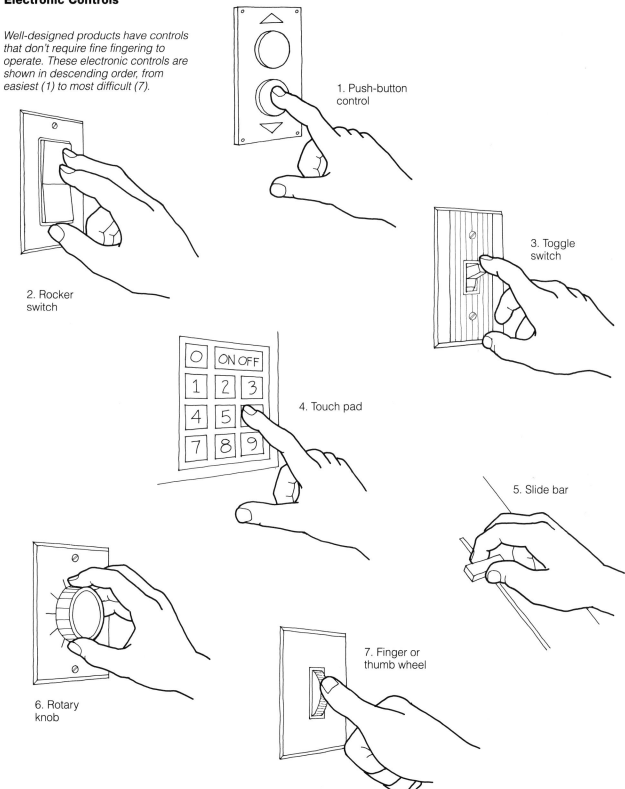

1. Push-button control

2. Rocker switch

3. Toggle switch

4. Touch pad

5. Slide bar

6. Rotary knob

7. Finger or thumb wheel

FUNDAMENTALS OF HOME DESIGN

There are four quality-of-life basics that should become a part of every house design:
• privacy
• sense of belonging
• sense of control
• sense of safety and security.

Each of these elements contributes to the sense of self-worth that people experience in their living environment. Homes should be designed to enhance self-worth. The quality-of-life basics should serve as fundamental measuring rods for assessing the design of living environments.

Privacy The degree to which privacy is important varies from person to person, but there are times when each of us wants to be left alone. Many may not consider privacy an issue — until it is taken from them. Unfortunately, many components of conventional home design are time bombs waiting to rob the occupants of their privacy. The bombs go off when the abilities of a family member changes. For example, multi-level homes where all of the facilities are not duplicated on each level may force significant changes in the household lifestyle in the event of an illness or injury. The ground-floor den may have to be converted into a bedroom so that the person who is unable to climb the stairs may be near the bathroom, kitchen and entry on that floor. Such a change will affect the patterns of privacy developed by all the members of the household.

We have seen house after house in which the ground-floor living room or den was turned into a sickroom, at a great loss of privacy to everyone. We have visited homes where the first thing one encounters upon entering the front door is someone in a hospital bed, with an oxygen tank, medicines and bandages littering what once was a coffee table.

Living rooms have to become sickrooms for a number of reasons. Perhaps the bedroom was too isolated or too small to accommodate a hospital bed. Perhaps the bathroom was too far away. Perhaps the doorway was too narrow, or the bedroom didn't have sufficient electrical power to handle all of the medical paraphernalia.

Ironically, doors, which are installed with the intention of providing privacy, are often one of the reasons it is lost. Far too many bathrooms have doors that are too narrow, with fixtures that are difficult to use and with space enough only for someone capable of walking erect. Don't build a bathroom that may force people who are temporarily or permanently disabled to seek help whenever they need to use it, making them more dependent than they need to be.

Because conventional home design does not plan for such contingencies, many people are forced by temporary or permanent physical limitations to turn public spaces in their house, here the front parlor, into a combination sickroom/bedroom.

Belonging   A sense of belonging in a living environment blends privacy with interaction with the other members of the household. Home design should create living environments that encourage belonging. When faced with a change in the abilities of a family member, a portion of the house may have to be remodeled so that the family member with a disability will have an area (bedroom and bathroom) that he or she can use. Many families build on a new barrier-free wing, which allows for individual privacy, but often at the loss of community. The individual becomes cut off from the rest of the house, and thus from the activities of the rest of the household. The separation serves as a regular reminder of the disability. The specially built environment takes away the person's sense of belonging.

Control   Having control over your surroundings provides a sense of competence and capability. Being defeated by your environment demoralizes and diminishes self-esteem.

People who can't go where they want and do what they want within a living environment are not in control. Being able to open doors and windows, go in and out of the house, insert a plug into a socket, get a drinking glass out of the cabinet, do one's own laundry and get something out the refrigerator are taken for granted by most of us. These seemingly insignificant acts provide us with an unquestionable sense of competence in our living environment.

Competence is often lost gradually, almost imperceptibly, with advancing age. Many slowly lose the ability to provide for the upkeep of their homes. They no longer feel capable of climbing a stepstool to change a light bulb. They feel less and less able to climb in and out of the bathtub. Loss of competence in a home makes it appear to be an increasingly more demanding and unfriendly place. An unfriendly home breeds a sense of loss and of loneliness, even if the aging person is living with others.

Safety and security   A home should make you feel safe and secure, whether you are in it by yourself or with others. Security comes from knowing that you are protected from the elements and intruders, that you can escape in the event of an emergency and that you can summon help.

Secure spaces in homes should be accessible to everyone living there. Door locks should be operable by all (except those for whom door locks are a protection, such as toddlers or adults with Alzheimer's disease). Any emergency spaces (tornado or earthquake shelters, for example) need to be planned for everyone. Everyone living in the household must understand what these spaces are for and must be able to get into them when necessary.

CONFRONTING THE DISABILITIES OF ARCHITECTURE

A disability is anything that puts a person at a disadvantage. Architecture can disable people. Change the design, and the disability disappears. In this section we discuss seven ways in which design can disable people, and we suggest corresponding rules for designing houses built for the lifetime.

Access to spaces   Architecture disables people when it limits their mobility, their access to spaces. Pathways are disabling when they require a change in level, when they are long rather than short, when they require turns when they could be straight, when their surfaces are rough rather than smooth and soft rather than hard. Access is denied when the opening is too narrow and when the door in the opening creates an obstacle someone cannot get around.

Rule 1. Assess every pathway and entry outside and within the home and ensure they are (to the greatest extent possible) flat, short, straight, smooth, firm and wide.

Demands on strength   Architecture disables when it demands that individuals exert more effort than they have the strength to accomplish. Unnecessary demands may be expected of people to travel distances, climb steps or stand in a particular place. When an environment doesn't provide options of working at different work surface heights, of sitting to accomplish a task instead of standing, it may put the occupant at a disadvantage.

A seated work space at the sink can help people who have reduced strength or are unable to stand. This woman uses crutches to travel short distances and a scooter for longer distances. With the seat at the kitchen sink she is able to work without being encumbered by her crutches. (Photo: Institute for Technology Development.)

Rule 2. Create environments that are easy to use. If traditional design standards typically involve standing, stamina and demands on strength, incorporate alternative methods for accomplishing the tasks. The best alternative may be less efficient than traditional design for some people, but for others the alternative may mean the difference between capability and disability. Some examples include providing two paths leading to an area, two different styles of doors, more than one work surface and more than one type of bathing system.

Demands on reach   Several architectural disabilities are created because components are designed and built without regard to the range of reach of the inhabitants. Cabinets, shelves, faucets, electrical outlets, windows and window hardware are the components whose location most frequently disables people who are unable to reach them.

Rule 3. Put everything within reach. Build and locate as many of the operational components of the living environment (the areas that the occupants manipulate) with-

in a zone 20 to 44 in. above the floor and with a maximum depth of 20 in., as shown in the drawing on the facing page. This area is called the optimal reach zone (ORZ), a term that will appear throughout the book.

Demands on dexterity   Limitations are created by architectural components that require pinching, gripping, grasping and twisting, turning motions of the fingers or wrists. Many architectural components in the house challenge human abilities, including doorknobs, faucet and drain controls, window hardware, cabinet pulls, electrical outlets and light switches.

Rule 4. Scrutinize operations of components and select those with less demand for fine movements.

Demands on cognition   Architecture creates real hazards for people if they are unable to comprehend the functions or recognize inherent dangers. Dangerous parts of the living environment may include areas around doors, stairs and other level changes. People can become confused in an environment with misleading clues — a window that looks like an open door, a door that swings in an unexpected direction, light switches that aren't oriented logically to the lights they control, the pattern on a floor covering that "hides" a step.

Rule 5. Reinforce the logical function of the environment and avoid using components that are located or operate opposite to expectations.

Demands on vision   Lighting is one of the least considered elements of the home, yet one of the most important in maintaining competence and preventing accidents. Frequently, the future owners of a house pick out light fixtures on the basis of appearance, congruence with the decor and cost, rather than on their ability to provide adequate lighting.

Windows are the other source of light in the house. But window placement is often more determined by the desire to have a house that looks symmetrical than by the need to provide good lighting. Poorly located windows create glare and shadows and increase reliance on artificial light. Also, a house that seems adequately lit to young eyes may seem dark to an elderly occupant.

Rule 6. The architecture of light must be planned for all of the spaces within the environment, taking into account the gradual erosion in vision that is experienced by nearly everyone.

Demands on hearing   People hear better in a quiet environment. A noisy environment, which can be the result of not planning for the control of noises generated within the household or outside the home, will impair the occupants' ability to hear significant sounds within the home.

People monitor their environments through hearing (a knock at the door, footsteps on the porch, the furnace kicking on). The placement of walls, doors and windows needs to be assessed in terms of their impact on sound monitoring within the house. Efforts should be made to supplement the need to hear with the ability to see. For example, a window placed next to an exterior door allows the occupant to see people approaching.

Rule 7. The home environment must be planned with consideration given to the control of interior and exterior noise. Sound monitoring should be supplemented with visual monitoring.

PRODUCT DESIGN

Architecture defines the boundaries of living spaces, but it is the products we select to put within these spaces that establish the domain, the realm of an individual's abilities. Well-designed (enabling) products have several important characteristics:

• Well-designed products can perform their intended function with the user remaining unaware of their "special" design.

• Well-designed products compensate for differences in human abilities. Poorly designed products require special adapters for people whose abilities differ from the norm. Two such adaptive devices are shown in

The Optimal Reach Zone

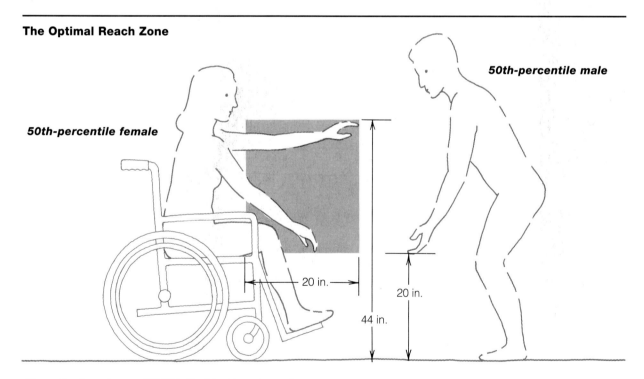

The optimal reach zone (ORZ) is the ideal target area for locating controls, shelving or other components and items that a person needs to reach. The ORZ is within a comfortable reach for tall people, short people and most people in wheelchairs.

One sure sign of a poorly designed product is the number of accessories it requires to function properly. The doorknob adapter (top) slips over a doorknob, turning a difficult-to-use item into a more functional household component. The universal turner (above) allows people to adjust a variety of knobs and switches.

the photos above. The doorknob adapter makes the traditional round doorknob, which is impossible for many people to grasp and turn, an accessible piece of hardware. The universal turner enables people with limited pinch and grip strength or wrist flexibility to operate knobs and other small objects that turn.

• Well-designed products continue accessible design throughout the product. Some products perform their primary function extremely well, but not their secondary functions. An example of discontinuous design is a door whose lever handle functions smoothly and effortlessly, but whose standard key lock demands good eyesight and considerable manual dexterity to use.

• Well-designed products do not require an effort. Poorly designed products require the user to be "on guard." The user is forced to pay attention while using the product because it is easy to make a mistake.

For example, a cook may have to hold a hand over the burner to check if it is on because the cooktop does not provide any other feedback.

• Well-designed products are simple to operate. Poorly designed products cannot be used without an instruction manual.

• Well-designed products enable; poorly designed products disable. A washing machine with a front-loading door and the control panels on the front rather than at the rear can be used by almost everyone. Top-loading washers (the only style commonly available in the United States) create insurmountable obstacles for people who can't reach down into the tub. One style lets the person do the laundry, the other style doesn't.

• Well-designed products are easy to maintain.

Evaluating products When evaluating products, look at the entire product and not just the primary function and price. Well-designed products may require added initial investment, which may well translate into long-term savings in maintenance costs and use. Consider a product from the standpoint of safety, ease of use and maintenance. Watch out for function controls that are located in potentially hard-to-reach areas, such as on the bottom, back or sides of the product. Function controls should be labeled clearly and unambiguously.

Well-designed products don't require fine fingering abilities. They allow alternatives, such as the use of a fingertip, a knuckle, the tip of a cane or an elbow. A good test of a product is if it can be operated with a closed fist or the palm of a hand. Look for products that can be operated with one hand.

Most household products are operated by a touch. Controls may provide feedback to the user through their shape, texture, size, method of actuation, color, graphics or labels and location.

There are several types of controls. They include knobs and switches that control electrical signals (push buttons, rocker and toggle switches, touch pads, knobs, slide bars and thumb or finger wheels). Mechanical controls include knobs, pulls, lever handles, wheels, thumblatches, magnetic catches and hook and eye latches. Controls should have enough space around them to allow their use by people with large fingers or who lack fine motor control.

The drawing on p. 21 shows seven types of electronic controls, ranked from the most flexible (preferred) to the least. Push-button, rocker and toggle switches are best for a two-position function (on and off). They are more difficult to use if they have a third or intermediate position. The rocker switch, with its large actuation surfaces, is especially convenient for someone with limited manual dexterity. The touch pad, which is appearing more and more frequently on appliances and other products, is desirable in that it is sealed into the unit and is easier to clean and maintain. On the other hand, some touch pads are hard to locate in dim light by people with visual limitations, and they don't provide tactile feedback. The slide bar is easy to move and doesn't require fine fingering. But sometimes people have trouble setting the level they want on the first try. If a rotary knob or thumb or finger wheel is large (1-in. diameter or more), has ribbed edges, is easy to turn and control and has position detents, it may be satisfactory.

Push-button and touch-pad controls should be at least ⅝ in. square or in diameter. Push-button controls that are 1 in. square or in diameter offer considerable choice in how they are actuated.

The drawing at right shows five types of mechanical controls, ranked from the least demanding (preferred) to the most. The efficacy of a pull is determined by the amount of space available for the hand. A large opening accommodates a single finger, all of the fingers, the crook of a cane or perhaps an elbow. A small opening eliminates alternatives.

The best control provides immediate feedback that it has been actuated. This feedback may be tactile (by feeling a click or spring action), auditory (a click or beep) or visual (a lighted display). A product will serve more users if it provides at least two, and preferably all three, forms of feedback.

Well-designed products have controls that are located within easy reach. Many bathtubs have faucets and drain controls located in positions that put the person preparing to take a bath at risk of falling headlong into the tub. Refrigerators with temperature controls on the back wall rather than the side also exceed the reaching capabilities of many users.

Warnings labels and instructions should be placed where they can easily be seen. A warning label placed on the back of a heavy appliance is next to worthless.

Manual Controls

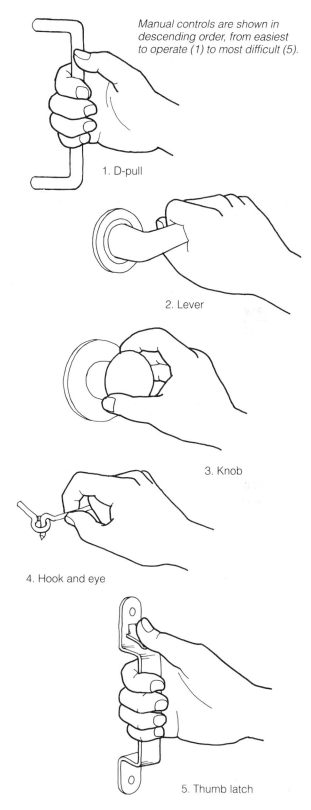

Manual controls are shown in descending order, from easiest to operate (1) to most difficult (5).

1. D-pull

2. Lever

3. Knob

4. Hook and eye

5. Thumb latch

Controls should be easy to see. Product showrooms are well-lit, and what seemed like easy-to-read graphics in the store may be difficult to discern in your dimly lit home or if you are operating in the dark. Important controls with distinctive functions should have a different shape from other controls. Humans can distinguish a variety of shapes and textures through their fingertips. Products that offer controls with distinctive shapes or knurled, fluted, squared or rounded edges provide that extra feedback in low levels of light to people with impaired vision.

Look for product displays that offer high contrast, that are arranged logically and that can be understood in poorly lit surroundings. Avoid products that have their operation symbols in graphics that are the same color as the background. Many people will be unable to detect such symbols. Be sure to evaluate the legibility of product graphics and displays from the angle and position that they are likely to be viewed in use. The most desirable product-operation graphics will include both a graphic symbol and legible text.

Laundry may be a routine chore, but for many people using a top-loading washing machine is a challenge. Reaching the controls or to the bottom of the tub is difficult for some, impossible for others. The knobs, which often require grasping and twisting, present another obstacle. The washer and dryer at top right have controls on the front, which makes them readily accessible (the top-loading washer, however, is not so accessible). The most convenient laundry unit (bottom right) loads from the front and has controls on the front. (Photo top right: courtesy Whirlpool; photo bottom right: courtesy Miele.)

The location and layout of controls affect the ease of use of the equipment. All of the controls for the combination microwave, cooktop and oven at far left are located next to the microwave. This product places high demands on being able to read the markings and understand the relationship of the control to the cooking units. The top cooktop at left has a safe arrangement of burners, but the relation between controls and burners can confuse users. In the bottom cooktop at left the relation between controls and burners is evident; it's obvious which control operates which burner. (Photo far left: courtesy Tappan White Consolidated Industries; photo top left: courtesy KitchenAid; photo bottom left: courtesy Roper Sales Corporation.)

Many products have sound signaling systems to alert the user that a function has been completed or an error has been made. Auditory feedback provides a valuable redundant cue for the operation of products. It allows the product operator to pay attention to something else and interact with the product only when required. It also provides feedback in low-light conditions.

Unfortunately, many people have difficulty hearing. Relatively faint, high-pitched beeps are not heard by people who have a loss of hearing sensitivity for the high pitches. High-pitched sounds don't travel around corners well. Low-pitched sounds, on the other hand, are likely to be masked by the background noise in the room. Product signals should fall within the range of 500 Hz to 1500 Hz. This range can be heard by a large group of people and has a pitch distinguishable from background noises.

WHAT NEXT?

Builders and designers need to understand more about human abilities and the ranges of and limitations to functioning of humans of all ages, sizes and abilities. Designers must begin to apply design criteria for universal design, for inclusive environments, to every project, not just to "special cases." Professionals in the construction industry must learn how to manage their projects so that inclusive design criteria can be implemented successfully by contractors and crews unfamiliar with the design differences. Universal design is about building houses that more people can live in, and thus it affects markets and profits. It is also about meeting human needs, and thus it affects the rights, comfort and happiness of people.

"Form follows function" is a familiar guideline for designers. We would like to modify this rule by adding the concept of "fit," that is, the fit of the product to human dimensions and abilities. To our way of thinking, form follows function, but foremost is fit.

CHAPTER THREE
MANAGING A BUILDING PROJECT

Someday universal design may be routine for designers, builders and subcontractors. Architects will automatically position houses with the first floor on a level with the parking place. Halls will be wide and bathrooms big. Doors 3 ft. wide will be standard, and 30-in. doors hard to find. Door knobs will be available only at flea markets, having been completely displaced by levers. Most thresholds in doorways will have been eliminated, and those that remain will be no higher than ½ in.

Kitchens with only one counter height and no place to work while sitting down will be considered funny looking. Standard sinks will be 5 in. to 6 in. deep, with drains located toward the back. Kitchen designers will

A Difference of Scale

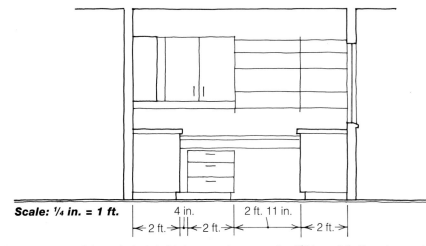

Scale: ¼ in. = 1 ft.

2 ft.   4 in.   2 ft.   2 ft. 11 in.   2 ft.

Large-scale drawings are useful, particularly in kitchens and bathrooms that contain nonstandard details. At a scale of ¼ in. = 1 ft., only minimal information can be conveyed; at a scale of ½ in. = 1 ft., there is room to call out the special dimensions and other features of accessible design, which may be unfamiliar to builders and contractors.

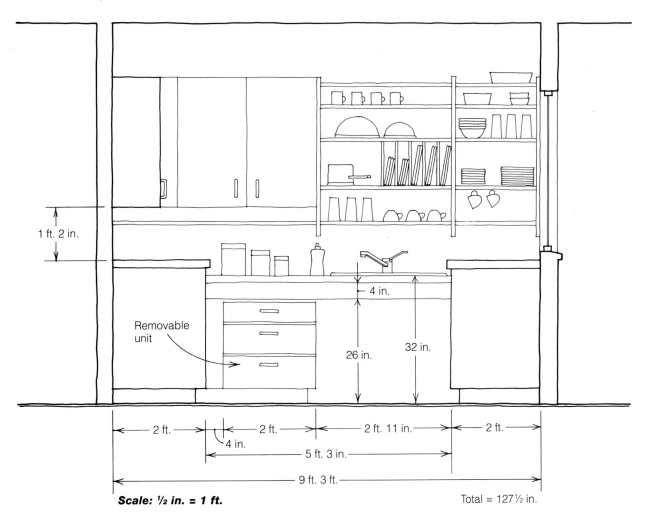

1 ft. 2 in.

Removable unit

4 in.

26 in.

32 in.

2 ft.   2 ft.   2 ft. 11 in.   2 ft.

4 in.

5 ft. 3 in.

9 ft. 3 ft.

Scale: ½ in. = 1 ft.

Total = 127½ in.

automatically provide lots of drawers and accessible cabinets. Electricians will insist on locating the service panel in an accessible spot on the first floor, and they will provide an abundance of outlets.

In short, houses will be designed for all people, for use over their entire lifetime. What we advocate is simply that those in the building field become as conversant with and committed to accessibility in the coming years as they have become with energy efficiency in the recent past. Until that goal has been achieved, however, those who are building for a lifetime will have obstacles to overcome. This chapter is designed to identify what some of these obstacles may be and devise strategies that reduce them to manageable dimensions.

FACING OBSTACLES

Most architects and builders have not yet taken a serious interest in accessible, or universal, design. Many who have some experience with accessible projects think of accessibility not as an essential or intrinsic feature of good design, but rather as a set of special features and products that must be grafted onto their already developed designs to comply with codes or specifications. Designers may work primarily from checklists based on national standards (ANSI and UFAS) rather than from ergonomic principles. They are likely to confuse minimum code compliance with optimum design.

Some builders actively resist accessible (universal) design features. Builders thrive by being efficient. They become efficient because they are thoroughly familiar with the materials and products they use, and because they use them the same way over and over. Unfamiliar features may be perceived as needlessly complex and costly, particularly if they require creative problem solving.

Builder resistance can take many forms. A time-honored method is to argue that an unfamiliar detail is unsound, costly or possibly not up to code. Builders may try to replace the designed feature with a more familiar one, whether it applies or not. Energy that should go into actual work can get dissipated defending the design from these challenges.

Builder resistance can also be inadvertent. Specifications or dimensions will be ignored or changed on site because the builder or installer doesn't understand their importance. A door may be moved 1 ft. for some perfectly logical reason that just happens to ignore the need for a side clearance on the handle side of the door. An overhead cabinet specified at 12 in. above the counter may be installed 18 in. or 20 in. up because the installer is sure the higher position is correct, since it always has been so. Perhaps most serious, a foundation specified at a certain grade to simplify entrance and eliminate the need for a ramp may get poured a foot or two higher for reasons that seem convincing at the moment.

Obtaining necessary materials and products can be a major challenge. Suppliers often know little about accessible products and applications. Identifying what you need is difficult because the regulations can be complex and confusing. Although many items (such as lever faucets and door handles) are now commonplace, other specialty items are hard to find. On the other hand, some "standard" products can easily be adapted to accessible applications. But finding them can take time and research.

Many products that are manufactured for the accessibility market cost significantly more than their conventional counterparts. So-called accessible cabinets, to take one example, are smaller than standard ones, but cost roughly 10% more. To complicate matters even more, some products specifically marketed for users with specific disabilities are not necessarily suited to every application — standard accessible toilets are too tall for some users.

The ideal project would involve a designer and builder with knowledge of, experience in and commitment to universal design, and who are also in tune with the clients' needs, resources and tastes. Until all builders and designers are conversant with universal design ideas and methods, people building or remodeling might want to follow some variation on the strategy described here to help their project succeed without needless delays and expenses.

Key elements of managing an accessible building project are as follows:
1. Build a team that includes people experienced with accessibility, both on the drawing board and on the building site.
2. Present the design to the team in a way that gets everyone involved with the idea of accessibility, and with the features that make it work.

3. Supply critical information to the various workers in a convenient form.

4. Have the special products selected and purchased when needed.

5. Institute a few controls — procedures to review the work done when it's still possible to correct it.

BUILDING A TEAM

The usual building team includes a designer, a builder, the primary on-site carpenters, and the subcontractors who do excavation, plumbing, wiring and other specialized tasks. Design and contracting may be combined in a single design/build firm.

Hiring a designer and a builder (or designer/builder) usually begins with making a list of the local practitioners with good reputations. One's acquaintances will always be eager to tell their stories. It might make sense also to search out people who specialize in accessible projects by running a little advertisement or by contacting local advocacy agencies.

Ask prospective designers and builders what their approach is, what relevant projects they've done and how they charge for their services. Ask all candidates for the job about their experience with and attitude toward accessible building. A willingness to do the job isn't always enough. A positive interest in and commitment to the subject are important. A designer who is merely willing to build accessibly will check the codes and incorporate the minimal requirements into the plan; a builder merely willing will follow the plans if they are clear enough. But people with a positive interest in accessibility will also be looking for ways to improve the project from the first day of planning right through moving day. They will take the extra steps to find the best product or detail. Fewer things will go wrong or fail to meet expectations.

Be prepared to ask some tough technical questions. How do you make door thresholds accessible? What's the best way to create a no-step entrance? Is it hard to make sink counters adjustable, and how is it done? Does an accessible house have to be more expensive? The answers to such questions would help you find the people who know what they are doing. Ask to visit their other projects.

The subcontractors are just as important as the general contractor, because they handle most of the nonstandard details. In the initial stages, the excavation subcontractor has the most influence on the success of a project by keeping the foundation low and the site level. Later, the plumber, electrician and kitchen installers carry out many critical functions.

The problem is that most subcontractors work under pressure and in a hurry. They always have another job where they are needed, and doing things the way they've always done them before gets them to that next job sooner. Finding subs who are comfortable with what you are doing, and willing to take the time to do it right, can be more difficult than finding a good designer or general contractor.

Often the home owner hires the general contractor, who then chooses the subcontractors with whom he or she has strong working relationships. That's a good approach. But sometimes it makes sense for the home owner to try to match particularly good subcontractors with the builder. For example, the home owner may know a plumber who has a reputation for flexibility and patience and has experience with or interest in accessibility. That person would be a good member of the team, even if the general contractor had never worked with him or her before.

Though expertise with accessibility is valuable, you probably wouldn't want to choose a designer or contractor on that basis alone. Experience, skill at estimating, good business practices and a willingness to listen to your ideas are crucial. It's important to feel comfortable with your builder or designer, to trust their instincts and to feel that their design ideas fit yours.

Adding specialists to the team If the designer and builder are relatively new to accessible projects, it's a good idea to add an accessibility specialist to the design and planning team. This person might be a another designer or architect, hired on as a consultant. It could be a person from a local advocacy agency or independent living center who does plan reviews. It should be someone who is thoroughly familiar with codes and the variety of workable solutions available. Ideally this person would also be familiar with accessible products and with building practices.

The accessibility consultant should participate at critical points in the design process. He or she should take part in the early discussions of siting and house layout, review sets of plans as they evolve and later go over details in the kitchen, bathroom and wherever else small dimensional changes and product choices are important. The consultant might also visit the building site at critical periods to check the work in progress.

When a residence is being built or remodeled to accommodate someone with specific limitations, it is useful to include as consultants the rehabilitation professionals (physicians, physical or occupational therapists) who have worked with that person. Accessibility codes are useful guidelines for designers, but there are many design issues that have to do with the particular needs of actual people. The rehabilitation professional may have important suggestions that could influence the layout. For example, a person with a strong left hand and a weak right hand will require a different bathroom layout from a person strong on the opposite side. The therapist might have a sense of how a person's abilities may evolve in the future, or know of special equipment or products that should be considered.

The client's role Ideally, the home owner will play a major creative role in designing a house or planning a major renovation. This involvement is especially critical if the design is intended to accommodate a particular person in the household. Universal design is a relatively new concept. The home owner can become a better-informed, more valuable member of the design/build team by reading books, studying codes and visiting accessible buildings. The basic concepts are not at all hard to understand. The Resources section on pp. 37 lists databases, catalogs and other useful sources of information.

It may also make sense for one member of the household to become the "designated shopper." The builder and subcontractors probably won't have the time to search out suitable faucets, sinks, door levers and appliances for the house. They may suggest expensive items aimed specifically at the accessibility market. Through a little research, the designated shopper may find more affordable items that work

just as well. This research should include shopping at local suppliers, calling manufacturers and wholesalers, inspecting catalog detail drawings carefully and consulting databases of accessible products.

PRESENTING THE DESIGN TO THE TEAM

In conventional building projects the designers, carpenters, backhoe operators, plumbers and electricians are generally familiar with each other's work. The backhoe operator will know a lot about foundation work, the electrician will have installed cabinets, the carpenters will have a good knowledge of plumbing details. This common knowledge is important; it allows everyone to interpret correctly the intentions of the plan drawings. It enables the framing carpenters, for example, to anticipate what the electrician and plumber will need to make their work easier. The plumber and electrician, in turn, can then anticipate the needs of the cabinet installer.

Because accessible construction requires small variations in foundation details, framing, door installation and many other things, the common assumptions people bring to the job need to be altered slightly. To put it another way, some of the assumptions people bring to the job will be wrong. Conventional building practice and wisdom can create confusion, errors, delays and frustration. With proper planning, these can be avoided.

One solution is to bring together the home owner, designer, contractor, head carpenter and the principal subcontractors for a single presentation of the whole design. At this meeting, organized by the contractor or home owner, all the special features of the design would be presented, along with an explanation of why they are important. The goal would be for everyone to understand the whole project, to reevaluate their assumptions and to create a synergy on the project. Few people in building have an intuitive understanding of the need for low switches, adjustable counters, stepless entrances and other features. Explaining the logic of the design enables the workers to use their intelligence to keep things moving and to help each other and devise smart solutions to problems that arise.

An accessible project may involve some learning for everyone. A design presentation to the whole group gives each member of the team the opportunity to get that education and to ask questions and make suggestions. The subcontractors can use this time to educate the clients or the designer about products or methods of work that hadn't previously been considered.

SUPPLYING CRITICAL INFORMATION

Building accessibly is building sensibly. It is no more complex or difficult than traditional building. Products and dimensions vary, but the skills are the same. The adjustments will be easier for builders if a few extra steps are taken to supply the information needed. It isn't necessarily sufficient to have the new dimensions or unusual framing details covered in the drawings or in pages of specs. Workers in a hurry, perhaps cold and dusty and probably listening to a radio, are not that likely to comb through drawings for a dimension they may not know is important. Instead, critical information should be presented in a way that is hard to miss and hard to get wrong. There are several simple ways to do this.

Highlighting The simplest device for presenting critical information is to highlight nonstandard dimensions and similar information on the plans with colored pencil or marker. Most people will pay attention to information emphasized this way.

Large-scale drawings House plans often present everything at a scale of ¼ in. = 1 ft. on a small drawing. The small drawing works when it's in a code everybody shares. But some parts of an accessible house design can benefit from larger-scale presentations that are more pictorial and allow for greater detail. Kitchen and bathroom plans are good examples. A scale of ½ in. = 1 ft. on a kitchen plan can clearly present information that would blur or simply would not fit on a ¼-in. scale plan (see the drawing on p. 31). This includes variations in counter heights, heights of drawers, locations of pulls or handles and plumbing details. The bigger format is also more like-

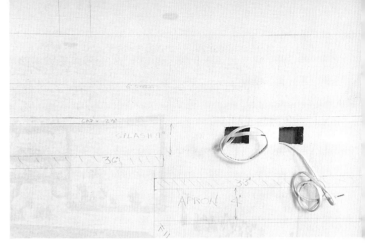

A simple way to clarify instructions and avoid confusion is to make full-size drawings to guide subcontractors. At top, the installation dimensions for kitchen cabinets are drawn right on the drywall. Above, a cross section detailing a sink installation is being drawn for the plumber on a scrap piece of drywall.

ly to remain legible after the rigors of site use have obliterated a smaller-scale version.

Even larger-scale drawings might be of use for some critical details. A door threshold, for example, might be drawn to a scale of 3 in. = 1 ft., which is the scale used in many door and window catalogs. Such a scale makes it easy to show precisely all the modifications needed to make a stock threshold work in a particular application.

Full-scale drawings   Full-scale drawings are standard in pattern shops, boatyards and furniture shops, where accuracy is essential. The full scale is more accurate, and allows the builder or designer to take measurements directly from the drawing. This approach can be an excellent way to communicate the most critical information with your crew.

Kitchen-cabinet locations can be drawn full scale right on the wall or on a scrap piece of drywall, along with blocking heights, sink-installation cross sections and other information (see the photos on p. 35). This form of presentation can save the subcontractor a great deal of time, and it almost eliminates the possibility of error.

SUPPLYING NEEDED PRODUCTS

Building efficiency always depends on getting the products to the site on time. If something isn't there when it's needed, the building sequence is thrown off. Workers lose their focus and rhythm.

In standard construction, most products are stocked locally and can be ordered a few days ahead of time. If an item is unavailable, a similar product can usually be substituted. Many purchases are left until the last minute. But some more specialized accessibility products are less common. Workable sinks (with the drain toward the rear so a wheelchair can roll under them), certain faucets and accessible exterior doors may not be immediately available. It may take quite a bit of research to find a shower enclosure to which grab bars can conveniently be attached. It's important for the designated shopper to start early so that products are delivered when needed.

CONTROLS AND REVIEWS

At several points in the construction process, it is useful to hold a formal walk-through or inspection of the job, similar to the reviews or sign-offs that occur on large construction sites. The home owner, designer, builder and accessibility specialist, if there is one, should participate.

It can be particularly important for a significant member of the team to be on site during foundation work. The finish height of the foundation is critical to the design of most stepless entrances. Foundation work often happens quickly — particularly if there are weather problems — and it is for all intents and purposes irreversible. It's not much trouble to reposition a kitchen cabinet, but once the foundation footings are located, it's hard to turn back. Even with a knowledgeable and sympathetic foundation crew it is possible to run into seemingly valid excuses for raising the level of the foundation. Excavation can reveal bedrock or water, for example. The best way to avoid these problems is for the designer to be on site at least twice a day during foundation work. The general contractor, excavator and concrete contractor should know that the grading will be checked before payment and that any change in the foundation height must be approved in writing.

Another review should take place right after the framing has been completed, at which time many critical dimensions should be checked (hall widths, door locations, provisions for thresholds). Another should follow plumbing and electrical rough-in. Critical details to check on this review would include the exact position of the toilet, the rough plumbing around a bathtub or shower, the heights of sink drains and electrical switches and outlets. Finally, an extra visit or two to inspect the bathrooms and kitchen will help ensure that cabinets, appliances and sinks have been installed correctly.

RESOURCES

These resources are places the project manager of an accessible building project can go to get help. Most provide information about products, barrier-free design or planning a home.

Abilities Expo
RCW Productions
1106 2nd Street #118
Encinitas, CA 02024
(619) 944-1122
An exhibition of products and services for individuals with disabilities. Held every year in California and New Jersey.

ABLEDATA
8455 Colesville Road
Suite 935
Silver Spring, MD 20910-3319
(800) 346-2742
A database information source on mobility, visual and hearing impairment, dressing, eating and computer aids.

Accent on Living
Cheever Publishing Company
P.O. Box 700
Bloomington, IL 61701
A monthly magazine that features articles and advertisements about assistive products and people with disabilities. Publishes a Buyer's Guide.

Access Real Estate
22 Sunset Avenue
Westhampton Beach, NY 11978
(516) 288-6244
Real-estate firm that specializes in marketing wheelchair-accessible homes. Has a national referral center.

Advanced Living Systems
Product Search Services
428 North Lamar
Oxford, MS 38655-3204
(601) 234-0158
A database of architectural and assistive products for barrier-free environments. For a small fee, provides architects, builders, developers and individuals with names and addresses of manufacturers and distributors of accessible products.

American Foundation for the Blind
National Technology Center
15 West 16th Street
New York, NY 10011
(800) 232-5463
(212) 620-2000
Information, referral and source of products for individuals who are visually impaired or blind.

AT&T Special Needs Center
2001 Route 46, Suite 310
Parsippany, NJ 07054-1315
(800) 233-1222
(800) 833-3232 (TDD)
Information about assistive devices for telephone communications and services.

Assistive Technology Sourcebook
Alexandra Enders and Marian Hall, Editors
RESNA Press Publishers
Suite 700, 1001 Connecticut Avenue NW
Washington, DC 20036
(202) 857-1199
A comprehensive directory of organizations, resources and technologies for individuals with disabilities.

National Organization on Disability (NOD)
2100 Pennsylvania Avenue NW, Suite 234
Washington, DC 20039
(202) 293-5960
Information about resources for individuals with disabilities.

Research and Training Center on Accessible Housing
North Carolina State University
School of Design
Raleigh, NC 27965-7701
(919) 737-7701
A research center funded by the National Institute on Disability Rehabilitation and Research that focuses on solving problems related to housing design for individuals with disabilities.

PART TWO
EXTERIORS

A house feels isolated from the nature around it, unless its floors are interleaved directly with the earth that is around the house.
— *Christopher Alexander*, A Pattern Language

CHAPTER FOUR
SITE PLANNING
AND FOUNDATIONS

The common refrain among architects, "You can't build a good house on a bad site," is especially true when building a house for a lifetime. The size and contour of the site have a great impact on the style of the house, the use of outdoor space and the overall costs of creating a universally accessible environment.

This chapter offers suggestions on how to select a site, orient the dwelling on the site, plan the foundation, approaches and yard and create outdoor spaces that can be enjoyed throughout a lifetime. As much attention should be given to planning the area around the house as to the design of the house itself.

Orienting The House on the Site

A level entrance is an important element of accessible design. Even if the site slopes, sometimes this goal can be achieved simply by changing the house's design or orientation to the site.

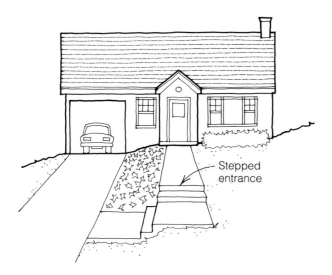

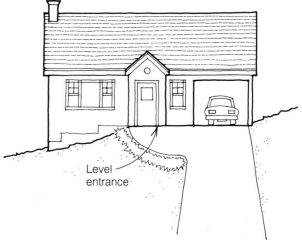

House across Slope (Parking Area at Low Side)

In this typical house-to-site arrangement, the driveway and carport are below the entrance. Steps are needed to reach the front door.

House across Slope (Parking Area at High Side)

With the driveway and carport located on the high side of the slope, the car does the climbing and the entrance to the house is level; no steps are needed.

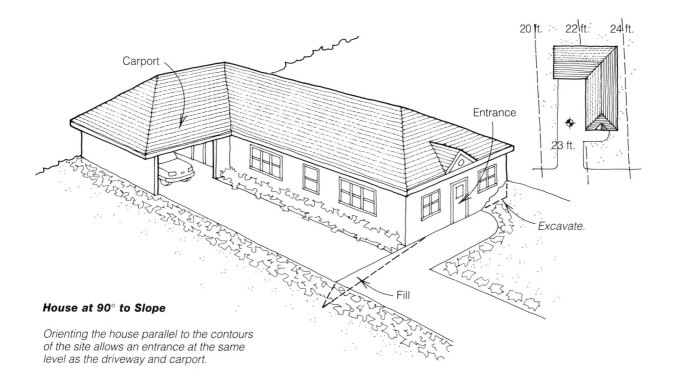

House at 90° to Slope

Orienting the house parallel to the contours of the site allows an entrance at the same level as the driveway and carport.

Outdoor spaces provide a transition from public property to private space, they offer entertainment and exercise and they support driveways and pathways to the house. It is sad to see so many homes built without regard to the future (and even potential) needs of the occupants; houses with unnecessary steps and steep or nonexistent sidewalks limit access to the site.

People often prefer to wait until they need accessibility before spending any extra time and money. However, this is a bit like waiting until an accident occurs before buying insurance. There are several drawbacks to this approach. First, remodeling costs a lot more than making the house and site accessible when the house is constructed. Second, just about everyone will at some point in life experience limitations in their abilities, but few people can predict when. Third, most people do not remodel their homes when they lose ability, they just lose access to portions of the house. Fourth, the less access that is built into and around the house, the greater the likelihood that those portions of the house will be neglected in terms of maintenance and repair. Fifth, changes that occur in abilities over time are gradual, yet pervasive. They affect the ability to get around, see, lift, bend, stoop, kneel and climb ladders or stairs. They gradually diminish one's capacity to deal with an insensitive (i.e. inaccessible) environment. The older you get, the more likely you will be less able to get about in or use your living environment.

SELECTING A SITE

People have many criteria for selecting a site for their home. They might choose a particular neighborhood because friends and family live there, because it has good schools, because there are children the same age as their own children, because the commute is convenient, and for a variety of other reasons. They choose a particular site because it is the only site left on the block, it's on the side of the mountain overlooking a bay, it's the last lot on the lake or the price is right.

These are indeed important reasons for selecting a site, but other criteria are important too. Consider the size of the lot. In places where the cost of land is high, the lots are likely to be smaller, which may force you to build a multi-story house. A house with more than one level dictates the need for stairs. If plans aren't made at the outset for dealing with an eventual inability to climb stairs, building on this lot today may force the owners to move to a more accessible site later.

Look at the slope of the site and determine if and how the variations in level are going to affect the style of house. Sites with fairly steep slopes often are most economically addressed with a split-level house (see the drawing on the facing page). However, a split-level house poses some of the greatest obstacles to accessibility because of the multiple levels. If a member of the household is unable to climb the stairs, it is unlikely that any one section of the split level house will have all of the necessary components for living (bedroom, bathroom and kitchen) on one level, and access to all areas of the house cannot be gained with a single stair lift or elevator. Each level would require a separate system.

Look at the entire site, not just that part of it where the house will go. Think carefully about your intended outdoor activities in light of the site. Steep slopes are difficult to mow. For a person lacking mobility or strength, a hilly site may make gardening difficult, may preclude coutdoor spaces such as patios and may limit access to the far reaches of the site.

If given the choice, opt for a site that is flat or has a gentle slope to it. It is certainly possible to build accessibly on difficult sites, as the drawings in this chapter indicate, but it costs money to move dirt, and that means you will have less money to spend on the house itself.

Spend some time learning the history of the land you are looking at. What has it been used for previously? Was it a landfill? If so, who monitored what was dumped on the site? Be sure you aren't building a house on top of a time bomb of chemical drums or otherwise contaminated soil.

If you are building on a sloping site, consider what might happen when someone builds next to and above you. Today the rainwater flows evenly through an adjacent vacant lot. A new building uphill can change all of that, often for the worse. Many disputes among neighbors can be avoided through proper planning. Obtain copies of the soil surveys

The Split-Level Solution

Section View

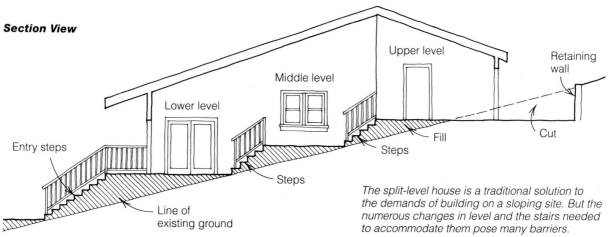

Upper level

Retaining wall

Middle level

Lower level

Entry steps

Fill

Cut

Steps

Steps

Line of existing ground

The split-level house is a traditional solution to the demands of building on a sloping site. But the numerous changes in level and the stairs needed to accommodate them pose many barriers.

from the soil and water conservation district. (Look in the Yellow Pages or contact your local cooperative extension service for assistance.) Among other things, the surveys will tell you about the possibility of seasonal high water, the depth to bedrock and the permeability, expansion and load-bearing capacity of the soil. Be sure to check the flood plain on the lot. If you have any concerns about the soil, have it tested.

Learn what the zoning ordinances are for the areas around the neighborhood. Might the vacant lot across the street someday become a highrise or a strip mall? Could the house next door be converted into a muffler shop? Towns, neighborhoods and individual streets change with the passage of time. Can you create your space so that these changes won't affect you?

Finally, consider how the site will lend itself to an accessible house and yard. From this perspective, the site should be able to provide:
• a transition into the house with minimal level change
• level or gently sloping smooth-surfaced routes to the far reaches of the lot
• conditions conducive to easy maintenance of the lot
• an orientation that maximizes accessible interior construction and the opportunity for all entrances to be accessible.

CREATING ACCESSIBLE ENTRANCES

One prerequisite for an accessible house is an accessible entrance, which can often be best accomplished with site work and foundation planning. It can also derive from a simple matter of orientation. Houses are usually situated on a lot so as to capitalize on a view, capture or block the sun's rays, satisfy zoning regulations and/or neighborhood conventions or simply for aesthetic reasons. One of the first things a designer should consider when orienting a house on the site is a way to create level or stepless entrances. When looking at house plans that call for steps, the builder and designer should automatically look for alternatives. If the orientation of the house cannot be changed, other possible solutions are ramps, bridges, berms, sloped walkways and moving the parking area from the low side to the high side of the house.

On sloped sites, often the driveway, garage or carport, and entrance are situated on the low side of the slope. This arrangement almost always dictates the need for steps. If the driveway and entrances were simply moved to the opposite side of the house, as shown in the drawing on p. 41, the climb to the entrance would be made by the car rather than the resident, and the grade into the house could be level. Another option would be to rotate the house on the lot so that the primary entrance is at the lowest point of the foundation. Instead of having stairs to climb with the house parallel to the street, the front door and garage door entrances are at ground level.

Obviously, not all site problems will be solved by the orientation of the house. But it is likely that more entrances to the house will be made accessible with fewer ramps or bridges if this planning is completed first.

If the house can't be rotated on the site to an accessible advantage, there are other means of avoiding steps at entrances. These can involve excavation and removing dirt or using some of the dirt as fill to level the site, creating berms out of fill, and building bridges. Ramps (which are discussed in Chapter 5)

offer yet another approach to stepless entrances. But ramps are often added on to houses because the siting, orientation and foundation planning discussed in this chapter were not done.

Ramps are important methods for creating accessible entrances. Unfortunately, however, they can still present problems for some people. A ramp with a 1:12 slope is fairly steep. Someone in a wheelchair, someone pushing a wheelchair or someone walking could have difficulty on a ramp with this grade of slope. Ramps are not as safe as level surfaces. If a level walkway and entrance can be provided, there is less likelihood of anyone encountering problems.

Leveling a Site by Excavation

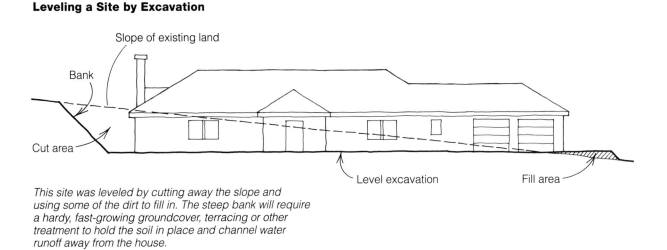

This site was leveled by cutting away the slope and using some of the dirt to fill in. The steep bank will require a hardy, fast-growing groundcover, terracing or other treatment to hold the soil in place and channel water runoff away from the house.

Top Access on a Downward Slope

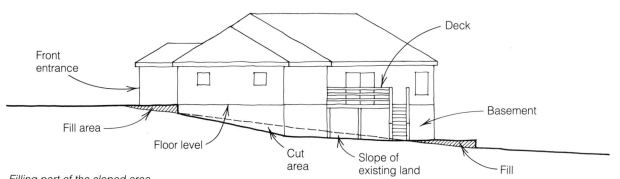

Filling part of the sloped area created level access to this house at the front entrance. Because the back yard is at a lower level, the house should be planned to include an elevator or lift.

In the top drawing on the facing page, a level house site was created cutting away the upper side of the slope and using some of the dirt for fill at the lower end of the slope. Although a considerable amount of dirt had to be moved, the entire house is now stepless. The area immediately adjacent to the house is level, so a sidewalk and patio can be built around the perimeter of the house, making each entrance accessible. However, maintaining the steeply sloping bank may be difficult.

In the bottom drawing on the facing page, a level front entrance was created by filling in the front side of this downward sloping lot. The front side of the house and the first floor are accessible. The deck is accessible to anyone from the house, but not from the back yard, except by a set of stairs.

The house in the photo at top right is a typical starter home built with framed floor construction over a crawl space. The floor is about 24 in. above ground, requiring three or four steps. These steps can be eliminated by creating a bermed entrance using fill, as shown in the photo at right. The berm could also extend across the entire front of the house.

In the drawing below, level entrances were created around the house on this upward sloping lot by building a berm and filling in around the house at the front and cutting away a small portion at the rear. The berm creates a level area around the house, but care must be taken to ensure that the grade of the driveway is not too steep. Planting the rise of the berm

The entrances to houses built over basements and crawl spaces are typically well above grade, requiring several steps, as on the house at top. Ramps are often tacked on to houses like this to make them accessible. A more attractive and less intrusive option is to use fill to create a bermed entrance, as on the house above, eliminating the need for steps.

Bottom Access

Front entrance

Cut area

Fill area

with a low-maintenance groundcover is a good idea. In this example, the trade-off for the berm and the level entrance may have been more difficult yard maintenance and a steep slope up to the level of the house.

Bridges can sometimes solve the problem of accessible entrances on a difficult site. Bridges can be incorporated into the walkway to bypass the need for steps in the walk or can eliminate the need for a ramp or sloped walkway. Bridges can be made part of a deck or porch and can be an architectural focal point. A bridge can be used to span a drainage area between the house and surrounding grounds that are higher. The bridge can also be used in combination with berming to eliminate the need for steps at the entrance of the house.

Keeping the House Low

Different foundation detailing can create stepless entrances by dropping the house closer to ground level than 16 in. to 20 in., which is common in standard construction (right). Two alternatives are shown below.

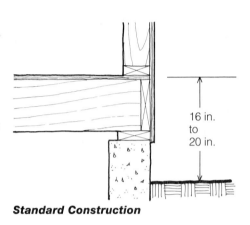

Standard Construction

Standard construction calls for a height of up to 20 in. from grade to floor level, which is spanned by stairs, a ramp or a sizable berm.

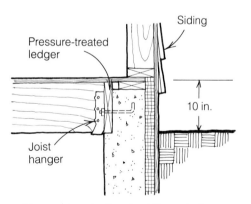

Siding

Pressure-treated ledger

10 in.

Joist hanger

Alternative A: Notched Foundation

A pressure-treated ledger resting on a notch in the foundation allows the joists to be hung low, reducing the distance from grade to floor level to about 10 in.

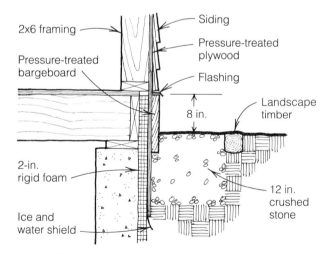

2x6 framing

Siding

Pressure-treated bargeboard

Pressure-treated plywood

Flashing

8 in.

Landscape timber

2-in. rigid foam

12 in. crushed stone

Ice and water shield

Alternative B: Bargeboard at Ground Level

Replacing the lowest courses of siding with a pressure-treated 2x12 bargeboard makes the distance between grade and floor level about 8 in., allowing for modestly graded pathways into and out of the house.

The floor of this house sits on top of a full basement, yet it is only 8 in. above grade, making it easy to berm the entries so the paths to the house would look entirely ordinary.

A stepless entrance can be also be created by dropping the entrance of the house closer to ground level, instead of raising the ground level up to the entrance. For example, the owners of the house shown in the photo above wanted the yard to be as accessible as possible, yet without excessive berming. However, standard framing (see the drawing on the facing page) calls for the entrance to be 16 in. to 20 in. above ground level. One way to lower the house, shown in Alternative A in the drawing, would be to notch the foundation. The solution arrived at for the house in the photo was to replace the bottom row of siding with a 2x12 pressure-treated bargeboard and a border of stone to facilitate drainage (Alternative B in the drawing). With either alternative the berms or other transitions at the entrances become short, inexpensive and unobtrusive.

PLANNING APPROACHES AND WALKWAYS

When considering the orientation and siting of the house, it is also important to plan the approaches to the house (driveways and sidewalks), parking areas and walkways around the yard. People may approach the property by driving up to the house, by parking their vehicle on the street, by foot or in a wheelchair or scooter.

Driveways   A well-designed driveway allows for an easy turn into the property, particularly if the drive is from a busy street. People should not have to worry about aiming for a narrow driveway when confronting oncoming traffic. As shown in the drawing on p. 49, driveways should be at least 12 ft. wide and flared at the end to accommodate the turn. Provide driveways with a turn-around space that will enable drivers leaving the house to enter the street driving forward. Add reflective markers at the entrance and on either side of a steep or curved driveway to help guide drivers when they are forced to back up, particularly if the ground is covered with snow.

Driveways should be graded to minimize the slope. In snow country the grade should not exceed 10%; the maximum recommended slope in warmer climates is 15%. If the driveway will be used regularly as a walkway from the street to the house, it should be graded to about 8% (maximum 1:12 slope) to accommodate people who use wheelchairs.

Driveways should be covered with a smooth surface material (concrete or asphalt). Gravel is difficult to walk on for many people and particularly difficult to maneuver a wheelchair over.

Driveways often reach the house at a garage under the house, necessitating stairs to reach the front door. A better scheme is to let the driveway provide level access to the house from the parking area on an otherwise unlevel site. If the house is going to sit on a hill, for example, establish the parking area at the same level as the foundation. Then run the driveway

The lot for the house at left was wide enough to have allowed the driveway to rise to the entrance level. Instead, a garage was built under the house, creating a steep climb for residents and guests. The house below left is a good example of how to let the car do the climbing.

The Well-Designed Driveway

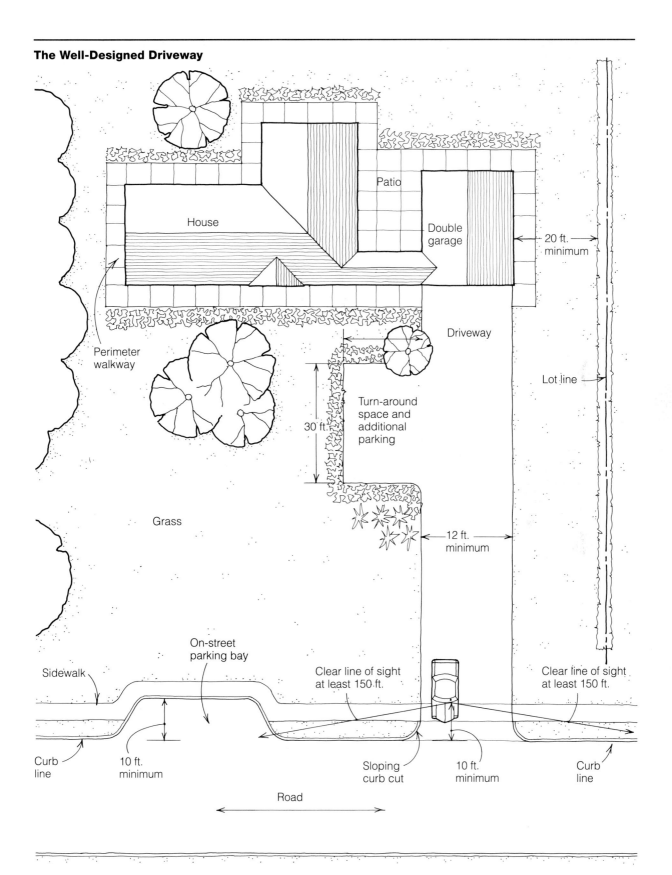

House

Patio

Double garage

20 ft. minimum

Perimeter walkway

Driveway

Lot line

30 ft.

Turn-around space and additional parking

Grass

12 ft. minimum

On-street parking bay

Sidewalk

Clear line of sight at least 150 ft.

Clear line of sight at least 150 ft.

Curb line

10 ft. minimum

Sloping curb cut

10 ft. minimum

Curb line

Road

up to the parking area. Let the car climb the hill, not the residents and visitors. The need for steps and ramps can be minimized, if not eliminated, by this rather simple solution.

Parking Building for a lifetime requires planning for the growth of the family. Many houses are built by young couples, with room allotted for only one or two cars. But as children grow, a four-person family can become a four-car family. Planning for the additional vehicles can be as simple as widening the driveway, but this might be difficult if the driveway is built right at the property line. Parking areas can be added behind the house or alongside the garage. Whenever possible, design the site so that these changes can be made easily at a later date.

Plan for the activities of the family. Consider the parking and storage requirements for boats and trailers, recreational vehicles, motorcycles and snowmobiles. If parking for the household is on the street, think of ways to make it easier to get to the house. Consider creating a parking bay along the street, as shown in the drawing on p. 49.

If the parking area and walkway to the house aren't sufficiently lit by street lights, put in yard and walk lights. Be sure that anyone who has to park on the street can get onto the property and up to the house easily. If you have ever spent a night trick-or-treating with your kids, you know how difficult it can be to find your way to many front doors in the dark. Resources on the facing page lists companies that make outdoor lighting.

Design the front walk to end in a curb cut at the street. Don't end the front walk at the city sidewalk, but rather cross that walk and provide an entrance from the street. The most desirable style of curb cut does not cut into the sidewalk, but creates an extension of the sidewalk to the street so that the uneven surface does not catch a walker off guard. Avoid curb ramps, which extend out into the street.

Responsibility for building sidewalks, curbs and curb cuts varies widely from town to town, and neighborhood to neighborhood. The city engineer or subdivision developer will be the best source for information. Many streets and sidewalks are still being constructed without curb cuts or with curb cut designs that are inefficient and hazardous. Be prepared to work with the responsible agency (if there is one) and to provide that agency with examples of good locations and designs for curb cuts.

Paths One of the ways to make the space around the house part of the usable living environment is to plan and build good walkways. It is amazing how many houses are built without a sidewalk leading even to the front door. Even small yards provide an enjoyable retreat if they include good walkways. Also plan walkways and paths that lead to the extremes of the lot in both the front and back yards. When the earth-moving equipment shows up to level and prepare for the foundation and driveway, go ahead and create smooth, graded sidewalks at the same time. Then, when the driveway is finished with concrete or asphalt, finish the walkways as well. The added costs will be negligible, and the value of the outdoor living space will be significantly enhanced.

Having walkways around the perimeter of the house and to the edges of the property opens up the outdoor space to everyone. A smooth walkway of asphalt or concrete, at least 36 in. wide, will provide access to people using wheelchairs or other assistive devices. A wider walkway (48 in. to 66 in.) will allow two people to pass each other without having to step off the walkway. Backyard sidewalks double as great play places for young children, too.

When building walkways, use solid surface construction, rather than landscaping blocks, flagstones or decorative rock. Walkway surfaces should be smooth but not slippery. They should have a small gradient (1%) to facilitate drainage and should not have expansion or contraction joints or gutters in them larger than ½ in. Some contractors brush concrete with a stiff broom to create a ribbed texture so the surface will not be slippery when wet. However, ribbed concrete can trap dirt or ice and become more slippery than smooth concrete. If gratings are used for drainage, put them off to the side in an area not likely to be used as a walkway. Select gratings that have openings ½ in. or smaller.

A brick walkway, though less desirable than concrete, can be constructed so that it can be used by people who are unsteady on their feet, wear high heels or use a wheelchair. To achieve a smooth sur-

Curb Cuts

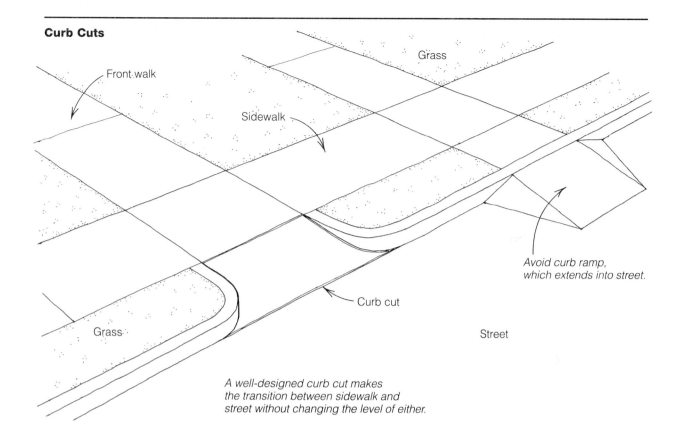

A well-designed curb cut makes
the transition between sidewalk and
street without changing the level of either.

face, the brick walkway needs to be built on a concrete base. The bricks should be laid together with
less than ¼ in. between them and at a uniform
height. The finished walkway will look like brick, but
should be as smooth as concrete or asphalt.

On all walkways, avoid creating seams or level
changes greater than ½ in. Anything larger can cause
people to trip and will be an impassable barrier for
someone in a wheelchair.

On large lots it may be too expensive to finish
the surfaces of every pathway. Nonetheless, the yard
should have a wide pathway that reaches the perimeter of the lot and connects the house and outbuild-
ing areas, if there are any. This pathway, if kept open,
can provide easy access for someone in a small truck,
all-terrain vehicle or large lawnmower with a garden
cart attached.

RESOURCES

Outdoor Lighting

Fiberstars
47456 Fremont Boulevard
Fremont, CA 94538
(800) FBR-STRS
*Fiber-optic cable lighting that
can be used to outline steps and
walkways outdoors.*

Hubbell Lighting
2000 Electric Way
Christiansburg, VA 24073
(703) 382-6111

Idaho Wood
P.O. Box 488
Sandpoint, ID 83864
(800) 635-1100
(208) 263-9521

raak
Lighting Inc.
1051 Clinton Street
Buffalo, NY 14206
(416) 886-6370

Roberts Step-Lite Systems
4501 North Western Avenue
Oklahoma City, OK 73118
(800) 654-8268
(405) 528-7738
*Low-voltage systems for lighting
steps and stairs.*

CHAPTER FIVE
EXTERIOR AND LANDSCAPE DESIGN

One of the greatest mistakes made in designing living spaces is to concentrate almost exclusively on the interiors. Yet from the choice of siding to the design and location of garages, decks and gardens, there are dozens of decisions to be made that can affect the comfort and convenience of the house. Building for a lifetime requires looking at all the exterior components of the house and making decisions with full knowledge of the consequences of each selection. Take time during the planning process to plan the outdoors. As the earth-moving equipment prepares the ground for the foundation of the house, it can also prepare the foundation for the outdoor spaces.

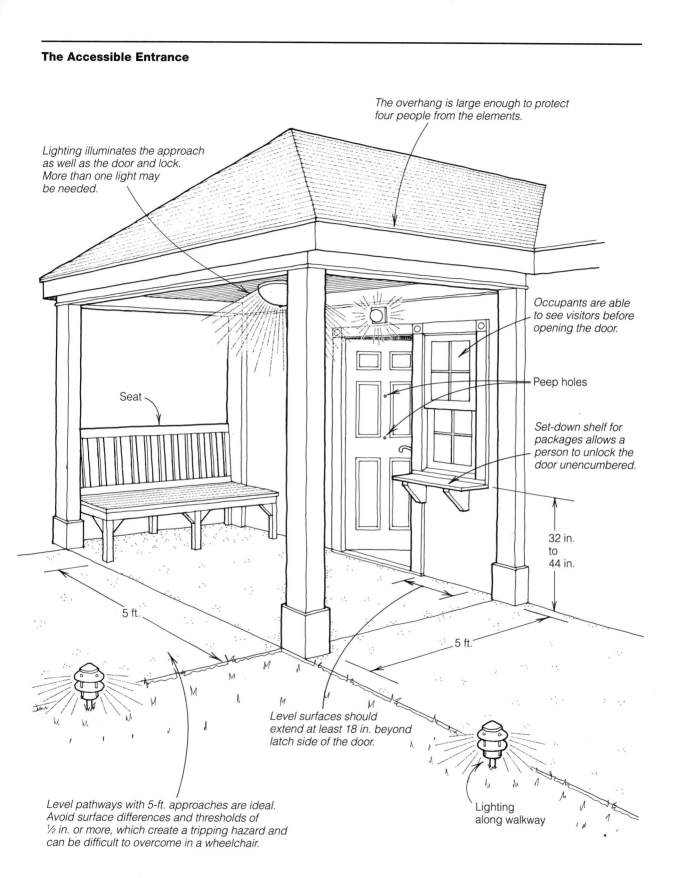

The overhang is large enough to protect four people from the elements.

Lighting illuminates the approach as well as the door and lock. More than one light may be needed.

Occupants are able to see visitors before opening the door.

Peep holes

Set-down shelf for packages allows a person to unlock the door unencumbered.

Seat

32 in. to 44 in.

5 ft.

5 ft.

Level surfaces should extend at least 18 in. beyond latch side of the door.

Lighting along walkway

Level pathways with 5-ft. approaches are ideal. Avoid surface differences and thresholds of ½ in. or more, which create a tripping hazard and can be difficult to overcome in a wheelchair.

THE FACADE

Studies have shown that 14% of people who are 60 and older believe they are paying too much for housing upkeep and maintenance, and 50% of these people are concerned about their future ability to pay for the upkeep of their homes (AARP, 1990). Other studies have shown that 25% of the homes of people 75 and older are in need of maintenance, repair or replacement work (Reschovsky and Newman, 1991).

Houses that are sided with wood (including hardboard, plywood, shingles and clapboards) may require regular painting or staining. Brick, stone and stucco homes generally require minimal maintenance, although they may have wood trim that needs painting or staining. Maintaining the trim around the eaves of the roof and upper windows can present formidable demands for someone who is a bit unsteady on a ladder.

Vinyl siding has improved in both appearance and quality in recent years, and is virtually maintenance free. Cedar shingles and some other wood sidings can be left unfinished, allowing for natural weathering and coloration.

As they age, many people lose the ability to maintain their homes. A low-maintenance siding such as brick, stone, stucco or vinyl is a better choice for the lifespan house than the wood clapboards shown here, which require paint.

ENTRANCES

Entrances to houses have various purposes, and it pays to review them when planning a house. Being aware of the many purposes and requirements of entrances, and of the differences among people who may use them, can inform and guide decisions on where to locate entrances and how to design them.

Entrances should be planned for specific uses and should be designed to support these uses. Entrances can be classified into two somewhat broad categories: resident or family ("private") entrances and guest ("public") entrances. Typically, residents use the back or side door (the door nearest the parking area); guests and strangers use the front door.

Entrances need to accommodate a variety of people: short and tall, wide and thin, people who walk, limp, shuffle or use a wheelchair. Entrances are also used to move goods in and out. These may be the stuff of daily life, such as garbage and groceries, as well as heavy furniture and appliances.

The primary resident entrance is generally close to the location of the automobile. Ideally, this entrance connects a covered parking area with the kitchen or other area that has plenty of space for packages. A well-designed resident entrance allows for goods to be brought into the house as efficiently as possible. People should not have to strain themselves to get the groceries into the house. A secondary resident entrance may connect the house with a patio or deck.

The guest entrance should be clearly defined and delineated. Strangers should not have to wonder which entrance is meant for them. The guest entrance should be visibly "public." As the authors of *A Pattern Language* observe, when guests use the resident entrance, they affect the privacy and functioning of the household. The guest entrance should be located near where guests are expected to park or otherwise approach the house. It should open into a "public" area of the house, such as a foyer leading to the living room, den or dining room, not into areas leading directly to bedrooms and bathrooms.

A multitude of entrances into a house can offer convenience and greater access to emergency egress, but too many can create confusion for visitors and the need to ensure that all locks are secured.

Accessible entrances are protected, easy to get to, well lit and roomy; they offer a dry spot to set down packages while opening the wide and easily operated door. (Photo right: Walt Mixon.)

Basic criteria for entrances All entrances should be well lit, safe and easy to use (see the drawing on p. 53). Each primary entrance (whether resident or guest) should provide protection from the elements. Secondary entrances, such as those leading to a patio, are generally used at one's discretion or convenience and do not require a protective overhang.

All entrances need lighting to illuminate the pathway, door hardware and the immediate surroundings. Good lighting helps prevent accidents, speeds access and allows for surveillance and a greater sense of security. Several manufacturers offer multiple light sets that include walk lights, floodlights, lights that turn on automatically at dusk and door lights. These sets improve the distribution of light around the entrance and are better than a single bright light located at the door.

All entrances around the house should provide easy access. Easy access means a smooth, firm and level or gently sloping pathway without steps termi-

nated by an easy-to-operate door in a doorway with a clear opening of at least 32 in. A 36-in. wide opening is better because it increases accessibility and options for people and people moving objects. A sufficiently smooth pathway has no surface differences greater than ½ in., preferably less than ¼ in. Firm surfaces are provided by concrete, asphalt or carefully laid brick or stone or other substance that won't move under foot or wheel. (For more on pathways, see pp. 50-51.)

Some accessibility guidelines suggest that a single accessible entrance into a house is acceptable. We disagree. Whenever possible, all entrances should be barrier-free. An accessible entrance is convenient for just about anyone and anything. An inaccessible entrance can create needless inconveniences and potential dangers. The idea of separate entrances for the people who are able bodied and people who are disabled is repugnant.

When a Walkway Becomes a Ramp

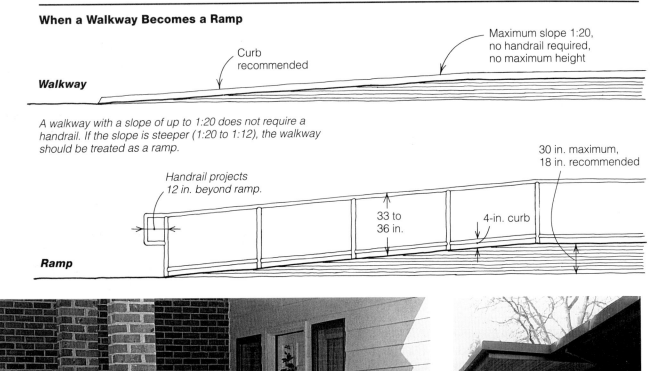

Walkway

Curb recommended

Maximum slope 1:20, no handrail required, no maximum height

A walkway with a slope of up to 1:20 does not require a handrail. If the slope is steeper (1:20 to 1:12), the walkway should be treated as a ramp.

Handrail projects 12 in. beyond ramp.

30 in. maximum, 18 in. recommended

33 to 36 in.

4-in. curb

Ramp

A well-designed ramped entrance can be as inconspicuous as it is convenient. The brick ramped entrance at left is nicely integrated with the entryway of the house. At right, a gentle slope, stone wall and bordering flower bed create a pleasurable walkway for everyone. (Photo at left: courtesy South Carolina Vocational Rehabilitation Dept., West Columbia, S.C.; photo at right: Kevin Ireton.)

RAMPS

The parking area and the walkway to the house should be level. Bridging and berming, discussed on pp. 43-47, are two ways to overcome level changes on a site without resorting to stairs. If the walkway must slope up to the entrance at a 5% grade (1 in. of vertical rise for every 20 in. of horizontal distance), it is essentially a ramp and should be built accordingly (see the drawing on the facing page).

Ramps can provide an architectural focal point and widely appreciated presence, enhancing a site rather than detracting from it. A ramp can be designed to complement the decor of the house. If the house is built with brick, for example, the ramp supports can be made of the same brick laid in a complementary pattern. A ramp on a clapboard-sided house with a porch might carry the line and structure of the porch. A ramp may create an opportunity for a raised bed planter to line the walkway and the porch or foundation. The ramped walkway should be designed with the house, not just be tacked onto it.

Ramps can be built from concrete or asphalt. But if it needs to rise more than 1 ft. above the ground, it may have to be constructed from wood or metal and suspended on a frame to reduce costs.

One researcher (Corlett, 1972) has found that ramps are easier to negotiate than any form of fixed stairway, particularly for people with knee, ankle or strength problems. A well-designed ramp is likely to serve more people longer than well-designed stairs.

A residential ramp that is built to minimum ANSI or UFAS standards (see Chapter 16) is not necessarily good enough. A ramp at a 1:12 slope can be very difficult for people to climb, either in a wheelchair or walking. We believe ramps should be built with a 1:20 slope (that is, a 1-in. rise for every 20 in. of run), which is much easier for people to traverse.

Some people say that ramps signify "disability," that they are an eyesore that detracts from the appearance and value of a home. This perception exists in part because talented designers have not been turned loose to create the well-designed ramp. Ramps, particularly those built for single-family homes, do not need to look like institutional accessories. Two nice-looking ramps are shown in the photos on the facing page.

If the ramp must be steep (1:12 grade), it must meet minimum standards. Many ramps added to homes lack important safety features such as guard rails to keep wheels and people from going off the side and handrails that may be grasped firmly. The guard rails and handrails may include planters, railings and decorative pickets that match the railings and pickets of the front porch. Handrails should not have diameters greater than 1½ in., a need that is too often ignored when the rails are chosen for aesthetic purposes only.

EXTERIOR LIFTS

If sloped walkways, bridges and ramps can't accomplish a required level change, the house could be equipped with an exterior platform lift. An exterior platform lift accommodates a wheelchair user, and in some instances a standing or seated rider. These lifts are generally unattractive and are difficult to incorporate into an aesthetically pleasing entrance. Manufacturers of exterior residential lifts are listed in Resources on p. 65.

Aging Technologies offers a lift system (the Everhard Lift) that is stored in the ground. This system, intended more for commercial applications, may be worth the added expense of installation and maintenance to preserve the exterior appearance of the home.

STAGING AREAS

Staging areas are transitional spaces around the house where the occupants move from outside to in and inside to out. These include garages, carports, porte cochères, porches, patios and decks. As *A Pattern Language* points out, these transition areas buffer the household from the cacophony of the street. They allow the person arriving at the house to begin to adjust and unwind.

Garages and carports Garages and carports protect vehicles and people from the elements. Additionally, they serve as storage areas for a wide variety of household possessions. Many garages contain laundry centers, freezers and home workshops. In houses that

A carport provides protection from the elements and plenty of room for people to pass from the car into the house. (Photo: Kevin Ireton.)

One-Car Garage

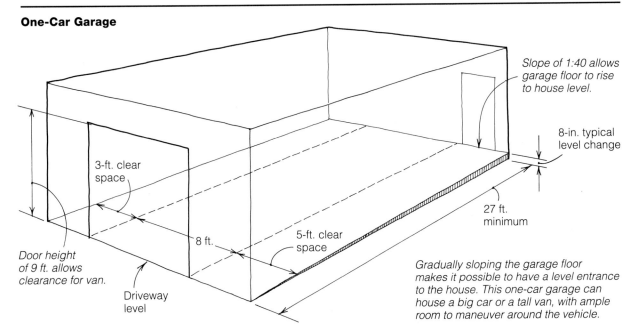

Slope of 1:40 allows garage floor to rise to house level.

8-in. typical level change

3-ft. clear space

27 ft. minimum

8 ft.

5-ft. clear space

Door height of 9 ft. allows clearance for van.

Driveway level

Gradually sloping the garage floor makes it possible to have a level entrance to the house. This one-car garage can house a big car or a tall van, with ample room to maneuver around the vehicle.

were not planned for adequate storage, the garage or carport can become a cluttered mess, presenting obstacles to accessibility and potential tripping hazards.

Garages and carports should be designed to permit safe access to the house. There should be wide pathways between cars and between the cars and the walls. These pathways should be at least 3 ft. wide,

and one side of the vehicle should have 5 ft. of clear space to allow for maneuvering a wheelchair or scooter in and out of a vehicle. This space would also allow enough room for a wheelchair lift, should one be needed. Even if these seemingly oversize spaces aren't needed for easier mobility for a household member, the space will almost certainly be appreciated for its storage potential. Ideally garage doors should be 9 ft. high, a height that should accommodate just about any vehicle a household would ever acquire, including a van with an elevated roof, which is preferred by many wheelchair users. The garage should be outfitted with an automatic door opener and automatic or motion-activated lighting.

The floor of the garage should be flush with the level of the entrance into the house. Although a single step may seem like a trivial obstacle, it prohibits someone in a wheelchair from using that entrance, and for others with reduced stamina or hip or knee difficulties it can become an almost insurmountable obstacle. Additionally, single steps have been known to trip up even the most agile.

The drawing on the facing page shows how the floor of the garage can be sloped to rise at a comfortable level to the entry level of a house. Whenever possible, it is best to let the vehicle do the climbing rather than the resident.

Some codes don't allow the garage floor to be flush with the floor of the house, because of the danger of carbon monoxide gases drifting into the house or because of possible flooding. Actually carbon monoxide fumes are lighter than air, so they rise to the ceiling of the garage (Smith, 1991). If codes require the garage to be separated from the house, leave a space between the wall of the garage and the wall of the house, rather than locating the garage floor at a different level from the house floor. The space can be turned into a small sheltered breezeway.

Porte cochères   The porte cochère began as a covered carriage entrance leading into a courtyard and later became a covered porch at the entrance to a building to shelter persons entering and leaving. Although not a common structure today, the porte-cochère offers significant advantages for households. It can provide a convenient and reasonably inexpensive area for residents visitors (who wouldn't normally use the garage) to get to and from cars while protected from the elements. This is especially helpful for individuals who are slower or who use a wheelchair or other assistive device. It is difficult to use crutches (or cane, walker or wheelchair) and hold an umbrella at the same time.

Porte Cochère

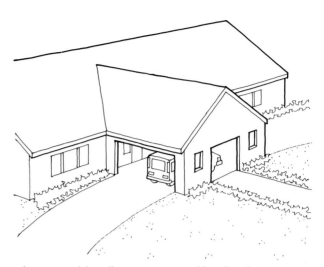

A porte cochère allows a person to drive directly to the entrance, leave the car and walk to the front door out of the elements.

The porte cochère should be long enough and wide enough to accommodate the vehicle and to shelter someone who is entering or exiting or moving around it. Someone using a wheelchair will require a 3-ft. wide pathway with at least a 5-ft. wide area for entering or exiting the vehicle.

Porches   Porches are a convenient staging area for entering and exiting the house. The requirements for a well-designed porch include the following: First, the porch should be at the same level as the door so that there are no entrance barriers. Second, the porch should be large enough to accommodate at least four people at one time, which means 5 ft. by 5 ft. at a minimum. This size would also accommodate someone using a wheelchair accompanied by others. A person should never have to step off the porch to open the door. Third, the porch should be covered.

A traditional screened-in porch provides a nice transition into a home. But if the porch is dark or doesn't have a clearly visible doorbell, visitors may feel uncomfortable and intrusive approaching the house through the porch. Good lighting should illuminate the spaces on and around the porch. The

This covered, cedar-decked porch will be flush with the yard when the landscaping is completed. Shims under the decking create a gentle 1:20 rise to the door sill, which improves drainage.

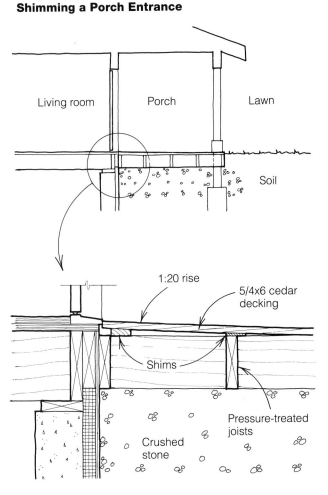

Living room

Porch

Lawn

Soil

1:20 rise

5/4x6 cedar decking

Shims

Pressure-treated joists

Crushed stone

doorbell should be placed in an obvious location and between 36 in. and 48 in. above the floor. A porch that provides a space to place packages other than on the ground offers convenience for the occupant searching for a key. The drawing and photo above offer one suggestion for constructing a porch made with cedar decking that slopes up to the entrance.

Patios A patio, like all the entrances to the house, should be designed as an accessible entrance and built so that it is flush with the threshold of the door. A slight slope (no greater that 1:50) away from the house will allow water to run off.

Patios that are constructed of bricks or flagstones should be smooth and should have no gaps greater than ½ in. Level changes should also be no greater than ½ in. — ¼ in. is recommended.

Decks A deck (or balcony) serves the same purpose as a patio except that it is built off of the ground. Decks are often constructed of wood planks and have steps leading to the ground. Decks can cause significant problems and dangers if they aren't constructed with people of all ages and abilities in mind.

Deck boards should be spaced no more than ¼ in. apart. Spaces greater than this may cause tripping or wheeling hazards. Decks should be bounded by railings with balusters no more than 4 in. apart. This spacing will protect children from climbing or falling through and will help keep someone in a wheelchair from rolling off the edge. Planters and seating around the edges of a deck also help keep people from falling.

An Accessible Deck

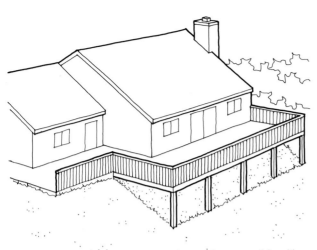

Inaccessible outdoor space can be made accessible with a deck, which can provide a level surface over rough terrrain.

A deck that encircles the house, particularly on an uneven site, can furnish a pathway around the house and create many options for entrances (see the drawing above). An exterior door on the far side of the house may be connected to a bridge or ramp on the other side of the house by way of the deck. A deck and a bridge can create accessibility on an uneven site and an attractive space for enjoying the outdoors.

LANDSCAPING

The trees, lawns, shrubs, flower beds, gardens and pathways to them should be planned to meet the same accessibility criteria that are used for designing and constructing the interior of the house. And, although the thought of spending vast amounts of time in our gardens in our advanced years may be pleasing to many of us, the rigors of maintaining gardens and yards should not be underestimated. The chart on p. 63 lists some routine outdoor chores and the physical challenges they can pose. Outdoor chores are great exercise, but the loss of the ability to do yard work should not have to result in a neglected yard or garden.

Some decisions are best made before construction on the house has even begun. A detailed site design showning grades, plantings, paths, retaining walls and other features will allow you to create an accessible and easy-to-maintain yard.

Trees Trees present two sets of problems on a new building site. First, what to do about existing trees on the site and, second, what new trees to plant and where. Some builders prefer to clear the lot entirely of trees and not be burdened by the obstacles they create when building the house. Others are more sensitive toward maintaining the existing environment. Be sure you and your builder agree on what will happen to the trees before the bulldozer shows up.

Trees of considerable size represent decades of growth and an extraordinary treasure. Mature trees add value to the site and can help reduce the costs of landscaping. Keep as many trees as possible and avoid injuring them in the excavation and construction process.

Trees are injured when too much dirt is taken away or when their roots or bark are cut. They suffocate if too much dirt is piled around their base, and they are damaged when the earth is compacted around their base by heavy equipment. Trees that are to be saved should have a fence constructed around them for protection. It may be a wise investment to contact an arborist to assist in developing plans for protecting the trees while the site work and construction are underway.

When selecting trees to plant or determining which trees to leave in place, it is worthwhile to consider the purpose of each one. Is it to provide shade, create a windbreak, bear fruit, provide decoration or offer camouflage? A shade tree may be a welcome complement to a patio, but it can also block out the sunshine needed to melt an icy sidewalk.

When shopping for new trees, consider the following:
• The expected height of the tree, relative to the height of the house. Will the tree grow tall enough to shade the areas of the house where shade is desired?
• The expected diameter of the tree and the amount of space needed around the tree to allow for its future growth.

Planning the Landscape

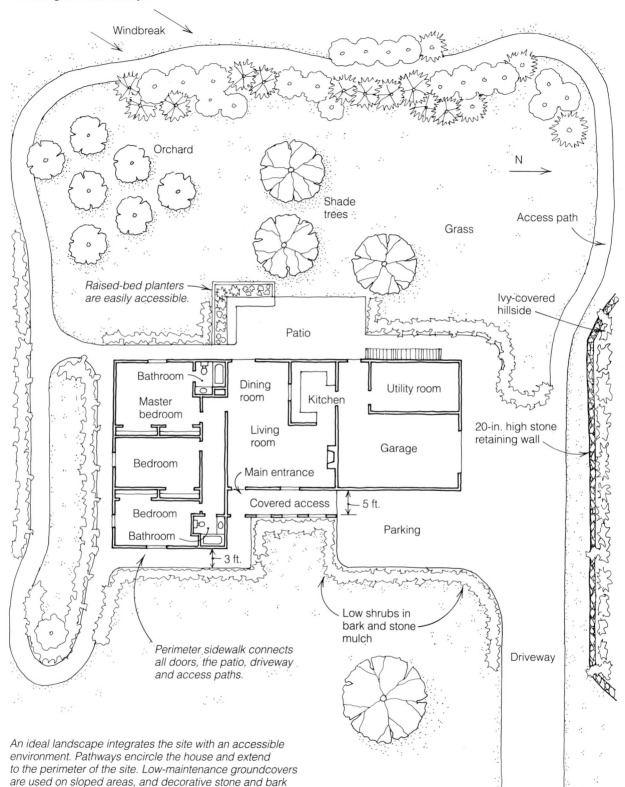

Windbreak

Orchard

Shade trees

N

Access path

Grass

Raised-bed planters are easily accessible.

Ivy-covered hillside

Patio

Bathroom

Dining room

Kitchen

Utility room

Master bedroom

Living room

Garage

Bedroom

Main entrance

20-in. high stone retaining wall

Bedroom

Covered access

5 ft.

Bathroom

Parking

3 ft.

Low shrubs in bark and stone mulch

Perimeter sidewalk connects all doors, the patio, driveway and access paths.

Driveway

An ideal landscape integrates the site with an accessible environment. Pathways encircle the house and extend to the perimeter of the site. Low-maintenance groundcovers are used on sloped areas, and decorative stone and bark surround shrubs.

• The typical root structure. As the roots grow, are they likely to interfere with foundations and water lines? Are they likely to grow close to the surface and disrupt a sidewalk or driveway? How far from the tree can the roots be expected to surface?

• The rate of growth.

• The amount of care the tree will require when it is first planted. Will it need fertilizing or pruning?

• The type and amount of debris the tree will produce? Will the debris be difficult to clean up? Could it be hazardous on walking surfaces?

• The fruit. Is it safe for a child to eat (even inadvertently)? Will it attract birds (and bird droppings)?

Trees can be used to create windbreaks and visual fences. If they are located on the outer edges of the property, consider building a pathway to them to allow access by a wheelchair and/or garden cart.

Orchards may require a considerable amount of attention. Young trees need to be fed, watered and pruned. On a large lot, it may be wise to run a water line to the orchard. Plan a path to and around the orchard for wheeled vehicles. This will be especially appreciated at harvest time. Consider planting dwarf fruit trees. Though they may still require a ladder or long-handled fruit picker at harvest time, they should be easier to manage than standard trees.

Lawns Americans have a real fetish for manicured lawns. Grass lawns are neat and attractive and can take a lot of abuse from active children, but they also require a lot of routine maintenance. Before planting the whole yard with the generic grass seed sold at the local discount store, consult your county cooperative extension office for advice on suitable grass species and mixes that resist disease and repel insects. Consider planting groundcovers or grasses that require almost no regular maintenance (especially mowing).

Groundcovers such as ivy, thrift and ajuga, among others, can create an almost maintenance-free yard. Although they may not be strong enough to handle a lot of traffic, and certainly would not be an

The Demands of Maintaining Outdoor Areas

Task	Demands
Preparing earth for planting	Using tiller, shovel, rake and hoe. Strength, bending, stooping, kneeling and fine fingering.
Planting seeds and bedding plants	Bending, stooping, kneeling and fine fingering.
Planting trees and shrubs	Strength, bending, stooping, kneeling and fine fingering.
Mowing with riding mower (electric start)	Fine fingering, climbing onto mower, grasping and strength in arms, vision.
Mowing with rotary mower	Fine fingering, pulling, strength in arms, walking, stamina, vision.
Cleaning up debris	Bending, stooping, kneeling, fine fingering, gripping, grasping, stamina and strength to lift and remove collection.
Watering	Depends on system and availability of water source.
Pruning, trimming	Gripping, grasping, reaching, strength in arms and fingers.
Weeding	Gripping, grasping, fine fingering, reaching, bending, stooping, kneeling.
Getting to areas on site	Depends on pathway and mode of walking or wheeling.

adequate cover for children to play on, they can fill in many areas that may be difficult to mow or that would be unlikely to be used as a walkway or play area. Most groundcovers, once they are established, help keep out weeds and need nothing more than an occasional trimming or redirection to keep them within their bounds.

Lawns that require weekly mowing and a regular dose of herbicides and pesticides are not the ideal outdoor oasis. Ask yourself if it is worth adding to the destruction of the environment to create perfectly coiffed lawns, and consider the amount of work involved. If a person begins having difficulty maintaining the yard, it can quickly turn into an eyesore.

Foundation plantings   Bushes and shrubs are often used to border the house and smooth the seam between the house and the soil. Your local landscaper will be able to provide you with the recommended plantings for these areas. These plants will need to be pruned and trimmed to keep them attractively shaped and prevent them from covering up more of the house than you would like. Two problems can arise in keeping the shrubs trimmed. First, the physical stamina required to use pruning shears, lopping trimmers or trimmers can be formidable. Even the electric-powered trimmers are too heavy for many people to operate safely. Second, it may be difficult to get to the plants that require trimming. Keep border plantings shallow, no deeper than 24 in., if they are accessible from only one side.

Foundation plantings can be easily pruned, cultivated and weeded from a perimeter walkway around the house, even by people who have walking difficulties or who use a wheelchair.

Gardens   Gardening is the most popular pastime of adults in the United States, and it should be accessible to all. However, normally flower beds and vegetable gardens are at ground level, which is out of reach of many people. Raised beds offer advantages for people of all ages and abilities. Raised beds can be built from large stones, bricks, railroad ties or wood. A height of 12 in. is helpful, but 18 in. to 24 in. will be within reach of people who use wheelchairs or who have problems bending, stooping and kneeling.

Raised beds offer efficient vegetable and flower gardening at an accessible height. (Photo: Jay O'Neil.)

Raised-bed gardens should be no more than 24 in. wide unless they can be approached from both sides.

Multiple raised beds should have pathways between them at least 36 in. wide to allow for garden carts and wheelchairs. Pathways 4 ft. wide would be even better.

An exceptionally attractive raised bed area can be created by using a ramped walkway as one of the borders. The raised beds can hold short shrubs and provide a space for flowers that will line the ramp to the house. A gradual curve in the walkway will provide a natural pocket for a small grotto, water garden or rock garden.

Porches, decks and patios are ideal locations for container gardening. Containers may be built from the same materials used for the deck or contrasting stone or wood. Some people purchase old whiskey barrels and planters designed for outdoor container gardening.

Gardening requires a place to store tools, a source of water, a place for a compost and smooth, solid surface pathways. If concrete or asphalt are too expensive for the budget, don't be tempted to use loose stones or wood chips. Soft, loose material is harder to move wheels through and is unsteady underfoot. Grass is preferred.

RESOURCES

The list below includes manufacturers of outdoor residential ramps and lifts. For manufacturers of indoor lifts, stairway lifts and elevators, see p. 133; for comprehensive catalog companies, see p. 221.

Aging Technologies
1329 Inverness
Lawrence, KS 66045
(913) 841-5036
The Everhard Lift, which is enclosed in a concrete pit and flush with the ground.

AlumiRamp
90 Taylor Street
Quincy, MI 49082
(517) 639-8777
Modular aluminum ramp systems.

American Stair-Glide Corporation
4001 East 138th Street
Grandview, MO 64030
(800) 383-3100
(816) 763-3100
Porch-Lifts, wheelchair carrier-lifts, inclined platforms, stair lifts, elevators.

Handi-Access Company
P.O. Box 3071
Littleton, CO 80161-3071
(800) 551-0525
(303) 795-9102
Aluminum ramp systems.

Handi-Ramp
P.O. Box 745
1414 Armour Boulevard
Mundelein, IL 60060
(800) 876-7267
(312) 816-7525
Galvanized steel or aluminum ramp systems.

Hiro Lift USA
510 North Belleview Avenue
Cinnaminson, NJ 08077
(800) 451-5438
(609) 829-4315
Inclined wheelchair lifts.

JH Industries
8901 E. Pleasant Valley Road
Independence, OH 44131
(800) 321-4964
(216) 524-7520
Aluminum ramp systems.

Quick Deck
P.O. Box 607
Livermore, CA 94550
(415) 516-0603
Modular steel ramp systems.

Rampus
P.O. Box 37
Coldwater, MI 49036
(800) 876-9498
Aluminum ramp systems.

Spectrum Pool Products
9600 Inspiration Drive
Missoula, MT 59802
(406) 543-5309
Lifts for in-ground swimming pools, above-ground pools and spas.

A GALLERY OF
ACCESSIBLE DESIGN

Accessible design doesn't have to look institutional. The houses shown on the following pages were designed for use by people with various disabilities, yet they don't sacrifice aesthetics.

Open Plan, Few Doors
Architect: *Chuck Williams*
Builder: *Jim Wolfer*

The owner of this house was skeptical of claims made for "barrier-free" buildings. At both the college where he teaches and at his church, he found himself unable to enter new, supposedly accessible buildings because of door closers, thresholds and saddles. In building his own home, he wanted to be assured of complete access to the house, garden and pathways.

The solution was found in an open plan with few doors. The carport provides easy access to the bedroom, bathroom and kitchen. The house is bathed in natural sunlight and has a covered breezeway and sunroom. Flush transitions are provided between rooms, and exterior doors are equipped with automatic door bottoms, which eliminate the need for thresholds.

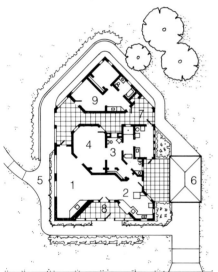

1. Living room
2. Kitchen
3. Bathroom
4. Bedroom
5. Pathway
6. Carport
7. Breezeway
8. Sunroom
9. Apartment for guest
   or live-in aide

The unusual kitchen design (top) has no upper cabinets, while the lower cabinets are actually mounted on casters. A cantilevered counter permits wheelchair access. The corner sink in the bathroom (above) was installed at a height that perfectly suited the home owner. He can also wheel himself into the shower. The shower pan extends across the floor to guard against water damage. (Photos: Kevin Ireton.)

A House on One Level
Designer: *Sam Clark*
Builder: *Peter Peltz Construction*

Karen Seeger and Michael Birnbaum had lived in a comfortable Vermont mountain house with their son Tyler, who uses a wheelchair, but the demands of carrying him up and down the stairs proved burdensome as he grew. There was simply no way to tame the steep site so that it could allow for the independence of a kid in a wheelchair. Everyone's comfort and independence required a new, level site and a level-headed design.

The open floor plan of the new house allows Tyler to get around easily in his wheelchair, indoors and out. Even though the new house sits on a full basement, the design allows for gradual, stepless entrances. The large porch is level with the interior floor, and the lawn area only slightly below. Large stones from the excavation, along with concrete pavers, were used as a berm to the front door and a path between the two main entrances.

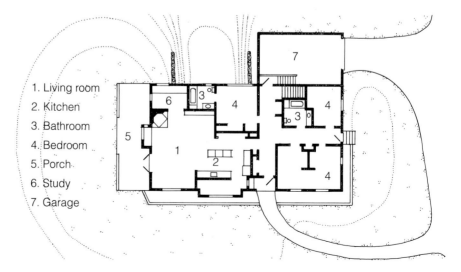

1. Living room
2. Kitchen
3. Bathroom
4. Bedroom
5. Porch
6. Study
7. Garage

Fourth Quarter
Designer: *Ted Brown*
Framer: *Ken Ash Construction*
Builders: *Sara Davidson, Jonathan Tate, Joel Little*

**Wobble Davidson used to scout for professional
football teams, so he and his wife, Sara, named their
"retirement" house Fourth Quarter. Although neither of
them has any trouble walking, they built their house to
accommodate them if one day they did. Both regularly
use the elevator, the entrance to which is in the foyer
between the two garages (above right). Wobble's
bathroom is equipped with a roll-in shower and an
18-in. high toilet. The bathroom on the third floor has
an old-fashioned sink that is wheelchair accessible
(right). (Photographer: Walt Mixon.)**

Barrier-Free Remodel
Architect: *William Dutcher*
Builder/Remodeler: *Tom Nowell*

Pauli and Sandy Muir needed more room and more color in their house.
And Sandy, who had polio in his youth and gets around the house mostly
in his wheelchair, needed more access. The house needed ramps along
both sides, and the two-step difference in levels between the house and
the garden had to be smoothed over. In the front of the house, truckloads
of fill raised the grade, and the new earth was held away from the house
with low retaining walls. Excavated earth was also recycled into the
garden to raise the grade at the back of the house. House and garden are
now linked by an equally accessible deck.

Inside, the bathroom (above right) is equipped with a bathtub with a wide, flat rim that makes it easier for Sandy to transfer from his wheelchair. Stainless-steel grab bars around the perimeter of the bathroom double as towel racks. The kitchenette (right) has a 6½-ft. counter with a sink, a small cooktop and an under-counter refrigerator at one end. This allows Sandy to prepare some of his famous specialties. (Photos: Chuck Miller.)

Spatial Complexity, Full Access
Architect: *Max Jacobson (Jacobson, Silverstein and Winslow, Architects)*
Builder: *Rangel Brothers Construction*

The Hoberts loved their previous home, with its wonderfully complex multilevel design. After Kent became paralyzed, however, the numerous sets of stairs became impossible for him to negotiate. When they acquired a flat lot just down the road, they provided architect Max Jacobson with the following criteria for their new home: spatial complexity and excitement similar to their old house; full functional accessibility, inside and out; and a house that doesn't "look" designed for people who have a disability.

This house was selected as one of six winners of the California State Department of Rehabilitation's 1989 Award of Merit for outstanding design providing handicapped access. (Photos: Jay O'Neil.)

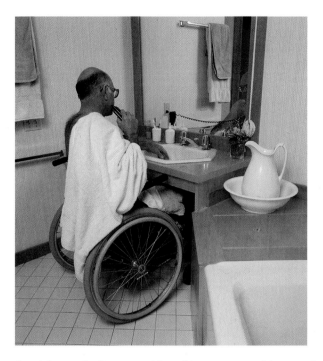

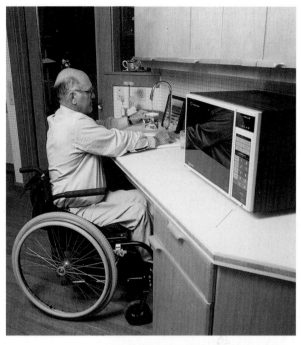

Spatial complexity was achieved by an outreaching, angled plan, by varying ceiling heights and slopes and by unusual lighting strategies. Full accessibility was provided for the workshop, kitchen, therapeutic hot tub, exterior gardens and even for mechanical maintenance items such as the landscape sprinkler system.

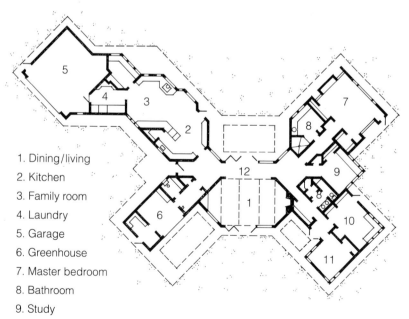

1. Dining/living
2. Kitchen
3. Family room
4. Laundry
5. Garage
6. Greenhouse
7. Master bedroom
8. Bathroom
9. Study
10. Bedroom
11. Guest room
12. Entry hall

An Accessible Two-Story Home
Designer: *Diana Moore, based on plans by Tim Treadwell*

Injured in Vietnam, William Moore lost his legs at the hip. Today he is a successful CPA and family man. Stepless entrances and an elevator near the front door allow him easy access, inside and out. (Photos: Walt Mixon.)

Accessible Multi-Family Housing
Architect: *Design Coalition*
Builders: *Connery Construction*

Twelve wheelchair-accessible units were included in a 28-unit mixed-income, resident-managed project. The building exteriors echo the massing and roof shapes of the neighborhood. Entry to the units is on grade. Four of the units are fully barrier free. The kitchen cabinets are a national manufacturer's standard line for accessibility, with minor modifications. (Photos: Lou Host-Jablonski.)

PART THREE
INTERIORS

Even in our city zoos we have created artificially a normal ecology for the animals. But we refuse to do it for our human brothers. For mountain goats, we make them some rocks to climb on; we give antelopes a park-like place with a moat around it; even the snakes enjoy air-conditioning. But we won't provide proper housing for human beings... — Ted F. Silvey, AFL-CIO

CHAPTER SIX
MECHANICAL SYSTEMS, FLOORS AND WALLS

The mechanical systems, floors and walls of a home form the infrastructure of the building: an underlying set of systems, structures and surfaces that appear in or interconnect every room. The purpose of this chapter is to describe the various elements of the infrastructure in relation to their support of and use by people of all ages and abilities. Topics to be addressed include the health and usefulness of the living environment and their relationship to building materials; electrical components and lighting; heating, ventilation and cooling systems; communications; and surface treatments of floors and walls.

Common Sources of Indoor Air Pollution

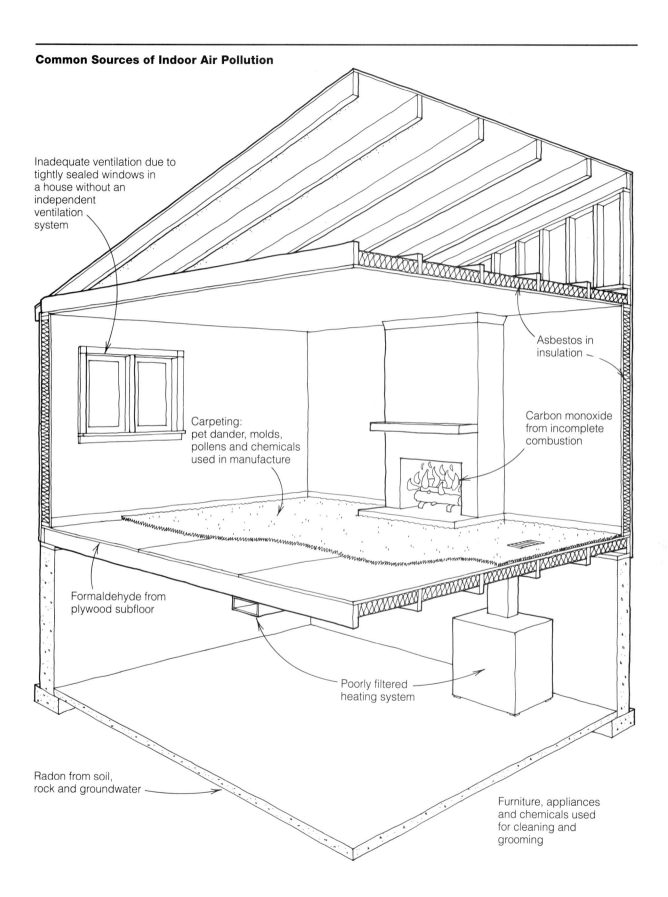

Inadequate ventilation due to tightly sealed windows in a house without an independent ventilation system

Asbestos in insulation

Carpeting: pet dander, molds, pollens and chemicals used in manufacture

Carbon monoxide from incomplete combustion

Formaldehyde from plywood subfloor

Poorly filtered heating system

Radon from soil, rock and groundwater

Furniture, appliances and chemicals used for cleaning and grooming

THE HEALTHY HOME

The lifespan house should be as healthy and comfortable to live in as possible, and that means free of indoor air pollution. The energy crisis of the mid-1970s led to improved energy efficiency in residential construction, but an unfortunate by-product of that worthy effort has been an increase in indoor air pollution. With the tightening up of houses and office buildings has come "sick building syndrome." For many people, the quality of the air inside their homes is now worse than the quality of the air outside. But the issue of energy efficiency vs. clean air isn't a matter of irreconcilable trade-offs. It is entirely possible, and increasingly necessary, to build energy-efficient houses that are also healthy to live in.

As a general rule, the longer a person is exposed to a toxic substance, the greater is the likelihood of suffering harmful effects from the substance. Thus, as our populace lives increasingly longer lives, it can be assumed that larger numbers of people will develop diseases or other reactions to the toxins in their homes. The drawing on p. 79 identifies some of the principal sources for pollutants.

It has been suggested that your clothes are your second skin and your living space your third skin, and that body/clothing/dwelling represent a single organism (Maciocha, 1987). Even if you don't subscribe to this holistic viewpoint, you would be wise to select building materials and all other components that will be going into your home with the same concern for health as you choose the food you eat.

Pollutants are categorized as particulates (solids or liquid droplets) or gases (vapors). Common particulate pollutants in the home include asbestos and various pathogens and allergens. Asbestos is a mineral fiber that has been used in hundreds of building materials over the years, especially for insulation and fireproofing purposes. The fibers, which are small enough to pass through a vacuum-cleaner bag, can lodge in the lungs and cause asbestosis (a disease of the lungs) or cancer. Unfortunately, the lag time between exposure and clinical manifestation of asbestos exposure can be anywhere from 15 to 30 years. Kane (1985) suggests that all children living in cities in the United States run the risk of asbestos exposure from the air, water or food.

Houses that were built after 1977 are much less likely to have asbestos-containing materials in them, although some vinyl floor coverings may contain asbestos. If you are planning to remodel a house built before 1978, it would be wise to identify and take proper measures for handling materials that might contain asbestos. Call your local building department for advice on current regulations and practices.

Pathogens are substances that cause disease, and allergens induce allergies. Bacteria, viruses, mold, pollens, insects, people dander and hair from pets collect in carpets, fabrics, duct systems, humidifiers and fan coil units and can cause colds, flu, pneumonia and allergies. People susceptible to colds and allergies may do better in homes with uncarpeted hardwood floors; air-conditioning systems with easy-to-access air filters that may be changed frequently also help.

Reports of illnesses believed to be related to indoor air environments have increased dramatically over the past decade. However, it is difficult to distinguish between problems resulting from indoor air exposure to chemicals and sensitivity that may arise from bacteria, mites, foods or allergens such as dust (Henry et al., 1991). Nonetheless, the increased incidence of asthma and deaths from asthma in industrialized nations (Jackson et al., 1988), the documentation that autoimmune diseases are caused by environmental chemicals (Bigazzi, 1988) and the suggested link in the increased number of cases of depression and environmental air quality (Klerman and Weissman, 1989) all indicate that homes should be built so that the occupants are able to control and clean the indoor air they breathe.

Common gaseous pollutants include radon, carbon dioxide, carbon monoxide, sulfur dioxide, oxides of nitrogen, cigarette smoke and volatile organic chemicals. Radon is a colorless, odorless gas that results from the decay of radium, a common element found in soil, rock and groundwater. Highly energy-efficient residences in regions where radon occurs can pose the greatest risk of long-term radon exposure, which can cause lung cancer. The Centers for Disease Control in Atlanta estimates that radon-related lung cancer is responsible for 5,000 to 20,000 deaths per year; the Consumer Federation of America suggests that the number may be as high as 30,000. The Environmental Protection Agency reported that exposure to radon may be the second leading cause of lung cancer, after cigarette smoking. Homes with high radon levels in which one or more occupants smoke are particularly dangerous. In areas where radon concentrations are high, houses can be designed to reduce the risk (check with your local building department).

The increasing use of woodstoves and kerosene heaters in the 1970s and 1980s has contributed to the buildup of toxic gases in the home. Gas ranges and appliances are also culprits. Gas appliances cost less to operate than electric appliances, but the savings may be offset by visits to the doctor and medication for colds and respiratory infections. The greatest danger from gas appliances is carbon monoxide poisoning. However, these appliances also emit nitrous oxides and other gases that have caused respiratory illness in young children and persons with emphysema and asthma. Young children who live in homes with gas ranges and appliances have higher rates of respiratory infection and illness than children in homes equipped with electric ranges (Kane, 1985).

Homes with gas appliances and fuel-burning stoves or fireplaces need a supply of fresh air, such as a slightly open window, while the fuel is burning. Carbon monoxide is produced when fuels do not burn completely and is especially dangerous when a source of fresh air is not available. Studies completed in the 1970s (Kane, 1985) revealed that as many as 25% of 372 homes included in the research were discharging carbon monoxide into the atmosphere at rates of 200 parts per million (ppm). This is more than 20 times greater than the Environmental Protection Agency standard of 9 ppm.

Volatile organic compounds (VOCs) include styrene, benzene, methylene chloride and xylene isomers. These substances are used in insulation, cleaning agents, spray paints, adhesives and many other materials. Formaldehyde is a dangerous VOC found in hundreds of products, including pressed wood, cosmetics, paper products, automobiles, draperies, permanent press fabrics, cigarettes and dry-cleaning chemicals. Formaldehyde is a depressant, mutagen and carcinogen. It is estimated that as many as 11 million people suffer the effects of elevated formaldehyde concentrations in the home (Vaughan, Strader, Davis and Daling, 1986).

Everyone involved in design and construction should stay informed on the issue of building homes that are healthy to live in (see Resources on p. 95 for some publications on the subject). Some simple steps that can be taken include:

• Test for radon emission on your prospective site before building.
• Select solid-wood flooring, cabinets and other materials that don't use urea formaldehyde adhesives. Avoid particleboard.
• If you must have floor coverings, investigate the materials they are made from before purchasing. Natural fibers such as cotton or wool are a better alternative than synthetics.
• Equip the house with a ventilation system that provides an adequate supply of fresh air.
• Understand the risks and trade-offs of installing gas-powered appliances.

WIRING

The electricity needs for houses today are quite different from the needs in the 1950s. Modern communications and home entertainment require extensive, reliable electrical wiring. There is also good reason to expect that health care will increasingly be administered within the home, and home health care will require special attention to electrical needs. Ever-increasing numbers of people with chronic illnesses are sustained by daily therapies (dialysis, medication infusion) and continual therapies (oxygen) that require electrical power. The lifespan house must be designed to meet the future medical needs of its occupants.

One way to prepare for the future is to be sure that the components of the electrical infrastructure are easy-to-reach and adaptable. There should be adequate outlets in rooms likely to be used for caregiving (bedrooms and bathrooms), and cables should be labeled for easy identification. A surface-mounted cable raceway would permit new wiring to be added simply and easily. For example, a new household sound system could be installed throughout the house by merely opening the raceway and laying the wire inside. Eliminating a system would require only a few minutes of work to unplug the ends of the wiring from the junction boxes and lift out the wire. The electrical wiring, service boxes and connections installed today are likely to need replacement or upgrading tomorrow. Install a cable race and label the cables to avoid fishing expeditions later.

Outlets and switches Apartment dwellers and home owners often complain that they don't have enough outlets. When people cannot find a convenient outlet they add extension cords and taps. These solutions, however, create the potential for overloaded circuits and fires. They are also tripping hazards.

The National Electrical Code (NEC) requires that no point along the floor line in any wall space be more than 6 ft. from an outlet. Although this regulation appears to ensure a sufficient number of outlets, the fact is that many of them become inaccessible because they are obstructed by furniture. Getting to these electrical outlets becomes more of a challenge with passing years. We suggest instead that at least two outlets be installed on each wall in positions that are unlikely to be obstructed by furniture.

The best way to avoid blocking electrical outlets is to install some outlets higher than normal, as shown in the drawing below right. Outlets at 30 in. to 44 in.

will clear most tables, desks, chairs and sofas. A combination switch and outlet at the entrance to each room is particularly useful for items that are regularly plugged and unplugged, such as vacuum cleaners. Outlets installed at a lower level can then be used only for items that are rarely unplugged, such as lamps. All outlets and switches should be within the optimal reach zone (ORZ) of 20 in. to 44 in. off the floor, where people of various heights and abilities can reach without exertion or assistance.

Pay particular attention to wiring in bedrooms. Common bedside appliances are a lamp, alarm clock, electric blanket, heating pad and television. With all this stuff plugged into one standard dual-outlet receptacle, the area becomes a tangle of electrical cords. Additionally, individuals who use assistive devices to communicate, who require a home health-care device or who add a home control system may have additional needs for electrical power near the bed.

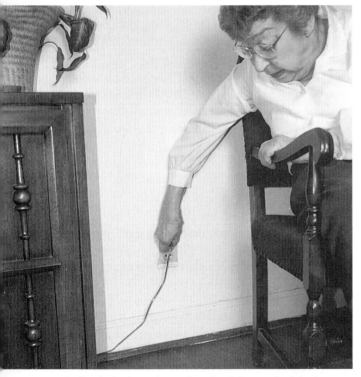

A simple task such as plugging into an electrical outlets becomes difficult if it requires moving furniture, stooping or kneeling and grasping the plug. Staggering the heights of outlets in a room can help eliminate these gymnastics.

Accessible Switches and Outlets

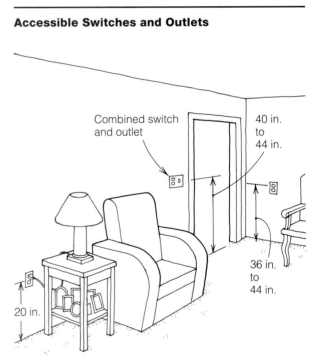

Combined switch and outlet

40 in. to 44 in.

36 in. to 44 in.

20 in.

Keep all outlets and switches within the optimal reach zone (20 in. to 44 in.). Outlets installed at the high end of this zone are handy for occasionally used appliances, such as vacuum cleaners, because they can be reached without moving furniture. Switch/outlet combinations at the entrance to each room are a good investment.

Bedroom walls that are long enough to accommodate a bed, and walls in other rooms where extra lamps, computers, televisions, answering machines and other electronic devices are likely to be located, should have four-outlet receptacles, ideally on two separate circuits. In the bedroom, one of the outlets should be wired to a three-way switch at the entrance to the room, allowing a bedside lamp to be turned on at the door and off at the bed.

Light switches must be located at all entrances to each room on the side nearest the door handle. The light switch at room entrances should be located the same distance from the door frame and at the same height. Switches are generally required to be located at a height of 36 in. to 48 in., but we prefer a range between 40 in. to 44 in. This height is just out of the reach of a toddler, and just within the reach of a person of shorter stature who may be seated or using a wheelchair. Wiring for adaptability should be the goal (see the drawing at right).

The National Electrical Code requires that every habitable room in the house have lighting that can be controlled by a switch. This can be in the form of permanently installed lighting outlets that are controlled by a switch. Switched outlets that can control lighting in far corners are particularly helpful to many people. They can also be much easier to use than the switches on lamps. For some individuals, a switch-operated outlet may mean the difference between using and not using a product.

Light switches must be located at both the top and bottom of stairs, and they should be located at least one full stride (36 in.), and preferably 48 in., away from the first step, so a person will not be at risk of stepping onto the stairs in darkness or immediately after the light level changes.

Switches with multiple controls, such as the typical three-way switches at the top and bottom of stairs, should be located so that one person cannot inadvertently put someone else into darkness. We have seen houses where a switch controlling the light on the stairway was located unwisely, on the other side of the door at the top of the stairs.

As with all products in the house, avoid toggle switches, dimmer knobs and other devices that require fine fingering (see pp. 26-27). Rocker or paddle switches are the easiest to operate for people who have difficulty using their fingers or hands. Some

Wiring for Adaptability

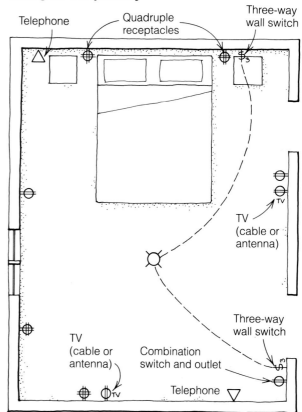

Rooms become more usable if they are adequately wired for electrical needs. In each room, provide multiple telephone and cable or antenna television hookups. Install quadruple outlets on either side of potential bed locations and where desks are likely to be placed.

large paddle switches can even be operated with an elbow or forearm. Light switches with an internal light help direct the user to them. They also act as a guide if someone is trying to move through a room in the darkness.

Automated lighting, which is activated by motion, sound or even body heat, can be a significant boon for people who are unable to move freely and easily around the room. Even though many of these devices are incredibly simple to use, people need to adjust them so that they are sensitive to appropriate levels of stimuli. Some systems do not have user-friendly controls for adjusting them and may require a magnifying glass and screwdriver to establish the appropriate sensitivity level. Hard-to use-adjustment controls make the device inconvenient to use in locations where activities may change, thereby requiring different sensitivity levels. An automatic lamp may be adjusted to suit the needs of a person living alone, but when the grandchildren visit, the lamp will blink on and off. If the setting can't be readjusted easily, the lamp may well be unplugged for the duration of the visit.

The type of sensing system needed depends on the device and where it will be used. Motion detectors adjusted to detect movement next to a bed would provide a lighted pathway as soon as someone's feet dangled over the edge. A sound-activated device in a bedroom, on the other hand, may cause problems if an occupant snores.

Automated light systems activate and deactivate automatically. Some automatically turn off after a certain period of time, which is usually adjustable. Some motion detectors turn the lights on when motion is detected and turn them off after a brief period of time without activity. Thus, a motion detector system may work well when you walk into a room, but after you are ensconced in a chair reading a book, you may be thrown into darkness because the system can't detect the movement associated with turning a page. Before deciding on an automated system, evaluate the controls, the ease of adjusting sensitivity and the ability to override the system.

Ground-fault circuit interrupters Ground-fault circuit interrupters (GFCIs) are now required by electrical codes in kitchens, bathrooms, garages and other areas inside and outside of the house. These devices shut off the flow of electricity when they detect an imbalance in the circuit, that is, when the current is running to an unintended ground, which could be through a person. Thus, if a person inadvertently came in contact with a hot conductor while grounded, the GFCI would sense the situation almost immediately and trip the circuit. The person would feel no more than a momentary shock, instead of possibly being killed. The expense of installing ground-fault circuit interrupters is negligible compared to the savings in human life.

Service panel The electrical service panel is traditionally installed in a dark, out-of-the-way location, such as the basement or the garage. This custom makes little sense. When a circuit breaker trips, throwing at least part of the house into darkness, the occupant needs to be able to find and reach the service panel easily. Also, placing service panels in remote locations requires extra wiring.

The service panel should be installed in a location that is easily accessible and has plenty of clear space (30 in. by 48 in.) in front of it. It should be located with the optimal reach zone and found easily when the power is off. A hallway between the kitchen and utility room or an area near a back entranceway may work well. The service panel could be located on a wall in the kitchen or utility room and "dressed up" by a small frame around the box and a cabinet door that matches other cabinets in the room, as shown in the drawing at left.

LIGHTING

Lighting serves several purposes in a residential environment. It allows us to see where we are going and what we are doing, of course, and it affects the mood of a room or space (dark and gloomy vs. bright and

---

Disguised Service Panel

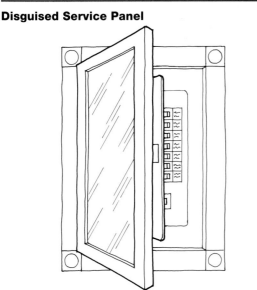

The electrical service panel should be placed in a prominent location in any easily accessible room, not stuck in a remote corner of the basement. A service panel can be integrated into the room's design; it can be concealed behind a mirror, chalkboard or wall hanging, or it can have a surface that matches adjacent cabinets.

The well-lit house combines abundant natural light with strategically located task lighting.

cheerful). A well-lit dining area can also help promote good health. People with seasonal affective disorders or other problems related to insufficient natural light are helped by well-lit living environments.

Adequate lighting becomes increasingly important as we become older, and houses should be designed to provide ample amounts of natural and artificial lighting for everyone. The lens of the human eye yellows over time, and the muscles of the eye weaken. The pupils of a 20-year-old dilate more rapidly and to a size twice as large as the pupils of an 80-year-old. Thus, research has shown, many older adults require two to three times the amount of light as do younger adults (Weale, 1961).

Natural light In several surveys conducted of hundreds of individuals, one of the most frequently expressed desires for the living environment was for lots of natural light. The use of natural lighting affects the aesthetics, work efficiency, health, safety and economics of the home. The availability of natural light is particularly important to people with limited opportunities to venture outside the house. Studies completed by the American Association of Retired Persons have shown that the average person age 60

and older spends 80% to 90% of the day in the home. Many older people report that they may go outside of their home only once a week, if that often (AARP, 1990).

Studies have shown that people who spend most of their days indoors under artificial illumination suffer increased fatigue, susceptibility to disease and other physical problems associated with prolonged deprivation of natural sunlight (Wurtman, 1975; Hughes and Neer, 1981). Unfortunately, very little research has been done on the lighting of houses. Artificial lighting in houses is usually treated as a means of extending the day in a decorative manner (Boyce, 1981).

Incandescent vs. fluorescent light Artificial lighting in most houses comes from incandescent and fluorescent bulbs. Incandescent bulbs provide an easy-to-concentrate beam and emit light at most wavelengths, which creates truer colors than standard fluorescents. But incandescents cost more to operate and don't last as long. Commercial establishments, and a growing number of houses, use fluorescent lighting for cost-saving and energy-conserving reasons.

Light Distribution

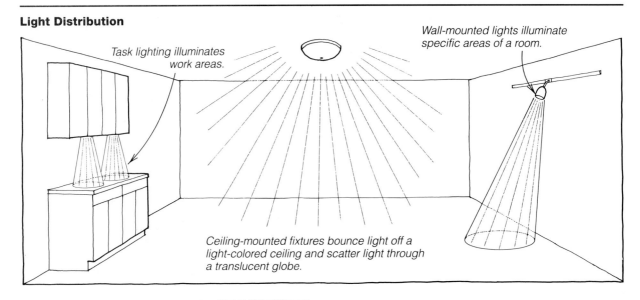

Task lighting illuminates work areas.

Wall-mounted lights illuminate specific areas of a room.

Ceiling-mounted fixtures bounce light off a light-colored ceiling and scatter light through a translucent globe.

Changing a light bulb should not be a major undertaking, but it is for many people when confronted with a fixture like this one. Removing the globe requires balancing on a chair or stepladder and twisting several small screws while simultaneously holding the globe with the other hand.

The frequency range of a light bulb is important because the eye's ability to perceive light changes with age. It becomes increasingly difficult to see and distinguish blue and green hues. Research has shown that half of the people over the age of 65 have defects in color vision (Bender, 1975). Thus, incandescent bulbs are preferred in environments serving people of all ages because of their wider spectrum of colors.

Fluorescent bulbs produce more of their energy in the frequency range that illuminates blue and green hues, which can cause older adults to see some natural colors as washed out or dull. Additionally, scientists with the U.S. Food and Drug Administration are concerned that excessive exposure to the narrow spectrum of ultraviolet light emitted by standard fluorescent tubes may increase the chances of getting skin cancer. In a 1982 Australian study (Merz, 1982), the researchers saw a doubling of skin cancer risk from long-term exposure to fluorescent lighting. Wing, 1990 suggested that diffusing materials, such as solid plastic, may be used that filter out the ultraviolet light.

Recently, compact fluorescent bulbs have become developed that fit into the standard table lamp and offer a full-spectrum of lighting. Although their initial cost is considerably higher than incandescent bulbs, these energy-efficient units last a long time and offer considerable energy savings.

Built-in light fixtures Plan lighting so that it will be bright and evenly distributed throughout the room, without shadows. Lighting that appears too bright for the young eye may be just right for the older eye, and the level can be controlled with a dimmer switch. All light sources should be shaded or diffused so no one has to look directly into the light source.

General room lighting is best provided through centrally located ceiling fixtures. Wall-mounted fixtures may be used to illuminate an area of the room, to provide task lighting or for decoration, but they generally do not distribute light evenly enough to serve as the sole light source. Ceiling fixtures that direct the light downward through translucent glass as well as upward to reflect off the ceiling are the best light sources. The translucent glass diffuses the light, and the reflected light is distributed over large parts of the room without shining directly into anyone's eyes. Ceiling-mounted canister light fixtures that focus the beam of light downward create shadows and are less efficient.

Task lighting should be provided by built-in fixtures or by tabletop or floor lamps. These lamps can direct the light onto a particular object or area. Task lighting should be provided in the kitchen, bathroom, study, living areas and at bedside.

Too often, light fixtures are selected to match the decor rather than for their ability to produce and direct light and their ease of maintenance. Designers of light fixtures have focused their talents more on aesthetics than on function. Built-in light fixtures should hold more than one light bulb, so that if one burns out there is still a light source. Fixtures should allow for bulbs to be changed easily. Older people often complain how hard it is to change bulbs in ceiling fixtures like the one in the photo on the facing page. One clever solution, out of style today, is the ceiling fixture on a retractable cord.

Select light fixtures whose bulbs can be changed easily and effortlessly. Many fixtures have been expressly designed to minimize the number of latches, screws and clamps. Some fixtures have cleverly integrated large clamps so that they are easy to open.

Select light fixtures that will be easy to keep clean. Fixtures lose some of their lighting power when they trap a lot of dirt and bugs or when the screen gets dirty. Globe fixtures keep bugs out and allow dirt to slide off, but many have only a single light bulb. Translucent light fixtures with a screen over the top keep bugs from collecting in the bowl of the fixture but don't prevent a build-up on the top. Translucent bowl or dish fixtures quickly accumulate dirt and bugs. Egg-crate screens allow dirt and bugs to drop through, but the light source may be annoying because the bulb is usually visible through the screen.

HEATING, VENTILATION AND COOLING

The type of heating, ventilation and cooling (HVAC) system chosen for a house depends largely on the local climate. This section of the book will offer some additional criteria for evaluating and installing HVAC components.

Some people are considerably more sensitive to temperature variations than others, especially older people and those with arthritis, heart problems and multiple sclerosis. About half of the American population over the age of 65 has some form of arthritis (National Center for Health Statistics, 1990), and many of these people are miserable during "arthritis season," which is the damp and cold winter months. People with multiple sclerosis, on the other hand, need to avoid becoming too warm.

The cruel irony is that for many, the more heat they need as they age, the less they can afford on fixed incomes. The most frequent complaint among individuals over the age of 60 about their dwelling units is the cost of utilities (AARP, 1990). Many people on fixed incomes turn down their thermostats to less than comfortable levels, shut off the heat to some rooms, and even resort to living in one or two rooms in their house during the winter to control utility costs. Frequently, they use a portable space heater or a small gas heater instead of the central heating system. Use of these heaters is probably one of the reasons that older people are seven times more likely to die in a home fire than young adults (Linn, 1980).

Overall comfort indoors requires a good HVAC system, but for that system to work best it needs to rest in a house that has been constructed with proper insulation and good-quality doors and windows. Compromises in quality generally translate into insufficient heating and cooling, increased maintenance and greater demands on the user for monitoring and functioning. These compromises may seem unimportant to young people, but they can significantly affect the quality of life for older residents. A zoned system allows for separate control over various portions of the house, which can significantly reduce energy needs.

The thermostat should be located in the room that is used the most, unless that room has another source of heat, such as a fireplace. It should be placed

The Honeywell Easy-To-See Round® Thermostat has enlarged and raised numbers, a clicking control dial and a large grip dial. (Photo: courtesy Honeywell.)

at a height comparable to a seated height for an individual, within the optimal reach zone (20 in. to 44 in. off the floor). Most activities within the home (with the exception of meal preparation, exercise and some forms of entertainment) are conducted while seated. Thermostats should monitor temperatures at this height.

While convention has placed thermostats at heights of about 60 in. there is no compelling argument that would prohibit their location at a height of 44 in. We do not need to assume that the user must be standing to adjust the thermostat. A height of 44 in. would be accessible to all.

The thermostat should be located in an area where there is clear space (30 in. by 48 in.) in front of it. If a builder or owner cannot accept the idea of sitting down to read and adjust the thermostat, we recommend a height of 52 in. This should improve access for short people, but not greatly inconvenience those who are tall. As usual, a tall person may stoop to read something that is lower, but a short person cannot stretch to read something that is higher without using a stepstool or a ladder.

The thermostat should be placed where it will not be affected by direct sunlight, but where there is a natural or artificial light source providing ample illumination of the control. The thermostat should be selected with ease of use and convenience in mind.

Many thermostats on the market are almost impossible to read for the healthy, normal eye. This does not bode well for the occupants as they get older.

Honeywell's thermostat designed for people with low vision (see the photo at left) has many desirable features. It has a large scale depicting the temperature settings, a large dial for control and click detents that tell the user how many degrees the temperature is being changed (three clicks equal six degrees when each detent is a two-degree increment). This thermostat is not perfect, however. Its thermometer is small and hard to see, and the temperature-adjustment dial is hard to grasp for a person who lacks manual dexterity.

When selecting an HVAC system, think beyond the initial installation costs and determine the demands on human capabilities to manage and maintain the system. Some systems require no more than changing a filter once or twice a year. Others require periodic provision of fuel, frequent cleaning and placement within the home in a location with low potential for a fire. A system that must be installed in the basement may be inaccessible to an resident who can't get up and down stairs. The woodburning stove that seems like an economical choice at the time can become a nightmare when the occupants get old, sick or injured.

Routine maintenance is likely to be neglected if the unit is difficult to reach, requires special tools, is hard to open or has an inadequate light source. HVAC systems have generally been designed to accomplish only their primary function as effectively and efficiently as possible, with little design consideration given to how or what someone with less than the normal strength, mobility, manual dexterity or vision would do to manage and maintain them. HVAC systems quite often last the lifetime of the house. They should be designed and installed to accommodate the lifetime needs of the house's occupants as well.

The best choice for a heating, ventilation and cooling system for the lifespan house is an efficient unit, installed in an accessible location, which requires a minimal amount of monitoring and maintenance. It should also be as safe as possible. Despite warnings, knowledge, experience and good common sense, HVAC systems regularly cause preventable injuries to home occupants. Systems that rely on the user to see, hear or smell potential problems may be dangerous for people who have diminished capacity. Amazingly, many warning statements and emergency instructions are placed on the bottom or back side of units. Often they are squeezed into a small space and are difficult to read.

Consider what tasks would be required in the event of an emergency, and how they could be accomplished by someone less than fully abled. For example, gas shut-off valves should be accessible to someone who uses a wheelchair or who has difficulty walking. Valves or other controls should be easy to operate by someone who has difficulty grasping and should not require tools that may not be available when needed the most.

Heating, ventilation and cooling systems vary in the amount of noise they make. Radiant systems are quieter, while forced-air duct systems can create considerable background drone. The University of Illinois Small Homes Council-Building Research Council recommends the following:
• Install the HVAC unit in an area away from the quiet areas of the home (bedroom, dining room) and acoustically treat the walls around it.
• If the unit is in a closet near the living area, the walls should be masonry or the finish materials should be mounted on resilient channels. The door should be solid (wood or metal) and weatherstripped. Combustion air should be taken from the attic or crawl space, not through the wall or door louvers to the living room.
• Use canvas connectors in the ducts to keep furnace vibration from being transferred to the ducts.
• Support the furnace on vibration-isolating pads.
• Line duct hangers with sound-absorbing material and seal all openings around the ducts.
• Wrap the pipes for hydronic heating systems to insulate them and reduce noise.

COMMUNICATIONS

The lifespan house contains a variety of constantly evolving communication systems, including telephones, room-to-room intercoms, home control systems, smoke alarms and other warning systems. When specifying or buying communications products, it is important to look beyond the primary function and select products that are logical, easy to understand and easy to use. They should have high-contrast and easy-to-see print and graphics, and you should be able to operate them with a closed fist. (For more on accessible product design, see pp. 25-29).

Telephones Telephone lines perform many new functions in the house. They provide links for computer modems, emergency response systems and health monitoring equipment. The one or two phone-jack house of the past is not sufficient in this age of evolving telecommunications. Adding sufficient telephone wiring when the home is constructed means low-cost assurance of future convenience.

Put at least one phone jack in every room where people are likely to be settled and to spend more than a few minutes at a time. If the room is likely to contain heavy furniture that could block the jack, install additional ones. To allow flexibility in the placement of furniture, put telephone jacks on at least two walls in every bedroom. Keep in mind that rooms often serve several functions over the years. Today's nursery may be tomorrow's home office. View each room as potentially requiring telephones, computer modems and family health stations, and wire them accordingly.

Locate telephone jacks near electrical outlets. Phones are often coupled with devices requiring electrical power, such as answering machines, computers and health monitoring equipment. All phone jacks should be installed within the optimal reach zone (20 in. to 44 in. off the floor) in locations that aren't likely to be covered by furniture or appliances. Bear in mind that equipment such as laptop computers with built-in modems may be regularly connected to and disconnected from the phone jacks.

Telephone sets come in every imaginable shape, size and form. The greatest flexibility and ease of use are provided by large back-lit buttons, adjustable volume control and simple memory storage and retrieval. Other desirable features include hands-free operation and a built-in emergency response function.

Intercoms Intercom systems greatly facilitate in-house communication, especially in large houses. They allow easy monitoring of children or an adult with Alzheimer's disease. They create a link between someone with restricted mobility in one room and

The Aiphone two-wired video entry security system consists of a door station (doorbell and camera) and room master station with a video monitor. Ringing the doorbell activates the camera, and a chime sounds inside the house. The resident picks up the receiver to talk to the person at the door and can see who it is on a 4-in. monitor. An electric release lock allows the resident to unlock the door from the master station. (Photo: courtesy Aiphone.)

the rest of the family. Intercoms can be used for both sound and visual communication, and they can be linked with other household systems such as door-bells and stereos.

Intercom systems may be hard-wired and installed while the house is being built, or they can be added on as plug-in units. Hard-wired systems are usually built into the wall, with the controls located near the light switch inside each room. Intercoms should be evaluated and located according to the same criteria as telephones (see p. 89).

(see p. 89)

One problem inherent in the built-in intercom system is lack of flexibility in situating the individual room units. A location adjacent to a doorway may not be the most convenient, but it will not conflict with furniture placement.

Add-on intercom systems are available that operate off carrier current. This means that the individual intercom units are plugged into the outlet receptacles in the home and that the communication signals (speech, music, but not video) are mixed with the line current and transmitted over the existing electrical wires. Individual add-on units can be plugged into any receptacle, but this feature could be a problem if there are too few receptacles in the house to begin with. Also, the sound quality in add-on systems may not be nearly as good as in built-in systems with dedicated wiring.

Video intercom systems, like the one in the photo at left, are available from several manufacturers. These phones allow someone inside the home to see and talk to visitors standing at the door from a remote location. The miniature camera and intercom units can also be located at other sites around the home. These systems offer tremendous advantages to people with mobility and hearing limitations.

Typically the doorbell unit of a video intercom system is slightly larger than a cigarette box and has a lighted button indicating the location of the push button. A miniature, wide-angle camera is mounted in the doorbell unit. The light from the backlit button dispenses sufficient illumination for the camera to capture the image of the visitor even if there is no other light source. When the visitor rings the doorbell, the camera is activated and sends the alerting signal and a video image to the receiver unit or units, which can be located anywhere in the house. The occupant can speak with the visitor and, on some units, even unlock the door, without having to move. Most of these systems also have a monitoring function that permits the occupant to push a button to turn on the camera at the entrance area, without the doorbell having been activated first.

Home control systems   Home control systems have outstanding flexibility and are capable of putting many household operations under the fingertip, voice command or remote telephone access control of the residents. While the functions of a home control system may seem unnecessary to some, they can serve as the arms and legs to many others. Using electrical signals from remote locations within or outside the house, a home control system can provide such functions as:

• turning on and off all appliances, lights and entertainment systems
• activating, answering and operating the telephone

Home Control System

Home control systems can operate virtually any device running on electrical current in the house by means of a central control unit, which can be activated by voice, touch screen, touch pad or telephone.

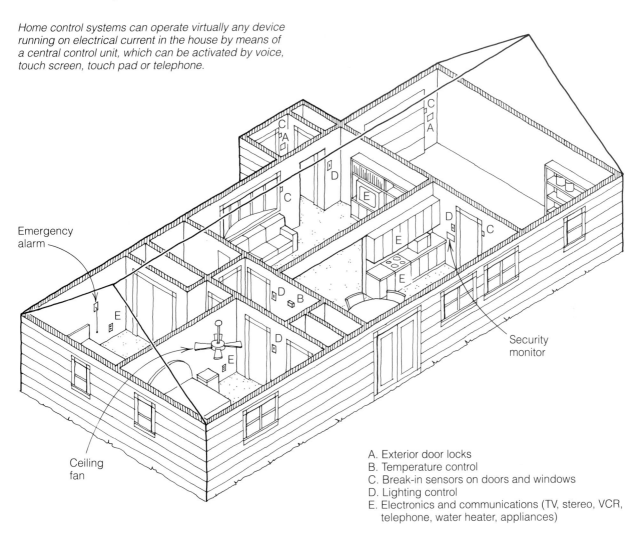

Emergency alarm

Ceiling fan

Security monitor

A. Exterior door locks
B. Temperature control
C. Break-in sensors on doors and windows
D. Lighting control
E. Electronics and communications (TV, stereo, VCR, telephone, water heater, appliances)

• adjusting the volume or intensity of audio or light sources
• monitoring, activating and deactivating locks on exterior doors
• monitoring for intruders via sound, motion or heat sensors
• activating, controlling and monitoring the HVAC system
• activating, controlling and monitoring water taps
• monitoring smoke and fire alarms.

Home control systems are great equalizers. They afford step-saving convenience, energy economizing control, monitoring capabilities and an increased sense of safety and security. The critical issue in selecting a system is to ensure that the occupant can be in the driver's seat. While many systems seem designed more for the technomaniac than the typical home owner, others have been developed for individuals with specific disabilities and offer a variety of interface options and switches. Several companies make these systems (see Resources on pp. 95-96).

Home control systems vary considerably, but three distinct types are available: hard-wired systems,

systems based on X-10 (or similar) modules that operate the various components via signals sent on the carrier or line current, and the Smart House, a product developed by a limited partnership headed by the National Association of Home Builders.

The Smart House is a system based on new wiring and product-interface concepts. Smart House systems must be installed when the house is built and must have appliances and other electrical furnishings that are compatible with the system. The home must have a single cable through which all products (televisions, stereos, communication devices and appliances) are fed their electrical current as well as the control commands. The products under control must have a computer chip installed that actively communicates with the central processing unit (CPU).

The Smart House can control both electrical and gas-powered components through the single cable and the CPU. It is a compelling concept that has received a great deal of publicity, but there are several problems. All of the electrical and gas products in the house must be compatible with the system, which severely limits the home owner's product choices and raises questions of affordability. Also, Smart Houses must be built by specially trained contractors and subcontractors, who are in short supply.

Home control systems generally offer direct or remote control means of communication. Direct control is provided by a computer mouse, keyboard, keypad or touch screens on a television monitor. Remote-control devices may include a hand-held key pad that sends either an infrared or frequency-modulated (FM) signal to the CPU, a telephone interface that communicates with the system with touch-tone signals, or voice-activation units. Voice-activation systems are programmed to respond to specific voice commands of single or multiple users. The user teaches the system its command vocabulary by speaking the commands into the system during a programming and setup operation. Once the computer has been programmed, the user merely says the word and the system responds. Many components in hard-wired and X-10 systems can be programmed to turn appliances on or off and to adjust heating and cooling systems at specific times.

The home control industry continues to evolve. In addition to selecting a system based on its ease of use and function, the home owner should try to determine whether the manufacturer and supplier of the system will be available to provide maintenance, repairs and replacement parts. One source of information about home control systems is a magazine called *Electronic House* (see Resources on p. 95).

Alarm and warning systems Although smoke detectors appear to be in general use, the sad fact is that one out of three smoke detectors fails in a fire. They fail because the batteries are dead, which often happens because the occupant doesn't routinely check the units, or because they are installed in difficult-to-reach locations.

There are several types of smoke, fire and gas detectors. Those with an Underwriter's Laboratory label should be acceptable. We recommend that any home serviced with gas be equipped with smoke and gas detectors.

Some smoke, fire and gas detectors are equipped with a strobe light as well as a sound alarm. The strobe light may help to awaken an extremely deep sleeper as well as someone with a hearing impairment. It is prudent to have redundant signals on an alarm or alerting device.

We recommend that at least one detector be installed within the optimal reach zone (20 in. to 44 in. off the floor). Smoke detectors generally work best when placed on the ceiling because many smoke and combustion fumes are lighter than air and rise to the ceiling, which means that a detector placed within the ORZ may not provide the best detectability. But in the event that all other smoke detectors fail because they were inaccessible and thus not maintained, this detector could be a life-saver.

First Alert makes a smoke detector that can be tested easily with a flashlight beam. This allows the unit to be installed at or near the ceiling, where it is most needed, while allowing for regular monitoring from the ground level.

A few companies make alerting products that are helpful to individuals with hearing impairments. Many of these systems convert the signal that would normally be sound into a light or vibration. Some of the available products include doorbells, telephone ringers, smoke and fire detectors, alarm clocks and monitoring systems. Some systems are designed to flash a single light in the house when someone is at the front door and another light when someone is at the back door. Some systems can flash every light in the house or selected lights in various rooms.

About 400,000 homes in the United States are equipped with a personal emergency response system (PERS). Most are used by older individuals who live alone. Some emergency response systems are also being installed for "latchkey kids," children who come home from school and are by themselves until their parents arrive after work.

Most personal emergency response systems consist of a "help button" worn by the occupant of the house, a central automated dialing unit that is connected to the telephone line and a response center. An occupant who needs help (due to an accident, medical problem, fire or intruder) pushes the help button. The central unit receives the FM signal transmitted from the help button and automatically dials preprogrammed numbers. Depending upon the type, manufacturer or supplier of the system, the central unit may dial a national monitoring center, a local monitoring center or a series of phone numbers belonging to family members or friends. Most systems allow two-way communication between the occupant and the emergency respondent answering the call through a speaker on the unit. For a list of manufacturers of personal emergency response systems, see Resources on p. 97.

In a study we completed in 1992 for the American Association of Retired Persons, we found that almost all PERS users are pleased with their systems. Almost three-fourths of the 2,000 users we heard from stated that at one time or another they had accidently activated their system. One-fourth of the users stated that they had used their systems in an emergency.

There is no doubt that personal emergency response systems are an important communication link and provide a sense of security for a growing number of people. The AARP provides a guide for selecting personal emergency response systems free of charge (see Resources on p. 97 for the address).

The central dialing unit should be installed in a central location in the home away from large metal objects and foil wallpaper. The system requires access to both a telephone jack and an electrical outlet. Be sure that the central unit can be activated by the help button from all rooms of the house. In our study we found that activation was sometimes a problem.

FLOOR SURFACES

Floor surface materials are chosen based on the purposes of the room, the type of traffic, budget, maintenance requirements and safety. It is best to select the most durable surface that the budget will allow. Hard-surface floors (such as wood or linoleum) are often the most durable, especially if the floor will be subjected to water spills or traffic from outdoors, but they may require more maintenance. Carpeted flooring generally demands fewer steps for routine maintenance in low-traffic households, usually only vacuuming. Only stain-resistant carpeting should be used.

Sixteen percent of the accidents that occur at home are caused by floors and flooring material (Buffalo Organization for Social and Technical Innovation, 1982). Some of the risks are tripping, slipping and lack of cushioning when falling.

Tripping is caused by uneven thresholds or surfaces; catching a heel, cane or walker on carpeting pile, loose threads or seams in the carpeting; and misperceiving changes in the floor surface when there are no changes. Misjudgment of the floor surface occurs frequently with patterned carpeting or the shadowing or pooling that occurs in solid-color carpeting. People with visual problems may be unable to identify real level changes from the appearance of changes in the pattern of the flooring. Other carpet patterns create a sensation of movement. Carpeting that has loosened from its backing can cause people to trip.

Slipping on a floor can result from a combination of three factors: the surface of the floor, extraneous material on the floor and a person's footwear. Slippery shoes or stocking feet on a smoothly polished waxed surface are about as dangerous as flat-soled boots on ice. Nonslip flooring is made by several manufacturers (see Resources on p. 97).

Cushioning of falls is important in any area of the home that has potential for tripping or slipping. Unfortunately, there is a trade-off between cushioning and durability. The greatest cushioning is offered by the softest floor surface, but soft surfaces aren't as easy to roll a wheelchair over as hard ones.

Select flooring that will facilitate movement. Consider how well wheels and casters will be able to move on the surface. Thick, plush carpeting creates a warm, sometimes elegant environment that becomes increasingly burdensome to maintain and traverse.

Floor, Wall and Ceiling Surface Treatments

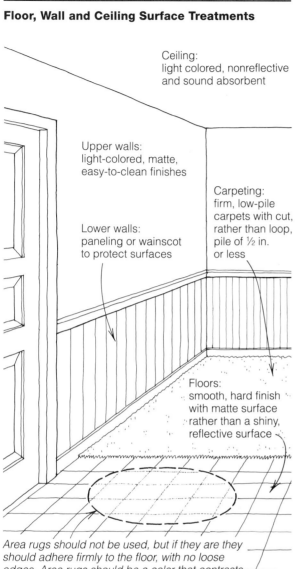

Ceiling:
light colored, nonreflective
and sound absorbent

Upper walls:
light-colored, matte,
easy-to-clean finishes

Carpeting:
firm, low-pile
carpets with cut,
rather than loop,
pile of ½ in.
or less

Lower walls:
paneling or wainscot
to protect surfaces

Floors:
smooth, hard finish
with matte surface
rather than a shiny,
reflective surface

Area rugs should not be used, but if they are they should adhere firmly to the floor, with no loose edges. Area rugs should be a color that contrasts strongly with the color of the floor.

Wheels and casters move better on low pile, tightly woven carpeting or hard surfaces. Some industrial-grade carpeting is ideally suited for high-traffic rooms with exterior entrances and wheeled objects. It usually has a short pile, thin backing and padding and easy maintenance requirements. Cleaning up dirt and moving wheelchairs or chairs with casters are relatively easy.

In 1990 we completed a study where we had research subjects travel a specific distance in a wheel-chair on three different floor surfaces. We measured the length of time it took them to travel the distance and the number of times they had to push or stroke the wheel of their chair; we also asked them how "easy" they thought the task was to perform. The research subjects reported that moving on a non-resilient hard-surface floor was about twice as easy as moving on carpeting with ½-in. pile.

The floor surface can affect the noise level in a room. Hard surfaces reflect sound waves and result in a noisier room. Soft surfaces absorb sound, cushion the impact between object and floor and make the room quieter. However, we often want the sound-absorbing capacity of a carpet just where we have the greatest need for a hard surface.

Many carpets are rated relative for antistatic capacity, an important consideration in rooms with personal computers (or other microprocessor-based products). People who use walking aids, particularly those that may be skidded over the floor like a walker, also appreciate anti-static floors.

WALL AND CEILING SURFACES

The properties of walls that influence selection decisions include maintenance, light reflectance and glare. Wall surfaces are most often painted, papered or paneled.

Maintenance demands vary, depending on what the room is primarily used for (cooking, bathing, playing, watching television, sleeping) and what moves through the room. If the pathway through a room is next to a wall, there is likely to be greater wear and tear on the wall surface.

Painted walls are the least expensive, but they may also be the least durable. Although generally easy to repair by washing, touching up or repainting, painted walls are likely to require more frequent maintenance because they are highly uniform in appearance and readily display their blemishes.

The longevity, costs and maintenance properties of papered walls depend on type of wall covering. Untreated wallpaper is the most fragile and may tolerate only a light wiping with a damp cloth. Vinyl and plastic coverings are more resistant to marring and tolerate washing well.

Wood paneling is the most durable of the three main wall surfaces. Most paneling may be scrubbed without losing its appearance and can be "repaired" using furniture polish or wood finish. Wheelchair and scooter users often prefer paneled or wainscoted walls because the lower half of the walls is better protected from the bumps and nicks caused by the wheels and footplates.

Light-colored walls reflect more light and brighten a room; dark walls absorb light and make the space look gloomier. On the other hand, light-colored walls generally require more frequent maintenance because they show dirt readily. When natural and artificial lighting cannot be increased, we recommend that the walls receive light-colored surface treatments (white, cream or pastel) to provide a better visual environment. Wainscoting is an excellent compromise for balancing the need for good lighting and low maintenance.

Painted, papered and paneled walls can all cause glare if they have a glossy surface. A matte or satin finish is preferred because it reflects less light. Mirrored walls, while not as common as the primary types, are used to make small rooms look larger. They can be a nuisance if the light sources (both windows and artificial lighting) in the room are not covered. On a bright sunny day, the blinds to the room may have to be closed because the mirrors reflect too much glare.

The primary functions of ceiling surfaces are to reflect light and absorb sound. Light-colored ceilings are recommended because they help distribute lighting evenly throughout a room. Acoustically treated surfaces (acoustical tile) are strongly recommended for rooms that are unlikely to have many soft surfaces such as carpeting, draperies or upholstered furniture. The more soft surfaces in a room, the lower the demand for acoustical treatment.

RESOURCES

The Healthy House

Building with Nature.
C. Venolia, P.O. Box 369, Gualala, CA 95445.
A bimonthly networking newsletter; $45 for six issues.

Electronic House: Advanced Housing & Home Automation.
Electronic House, P.O. Box 399, Stillwater, OK 74076.
A bimonthly magazine; $16.95 for six issues.

Environmental Building News.
A. Wilson, editor, RR 1, Box 161, Brattleboro, VT 05301.
A bimonthly newsletter; $60 for six issues.

Environmental Hazards to Young Children by D.N. Kane. Phoenix: The Oryx Press, 1985.

Healing Environments by C. Venolia. Celestial Arts, California: 1988.

Healthful Houses by C. Good and D.L. Dadd. Bethesda, Maryland: Guaranty Press, 1988.

Healthy House Building: A Design and Construction Guide by J. Bower. Available from The Healthy House Institute, 7471 North Shiloh Road, Unionville, IN 47460. This 1993 book includes house plans for a model healthy house, which Bowers recently built and sold.

The Human Ecologist. Human Ecology Action League, 2250 N. Druid Hills Road, NE, Atlanta, GA 30329. A quarterly publication; $20 for four issues.

The Inside Story: A Guide to Indoor Air Quality. Washington, DC: U.S. Environmental Protection Agency, Office of Air and Radiation, 1988.

The Nontoxic Home. by D.L. Dadd. Los Angeles: Jeremy P. Tarcher, 1986.

Save Our Planet: 750 Everyday Ways You Can Help Clean Up the Earth. by D. MacEachern. New York: Dell Publishing, 1990.

Lighting, Switches and Electrical Controls

Artemide Company
1980 New Highway
Farmingdale, NY 11735
(516) 694-9292
Pull-down lighting fixtures.

Honeywell
Home and Building Control
1985 Douglas Drive North
Golden Valley, MN 55402
(800) 345-6770 ext. 7200
Easy-To-See Thermostat, automatic lighting, nightlights, lighted switches, air cleaners, home control systems, braille home owners' guide.

Leviton Manufacturing
59-25 Little Neck Parkway
Little Neck, NY 11362-2591
(718) 383-4500
Lighting and electronic controls, rocker switches.

Lutron Electronics
205 Suter Road
Coopersburg, PA 18036-1299
(800) 523-9466
(800) 222-4509 (In PA)
Slider and rocker paddle switches and controls.

Tempo Industries
2002 A South Grand Avenue
Santa Ana, CA 92705
(714) 641-0313
Floor lighting strips.

Environmental Controls

Consultants for Communication
508 Bellevue Terace
Pittsburgh, PA 15202
(412) 761-6062
Controls up to 16 appliances or outlets with one switch. Sends signals over house wiring using an X-10 or other carrier current.

Custom Command Systems
115 Paint Branch Drive
Suite 3181
College Park, MD 20742-3261
(301) 454-7158
Custom home entertainment, security and automation systems.

Cybercom Systems
P.O. Box 62223
Bloomington, IN 47401
(812) 339-3009
Communication and control systems for physically and/or neurologically impaired people.

Enerlogic Systems
P.O. Box 3743
Nashua, NH 03061
(603) 880-4066
A home automation hardware and software package that is used with a home computer and compatible with home wiring.

Heathkit / Heath Company
Benton Harbor, MI 49022
(800) 253-0570
Catalog sales of home automation systems.

Home Automation Laboratories
5500 Highlands Parkway
Suite 450
Smyrna, GA 30082-5141
(800) YEL-4-HAL
(404) 319-6000
Catalog sales of home automation equipment.

Hypertek
Salem Industrial Park
P.O. Box 137, Route 22 East
Whitehouse, NJ 08888
(201) 534-9700
System is compatible with home computers or available as a stand-alone system.

Innocomp
33195 Wagon Wheel Drive
Solon, OH 44139
(800) 382-VOCA
(216) 248-6206
System's transmitter is intended for use by those with limited hand and finger dexterity.

JDS Technologies
17471 Plaza Otonal
San Diego, CA 92128
(619) 487-8787
System can be operated through telephones; uses carrier current.

LC Technologies
Eyegaze Systems
4415 Glenn Rose Street
Fairfax, VA 22032
(800) 733-5284
(703) 425-7509
System can control appliances, communication devices, lights or telephone; designed to operate by infrared light reflected from the cornea. Full system costs about $25,000.

MasterVoice
Butler in a Box
10523 Humbolt Street
Los Alamitos, CA 90720
(213) 594-6581
System can be controlled by voice, remote telephone, timer or keyboard. Interfaces with carrier-current control systems.

Plexus Corporation
55 Jewlers Park Drive
Post Office Box 156
Neenah, WI 549557-3451
(800) 236-7597
(414) 722-3220
Plexus makes the primary control unit for the Smart House.

Quartet Technology
52 Davis Road
Tyngsboro, MA 01879
(508) 692-9313
Voice-controlled system uses carrier-current modules to control lights, appliances, telephone and entertainment systems.

tash
91 Station Street, Unit 1
Ajax, Ontario
Canada L1S 3H2
(416) 686-4129
Catalog sales of technical aids for people with disabilities.

X-10 (USA)
185A LeGrand Ave.
Northvale, NJ 07647
(800) 526-0027
(201) 784-9700
Systems that use carrier-current modules, sensors (sound, motion, infrared) and controllers.

Intercom Systems

Aiphone
1700 130th Ave., N.E.
Bellevue, WA 98005
(206) 455-0510
Video entry systems that operate as a doorbell, security camera and audio intercom.

Broan Manufacturing Co.
Hartford, WI 53027
(414) 673-4340
Built-in electronic intercoms, range hoods, vacuum, ironing, bathroom vents, fans.

Crest Industries
300 East Meridian
Puyallup, WA 98371
(206) 927-6922
Doorbell and intercom that interface with telephone hardware.

Fisher-Price
620 Girard Avenue
East Aurora, NY 14052-1879
(716) 652-8402
Electronic nursery monitor.

.

Gerry Baby Products
12520 Grant Drive
P.O. Box 33755
Denver, CO 80241
(303) 457-0926
Electronic nursery monitor.

Intelecom
6488 Avondale Drive
Suite 125
Oklahoma City, OK 73116
(405) 842-0163
Door intercom, music intercom, voice-activated system.

M & S Systems
A Nortek Company
2861 Congressman Lane
Dallas, TX 75220
(800) 877-6631
(214) 358-3196
Doorbell and home intercom system that can interface with telephone hardware.

NuTone
Madison and Reed Bank Roads
Cincinnati, OH 45227-1599
(800) 543-8687
Video door answering systems, lighting, intercom, range hoods and other built-in electronic products for the home.

Siedle/Intercom/USA
780 Parkway
P.O. Box 520
Broomall, PA 19008
(800) 874-3353
(215) 353-9595
Video entry intercom, door entry intercom, music intercom systems.

TekTone
27 Industrial Park Drive
Franklin, NC 28734
(800) 448-1811
(704) 524-9967
Video entry intercom, door entry intercom, music intercom systems.

Signaling Systems for the Hearing Impaired

American Phone Products
5192 Bolsa Ave., Suite #5
Huntington Beach, CA 92649
(714) 897-0808
An alarm notification device that detects smoke, the doorbell, telephone, etc. It activates a strobe light, bed shaker and buzzer.

Clarke School for the Deaf
McAlister Building
Round Hill Road
Northampton, MA 01060
(413) 584-3450
Catalog sales of products for people who are hearing impaired.

Compu-tty
4301 Rowan Drive
Fort Worth, TX 76116
(800) 433-2126
(817) 738-8993
Catalog sales of telephone typewriter devices, door bell, telephone, burglary alarms.

First Alert
780 McClure Road
Aurora, IL 60504
(708) 851-7330
A smoke detector/alarm that can be mounted in the ceiling and tested with the light beam of a flashlight.

Fourth Dimension
Instruments
P.O. Box 376
Spring, TX 77383
(713) 288-9366
Knock Light, a light that attaches to the door and flashes when someone knocks on it.

Guardian Angel Products
401-417 Fayette Avenue
Springfield, IL 62704
(217) 753-2505
A sound pick-up device that flashes a light when a sound is present in the monitoring room.

HARC Mercantile Ltd.
3130 Portage Street
P.O. Box 3055
Kalamazoo, MI 49003
(800) 445-9968
(616) 381-0177
(616) 381-2219 (TDD)
Catalog sales of assistive listening and sound signalling products.

Hartling Communications
7 Sunset Drive
Burlington, MA 01803
(617) 272-7634
Catalog sales of assistive listening and sound signalling products.

Hear You Are
4 Musconetcong Avenue
Stanhope, NJ 07874
(201) 347-7662
Catalog sales of assistive listening and sound signalling products.

Heidico
1226 Westfield Avenue
Reno, NV 89509
(702) 324-7104
Catalog sales of assistive listening and sound signalling products.

HiTec Group International
8205 Cass Ave, Suite 109
Darien, IL 60559
(800) 288-8303
(708) 963-5588
Catalog sales of assistive listening and sound signalling products.

Let's Talk
915 Lloyd Building
603 Stewart
Seattle, WA 98101
(800) 237-TALK
(206) 340-8255
Catalog sales of assistive listening and sound signalling products.

Mid-Audio
120 East Ogden
Hinsdale, IL 60521
(708) 323-7970
Distributor of assistive listening and sound signalling products.

NFSS
8120 Fenton Street
Silver Springs, MD 20910
(301) 589-6671
Manufacturing and distribution company of assistive listening and sound signalling products.

Phone-TTY
202 Lexington Avenue
Hackensack, NJ 07601
(201) 489-7889
Manufacturing and distribution company of assistive listening and sound signalling products.

Sonic Alert
1750 West Hamilton Road
Rochester Hills, MI 48309
(313) 656-3110
Manufacturing and distribution company of assistive listening and sound signalling products.

Sound Involvement
6529 Colerain Avenue, Suite A
Cincinatti, OH 54239
(513) 923-3353
Catalog sales of assistive listening and sound signalling products.

Sound Resources Hearing Center
201 East Ogden Avenue
Hinsdale, IL 60521
(312) 323-7970
Catalog sales of assistive listening and sound signalling products.

Personal Emergency Response Systems

The companies listed below offer personal emergency response systems and a nationwide monitoring network. Other companies operate within a community or region. Check the Yellow Pages for these listings.

AARP Product Report: PERS (Personal Emergency Response System), Vol. 2, No. 1, available from American Association of Retired Persons, 601 E Street NW, Washington, DC 20049. Ask for PF 3986(592)-D12905.

American Medical Alert Corp.
3265 Lawson Blvd.
Oceanside, NY 11572
(800) 645-3244
(516) 536-5850

Colonial Medical Alert Systems
22 Cotton Road
Nashua, NH 03063
(800) 323-6794
(603) 881-8351

Communi-Call
2661 Whitney Avenue
Hamden, CT 06518
(800) 841-3800
(203) 281-1149

Emergency Response Systems
5777 W. Century Blvd
Los Angeles, CA 90045
(800) 833-2000
(213) 215-9600

Knight Protective Industries
7315 Lankershim Boulevard
Hollywood, CA 91605
(800) 356-4448
(818) 765-0612

Lifecall Systems
1300 Admiral Wilson Boulevard
Camden, NJ 08101
(609) 963-5433

Lifeline Systems
One Arsenal Marketplace
Watertown, MA 02172
(800) 387-8120
(617) 972-1361

Link Technologies
1421A Arnot Road
Horsehead, NY 14845
(800) 338-4176
(607) 739-6262

Medic Alert
2323 Colorado Avenue
Turlock, CA 95380
(800) 423-6333
(209) 668-3333

Mytrex
7050 Union Park Avenue
Midvale, UT 84047
(801) 561-9576

PERSYS
1017 Walnut Street
Roselle, NJ 07203
(800) 631-7370

Pioneer Medical Systems
37 Washington Street
Melrose, MA 02176
(617) 662-2227

Protect Emergency Response
100 Park Place, Suite 250
San Ramon, CA 94583
(800) 548-8805
(415) 820-0949

Pulsar Security Corp.
31 Volunteer Drive.
POB 1470
Hendersonville, TN 37077
(800) 245-7255
(615) 822-6200

Tele Larm
4020 Capitol Blvd., Ste. 90
Raleigh, NC 27604
(800) 835-5276
(919) 878-1101

Transcience
179 Ludlow Street
Stamford, CT 06092
(800) 243-3494
(203) 327-7810

Nonslip Floor Products

Altro Safety Floors
399 Main Street
Los Altos, CA 94022
(415) 941-1961
Vinyl with silicon carbide, aluminum oxide and colored quartz crystals dispersed throughout thickness.

Arden Architectural Specialities
1943 West County Road C-2
St. Paul, MN 55113
(800) 521-1826
(612) 631-1607
Building entrance mats surface mounted or recessed.

Azrock Industries
10999 IH-10 West
P.O. Box 696060
San Antonio, TX 78269
(512) 558-6400
Slip-resistant vinyl composition tile.

Florida Tile
Division of Sikes Corporation
Sales Office
1 Sikes Boulevard
Lackland, FL 33802
(813) 687-7171
Ceramic tile.

Institutional Products Corp.
S. 80 W. 18766 Apollo Drive
P.O. Box 406
Muskego, WI 53150
(800) 222-5556
Anti-Skid Tape (a pressure-sensitive tape used for stairways, ramps and showers).

Matting World
P.O. Box 1333
Pleasantville, NJ 08232
(800) 257-8557
(609) 641-7766
Surface floor mats.

Musson Rubber Co.
1320 Archwood Avenue
Akron, OH 44306
(216) 773-7651
Aluminum-framed recessed entrance mats.

R.C.A. Rubber Company
1833 East Market Street
Akron, OH 44305-0240
(800) 321-2340
Stair treads with an abrasive strip that is of a contrasting color, which helps to alert a person to the edge of the step.

Roppe Corporation
1602 North Union Street
Box X
Fostoria, OH 44830
(800) 537-9527
Stair treads with abrasive strips.

Tarkett
800 Lanidex Plaza
P.O. Box 264
Parsippany, NJ 07054
(201) 428-9000
Nonslip vinyl flooring.

VPI FLoor Products Division
P.O. Box 451
Sheboygan, WI 53082-0451
(414)458-4664
Slip-resistant rubber tile and stair treads.

CHAPTER SEVEN
DOORS, DOORWAYS AND WINDOWS

The lifespan house requires that the occupants control the built environment. Unfortunately, when confronting doors, doorways and windows, it is often the environment that rules. The selection, placement and design of doors, doorways and windows and their hardware are critical to house design because in many instances they are the bottleneck, the one feature that severely limits the use of a space for an occupant.

There is a widespread belief that the essence of barrier-free design is constructing wide doorways to allow wheelchair users access to the house. In fact, the selection, placement and design of doors, doorways and windows and their hardware affect a wide range of people besides

Emergency Egress

Bedrooms and basements require an emergency exit, which should be accessible to people of all ages and abilities. Clear areas in front of escape egress should be accessible from all parts of room (nothing should get in the way).

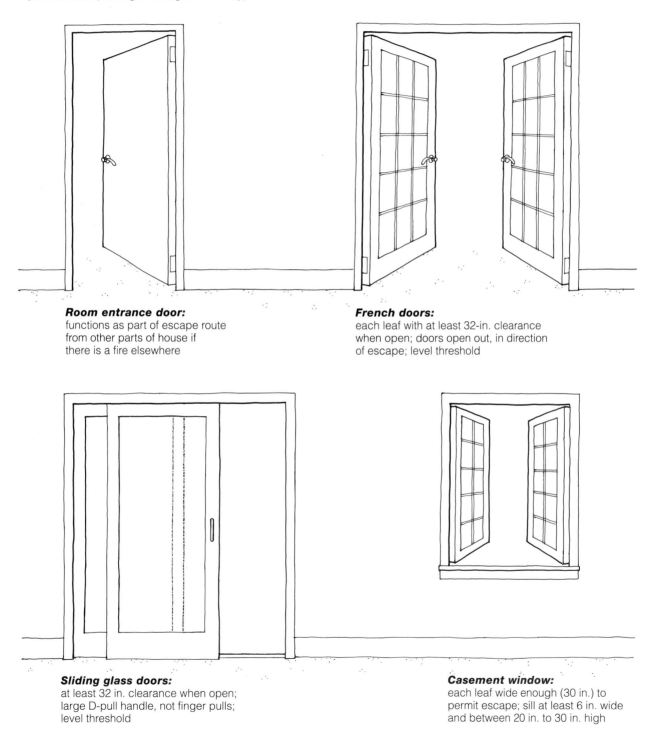

Room entrance door:
functions as part of escape route from other parts of house if there is a fire elsewhere

French doors:
each leaf with at least 32-in. clearance when open; doors open out, in direction of escape; level threshold

Sliding glass doors:
at least 32 in. clearance when open; large D-pull handle, not finger pulls; level threshold

Casement window:
each leaf wide enough (30 in.) to permit escape; sill at least 6 in. wide and between 20 in. to 30 in. high

wheelchair users. For example, people lacking in agility or strength may be unable to manipulate door or window hardware, open or close a door, or get over a threshold or through a doorway simply because of bad design, which denies them access to major components of the living environment.

Poorly designed doors and doorways impair the efficiency and safety of people moving into and throughout the house, the sense of security people have while in their homes, their potential for a safe escape in the event of a fire or other emergency, the size of objects that can be moved into and throughout the house, the quality of the environment achieved through the regulation of temperature and ventilation and the overall ease of use of the house.

Additionally, the type, location and size of doorways and windows affect furniture placement and the amount of usable space in a room. Furniture placement and usable space affect the clear space and pathways within the environment, which in turn affect the usability of the environment for someone with mobility problems or for a household with more than one member.

DOORS AND DOORWAYS

Doors are such an obvious part of the house environment that we rarely stop to think about their purpose and necessity, and whether they are a help, a hindrance or an unnecessary expense. Before a door is specified and installed in a specific location, its purpose should be clear. If a legitimate purpose can't be found, don't install the door. The principal legitimate functions of a door are safety, security, privacy, climate control and aesthetics. If a door won't satisfy one or more of these functions, it may not be necessary. Not every room needs a door to separate it from other rooms. Many homes are better served by open spaces — a doorway, but no door. Once a legitimate purpose has been found for a door, it then needs to be located and installed so that it can be used easily by all occupants of the house.

Doorways, too, are barriers. Think about who goes through the doorway and how they do it. People vary widely in size, strength and manual dexterity. People may go through the doorway with one or both arms encumbered by groceries or children. The doorway is a portal for children, pets, toys, baby carriages, bicycles, groceries, vacuum cleaners, laundry baskets, furniture and appliances. Often, the larger and heavier the object, the more people who will be needed to try and get it through the doorway. Bounding pets and racing children frequently clog doorways. All this traffic and activity mean that a narrow doorway is likely to encounter more bumps and cause more problems than a wide doorway.

A door equipped with difficult-to-use hardware is more likely to be pushed against, kicked and otherwise abused than a door with easy-to-use hardware. Doorways with smoothly transitioned thresholds will accommodate the wheels of baby carriages, casters on chairs and the portable television set.

Basic specifications for doors and doorways are shown in the drawing on the facing page. The main issues to be considered when selecting and placing doors are:
• the necessity and function of the door
• the swing of the door
• the handedness of the door
• the access space (clear space) in front of the door and on the side with the latch set
• the style of the door
• the width of the doorway
• the dimensions of the threshold
• the location of the door relative to the pathways within the room and between rooms
• the door hardware.

The swing of the door affects its ease of use and safety. Will the door swing in or out? The outside of a room is either the exterior of a house, the corridor or another room. When considering the swing of the door, ask yourself the following questions: Is there adequate space to maneuver around it? Does the door swing into the path of people passing by? Does the door swing into the path of or create obstacles with other swinging doors or objects?

The handedness of the door is important for ensuring that there is adequate clear space on the latch or pull side. Doors are either right- or left-handed. When the door opens toward you and the door knob is on the left, the door is left-handed. There should be at least 18 in. of space on the latch side of the door swinging inward to ensure that the door can swing past the person.

Clear space in front of and adjacent to the door refers to where the enterer is positioned when opening the door. Individuals who use wheelchairs as well as people carrying a child or a sack of groceries are affected by the clear space. Hinged doors that don't allow at least 18 in. of clear space on the latch side can be extremely difficult to open and close.

All doorways should have a minimum of 32 in. of clear-width opening. In order to achieve a clear opening of 32 in., a 2-ft. 10-in. or 3-ft. door may be required, depending on the style of door, the type of hinge and the size of the door stop on the frame. While the 32-in. wide doorway is routinely viewed as a requirement for people in wheelchairs, it has a much broader application. Many large, awkward objects (sofas, beds, pianos, refrigerators) that are moved into and through the house require a wide opening. Also, people carrying coats, packages, briefcases and/or children who enter the house would appreciate a little extra space to squeeze through.

All doors should have a minimum of 18 in. of clear space on the latch side for maneuvering. This space should be covered on the outside, and the sidewalk or porch should extend at least 18 in. beyond the door, preferably more. A clear space and roof overhang of 24 in. to 30 in. would afford better protection against the elements yet not cost much more than an 18-in. sheltered area. (For more on designing the entry to the house, see pp. 54-61.)

The lifespan house is planned so that every occupant can access all closets, all rooms and all spaces. The lifespan house seeks to minimize, if not eliminate entirely, the frustrations caused when an individual is kept out of a linen closet, pantry or bathroom because the designer or builder failed to consider human differences.

Doors and Doorways — General Guidelines

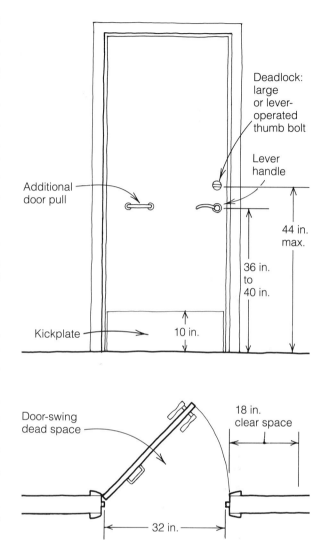

Exterior doors   There are several types of exterior residential doors: side-hung entrance, sliding glass entrance, overhead or sliding garage and bulkhead or cellar. The garage door and cellar door are rarely discussed in terms of ease of use, and to our knowledge have not been evaluated in research studies.

In our research we evaluated both side-hung and sliding glass exterior doors. We found that people rated the sliding glass doors as easier to open and pass through than hinged doors (regardless of whether

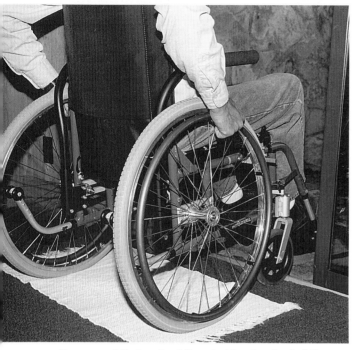

Because of their raised thresholds, standard sliding doors are barriers to wheelchair access.

they were hinged on the right or left). This finding is a bit paradoxical: although many people can open the doors more easily, they often have more difficulty getting through the doorway because of the slide channels. People in wheelchairs, especially, have less difficulty opening a sliding glass door because they can do so without having to maneuver their wheelchair around it. Unfortunately, the slide channel threshold is usually higher than ½ in., which makes moving over the threshold virtually impossible. Also, the locks and door pulls on sliding glass doors are often difficult to manipulate.

Two ways to provide a good transition over the channels on standard sliding glass or French doors are shown in the drawing below. If the door is in an area where water is unlikely to accumulate, such as on an above-ground deck or in a covered entrance, the slide channel can be recessed into the subfloor, with a filler block added as needed (A in the drawing). The screen (if needed) will in effect be recessed into the floor. The second method (B in the drawing) is to install the door conventionally, but build a wood

Doors and Wheelchairs

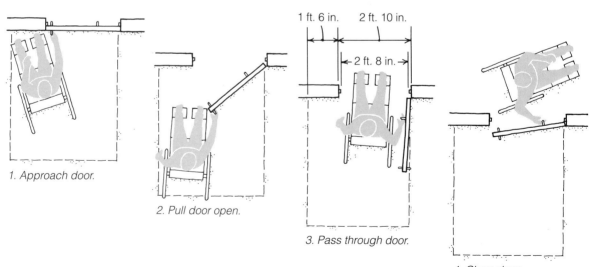

1. Approach door.

2. Pull door open.

1 ft. 6 in.　　2 ft. 10 in.

←2 ft. 8 in.→

3. Pass through door.

4. Close door with door pull.

For a person in a wheelchair, negotiating a doorway can be a complex operation that requires adequate clear space and door pulls that are easily gripped.

Threshold Treatments for Sliding Glass Doors

Standard Installation

On most major brands of sliding glass doors and French doors, the slide channel or channels present major obstacles, especially for people in wheelchairs. On a double patio door, the height difference from bottom to top of the track can be as much as 2 in.

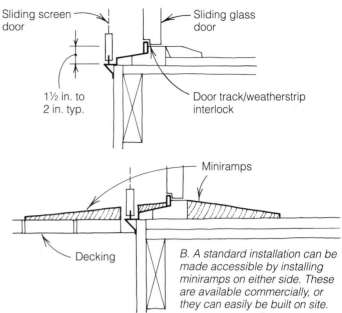

Two Accessible Solutions

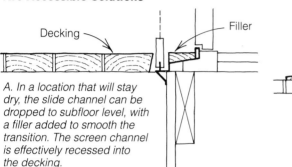

A. In a location that will stay dry, the slide channel can be dropped to subfloor level, with a filler added to smooth the transition. The screen channel is effectively recessed into the decking.

B. A standard installation can be made accessible by installing miniramps on either side. These are available commercially, or they can easily be built on site.

miniramp on both sides of the channel, again leaving a slot for the sliding screen.

Significant problems are encountered by people trying to enter doors when they are burdened with packages or when they are assisted by walkers, wheelchairs, canes or crutches. Their difficulties are multiplied when a screen or storm door with a conventional spring closer is added to the obstacle course. Two doors would not be impossible to handle if the door with the closing device opened a full 90° and if it closed after the individual had passed through. Unfortunately, mechanical door closers usually increase the amount of force required to open the door, they do not allow the door to open fully and they make it difficult to keep the door open while passing through the doorway. Closing the door after crossing the threshold is difficult because many people do not have arms long enough to reach back and grasp the door to pull it closed.

One solution for this problem is to use specially designed automatic closers that allow the door to be opened fully, then have a short delay before they begin to close automatically. Another solution is to avoid the use of double doors. Essentially the same benefits of storm and screen doors may be gained through the addition of a screened-in or glassed-in porch. This solution, although significantly more costly than the installation of a storm or screen door, could also help to keep the house warm and/or cool. Additionally, people would be spared having to negotiate two doors at the same time. A third solution to pulling the door closed is to add a handle near the hinges to make it easier to shut the door.

Most exterior doors are made of wood, aluminum or steel (some are also made of fiberglass). Although the type of material does not significantly affect how easily the door can be used, it does affect durability and maintenance, which in turn affect the ease of use of the door over time.

Most people find wood doors to be the most attractive choice. Beautiful wood entry doors often become the focal point of a house. But wood doors are likely to require more maintenance than steel or aluminum doors, and they are more likely to be damaged by weather, scrapes and bumps. They can, however, be protected somewhat from wheelchair footrests and impatient dogs with brass kickplates. Also, wood doors can be repaired easily when they are damaged. Solid wood doors insulate better than aluminum, although generally not as well as insulated steel doors.

Aluminum doors are generally less attractive than wood or steel and are often used as less expensive

Easing Threshold Barriers

Standard raised thresholds are designed to keep mud and dirt out of the house, but in so doing, they also keep out people in wheelchairs and can cause people who are unsteady on their feet to trip (A in the drawing at right). ANSI accessibility standards call for square-edged sills no higher than ¼ in., and beveled thresholds no higher than ½ in. (B in the drawing). There are various ways to make accessible thresholds, depending on the type of door. The first step is to raise the exterior decking to the same level as the threshold.

A traditional wood door sill is relatively easy to adapt since it is flat to begin with. Instead of setting the sill on the subfloor, it can be set on the framing or shimmed up slightly, creating a rise of ½ in. (C in the drawing). Bottom mounted, adjustable bulb-type weatherstripping works best with this installation.

Prehung wood and insulated steel doors can be ordered with what is referred to as a "handicap sill," a low-profile aluminum or brass sill (D in the drawing). The sill is fit on site.

Many insulated steel doors come with an aluminum sill and a wood insert whose height can be altered by means of adjusting screws. These can be almost flat on the outside and as little as 1⅛ in. high overall (E in the drawing). By adjusting the threshold down, some versions can be made accessible without modification. Other versions can be adapted by recessing the sill into the subfloor.

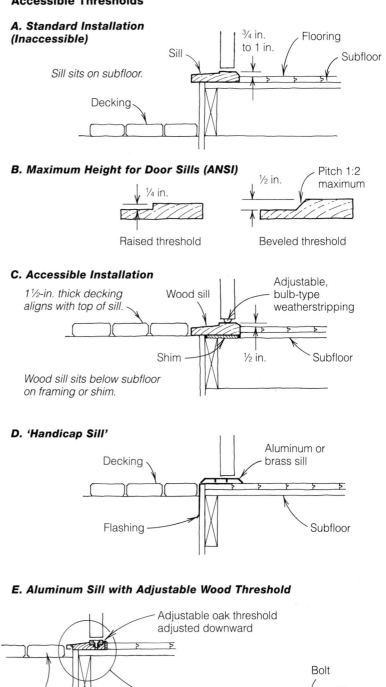

Accessible Thresholds

A. Standard Installation (Inaccessible)

Sill sits on subfloor.

¾ in. to 1 in. — Sill — Flooring — Subfloor — Decking

B. Maximum Height for Door Sills (ANSI)

¼ in. — Raised threshold

½ in. — Pitch 1:2 maximum — Beveled threshold

C. Accessible Installation

1½-in. thick decking aligns with top of sill. — Wood sill — Adjustable, bulb-type weatherstripping — Shim — ½ in. — Subfloor

Wood sill sits below subfloor on framing or shim.

D. 'Handicap Sill'

Decking — Aluminum or brass sill — Flashing — Subfloor

E. Aluminum Sill with Adjustable Wood Threshold

Adjustable oak threshold adjusted downward — Decking — Bolt — Flange — Oak insert — Socket

alternatives to save money. But aluminum doors don't necessarily save money in the long run. They typically don't insulate as well as steel or wood doors, and if damaged they are nearly impossible to repair.

Steel doors with a foam insulation core provide excellent insulation. They are durable, require little maintenance and can maintain their appearance for a long time. Steel doors are available that look almost like wood. They are, however, difficult to repair if they are damaged.

Whatever kind of door you choose, your entrance won't be fully accessible unless you provide a threshold that is barrier free. Raised thresholds can cause tripping hazards and prohibit passage by people in wheelchairs. The sidebar on the facing page offers suggestions for smoothing out thresholds.

Interior doors Interior doors offer privacy, protection and climate control. If a door isn't needed for one of these functions, don't install it. It has become the custom to install hinged doors throughout the house, even though the only reason many of them are moved is to sweep behind them.

In our research we evaluated several door styles with people of all ages, abilities and assistive devices. We found that the pocket door with a D-pull handle, rather than the standard recessed finger pull, was the easiest for everyone. The next easiest was the sliding closet door followed by double-leaf doors, standard right- and left-hinged doors and bifolds.

The standard hinged door is ubiquitous in contemporary home construction. Hinged doors are generally inexpensive and simple to install. Their biggest drawback is that they take up space and create unnecessary obstacles. They interfere with other doors, cabinet drawers and doors, passages and maneuvering through a space. Depending on the direction of the swing, hinged doors can hinder the quick evacuation of a room or house.

Pocket doors are excellent space savers. A standard hinged door requires over 16 sq. ft. of clear floor space for its swing. In a house with 10 hinged doors, roughly 165 sq. ft. of space can be lost to the swing of doors. In contrast, pocket doors have no swing. Pocket doors require about half of the clear floor space of hinged doors. Replacing half of the hinged doors in a house with pocket doors could result in a substantial increase in usable space.

Hinged Doors vs. Pocket Doors

Hinged Door

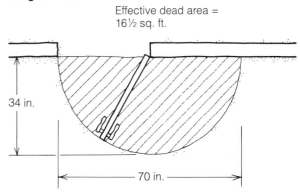

Effective dead area = 16½ sq. ft.

34 in.

70 in.

A standard hinged door can monopolize 16½ sq. ft. of floor space. Hinged doors also block passageways, create maneuvering problems and block wall space.

Pocket Door

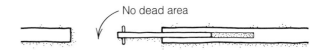

No dead area

For many people, pocket doors are easier to operate than hinged doors. They also free up wall and floor space.

Many builders despise pocket doors and refuse to consider their applications. The bad reputation of pocket doors is due to the use in the past of low-quality door kits, with weak tracks, hangers that jumped off the tracks and sides made from cheap wood that warped easily and caused the door to become misaligned. Furthermore, once installed, pocket doors can be difficult to repair. Also, some builders don't like pocket doors because they are not part of their ordinary routine and must be installed during framing, before the drywall is installed.

A number of companies now offer high-quality pocket-door kits, sometimes referred to as universal pocket-door kits (see Resources on p. 119). Universal kits provide all the special parts needed to build a high-quality pocket for any door and are easier to work with and more reliable than lightweight kits.

The sidebar below offers suggestions on choosing and installing pocket doors.

All interior doorways should have a minimum clear width of 32 in., which means a 2-ft. 10-in. or a 3-ft. door. Avoid the temptation to use smaller doors on closets, linen closets and other small spaces. It makes no sense to make a bedroom accessible by using wide doors only to create a barrier at the closet with a narrower door (see pp. 196-198).

Double-leaf doors are often put in a space when one larger door may occupy too much room. A double-leaf door takes two hands to open, but it takes up less room when opened. While not efficient from the viewpoint of human movement, double-leaf doors may be a good compromise for providing full access to closet space. A standard 34-in. door on a 48-in. wide closet would provide a clear opening of 32 in. to the closet space. Two 24-in. doors would provide

Choosing and Installing Pocket Doors

When shopping for pocket-door hardware, look for units rated for doors that weigh 125 lb. to 150 lb. Rather than suspending the door from two single wheels, riding in a track open on one side, these units will have two hangers or "wheel carriers" with three or four wheels each, which ride in a track that surrounds the hanger. The wheels can't jump off. The hanger is typically composed of two parts. A mounting bracket attaches to the door. The wheel set enters the track from a drop-out at the very end, then hooks onto a bolt on the mounting bracket. The bolt also allows for vertical adjustment (see the drawing below).

Many manufacturers offer models with ball-bearing wheels, which reduce the force needed to open the door from about 7 lb. to about 3 lb.

Since standard opening hardware can be difficult to grasp and pull, the ball-bearing units are preferred.

You can buy a hardware kit and build the pockets yourself, or you can by a universal kit, which also includes parts for the pocket. In addition to the rolling hardware and track, the hardware kit should also include a bottom door guide, a bumper and an installation wrench. The universal kit would include steel-reinforced studs to go around the door and steel stiffeners for the split jamb.

A typical installation is shown in the drawing at left on the facing page. The framing around the door is thin (at most, ⅞ in. for a 3½-in. wall), so it has to be very straight. There isn't space for wires or outlet boxes, and drywallers and carpenters have to be careful not to drive nails or screws into the door. The split jamb is screwed in place on one side, so it can be removed to service the hardware or remove the door itself.

Installing a pocket door in a 2x6 wall allows you to beef up the framing around the door considerably and provides room for wiring. In this case, it's best to buy only the hardware and build the rest of the unit yourself.

Heavy-Duty Pocket-Door Hardware

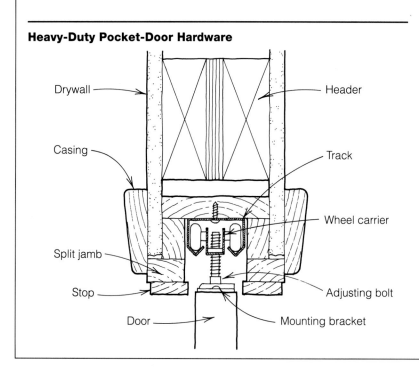

approximately 44 in. of clear opening into the closet space and would not require as much swing in the room. A single sliding door on a 48-in. closet would not be an acceptable alternative because the doors would be 24 in. wide, thus providing only 23 in. of clear space at the opening (see the drawing on p. 108).

Bifold or folding doors are often used to conceal laundry areas, bookshelves and small storage closets. They can be decorative and they require less clear floor space than a hinged door, but most bifolds are not high quality, and they tend to jam and can be difficult to operate. They also often may require two hands to operate them, especially if their pulls aren't installed correctly. When open, they occupy part of the clear opening, thus reducing access to the area behind. Some folding doors (series 1601 by L.E. Johnson Products is one example) open fully and the doors fold back flush against the wall.

Many of the problems with pocket doors can be eliminated by surface mounting the door (see the drawing below right). After drywalling, the track is mounted on a simple cleat, perhaps 1½ in. by 2 in., screwed into the wall.

Similar cleats act as stops both left and right. The track at the top is concealed with a trim piece or casing, screwed in place for easy removal. Both repairs and installation are extremely easy — easier than a hinged door. The only drawbacks are that about 2 in. of floor space is taken up by the door, and some wall space is lost. Furniture can be placed in front of the door, however.

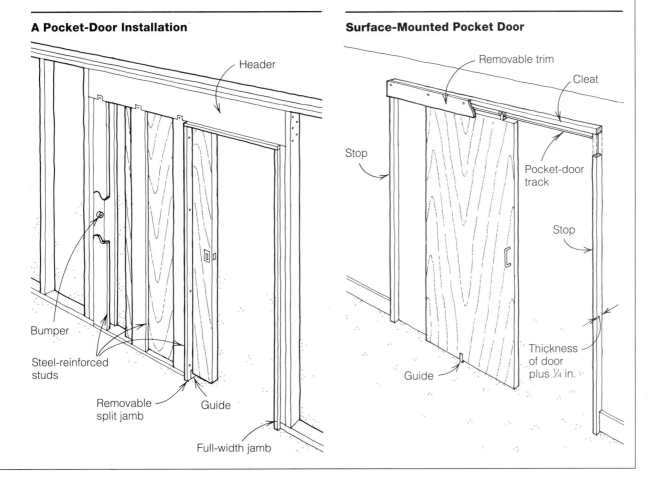

A Pocket-Door Installation

Header

Bumper

Steel-reinforced studs

Removable split jamb

Guide

Full-width jamb

Surface-Mounted Pocket Door

Removable trim

Cleat

Stop

Pocket-door track

Stop

Guide

Thickness of door plus ¼ in.

Some inexpensive models of folding doors are mounted on tracks and constructed of vinyl or reinforced canvas. They work best with a floor track, which tends to fill with debris and causes the door to jam. The track itself could be a barrier to getting into the closet area inside. These folding doors aren't particularly durable, and they often require considerable strength and agility to push them open or pull them shut. They also tie up space in the doorway.

Stable or dutch doors are usually found only on kitchen doorways. They allow the top half to be open while the bottom half is closed. Often they are unnecessary. If a door is truly needed for the kitchen, many will prefer the greater convenience of a pocket door or full-sized swinging door. Dutch doors do allow communication, ventilation and light to pass through the upper half of the doorway while the lower half serves as a gate to children and pets. They cause problems because people are unaccustomed to them, and they invite fingers to be pinched between the sections.

The location of doorways affects furniture placement and traffic flows. Any regular pathway should be at least 36 in. wide, and it should be as direct a route as possible. People should not have to make tight turns. The authors of *A Pattern Language* recommend placing doorways at the corners of rooms, so there will be more uninterrupted wall space for furniture placement. If the doorway is part of a through pathway, the connecting doorway should be on the same end of the room or on the wall adjacent to the corner. Finally, locating doors on the side of the room that is used most frequently will reduce the number of steps.

Door hardware   Many people can't open doors with standard hardware, even hardware that meets ANSI 117.1 standards for accessibility. Many people, particularly older women, are unable to open the doors of their homes because they do not have the strength or manual dexterity. Many doors become difficult to open because the hardware sticks or because the doors swell in hot, humid weather. Even new doors are often outfitted with hardware that requires twisting and turning of the wrist, fine fingering or depression of a thumb latch. For many people, these tasks are next to impossible. People can literally become trapped in their homes during a fire because their exit was too difficult to open.

Door hardware includes knobs and handles, pulls, locksets, dead bolts, mortise locks, kickplates and door closers. For maximum accessibility, select door hardware that can be operated by hands and fingers that are not nimble, that lack strength or for that matter essentially don't work well at all.

Traditional door knobs should be assigned to a museum for poorly designed objects; they just shouldn't be used. Attractive, effective and economical lever door handles are available from a wide variety of manufacturers, in styles and finishes to fit any decor. Lever handles that work when the handle is pushed either down or up offer the greatest flexibility. The shopper burdened with two or three gro-

Closet Doors: Bypass vs. Double Leaf

Bypass sliding door

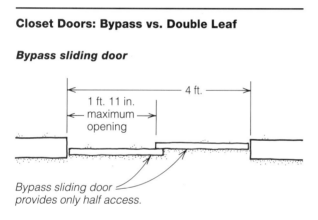

Bypass sliding door provides only half access.

Double-leaf hinged doors

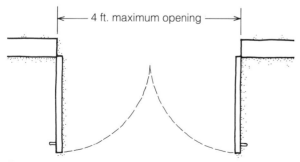

Double leaf-doors provide full access.

The traditional round door knob should be abandoned. It requires fingering, grasping and twisting — maneuvers that many people find difficult to perform. Good lever handles are much easier to use for virtually everyone. They can be opened with a closed fist, or even with a knee or elbow. A lever that curves back toward the door (above) is less likely to snag clothing and other items. (Photo above left: Kevin Ireton.)

cery bags can lower one of the bags onto the handle to release the latch, or, if nimble enough, could lift a knee to open the door. Meanwhile, the person with arthritis doesn't have to grasp and turn the lever to open the door.

Lever door handles need at least a 5-in. handle or blade. The longer handle provides greater leverage, which aids the person with loaded arms or limited movements. Levers whose ends curve back toward the door are less likely to catch the coat pocket or sleeve of someone who passes by.

Many exterior door locksets include an inaccessible thumb latch set and keyed lock on the outside and a lever door handle on the inside. This arrangement implies that the individual who is physically challenged will always be inside the house and only able-bodied individuals will be opening the doors from the outside. Both sides of a lockset should be

equipped with lever handles. The thumb-latch set demands too much manual dexterity for easy use.

Grasping, inserting and turning a key in a lock is a difficult maneuver for some people and an impossible one for others. For these people keyless locksets are a godsend. Keyless locksets include those with a mechanical or electrical numerical combination, magnetically controlled electrical locks and voice-actuated electrical systems.

Another big advantage to keyless locksets is that you don't have to keep track of a key. You simply need to be able to remember the combination. Except for the systems that operate by magnetic card, you won't have to fumble with anything to open the door. The principal shortcoming of the combination systems is that anyone needing to unlock the door has to remember the combination. However, some keyless mechanical systems require as much or more

Keyless locksets do not require the fine-fingering capabilities that are required to hold, insert and turn a traditional key in a lock. This electronic entry system operates on household current with a battery backup. Photo: Essex Electronics.)

manual dexterity as keyed systems. Several companies that manufacture keyless entry systems are listed in Resources on p. 119.

In addition to ensuring that the handles of the locksets are usable, extra security locks should be selected and installed so that all the members of the household are able to open them without difficulty, particularly in an emergency situation when a panicked person may not be thinking clearly. Deadbolts and door chains should work easily and should not bind. Avoid chain locks, which require fine fingering and are difficult for many to operate. HEWI manufactures a line of door hardware that is exceptionally attractive and is designed for ease of use. There are three styles of lever handles and large thumb turns that operate the dead bolt. Their hardware system also includes matching mail slots, numerals, doorbell buttons, pull handles and hinges.

Door hardware should be at a height everyone can reach. Do not install any hardware higher than 48 in. on the door; 40 in. to 44 in. is better. Many

keyed cylinder locks have traditionally been located at heights of 50 in. to 54 in., which is the maximum height that someone seated in a wheelchair can reach, let alone insert and turn a key.

Locks should be operable with one hand. The best lock is a deadbolt with a "panic release" operable by a lever door handle. That is, the deadbolt is released with the activation of the lever handle (on the inside) as opposed to a deadbolt that operates separately from the handle. The separate lock system requires a person to release both the deadbolt and the door latch, if indeed those are the only locks on their doors. Many people install multiple locks for an added sense of security, but these can hinder rapid egress in the event of an emergency.

On many sliding glass doors, the pulls are mounted on the frame at the edge of the door. Be sure there is adequate clearance (at least 1 in. of space) between the door handle and frame so that the palm of the hand (as opposed to the fingers) may be inserted into the area to push the door open. The locks on sliding glass doors vary considerably from manufacturer to manufacturer, so these too must be evaluated carefully. Look for large latches that can be operated using a closed fist. Avoid locks that are embedded in the interior of the pull, particularly those that require the use of a fingertip to push the lock up and down.

Many sliding glass doors are equipped with locks (lever bolts) located at both the top and bottom of the door. Although these do provide added security, they may also create a barrier for someone unable to reach or operate them. Always keep in mind that people of different sizes, strengths and abilities are likely to be living in the house, and all doors should be operable by the person with the least capability.

On pocket doors, the most common opening and closing hardware consists of a flush pull recessed into the face of the door or a retractable edge pull, mortised into the edge of the door, which allows the door to be opened from a fully closed position. Stanley and other manufacturers provide a unit that combines both functions (see the drawing at top left on the facing page). This hardware is far from ideal. The finger openings are small, and some people have difficulty releasing the edge pull.

A better solution is to mount a simple 5-in. D-pull on both sides of the door (see the drawing at bottom left). Positioning the pull 1½ in. from the door edge preserves hand space when the door is closed. Stopping the door 1½ in. shy of the D-pull leaves sufficient finger space when the door is open. This arrangement reduces the net clear opening by roughly 3 in., meaning that a 36-in. wide door would be required for a net opening of 32 in. A 40-in. door could be used for a wider opening.

A variation on the D-pull is shown in the drawing below right. Ordinary D-pulls are recessed into the wall, allowing the door to be shut flush with the jamb. This detail requires a 2x6 wall frame in the door area. Also, the door must be 4 in. larger than the finish opening to cover the recess when the door is closed (a covering block could be fastened to the door at the recess).

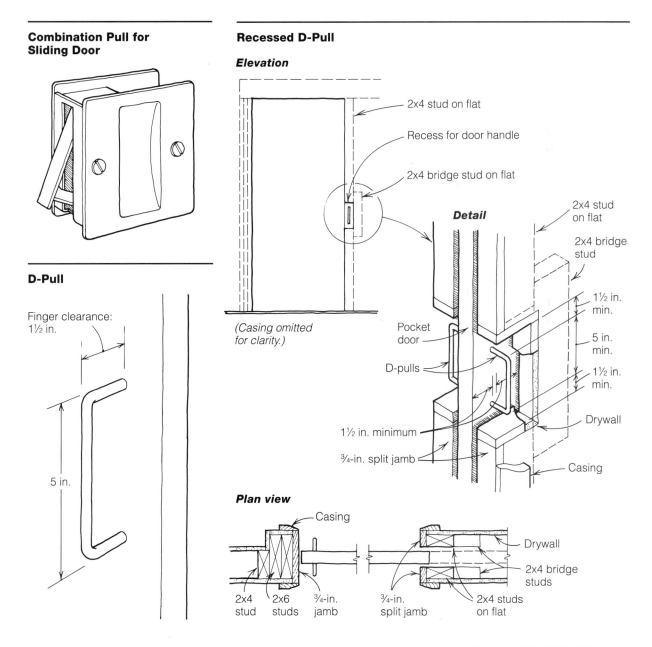

Combination Pull for Sliding Door

D-Pull

Finger clearance: 1½ in.

5 in.

Recessed D-Pull

Elevation

2x4 stud on flat

Recess for door handle

2x4 bridge stud on flat

(Casing omitted for clarity.)

Detail

2x4 stud on flat

2x4 bridge stud

1½ in. min.

5 in. min.

1½ in. min.

Pocket door

D-pulls

1½ in. minimum

¾-in. split jamb

Drywall

Casing

Plan view

Casing

2x4 stud   2x6 studs   ¾-in. jamb

¾-in. split jamb

2x4 studs on flat

Drywall

2x4 bridge studs

WINDOWS

In study after study we have found that people often equate the quality of their living environment with the amount of natural light it receives. Homes that let the sun shine in are considered cheerful, airy, peaceful and happy. People repeatedly tell us that one of the changes they would most like in their homes is more windows, more natural light.

Windows serve several purposes. First, they provide light, warmth and fresh air, if the house is designed right. The light improves the visual work space and a sense of orientation to the time of day and weather. Many people who remain indoors for long periods of time without good sources of natural light lose their sense of orientation and connectedness to the world around them. Some have suggested that the sleeping problems many older persons experience may be a result of confusion in their "internal clocks" because of an inadequate amount of daylight. In a house, windows are the principal source of fresh air and natural ventilation. Well-placed windows can substantially improve the climate and air quality in a house.

Windows also serve several safety functions. Windows are incorporated into doors or located near them to allow occupants to see persons on the other side. Windows can also be life-savers when they are used as a means of escape from a burning or collapsing structure.

Windows are used for surveillance, and for many people this surveillance is a form of entertainment. Studies by Sandra Howell, an architectural researcher at Massachusetts Institute of Technology, have shown that more than half of the individuals living in a retirement community reported that the longer they lived in the community (i.e., the older they became), the more time they spent watching events through their windows.

Windows provide a sense of security. It can be discomforting to hear a sound and not be able to find out what's causing it. Well-placed windows that provide views of the areas surrounding a home allow the residents to monitor children, pets and unexpected visitors from a comfortably located armchair.

Selecting windows In order to select an appropriate type of window for a specific setting, you need to consider the window's purpose or purposes. Will it be used for surveillance, as a primary source of light and/or ventilation, as an emergency exit? If the window is solely for ventilation, then it is unimportant if the occupants are able to see out. It is important, however, that they be able to control the ventilation. If the window is for observation, ventilation, light and emergency exit, it must satisfy several criteria.

Window Styles

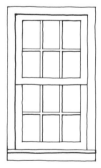

Vertical sliding sash (single/double hung)

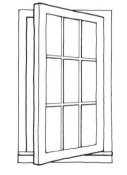

Casement

Awning

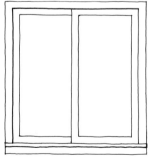

Horizontal sliding sash

There are various designs for windows, and each has its pros and cons. The most common, shown in the drawing on the facing page, are single and double-hung sliding sash, casement, awning and horizontal sliding sash.

People often choose a window style on the basis of aesthetic considerations. In some instances, the energy efficiency of a window will be a factor in its selection, but for the most part windows are selected without special consideration for their suitability relative to their purpose (viewing, ventilation, light or escape).

Vertical sliding sash windows   The single or double-hung vertical sliding sash is one of the most common windows in use. It is readily available in a variety of standard sizes. It comes in forms that meet most construction budgets. It comes in wood, wood clad in aluminum or vinyl, or all aluminum or steel. Many products have significantly improved hardware that make the operation of the window easier. Its style allows it to function as an escape route if it is located and sized properly. A sliding sash window accepts an air-conditioning unit. It can accommodate screens in the summer and storm windows in the winter.

Despite all of these advantages, the vertical sliding sash puts up a few obstacles and is considered the most difficult window to use for individuals with physical challenges. Many are able to operate the bottom half of the window, provided it moves easily, but have significant difficulty reaching and maneuvering the upper half of the window, even if it is well-built.

Some vertical sliding sashes have a tendency to bind and stick if they are not raised and lowered using two hands with essentially equal force on both hands. The demand for two hands eliminates some people, the requirement of equal force creates problems for still more and the extra strength dictated by a sash jammed in the frame may beyond the capabilities of still others. Lifting hard-to-open double-hung windows becomes more and more difficult over the years. And they are rarely replaced; they just get opened less and less often.

A window over the kitchen sink is always welcome. But this double-hung window is difficult to reach and even harder to open.

Vertical sliding sashes are easier to operate if the hardware provides adequate space for pushing the window up and down. However, many window manufacturers do not include sash lifts, and those that are provided often are too small to be of much assistance. Often the window has to be opened and closed by pushing on the horizontal sash, which is difficult to grip and push or pull with the fingertips.

Many vertical sliding sash windows (aluminum in particular) have rails that do not provide enough room for grasping. Some have a lift or pull at the bottom edge, but this location requires the user to rotate the hands palms up and lift the window by inserting the fingertips under the lift. Many people with arthritis can't rotate their wrists to this degree.

A separate handle or lift can be applied to wood windows and some vinyl-clad windows. Ideally two handles would be put on the window, one on the top rail and one on the bottom rail of the sash. The user could then begin to open the window by pushing up on the top rail; when adequate space was available at the bottom of the window, the user could continue the push using the handle on the bottom. The best location for accessory handles would be in the center of the window, which would permit one-handed people to operate the window independently.

Ease of cleaning is another consideration in selecting a sliding sash window. Different types of windows are cleaned differently. Some have sashes that tilt inward, others have sashes that are claimed to be easy to remove from inside the house and others are fixed in their frame. Tilting windows offer the greatest advantages because they can be cleaned from within the house and a person with limited strength may be able to operate them. Windows with removable sashes require the user to be strong enough to lift the window out of the frame, generally while releasing the small clip that holds it in place. Many people don't have sufficient strength and dexterity to accomplish this feat. Windows fixed in their frame, particularly those with screens, require added effort because the screen must be removed before the exterior side of the pane can be washed from the outside.

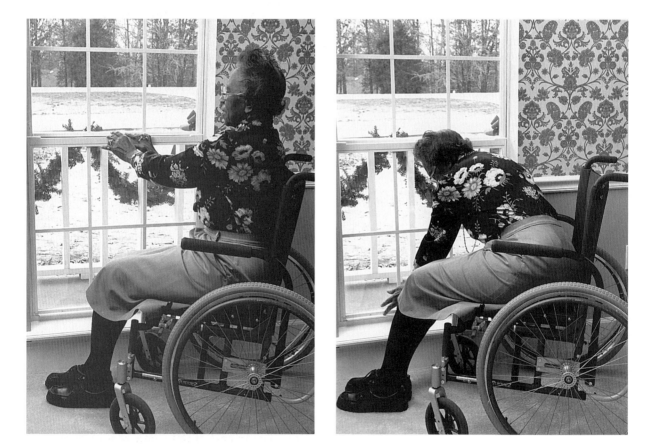

The lock on this double-hung window is located within the optimal reach zone, making it accessible to just about everyone. However, once the lock has been released, the only way the window can be opened is by reaching down nearly to the floor to grab the pull. Slightly thicker sash and/or the addition of sash lifts would make this window much easier to open.

Casement windows   Casement windows have many positive features. They are easy for most people to operate, especially one-handed. They generally provide a good seal against air and water leakage. And the design of the casement window is well-suited for an electrical window opener.

Researcher Sandra Howell asked 157 elderly residents living in 14 multi-family (apartments) housing sites across the country what they thought of various window types. The fewest complaints concerning air leakage and operation came from people whose apartments had casement windows. Double-hung windows were used in nine sites, casements in two, sliding sash in two and awning windows in one. Although it was a small study, the results provided some good information. Only 6% of the participants in apartments with casement windows reported problems with drafts, but about 20% with each of the other types of windows had complaints.

Casement windows have some drawbacks, too. They will not accept air conditioners, but in homes with central air conditioning that is not a problem. Although the opening hardware is usually easy to operate, some may be harder and require more cranking than others. Narrow casements may not be useful for emergency egress; extra-wide units, sometimes with special egress hinges, may be needed. Perhaps the biggest problem with casements is that unlike awning windows, they can let the rain in. A final problem is that casements (and awnings) protrude from the building. They should not be used in locations where they would obstruct a walkway. People can be seriously injured walking into windows.

Awning windows   Awning windows are hinged at the top and open outward at the bottom. They provide good weather protection, but the latches on some awnings are difficult to operate. Awning windows may demand more strength to open and close than casement windows. Like casements, awnings do not accept air conditioners and they protrude from the building when open. Awning windows may not serve well as escape windows if the hardware prevents them from opening fully.

An electrical window opener attaches to the window and opens and closes it at the turn of a knob. The one shown here is made by Andersen Windows.

Horizontal sliding sash windows   The horizontal sliding sash window has several attributes that make it a good choice, if it is a well-built model. The window is easily screened, and the hardware generally can be positioned in an easy-to-reach location. Unlike casement or awning windows, the horizontal sliding sash does not protrude from the building and will not create an obstacle or hazard. It may be easier to open for some people than a comparably located vertical sliding sash because it may not require reaching above the head. If necessary, an extra handle can be applied to the vertical rail to facilitate pushing or pulling.

Problems may arise in opening and closing horizontal sliding sash windows if debris collects in the track or if the window is heavy. Especially large windows may require rollers. Horizontal windows may provide the best escape window because they usually open fully and stay in the position in which they were opened.

Fixed windows   Fixed windows are not intended to be opened, so ease of operation is not a consideration. But, by design, their exterior surfaces are accessible only from the outside. Before designing a house

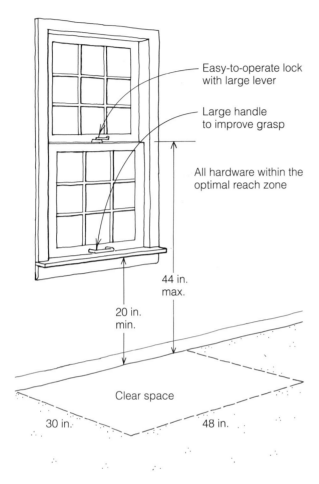

Easy-to-operate lock with large lever

Large handle to improve grasp

All hardware within the optimal reach zone

44 in. max.

20 in. min.

Clear space

30 in.   48 in.

A sill height of 20 in. is good for emergency egress and for looking outside while lying in bed.

with fixed windows, consider how they will be cleaned and repaired. Try to keep them within easy reach of the ground or a balcony. Often, fixed windows are placed in stairways and on high walls, where they are accessible only to someone able to climb a ladder.

Skylights   Fixed skylights, like other fixed windows, do not pose operability problems but they do often require extraordinary efforts to keep them clean. Unless they are placed on a roof adjacent to a balcony,

someone will have to climb onto a ladder or onto the roof to clean them. Skylights that open have a mechanical, electrical or automatic opening/closing mechanism. Like everything else in the house, these operating mechanisms should be located within the optimal reach zone (20 in. to 44 in. off the floor).

Storm windows   Storm windows are available in systems that are self-storing and systems that require removal and storage during warm weather. Combination storm and screen windows that are self-storing offer the advantage of not having to be put on and taken off every year. (Energy-efficient insulated windows have obviated the need for storm windows, and are recommended for that reason.)

Storm windows often take strength and manual dexterity to manipulate, and so present problems for many people. Many self-storing storm window systems have small, fingertip-actuated spring-loaded clips that the user must pinch while sliding the window. This maneuver is beyond the capability of many people. Unfortunately, we are unaware of any storm-window systems that have larger locking and handle systems that would enable someone with hand problems to operate them.

Window size and location in a room   Windows come in many sizes and shapes, and these dimensions, considered with the window's location in the room, are critical to the window's effectiveness. A window's height and width govern its use as an emergency exit and its maintenance requirements. The depth of the sill is also important. A window that has a sill narrower than 3 in. or one that does not have a sill may not provide adequate support for a person attempting to use the window as an emergency exit. A sill depth of 6 in. or more, on the other hand, provides a ledge that can help steady the person who needs extra support and time exiting through a window.

General guidelines for window dimensions and placement are shown in the drawing at left. The minimum criteria for a window are as follows:
• Window placement should allow people of all ages and abilities to use the window as intended.
• All operable components should be within the optimal reach zone (20 in. to 44 in. above the floor).

• The hardware should not require fine fingering, grasping, turning or twisting.

• Window dimensions should be appropriate to the window's purpose, taking into consideration differences in abilities. Windows used as auxiliary emergency exits should have a minimum width of 30 in. (only 20 in. is required by fire regulations, but this will not be wide enough for many people with disabilities, particularly if they have limited use of their lower extremities).

• The sill will enable passage and will have a height at its base no greater than 30 in.

• Clear space (30 in. by 48 in.) must be available to allow clear access to the window-treatment controls, which should be within the optimal reach zone.

The best location for a window will depend on its purpose or purposes, which should be considered with respect to furniture placement and clear space. These include climate and ventilation, viewing, security, safety and emergency egress.

Conflicts can occur in trying to balance these objectives. A good location for ventilation may be a bad location with respect to furniture placement. A window height that would allow a child or bedridden individual to see out of the window and to escape the house during an emergency is likely also to be low enough to be dangerous for young children. A combination of window heights and fixed and opening windows in the room may satisfy the purposes of ventilation (high opening window, sill 36 in. to 44 in.) and viewing (low fixed window, sill 28 in. to 30 in.). Tempered glass in the windows of a children's playroom may be a wise investment.

In most rooms, a window-sill height of 28 in. to 30 in. will put the window panes within the viewing region of children. In bedrooms, a window at this height will put the world on display for a person confined to bed. Privacy can come from window draperies or curtains, instead of from a window someone can't use.

In her study, Sandra Howell found that only 19% of the apartment dwellers reported problems cleaning their double-hung windows if the sill height from the floor was between 24 in. and 30 in. More than half (56%) of her elderly study participants reported difficulty cleaning windows with sill heights of 33 in. to 35 in.

Many people are concerned about a neighborhood that doesn't seem as friendly as it was 30 years ago when they moved to it. Windows strategically located so that the entire perimeter of the house can be observed will help ease the jitters over strange noises from outside. These window locations will likely aid in cross ventilation, too.

Too many tragic tales are told of young children falling out of windows from multi-story buildings. Gleeful roughhousing in a playroom turns into an ugly scar when a hand or foot goes through a window pane. In a playroom or a child's bedroom, a sill height of 44 in. would be high enough to prevent a child from climbing out or falling through it.

Codes require that basements and bedrooms have at least one emergency exit or rescue (door or window), which is at least 20 in. wide and 24 in. high, or have at least 5.7 sq. ft. of clear openable area. The sill height of an emergency window should not be more than 44 in. from the floor. These dimensions are appropriate for rescue personnel and much of the rest of the population, but they aren't adequate for everyone. Windows designated as escape routes should be lower and wider. A 20-in. wide window may be inadequate for a large man who does not have the use of his legs. The drawing on p. 99 gives general guidelines for emergency egress.

Not every room of a house will have or should have an escape door. Still, every room of the house should have an escape route, especially the bedrooms. Windows shouldn't just happen to offer an escape route in the event escape through the doorway of the room is blocked; a window (or door) should be planned as an escape route.

A conventional window designated as an escape should have a sill height between 20 in. and 30 in. This height will accommodate a short person or a wheelchair user. The sill should be wide enough and strong enough to function as a seat. However, this low height is in direct conflict with the suggested height of windows in children's bedrooms and playrooms. Rather than place low windows in these

A windowed exterior door can provide emergency egress from the first-floor bedroom, and be welcomed for other reasons as well, should the bedroom be converted at some point to an efficiency apartment or a home office (see pp. 198-199). On this house, the door installation cost no more than a window.

rooms, it may be best to have two doors at opposite ends of the room. That way, if one doorway is blocked, the other door will be available for escape.

Finally, the emergency-egress window needs to be operable. Many people lack the strength and dexterity to operate the locks on their windows and doors, and precious moments may be lost while someone is struggling to move a latch. A sliding glass door or a windowed hinged door can be ideal emergency exits that also function as windows.

Window hardware New and well-maintained locks are easier to use than old, rusted ones. Often, windows are installed and forgotten; dirt and corrosion accumulate over the years, making the windows harder and harder to open. Cam locks may work easily and well when new, but they tend to become quirkier as they age. The cam lock requires the operator to use the fingers in a tight space, with a tight pinch and rotation of the wrist. These movements are difficult, and often impossible, for someone with arthritis. Choose cam locks with a handle large enough so that they don't have to be grasped with the fingertips.

Crank hardware, common on casement and awning windows, is generally easy to use. Many cranks may be operated without using the fingertips or without a tight grasp. Be sure that the locking mechanism on a casement window is operable. Some window manufacturers offer a single lever lock on casement windows that connects a series of locks the length of the window. Some have very small cam latches on either side, and tall windows have latches at the top and bottom. The lock on the top assumes that everyone is able to reach and operate it.

RESOURCES

Pocket-Door Kits and Related Hardware

Acme (Stanley)
195 Lake Street
New Britain, CT 06050
(800) 622-4393

Lawrence Brothers
2 First Avenue
P.O. Box 538
Sterling, IL 61081
(815) 625-0360

L. E. Johnson Products
P.O. Box 1126
Elkhart, IN 46515
(219) 293-5664

National Manufacturing Co.
1 First Avenue
Sterling, IL 61081
(815) 625-1320

John Sterling Corporation
11600 Sterling Parkway
Box 469
Richmond, IL 60071-0469
(815) 678-4360

Door Hardware, Lever Locksets and Keyless Lock Systems

Best-Lock Corporation
P.O. Box 50444
Indianapolis, IN 46250
(317) 849-2250
Lever locksets.

Dor-O-Matic
7350 West Wilson Avenue
Chicago, IL 60656-4786
(800) 543-4635
(312) 867-7400
Automatic door closer with delayed action (adjustable delay time), reduced opening force, automatic door openers. Available for both interior and exterior doors.

Dryad Jebron
Architectural Hardware
Suite 202
249 Ayer Road
Harvard, MA 01451
(800) 445-5388
(508) 772-6005
Large entrance door handles, push-pull sets and door closers.

Duro-Med Industries
138 Kansas Street
Hackensack, NJ 07601
(201) 488-5055
Offset hinges and other door hardware.

Essex Technologies
Corporation
1130 Mark Avenue
Carpinteria, CA 93013-2987
(800) 628-9673
(805) 684-7601
An electronic touchpad keyless entry system that operates with the locks already on the door.

Genie Company
3515 Massillon Road
P.O. Box 6352
Akron, OH 44312
(216) 896-5200
Keyless garage-door entry system.

HEWI
2851 Old Tree Drive
Lancaster, PA 17603
(717) 293-1313
Complete decorative line of nylon-coated steel-core bathroom and door hardware products. Lever locksets, door pulls, hinges and accessories.

Kwikset Corporation
Emhart Hardware Group
516 East Santa Ana Street
Anaheim, CA 92803-4250
(714) 535-8111
Entrance, exit, passage and privacy lever sets. Entry lever set with deadbolt and deadlatch retract with the turn of the interior lever, ensuring exit in case of emergency.

Ply Gems Barrier Free
6948 Frankford Avenue
Philadelphia, PA 19135
(215) 331-3434
Offset hinges, grab bars and full line of accessories.

Schlage Lock Company
P.O. Box 193324
San Francisco, CA 94119
(415) 467-1100
Lever locksets and electronic locking systems.

Simplex Access Controls
P.O. Box 4114
2941 Indiana Avenue
Winston-Salem, NC
27115-4114
(919) 725-1331
Keyless entrance controls for electrical door locks and touch-button combination locks.

Stanley Magic-Door
Division of the Stanley Works
Route 6 & Hyde Road
Farmington, CT 06032
(203) 677-2861
Power access operator for interior and exterior doors. Can be operated through touch control or radio-transmitter control.

Yale Security
PO Box 25288
Charlotte, NC 28229-8010
(800) 458-1951
(704) 283-2101
Touch-code electronic locks. Power-matic door controls primarily for commercial or institutional applications.

Windows, Automatic Controls for Window and Treatments

Andersen Windows
100 Fourth Avenue
Bayport, MN 55003-1096
(612) 439-5150
Comprehensive line of windows and doors; electric window opener.

Bautex USA
10860 Alder Circle
Dallas, TX 75238
(800) 422-8839
Automated windows.

FASIRAND Corporation
P.O. Box 4425
Helena, MT 59604
(406) 449-6635
Automated windows.

Leviton Manufacturing
Company
59-25 Little Neck Parkway
Little Neck, NY 11362
(800) 232-8920
Automated windows.

Makita USA
14930 Northam St.
La Mirada, CA 90638-5753
(800) 4-Makita
(714) 522-8088
Automatic drapery opener.

Marvin Windows & Doors
2020 Silver Bell Road
St. Paul, MN 55122
(800) 328-0268
Automated windows.

Silent Gliss USA
29421 Kohouter Way
Union City, CA 94587
(510) 487-8305
Electronically controlled window opening system.

Somfy System
47 Commerce Drive
Cranbury, NJ 08512
(609) 395-1300
Automated windows.

Spectus Systems
P.O. Box 1145
Superior, WI 54880
(715) 394-9600
All-vinyl casement window, bottom-mounted locking handle and easy-to-control window.

Velux-America
Several offices throughout the United States; call for the one nearest you.
(800) 88-VELUX
Electronically controlled window openers and window blinds built-in; electronically controlled and easy-to-open roof windows and skylights.

Wintrol
1015 Poplar Street
Helena, MT 59601
(406) 449-6616
Automated windows.

CHAPTER EIGHT
STAIRS, RAMPS, LIFTS AND ELEVATORS

Steps and stairs, an integral part of architectural language, are a tool to get people from one plane to another. For many people, however, stairs are the ultimate barrier. They prevent people from visiting the homes of friends and relatives. They often restrict people to the use of a single floor or wing of their own home.

The challenge facing architects and home planners and designers is to develop an accessible system of changing levels within a home, and while doing that to create a new language, image and drama around the ramp or lift system. Stairs are the easiest, least creative and perhaps the most dangerous solution to a level change. Before deciding that a step

Stairs — General Guidelines

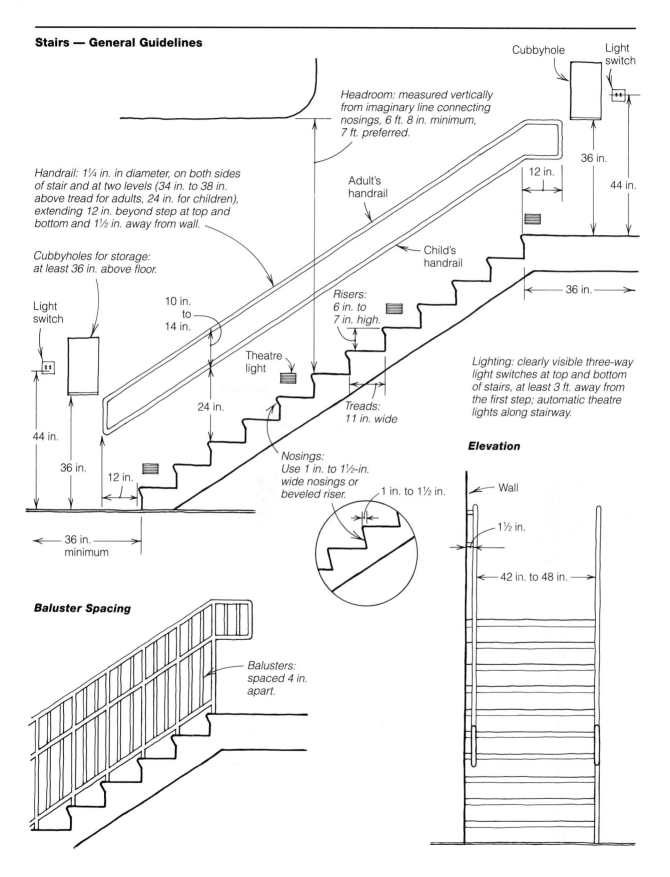

Cubbyhole

Light switch

Headroom: measured vertically from imaginary line connecting nosings, 6 ft. 8 in. minimum, 7 ft. preferred.

36 in.

12 in.

44 in.

Handrail: 1¼ in. in diameter, on both sides of stair and at two levels (34 in. to 38 in. above tread for adults, 24 in. for children), extending 12 in. beyond step at top and bottom and 1½ in. away from wall.

Adult's handrail

Child's handrail

36 in.

Cubbyholes for storage: at least 36 in. above floor.

Light switch

10 in. to 14 in.

Risers: 6 in. to 7 in. high.

Theatre light

Lighting: clearly visible three-way light switches at top and bottom of stairs, at least 3 ft. away from the first step; automatic theatre lights along stairway.

24 in.

Treads: 11 in. wide

44 in.

36 in.

12 in.

Nosings: Use 1 in. to 1½-in. wide nosings or beveled riser.

1 in. to 1½ in.

Elevation

36 in. minimum

Wall

1½ in.

42 in. to 48 in.

Baluster Spacing

Balusters: spaced 4 in. apart.

will be required to transcend a small level change, try a new challenge — design a ramp with the inventiveness, grandeur and aesthetic effect that would have been invested in the staircase.

Level changes can also be overcome by stairway lifts (platform or chair) and elevators. This chapter will describe how you can plan ahead to be able to add these accessories-turned-necessities when it becomes prudent to do so.

Where will you be when you reach the age of 100? Today, a majority of the people over 100 still live at home. More than 30% of people over 85 cannot walk up and down stairs to the second floor of their house without help (Cornoni-Huntley et al., 1990). However, although many of us are doing a great job of keeping a healthy heart, we haven't come up with a way of keeping our knee joints and hip sockets from wearing out. The lifespan house is planned to support changes in the abilities of its occupants. In a multi-story house, this planning calls for ensuring that one accessible floor contains everything the occupants require for bathing, eating, sleeping, toileting, getting in and out and moving about. The alternative to a self-contained floor is to design a home that will accommodate a lift or an elevator.

STAIRS

Stairs are the most common architectural structure for getting from one level to another. They help transport people of all ages, sizes and abilities, as well as quantities of household goods, including furniture, vacuum cleaners and laundry. Good stairs should be safe, easy to use and aesthetically appealing.

Stairs and steps contributed to more than 1,693,175 injuries that led to a hospital emergency visit in 1990 (NEISS, 1991). Leading the list of injuries (and deaths) from stairway accidents were children and older adults. An earlier study (BOSTI, 1982) revealed the following: "Among the accidents that occur at home, the greatest number are those that involve floors and flooring materials (16%) and stairs or steps (25%). These two product categories are also the two most hazardous to elderly people."

The BOSTI report found that women are three times more likely than men to suffer accidents on stairs. Two-thirds (66%) of all stair accidents occur at home, some occur at other residences and 9% occur in public places.

The BOSTI report lists five typical conditions for accidents on stairs. First, the individual may lose balance while using the stairs and fall. Loss of balance can be compensated for if the victim holds onto a handrail. If there is no handrail or if the handrail is ungraspable, the hazard still exists.

The second condition has to do with awareness and perception. An accident occurs because the victim is unaware of the presence of the stairs, because the area is dark, because the eyes have not adjusted to a change in lighting levels or because the surroundings are unfamiliar.

The third condition involves miscalculation. People miss a step on the stairs because their vision was obstructed by packages they were carrying or they thought they had reached the last step when in fact they hadn't. Miscalculations also occur when the height of one riser is different from the height of all the other risers. The victim expects the last step to be the same height as the others and is not prepared for the change.

The fourth condition is slipping on the surface of the stairs. Both smooth-surface stairs and carpeted stairs present this potential hazard, depending on the person's footwear: some stair surfaces are fine for shoes, but extremely hazardous for stocking feet.

The fifth condition occurs when lack of energy and strength prevent an individual from negotiating the steps, and a limb or joint "gives way." Again, if the person has a firm hold on a handrail, the fall may be preventable.

Elements of a stairway Stairways are composed of steps, landings and railings. Steps are made up of a tread, a riser and a nosing (see the drawing on the facing page). Stairs can be straight, L-shaped (one 90° turn), U-shaped (two 90° turns), curved or spiral. Stairways can be open (with no riser, like most cellar stairs) or closed (with a built-in riser, as shown in the drawing). Safe and efficient stairs result from the careful consideration of each of these elements.

A straight flight of stairs presents the fewest difficulties for people and the fewest obstacles for moving large objects. It is also much easier to install a lift system in a straight stairway. L-shaped and U-shaped stairs have landings that allow for a change in direc-

Parts of a Stair

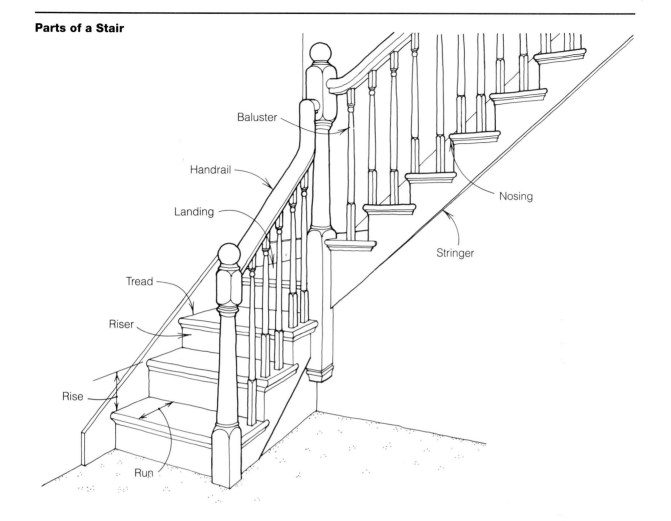

tion. Many people appreciate a landing as a place to catch their breath.

Turns in a stairway should not be accomplished with irregularly shaped steps. All treads and risers should be the same dimension on the entire stair. Curved staircases, even those with gradual curves, dictate that the tread depths will not be the same on both sides of the step. The steps on spiral staircases are particularly irregular, and spiral staircases are impractical for moving objects up and down.

Stairwells that are open underneath or suspended stairs present a hazard for individuals who are visually impaired and others who aren't looking where they are going. You can easily knock your head on the underside of the stairs if you are unaware of their presence above you.

Dimensions Stair dimensions are usually dictated by local codes. But most code restrictions are intended to be minimally acceptable standards. Our minimal recommendations, shown in the drawing on p. 121, are as strict as or stricter than typical code guidelines.

Narrow stairs are cheaper to build and take up less room than wide stairs. Codes generally require a minimal 36-in. width from finished wall to finished wall; 30-in. widths are allowed on little-used, "private" stairs. A width of 42 in. to 48 in. between handrails accommodates the movement of furniture and lets two people negotiate the stairs at the same time. You have enough room to carry a child up and down the stairs without bumping into the wall. A wider stairway (minimum of 42 in.) will also make a stairway lift easier to install (see pp. 128-131) and be less cramped for people walking up and down the stair, should a stairway lift be needed in the future.

A minimum head clearance of 6 ft. 8 in. is required, as shown in the drawing on p. 121. Very tall people might be better served by 7 ft. of headroom.

Risers, treads and nosings   The steepest stairs require the greatest expenditure of energy to climb. Archaeologists have long been trying to determine why the Mayans in Central America abandoned their great cities. Many blame drought, others pestilence. Perhaps they simply wore themselves out going up and down the incredibly steep pyramid stairs, with risers of about 20 in. and tread depths of about 8 in.

Research has shown that walking up steps requires less energy than walking up a ramp (Corlett, 1972), but the subjects of this study were young, able-bodied adults. Corlett studied the effects of slope of steps and heights of risers on oxygen consumption, heart rate and knee joint and ankle angles. He studied two riser heights (4 in. and 6 in.) and six different ramp and stair slopes ranging from 10° to 30°. He concluded that stairs with a 30° slope and 6-in. high risers required the least expenditure of energy. Stairs with 4-in. high risers actually required a greater energy expenditure and were more tiring to climb.

Riser height on interior stairs should be from 6 in. to 7 in. (check your local building code). All risers should be equally spaced, and landings should be located at a height that is an exact multiple of the risers. Nosings should be between 1 in. and 1½ in. wide and should be sloped, angled or rounded. Treads on interior stairs should be 11 in. deep, even though codes often allow a 9-in. minimum.

More than 15% of the population over the age of 65 uses a cane (AARP, 1992). In a recent study of 100 older cane users , we found that many of the subjects refused to climb our two-step staircase designed to ANSI standards. Those who used large quad-base (four-prong) canes had considerable difficulty because all four cane tips did not fit on the step. Despite these drawbacks to the 11-in. tread, we do not advocate a deeper step because it would interfere with the stride of the user.

Treads should have a stable, nonslip surface, preferably one that "grips" stocking feet, such as a vinyl with a high coefficient of friction or a carpet made of natural fibers. (Highly polished wood floors and stairs can be treacherous to the stocking foot.) Treads should be glued to stringers with a long-lasting adhesive. If the stairs are to be carpeted, care should be taken to choose a durable and nonslip variety.

Handrails and balusters   Handrails and balusters are first and foremost important safety features on stairs, both interior and exterior. Too often, however, they are treated more as architectural "statements," with safety taking a back seat. There are some incredibly bad handrails in existence. The companies that make them and the architects that specify them should live in fear. We recently visited a busy convention center where the long stairways were equipped with beautiful brass handrails that were at least 6 in. in diameter — too large for almost anyone to grasp. In this case, our rule for the designers (first fit, then function, then form) was turned on its head.

Handrails should not be more than 1½ in. in diameter, and 1¼ in. is preferred. Handrails need to be designed so that a person can grab onto them to keep from falling down the stairs. Rounded handrails best fit the human hand. In studies of hand strength (Czaja, 1983), users determined they had the greatest control or strength when they could completely encircle the grip and touch the fleshy part of their thumb with their fingertips. Note the geometry of your hand when you touch the tip of your middle finger to the tip of your thumb. Two-by-fours are not advisable because most users cannot curl their fingers all of the way around them (see the photos on the facing page). Additionally, handrails should be able to support the weight of a full-sized adult, so they must be firmly anchored to the wall framing.

A handrail should extend 12 in. beyond the steps at both the top and the bottom, so the user can get a firm hold and be well-balanced for initiating the first or last change in level. A good grip allows people to correct for an error in their calculation of the height of the step. In some homes it will be impractical to extend the handrail 12 in. beyond the last step because the handrail would then extend into a passageway. One alternative would be to have the handrail turn a corner, again to provide the person using the stairs with added stability at the point of transition to and from the first or last step. Free-standing handrail extensions beyond the steps that are not bound by walls should have a continuous extension to the ground and rounded corners (as shown in the drawing on p. 121). There should be no loose ends or sharp edges for someone to run into.

Handrails should have a 1½-in. clearance from the wall. Less than this will be too narrow for people to curl their entire hand around the rail. More than this, and someone's arm might get caught between the rail and the wall.

Handrails should be located on both sides of the stairways and at heights compatible with the users. Heights ranging from 34 in. to 38 in. are appropriate for most adults. Children are best served by a handrail about 24 in. high. The well-equipped stair would include four handrails: one on each side at an adult height and one on each side at a height suitable for children.

Balusters should be spaced no more than 4 in. apart, to prevent a baby's head from getting stuck between balusters. If an open appearance is desired, a clear, shatterproof plastic shield could be mounted the length of the stairway, instead of balusters. The plastic shield would provide light and visibility, yet keep kids from falling through.

Landings and demarcations   Stairways need to be well defined. The presence of a level change should not be a surprise behind a doorway. As shown in the drawing on p. 126, basement stairs should have a landing at the top of the stairs that allows the user to grasp the handrail, adjust to the different light level and prepare for the descent. Stairs that begin at the door threshold, which are common in many homes with basements, are dangerous. If at all possible, try to mark the beginning of the stairs (the landing) with a change in the floor surface or color.

Handrails should be graspable and at a height to offer support to a person going up or down. The original handrail on this ramp (top) was a 2x6 laid flat and installed too high to be or much good. Later, a graspable 1½-in. round handrail was added on at a more appropriate height (above).

Safe and Unsafe Landings

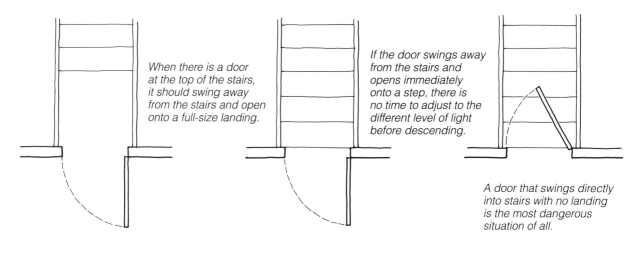

When there is a door at the top of the stairs, it should swing away from the stairs and open onto a full-size landing.

If the door swings away from the stairs and opens immediately onto a step, there is no time to adjust to the different level of light before descending.

A door that swings directly into stairs with no landing is the most dangerous situation of all.

The glare from windows placed at the top of stairs makes it difficult for a person's eyes to adjust to the dimmer light near the stair treads.

Stairway lighting From top to bottom, steps should have even lighting that does not create any shadows. Because shadows may look like steps, they create the potential for a misstep. Lights that illuminate the stairs just below the riser are the best, but these are rare in homes. Lighting along the stairway (like theatrical lighting) that illuminates the treads will provide the greatest help.

Light switches should be located at the top and bottom of the steps and should be at least 36 in. from the beginning of the steps (see p. 83). Stairways located behind doors such as those leading to basement stairs or second-floor sleeping areas would be best served by automatic lighting (lights that are activated either by the opening of the door or by movement sensors). An automatic setup of this sort will keep an individual unfamiliar with the terrain from taking an unexpected trip.

Although we continually advocate for natural light in the home, the placement of windows near stairs needs to be done with considerable care. Locating windows directly at the top or bottom of the stairs may mean that the user will be looking into an area of bright light and the steps will be obscured because they are in less light. The eye will not be able to adjust quickly enough from the bright light of the window to the dim light near the steps.

If windows are going to be placed along the stairway, locate them at stair height to illuminate the steps. Any windows placed along stairways should be set back away from the steps. When objects are being transported up and down the stairs, the windows are vulnerable, especially at turns.

INTERIOR RAMPS

The home owner interested in a sunken living room today, or the builder who overcomes a grade change in the lot by incorporating a change in floor levels in the house and adding a step or two to bridge the difference, should plan ahead for the day when a ramp may be required to allow all of the family members to enjoy the sunken living room or get from one area of the house to another.

A ramp to overcome a level change of a step or two may be feasible. We recommend that the ramp be built adjacent to a wall, which can provide a natural barrier on one side, with a railing and balusters on the open side. Alternatives to the railing include using a bookshelf, planter or half-wall along the length of what would be the open side of the ramp to protect the user from driving over the edge and to incorporate the ramp into the decor of the home, as shown in the drawing below.

Ramps, though useful for overcoming a level change of a step or two, can't solve all level-change problems. An interior ramp is not usually a feasible solution for a split-level home because a ramp with a usable slope (1:20 is preferred) would have to be longer than the rooms connecting it. (For the dimensions and requirements for ramps, see pp. 56-57.) For a house with many level changes, such as a split-level house, multiple stairway lifts or elevators may be required to get to all levels.

An Interior Ramp

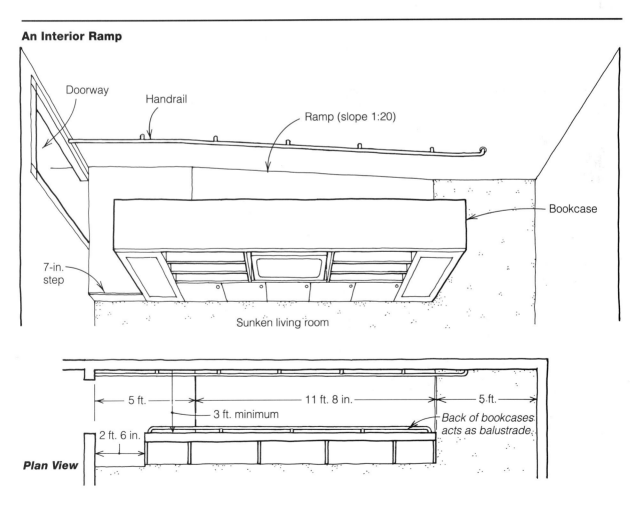

Doorway
Handrail
Ramp (slope 1:20)
Bookcase
7-in. step
Sunken living room

5 ft.
11 ft. 8 in.
5 ft.
3 ft. minimum
2 ft. 6 in.
Back of bookcases acts as balustrade.

Plan View

LIFTS

The odds are fairly high that someone in a multi-story home will be unable to climb the stairs during his or her tenure in the home. The choices are to abandon the portion of the house at the other end of the stairs or to install a conveyance system that will overcome the problems caused by weak hearts, arthritic knees and ankles or paralysis.

There are various lifts available for different purposes. Here we will discuss interior lifts that transport people from one floor to another in their homes.

Stairway lifts Stairway lifts (also known as stair lifts, seat lifts and chair lifts) feature a seat that moves up and down a stairway on a track. Stairway lifts are most often added to a house when an occupant is no longer able to climb or descend the stairs. Wheelchair users must transfer onto and off of the lift and have a wheelchair stationed at both the top and bottom of the stairs. (A platform lift, discussed on pp. 130-131, may be a better choice for wheelchair users.)

Stairway lifts need to be evaluated according to the type of stairway in which they will be installed, the budget and the abilities of the individuals who will be using them. Lifts are available that can traverse curves, corners and bends created by landings. Straight stairway lifts, however, are less expensive, easier to install and more widely available than those that curve. All of the companies listed in Resources (p. 133) make straight stairway lifts.

To allow for a possible future stairway lift, widen the stairs. A 36-in. wide staircase will be too narrow. A 48-in. wide staircase will be less obstructed by the lift and would allow someone to walk comfortably on the stairs while the lift was in use. A stairway lift is easiest to install on a straight-run stair. There will also be more options for future equipment if there is a landing no smaller than 30 in. by 36 in. at both the top and bottom of the stairs.

Be prepared to purchase a stairway lift sight unseen. We recently looked for a stairway lift in Memphis, Tennessee, a city with a population of over 1,000,000, and neither of the two dealers had a model that we could look at. Most manufacturers have videos, but few have locations where the lift systems could be "test driven."

The major components of a stairway-lift system are the seat assembly, the track and the motor. Most systems have a swivel seat that must be locked into position before the lift will move. A few have fixed seats that require the user to swivel into the seat. Other models offer seats, armrests and footrests that swivel as a unit. Generally, the more expensive models offer a wider choice of colors and padded seats. Many of the manufacturers have several models but only one or two motor and mechanical assemblies. Thus, the less expensive models are built more or less the same as the more expensive models; they just aren't as pretty and don't have as many options (swivel seats, choice of colors, remote hand-held controls).

Choose a seat whose dimensions fit the individual using the system. Seat widths range from 17 in. to 23 in. The depth of the seat is usually about 14 in. The height of the seat may be one of the most important dimensions for determining the ease of use of the system. Many are 24 in. to 25 in. high, while a standard wheelchair with a cushion is about 20 in. high. These seats require wheelchair users to manage a 4-in. or 5-in. lift in addition to the lateral transfer. Shorter people may also have some difficulty with the seat heights. Lower seat heights of 18 in. to 20 in. will be easier for the primary users (older women) to get on and off. Because there are twice as many women as men in the oldest age groups (U.S. Bureau of the Census, 1990), it's much more likely that the person using the lift will be of short stature (average height of 5 ft. 3 in.), and even an 18-in. high seat will be a stretch for getting on and off easily.

All of the seat assemblies are equipped with a seat belt. It is likely, however, that many users won't bother to use this safety feature. Assemblies with retractable seat belts may encourage more frequent use and will be less likely to become tangled.

Seats are available facing one of two directions (downward or sideways). Most fold up so that they occupy a space of from 9 in. to 12 in. from the wall. A few automatically fold and unfold when the user presses a button.

On stairway lifts virtually all the controls are the constant-pressure type, requiring the rider to press the button continuously in order for the lift to continue to move, but their location varies. They may be mounted at the end of a cable, on the arms or

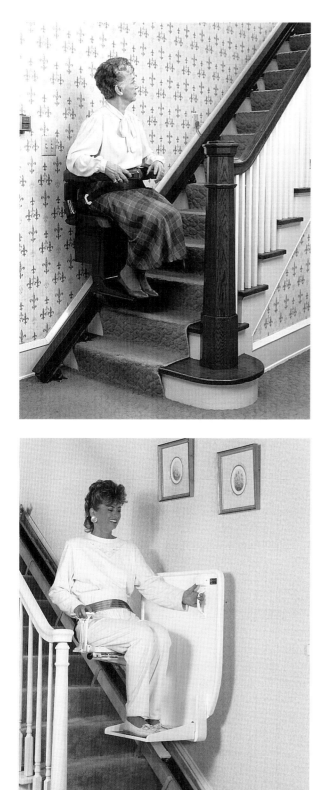

Stairway lifts come in various sizes and designs. The Cheney Liberty II (above left) is designed for straight stairs and has the controls located in one arm. The passenger rides sideways, but the seat swivels at the top landing to make getting on and off easier. The Cheney Liberty LX (above) is designed for a straight or curved two-flight stair with a landing or a spiral staircase. The controls are located in the arms, which swivel up and out of the way to assist in sitting and standing. This model folds up to within 12½ in. from the wall. (Photos: courtesy Access Industries.)

The Inclinette (left) is for straight stairways and comes in a variety of colors or wood-grain finishes and folds to within 9½ in. of the wall when not in use. The rider rides facing down the stairs, but the seat swivels 360° at the top landing. The track extends 7½ in. from the baseboard. (Photo: courtesy Inclinator Company of America.)

on the side wall of the seat assembly. Most of the systems have call buttons that are placed on the wall at the top and bottom of the stairs. Most of the systems can reverse direction.

Some armrests are fixed in place and the rider slips in between them, while others rotate or swivel independently of the seat. Movable armrests make it easier to get into and out of the chair. The American Stair Glide Liberty LT has arms that rotate out of the way and lock into the raised position. This lock-in feature provides the user stable support when transferring into or out of the lift.

Footrests or footplates vary in their dimension and shape, but all of the seat assemblies have them. Most footrests are located under the seat. People who have difficulty controlling their legs or bending them directly beneath the seat will want larger footrests.

Most of the stairway-lift systems have an obstacle detection system, usually mounted under the footplate. The lift will stop automatically if it encounters something beneath the footplate.

A platform lift, such as this Liftette, lets a wheelchair user change levels without leaving the chair. (Photo: courtesy Inclinator Company of America.)

Track units vary from system to system in the amount of space they require and in the way they are mounted. Some are mounted to the stairs while others require both stair and wall mounting. Some tracks have a single rail (monorail) that rests close to the wall, while others have up to three steel rails that occupy about 12 in. of step space. Some systems have tracks that can go around curves.

All the stairway-lift systems run on standard house current, although some of the systems transform the current to low voltage. The motors vary in horsepower. Motors can be located in a remote location, such as a nearby closet or at the top or bottom of the stairs. The Inclinator Model SC has a motor mounted within the seat assembly.

Stairway lifts are categorized by the distance and speed they travel and the maximum weight they carry. Most travel at a speed ranging from 20 ft. to 25 ft. per minute and can transport a person weighing up to 300 lb. using a ⅓-hp to ½-hp motor. A few have a maximum weight limit of 250 lb.

The greatest differences among the systems is in whether they can accommodate curves and landings (have a bend in the track), the type of driving mechanism, the location of controls and appearance. There is considerable variation among systems in the driving mechanism, which may be a steel cable, roller chain, rack and pinion, I-beam, ball-bearing worm-gear or screw-drive mechanism. If a system seems to meet the user's needs, the prospective owner may want to question the dealer (or if possible observe the system) to assess the smoothness of the ride, noise and sense of stability (wobble) as the chair moves up and down and the rider shifts weight or leans from side to side.

Platform lifts Interior platform lifts transport people sitting in a wheelchair from one floor to the next. (Exterior platform lifts are discussed on p. 57.)

There are two types of platform lifts: vertical and inclined. A vertical lift is much like an elevator in that it travels in a vertical line. Vertical lifts often have a small cab in which the passenger rides. Unlike an elevator, however, the vertical lift is not built into a shaft. An inclined platform lift, in contrast, travels along a stairway.

Unlike stairway lifts, the platform lift does not require the wheelchair user to transfer to and from the wheelchair. Some platform lifts have a track or rail on each side of the stair that encases rollers and a roller chain to hoist the lift. The lifts are left in position at the top or bottom of the stairs. Ambulatory people would walk on them when using the stairs. (A platform lift at the top of the stairs can be a serious hazard, as the platform rests about 2 in. off the floor.) Although this system has the advantage of keeping the occupant with his or her wheelchair, the rails reduce the available foot space on the steps and may cause people to trip and fall.

The platform lift has a small guard that automatically raises to help prevent the wheelchair from rolling off of the platform. Most platform lifts have a constant-pressure switch and operate on standard household current. Speed varies among systems, but generally they travel about 20 ft. per minute.

This system, while an important retrofit product for an existing home, is not one that you would plan as an alternative system if building a home because of the amount of space that it occupies and because of its looks. An elevator (vertical lift) would accomplish the task more efficiently with fewer hazards for others.

ELEVATORS

Some people think planning for the possibility of an elevator is macabre or defeatist, but we think it's an investment in yourselves and your future. The cost of building a home that is ready to receive an elevator or a lift is negligible compared to the cost of installing an elevator in a home that is not. You may never complete the conversion, but that's fine because you will have been using the space anyway. If, for example, you build two closets one above the other that are the right size (about 4 ft. 6 in. by 4 ft. 6 in.) for an elevator shaft to be installed at a later date, people in the house may have the use of the closet space for years before the area is needed for the elevator.

Should you sell your house, you have an additional advantage. Your multi-level home can attract the entire marketplace, not just able-bodied people. Retirees concerned about moving to a home with stairs or people who have always lived in single-story homes may find your elevator-ready home a delightful alternative.

A residential elevator can make a multi-story house accessible to everyone. The decor can be built to match any house design. (Photo: courtesy Cheney.)

A residential elevator should convey a residential appearance; it does not need to look or feel institutional. Planning for this elevator when you design the home will help ensure that it can meet aesthetic and other criteria.

Think of the elevator system as a pathway in the home. It should be reached easily from the primary entrance used by the residents, and it should begin and end in public space. Don't plan the future elevator to rise from the first-floor foyer to the master bedroom. It may not be the people occupying the master bedroom who are the primary users of the elevator. Design the house as if the elevator is part of the circulation plan, not an afterthought.

A residential elevator has a fully enclosed cab like a commercial elevator. It has an outer door at

Planning for a Future Elevator

On the first floor of this two-story house, space has been created that can be transformed into an elevator in the future with minimal disruption of the other spaces and functions in the house. An ideal first-floor location for an elevator is in a public area with clear access to the house entrances. An ideal second-floor location is near a wide landing at the top of the stairs, with clear access to the entire floor.

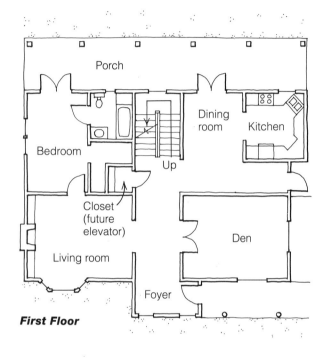

First Floor

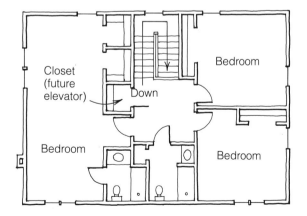

Second Floor

each stop that matches the house decor and an interior folding or accordion door that moves up and down with the car.

Exact dimensions for residential elevators vary widely with manufacturers, but most have a footprint of roughly 4 ft. 6 in. square. This accommodates a platform of 12 sq. ft., plus doors and gates, enclosure and lifting machinery.

The "pit," which allows the elevator platform to stop flush with the lowest floor, usually has a depth of from 6 in. to 12 in. Space is also needed nearby for the equipment. For some elevators, this may be a winch system in the attic or a channel built into the wall for a hydraulic system.

To plan ahead for a residential elevator, find an appropriate area on each floor that is roughly 4 ft. 6 in. square. The best location on each floor will be halls in public areas, such as a foyer (the drawing at left shows one possible design). On the ground floor the elevator should be near the most used entrance. Until it is needed, the designated space for the future elevator can be an open area, a storage room or a pair of stacked closets that can be altered later. Work with a local vendor to identify the product that best fits the location and configuration in your layout, and then adjust the layout and detailing accordingly.

The elevator supplier should be able to provide drawings and specifications showing where support will be needed, blocking locations, framing openings and door locations. Use these as guides for making the home ready for the elevator.

Head off and frame the floors as if framing for the elevator, including needed basement supports, then add framing to close over the rough opening and finish off the space as if the opening weren't there. If closets are incorporated into the design for now, their doors can be framed where the lift shop drawings specify.

Choosing an elevator You will need to make several determinations when deciding which elevator is best for your home. Since the elevator is a tool for independence, be sure to look at each of the operation features to be sure that the elevator you select best fits the abilities of the user.

Critical components of elevators include the door or doors, the call and operating controls and the cab. The elevator system has two doors. One is a standard swing door that matches the other doors and decor in the home. The second is the hatchway door. Most of these are folding or accordion-like. This style of door can cause problems in its ease of use. Try the door in the showroom and learn the best way to keep the door moving freely in the track. Be sure that the door can be opened wide enough (32 in.) to get in and out. Some systems have an automatic door. Be sure the door provides plenty of time for exiting and entering and that it is equipped with an electric eye to stop the door if the opening is not clear. Virtually all of the elevator systems have a door interlock, which prevents movement of the cab unless the hatchway doors are closed and locked.

Some elevators are available in several door opening configurations. You may enter on one floor from one direction and exit on another floor in the opposite or perpendicular direction.

Most residential elevator cabs have approximately 12 sq. ft. of interior space. The exact square footage could be a critical consideration if the user has an oversize wheelchair and is to be accompanied by an attendant.

Most elevators have a single-push, automatic push-button call and control system. A single push on the button will actuate the control. Others have keyed controls that require the user to turn the key at the call station or within the cab before pushing the button. Many people will have trouble turning the key. Some elevators have constant-pressure push buttons that must be actuated for the car to operate. For some, this sustained activity will be too difficult.

Be sure that the controls are located within the optimal reach zone and in a position comfortable for the person who will be using them most frequently. Sometimes location at the front of the cab will require the user to reach forward to operate them.

All elevator cabs have a light, generally an incandescent fixture located in the ceiling. Most systems can be equipped with a telephone, which can be a great comfort to someone living alone.

Many elevators are available with a variety of choices of paneling. They come in various colors or wood grains. Cab floors may be carpeted, wood or finished in other surfaces. Most of the companies provide options.

RESOURCES

American Stair-Glide Corp.
Access Industries
4001 East 138th Street
Grandview, MO 64030
(816) 763-1300
Stairway lifts, vertical and inclined platform lifts and residential elevators.

CemcoLift
P.O. Box 368
5191 Stump Road
Plumsteadville, PA 18949
(800) 962-3626
(215) 766-0900
Residential elevators.

Cheney
2445 South Calhoun Road
P.O. Box 51188
New Berlin, WI 53153-0188
(800) 568-1222
(414) 782-1100
Stairway lifts, vertical and inclined platform lifts and residential elevators.

Concord Elevator
10 Whitmore Road
Woodbridge, Ontario
Canada L4L 7Z4
(800) 661-5112
(416) 856-3030
Vertical and inclined platform lifts and residential elevators.

Econol Stairway Lift
Box 854
Cedar Falls, IA 50613
(319) 277-4777
Stairway lifts, vertical and inclined platform lifts and residential elevators..

Flinchbaugh
390 Eberts Lane
York, PA 17403-0330
(717) 848-2418
Stairway lifts, inclined platform lifts.

FlorLIFT of New Jersey
41 Lawrence Street
East Orange, NJ 07017
(201) 429-2200
Electric hydraulic lifts.

Garaventa (Canada) Ltd.
7505-134A Street
Surrey, British Columbia
Canada V3W 7B3
(800) 663-6556
(604) 594-0422
Inclined platform lifts.

Inclinator Company of America
2200 Paxton Street
P.O. Box 1557
Harrisburg, PA 17105-1557
(717) 234-8065
Stairway lifts, vertical and inclined platform lifts and residential elevators.

National Wheel-O-Vator
P.O. Box 348
Roanoke, IL 61561-0348
(800) 551-9095
Vertical platform lifts, stairway lifts.

Robertson Custom Aids
777 Warden Avenue, Unit 12
Scarborough, Ontario
Canada M1l 4C3
(416) 751-3352
Platform lifts.

Shugarman Surgical Supply
3134 Dorr Street
Toledo, OH 43607
(800) 321-8879
(419) 536-3767
Catalog company offering stairway lifts and porch lifts.

Waupaca Elevator Company
P.O. Box 246
Waupaca, WI 54981
(715) 258-5581
Residential elevators.

CHAPTER NINE
KITCHENS

At one time or another, virtually all kitchens are used by people of all ages and sizes, with a variety of physical abilities. Yet kitchen design has long been locked into kitchens plans that are suitable for the "average" person. This "one size fits all" approach works only for a certain proportion of the population, for a certain portion of their lives. Because people are living longer, often in multi-generational households, and because millions of people with physical and sensory disabilities aren't accounted for in the "average person" statistical mix, traditional kitchen designs based on the well-known concept of the work triangle need to undergo some changes. Kitchens should be designed to accommodate a broader

Planning the Kitchen

Traditional kitchen design, based on the work triangle, does not take into account differences in size and abilities among people. Key elements of the accessible kitchen are work surfaces at various heights with leg room underneath and strategically located set-down spaces.

Traditional Work Triangle

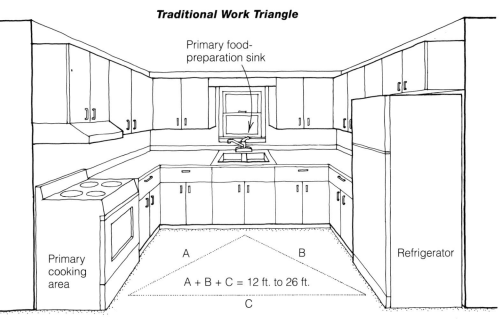

Primary food-preparation sink

Primary cooking area

A

B

A + B + C = 12 ft. to 26 ft.

C

Refrigerator

In traditional kitchen design, the stove, sink and refrigerator form a triangle whose perimeter should be less than 26 ft.

No leg of the triangle should be shorter than 4 ft. or longer than 9 ft.

Work-Surface Recommendations for an Accessible Kitchen

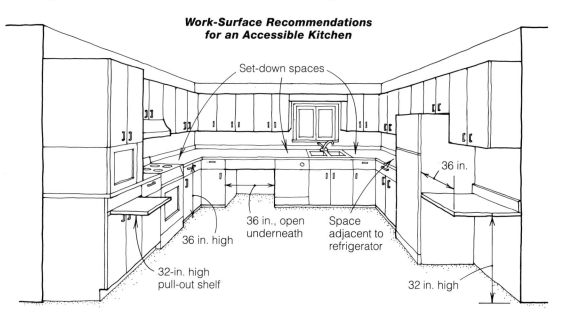

Set-down spaces

36 in.

36 in. high

36 in., open underneath

Space adjacent to refrigerator

32-in. high pull-out shelf

32 in. high

An accessible kitchen provides counters and work surfaces at various heights. Ideally, work surfaces should be located on both sides of the sink, cooktop, oven and refrigerator.

Where countertop space is not available, pull-out shelving can substitute. Counters and work surfaces should be open underneath (minimum height of 30 in.).

range of human sizes and abilities. Once they are, they will serve a greater number of people over a longer period of time.

The kitchen has evolved from a simple meal-preparation site to the center of family activities in many households. In a study of 602 female and 300 male heads of households interviewed by Market Response (Yuen, 1991), the respondents were asked about what goes on in their kitchen. They cited conversation (78%), getting together during meal preparation and cleanup (76%), eating meals (70%), entertaining guests (62%), spending quiet time (36%) and doing homework (29%). Twenty-nine percent said that household members spend more time together in the kitchen than in any other room in the house.

Families are using the kitchen and kitchen work time for togetherness, which the Market Response group calls "hearthing." But hearthing isn't really hearthing unless everyone in the household can participate fully. A kitchen that is designed for different uses and different users will accommodate various lifestyle and generations. This chapter provides guidelines for creating such a dynamic kitchen, the lifespan kitchen.

Kitchens require people to perform deep-knee bends, kneel on the floor and climb on stools and chairs to reach into cabinets. They contain cooktops, vent-hood controls, electrical outlets and large amounts of storage space that are beyond the reach of many people. Many of the appliances are difficult to clean and have physical and sensory demands beyond the capacities of many who could benefit from their conveniences.

In the early 1950s, kitchen researchers at Cornell University and elsewhere worked out the main features of "user-friendly" kitchens based on ergonomic principles (although the term "ergonomic" did not yet exist). About the same time (1954), Lillian Gilbreth, Orpha Mae Thomas and Eleanor Clymer wrote *Management in the Home: Happier Living through Saving Time and Energy,* which applied scientific management principles to work in the home. In this book they coined the term "motionmindedness."

In 1973, Etienne Grandjean published *Ergonomics of the Home,* which provided a wealth of information on planning the home for efficiency and convenience, with recommendations based on the dimensions of the average-sized woman. Although this book is an outstanding reference on designing kitchens to fit the abilities of a standardized primary user, it follows the conventional practice of describing adaptations for people with disabilities and older adults in a separate chapter at the end of the book.

Designing the kitchen for tomorrow requires that we abandon today the concept of the "average" person and dimensional standards built around preconceived "primary" users. Kitchens serve a variety of functions, but above all kitchens are work centers. Designed for safe and efficient work, they can make life easier for the whole household. Lifespan kitchen design includes the following:

• work centers and spaces that support multiple uses
• sensible location of the kitchen within the house
• efficient pathways for the movement of people, goods and foodstuffs in, out, around and through the space
• allowance for use by more than one cook at a time
• accommodation for the sizes, abilities and handedness of all users
• work surfaces at appropriate heights and of appropriate materials
• storage for perishable and nonperishable foods, cookware and numerous other items.

WORK CENTERS

The primary kitchen work centers are the sink (clean-up area), the refrigerator, the work surfaces (preparation area) and the stove or cooktop (cooking area). Other significant items include a microwave or alternative cooking device, the pantry or other storage areas, a secondary sink, and convenience or gourmet small appliances such as the toaster, food processor, bread maker, automatic coffee maker, coffee grinder, espresso coffee machine, blender and indoor grill.

Traditionally, kitchen layouts have been based on the concept of the "work triangle," shown in the top drawing on p. 135. The National Kitchen and Bath Association defines the work triangle as the shortest walking distance between the refrigerator, the primary cooking surface and the primary sink. The NKBA recommends that the triangle's perimeter be less than 26 ft., with no single leg of the triangle shorter than 4 ft. or longer than 9 ft. (The distances are measured from the center front of each appliance.) Additionally, no two primary work centers should be separated by a full-height, full-depth tower, such as an oven cabinet or pantry.

Technology and the diversity of electronic appliances are changing the fundamental relationship of the traditional work triangle. Prepared foods, microwave ovens, gourmet cooking appliances and dishwashers have eliminated kitchen steps and added pathways. Food now may go from the storage area or refrigerator to the microwave to the table. The reliance on prepared foods is likely to increase as women continue to enter and remain in the work force. Also, a lot of adults (approximately 25% in the United States) live, and dine, alone (U.S. Bureau of the Census, 1990).

The work triangle is still a useful tool for locating the primary work centers, but the kitchen planner needs to take its underlying principles and extend them to the entire kitchen. An efficient kitchen is compact, but not cramped. If appliances are too far apart, too many steps are required to get from one to another, and efficiency suffers.

Some additional work areas in the kitchen include the recycling center, a communications and/or entertainment center and, yes, a pet center. In some states and municipalities recycling is now mandatory. While yesterday's kitchen made do with one garbage can, today's well-designed kitchen must allow for storage of the refuse for longer periods in a variety of containers. Bins for glass, plastic, recyclable paper, aluminum, compost and real trash should be located in the kitchen or immediately adjacent to it. The kitchen should have a bare minimum of two waste receptacles, one for garbage and one for recyclables.

A communications area, which may include a telephone, a writing desk or a computer, and an entertainment center, which may include a television or a radio, are best located some distance away from the cooking areas, garbage disposal, dishwasher and sink to avoid interference with noise and to avoid splashing and spills. Most kitchens include telephones, many have televisions and more are being outfitted with a personal computer.

Pet centers should be located out of the primary lines of traffic, yet near a source of water for ease of filling the water dish and setting it down. Pet centers are for feeding the pets and storing the pet food. Because people with several pets or large pets often purchase food in 25-lb. or 50-lb. sacks, the storage area may need to be fairly substantial.

PATHWAYS AND ADJACENCIES

The kitchen should be near an exterior entrance that is close to where the car is parked, so groceries can easily be brought inside and trash can easily be taken out. As shown in the drawing on p. 138, the kitchen should also be adjacent to the areas or rooms of the house where food will be consumed (dining room and family room).

Individuals with reduced physical strength and people who use wheelchairs are hampered by having to turn corners while lugging grocery bags or containers. Each corner or turn requires extra effort. In our studies (see pp. 3-7), we found that people who use a cane, crutch or walker need to make almost three times as many trips as able-bodied people and people in wheelchairs to move the same objects from one point to another. In one study we asked participants to move two place settings from the kitchen counter to the dining-room table. Those without physical limitations and those who used wheelchairs were able to complete the task in one trip. The wheelchair users had the advantage of being able to pile everything into their laps. Those who used other ambulation aids, however, required an average of three trips, and a few required four or five.

The important pathways in a kitchen are the pathway for bringing groceries in and taking trash out, the pathway from the food-preparation areas to the dining area and the pathways used by those who are merely passing through the kitchen.

The pathway for bringing groceries into the house should be as short and straight as possible. Steps and uneven thresholds should be avoided because they are barriers to people who use a wheelchair or other assistive device. They may also trip an ambulatory person whose vision is obstructed by full grocery bags or low-light conditions.

The requirements for bringing groceries into the house also apply for taking trash out. It is best to have a straight pathway only a short distance from the trash bin. The trash should not have to be carried through the living area or dining room.

All entrances to the kitchen should have a minimal clear width of 32 in. If a door is not required, it shouldn't be specified and installed. Work aisles (pathways with a work center on at least one side) should be at least 42 in. wide and as short as possible without violating work-triangle rules. That way a person using an assistive device will be able to move about the kitchen, and a person who tires easily and who may need to hold onto surfaces for support will not have too far to go to get from one work center to another. Secondary passageways should be 36 in. wide in one-cook kitchens. In two-cook kitchens, work aisles should be from 48 in. to 60 in. wide. We recommend that kitchens be built to accommodate more than one cook (see the discussion on the facing page). These guide-lines exceed ANSI 117.1 standards, which specify 40-in. work aisles and don't address two-cook kitchens.

To allow everyone ample space to work and maneuver, there should be 30 in. by 48 in. of clear space in front of appliances and work centers. Since a wheelchair needs about a 5-ft. diameter circle to turn around, the center of the kitchen needs to have either a 60-in. diameter open area or wide pathways that will allow a wheelchair user to maneuver or turn. Pathways of 48 in. provide ample room for everyone.

The kitchen should also be designed so that noncooks can use and pass through the kitchen without interfering with cooking chores. Kitchens serve a multitude of functions that are unrelated to cooking. They are often centers of family socializing and entertainment. Pathways through the kitchen should not interfere with work centers, that is, traffic should not be directed through the work triangle.

Pathways and Adjacencies

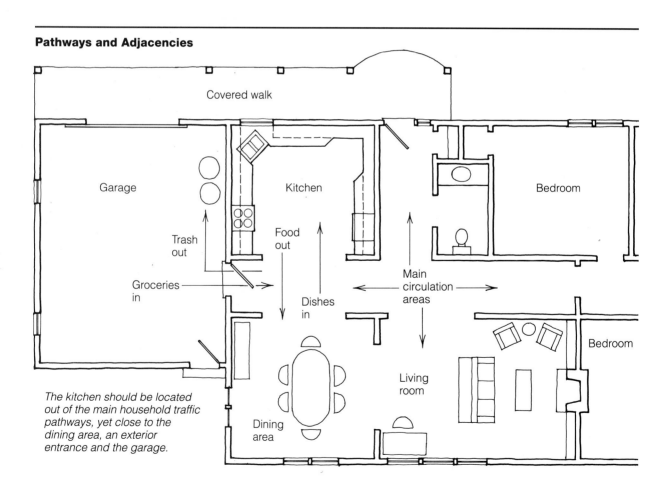

The kitchen should be located out of the main household traffic pathways, yet close to the dining area, an exterior entrance and the garage.

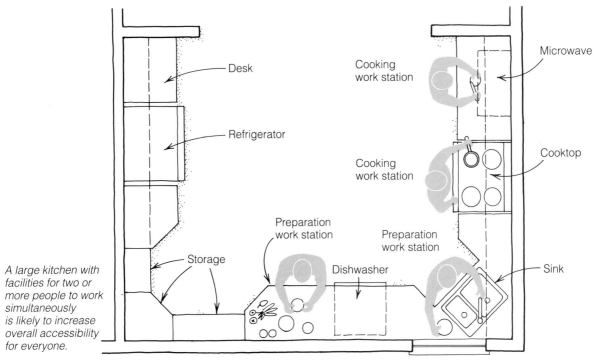

A large kitchen with facilities for two or more people to work simultaneously is likely to increase overall accessibility for everyone.

THE TWO-COOK KITCHEN

The lifespan kitchen should be built to accommodate at least two cooks. The one-cook kitchen is restrictive and is likely to inhibit the sharing of chores. As families change, roles and responsibilities change. Further, the careful spacing and planning that goes into a two-cook kitchen is likely to increase the overall accessibility of the kitchen. As shown in the drawing above, spaces and passageways built for two happen to offer fewer barriers to everyone.

A good two-cook kitchen has the following:

• wide (60-in.) aisles that allow two people to pass with ease

• at least two preparation areas a minimum of 36 in. wide and separated so there is plenty of elbow room for each cook

• storage areas located so that a cook at the preparation area doesn't block access to frequently needed items

• multiple sources of direct lighting focused onto work centers so one cook won't create shadows on the other cook's work surface.

Two-cook kitchens are generally large. The available work space in the kitchen is a function of its overall size, what you put in it and where you put it, and the entries and aisles through it. It is usually easier to achieve accessibility in a larger kitchen because more space is available for wide aisles and to provide clear space in front of each appliance. The Maytag Company recently published a kitchen design survey of 100 certified kitchen designers, which was completed in 1991. These designers stated that the sizes of the kitchens they have designed in the last five years have increased and that, although they agreed there is not an average size, the most frequently cited size was 12 ft. by 15 ft. (180 sq. ft). There is no excuse for kitchens of this size not to offer universal accessibility.

HANDEDNESS

Handedness refers to the hand or side whose use is dictated by the placement of furnishings, objects or appliances. An appliance is right-handed if it requires users to use their right hand or to approach it from their right side. Most kitchens are designed for right-handed users or without attention to handedness. For a sizable proportion of the population a right-handed approach is fine, but for a significant minority it isn't. The best handedness is neutral. That is, objects should be designed and located so that they can be approached from the right, left or front.

The issue of handedness is particularly important in the kitchen because of the abundance of built-in features. We have seen people perform unbelievable contortions just because the handedness of a kitchen was opposite to their "strong" side.

Dishwashers and ovens normally have pull-down doors. It is therefore essential that these appliances be approachable from either side. Part A of the drawing below shows a left-handed approach to the oven. When open, the door of the oven blocks the approach from the front; the person using the oven must work from the side.

In our research studies, we watched one woman who uses a wheelchair attempt to use the oven in this particular layout. She had to situate her wheelchair in the hallway in order to access the oven using her right hand, because her left hand wasn't strong enough to open the oven door or put a pan in the oven. There is no space to the left of the stove, so she had to balance the pan on her lap as she carefully maneuvered her chair into the hallway to open the oven door.

Ovens and microwaves should always have a neutral handedness. People should be able to approach and handle hot pots from their strong or dominant side. Moving the oven to a more central location (just to the right of the sink) makes it approachable from either side, as shown in Part B of the drawing below.

In the lifespan house, everything should be designed so that it is easy to use by those who are naturally right- or left-handed or by those who have lost the use of their "natural handedness." If possible locate the oven, cooktop and dishwasher in places that are approachable from the right, left and front.

Handedness

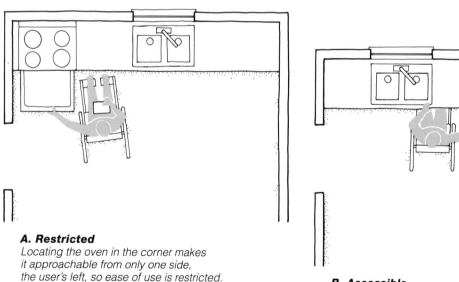

A. Restricted
Locating the oven in the corner makes it approachable from only one side, the user's left, so ease of use is restricted.

B. Accessible
If the oven is located between a sink and a counter area that can be adapted for wheelchair use, the oven can be readily used and approached from either side.

WORK SURFACES

The term "work surfaces" generally refers to countertops, although it can also include pull-out counters and work tops (such as cutting boards) that can be placed on top of the sink. Work surfaces in the kitchen are used primarily for preparing and eating meals and for temporarily storing goods. The important decisions that need to be made regarding work surfaces include how many square feet of countertop to provide, at what heights and locations, and of what construction and materials.

The National Kitchen and Bath Association specifies requirements for usable countertops (defined as a countertop that is at least 16 in. deep and not in a corner). Kitchens of 150 sq. ft. or less should have 132 in. (11 ft.) of usable countertop; kitchens of more than 150 sq. ft. should have 198 in. (16½ ft.) of usable countertop. We recommend that kitchens have at least 12 sq. ft. of countertop. People rarely complain that they have too much countertop space, but they often grumble about having too little.

The depth and height of the countertops are important considerations, too. At a minimum the kitchen should have 30 in. (36 in. is preferred) of countertop space that is at a fixed height no greater than 34 in. (32 in. is preferred) and open underneath with a minimum depth of 19 in. and a maximum depth of 24 in. The floor space under the open counter should be finished. Recommended heights for kitchen work surfaces are shown in the bottom drawing on p. 135.

The sink and appliances should be bounded on both sides (if possible) with countertops. Counter space should be provided on both sides of the cooktop/oven, on both sides of the sink and adjacent to the refrigerator. These surfaces are required for setting down an object that may be too hot or too heavy to handle. If compromises must be made, countertops may be omitted adjacent to the refrigerator, but they should always be next to the sink, stove and/or oven.

The NKBA guidelines call for at least 36 in. of continuous countertop for each cook. We recommend at least 36 in. of preparation-center countertop, at a height of 32 in. and open underneath, and an additional 36 in. at a height of 36 in., regardless of the number of cooks.

Most of the NKBA rules for countertop space are appropriate for the lifespan house, with the exception of the closed-end kitchen (such as a U-shaped kitchen, which is closed on one end). The NKBA rules suggest that the cooktop or range may be placed within 3 in. of a wall that is covered with a flame-retardant material. However, it is unwise to place a cooktop or range in a corner, because that placement limits the handedness and approach to the appliance (see pp. 139-140). If at all possible, allow at least 18 in. on each side of an appliance.

Set-down spaces should be built within easy reach on both sides of the oven and/or microwave oven, or next to or above the oven if the appliance door opens into a primary traffic pattern. Although the NKBA guidelines suggest the space may be placed "above," be sure the height of this set-down area is within easy reach (within the optimal reach zone). Lifting a hot dish to a shelf above a microwave oven may be dangerous or impossible for many people.

The work surface areas in the primary cooking area (cooktop or oven/range) should provide a continuous surface to enable an individual with little muscle strength or who uses an assistive device to drag or push a heavy container on the countertop. U-shaped and L-shaped kitchens are best for this purpose. If alternative working heights are provided they should be located at the ends of the primary food-preparation areas and/or at the sink.

Countertops should have rounded (radiused) edges, and the countertop surrounding the sink should have a lip to catch liquid. Nonstaining, heat-safe surfaces, such as Corian and similar solid surface materials and stainless steel, are the best for countertops. They also allow the sink to be integral with the countertop, which we consider desirable. Some types of plastic laminate are heat safe and can be used next to the cooktop and oven. Countertops with a light-colored, dull or matte finish provide a good contrasting background that does not reflect excessive light and cause glare.

Pull-out work surfaces provide the opportunity to accommodate more work stations in the same amount of floor space and to meet the needs of workers of various heights, seated or standing. A pull-out work surface located 2 in. below a countertop will be at a height of approximately 32 in. This height is convenient for seated or standing work, particularly if

the person is using a large mixing bowl or kneading bread dough.

Pull-out surfaces located under a side-opening wall-mounted oven or microwave are a must. And, they are convenient and excellent alternatives to base cabinets, which are often eliminated when trying to provide greater seated access in the kitchen.

One of the better solutions to "fitting" the needs of individuals of various heights and abilities is to provide multiple work stations within the kitchen that are of different heights and to provide work stations that are designed for the seated user. A seated area (open counter) can be the great equalizer among people of varying heights and abilities.

It is relatively simple to purchase inexpensive stools and chairs that meet the height requirements for built-in seated work spaces in the kitchen. Thus, if the open work-space height is 32 in. (the height wheelchair users felt most comfortable with), stools could be purchased that fit this dimension. These spaces are of benefit to individuals who use wheelchairs and workers of different heights. All will be accommodated without having to modify the kitchens or have special units. A dining counter open underneath with a clearance height of 32 in. may be used as a work surface or a dining area.

Different work surface heights are better for some activities than others, and installing more than one work surface height will accommodate a variety of activities. Many people prefer to stand while working in the kitchen, particularly while preparing a meal. The need to move between the refrigerator, cooktop, sink, microwave and countertop sometimes makes seated work impractical for the person in a hurry. The 36-in. countertop height meets the needs of the average-height adult for most food-preparation and small-appliance activities. A counter height of 30 in. is more convenient for filling large containers and emptying grocery bags.

Long, tiresome chores such as polishing silver, chopping a large quantity of foods by hand and frosting or decorating cookies and cakes are sometimes easier when seated at a work surface. A kitchen with more than one work-surface height can accommodate seated or standing workers, and youngsters or individuals of various heights. Spaces for a built-in kitchen desk and a dining counter provide perfect opportunities for incorporating more than one work-surface height.

These kitchens demonstrate the utility and
accessibility of multiple counter heights. The counters
double as dining tables and sit-down work surfaces.
Also note that all of the lower cabinets are drawers
mounted on full-extension slides. (Photos above and
at right: courtesy Whirlpool Corp.)

NKBA Seating-Space Recommendations

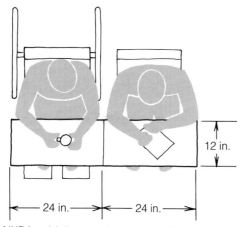

The NKBA guidelines are too cramped for comfort; allowing a bit more room, as shown at right in the drawing, makes the countertop more usable.

ITD Seating-Space Recommendations

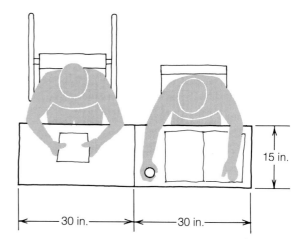

A table in the kitchen, in a position that does not interfere with ease of movement, provides a work surface for individuals who sit while working and frequently helps when transporting items from one counter to another, particularly in a large kitchen. A dining counter at a height of 30 in. to 32 in. separating the kitchen from a formal dining room or a den provides a space for seated work, an area for meals to be eaten in the kitchen, and a surface to aid in transferring items from the kitchen to the dining room.

The NKBA guidelines suggest a minimum space of 24 in. wide by 12 in. deep for each seated diner at a table or counter, as shown in the drawing above. We at the Institute for Technology Development think these dimensions are too skimpy and are likely to lead to more consternation than convenience. The 24-in. width barely allows enough room for somewhat restricted movement of the elbows, and two people seated side by side are likely to knock elbows at times. A 12-in. depth will not allow someone to pull up to the counter and have adequate room for knees and feet. Neither the 24-in. width nor the 12-in. depth would accommodate someone seated in

a wheelchair. We recommend a minimum space of 30 in. wide and 15 in. deep for each seated diner — this is barely enough to accommodate a wheelchair.

CABINETS AND OTHER STORAGE

Kitchen cabinets and their dimensions create the framework for the location of work surfaces, appliances and other storage. Recently, we asked a group of 77 people representing a wide variety of ages and abilities to name the one feature in their entire house that they most wanted to change. Almost without hesitation, more than half of the subjects named their kitchen cabinets.

Storage areas in kitchens includes cabinets, shelves or pantries, drawers, appliance garages and closets. If you take a moment to consider traditional kitchen cabinets you can quickly visualize their inefficiencies. First, think about the bottom shelf of the base cabinets and the back half of the top shelf. The only way you can reach these spaces is to kneel on the floor or do a deep knee bend. They are deep, dark, almost inaccessible spaces.

The features most disliked about kitchens are the unreachable spaces (see the photos at right). For many people these include about three-fourths of the base cabinets and two-thirds of the above-counter cabinets. Given the many disadvantages of traditional kitchen cabinets, it's time to challenge some of the standard cabinet dimensions and consider some alternative products that better "fit" different users.

Standard kitchen cabinets are sold by distributors, as are accessible kitchen cabinet and appliance systems (see Resources on p. 161). Cabinets may also be custom made by a cabinetmaker. Standard kitchen cabinets can be installed to improve their accessibility, but greater universal access may be planned using custom cabinets. The cost of the cabinets will depend on the materials from which they are built, the number of cabinets and the type and number of special features, such as systems that move the cabinets up and down or pull-out baskets or shelving.

Ideally, most kitchen storage space should be located within the dimensions of the optimal reach zone (20 in. above the floor, 44 in. high and 20 in. deep). Given the amount of storage space required in a kitchen and the amount of clear counter space required for working, this goal may be difficult to accomplish. Deep cabinets are dark and difficult to reach, shallow cabinets are open to view and simple. Standard-depth (24) in. cabinets are not a problem if they include drawers, pull-out shelving or baskets that bring their contents into the optimal reach zone.

Fixed shelving in base cabinets requires more effort from the user than drawers and pull-out shelving. Drawers and pull-out shelving help by bringing the stored items into the light in an easy-to-reach position. With pull-out shelving, the user merely pulls open the bottom drawer and reaches down to lift the object to the working surface. Although bending is required to get to the object, this movement is much less than that demanded by fixed shelving.

Drawers that reveal all of their contents to the light impose a degree of order. First, the space is defined. Unlike a continuous shelf, the drawer has boundaries that impose limits to the amounts that may be stored. Second, the drawer brings all of its contents to the user, so the back half of the storage space is as valuable as the front half.

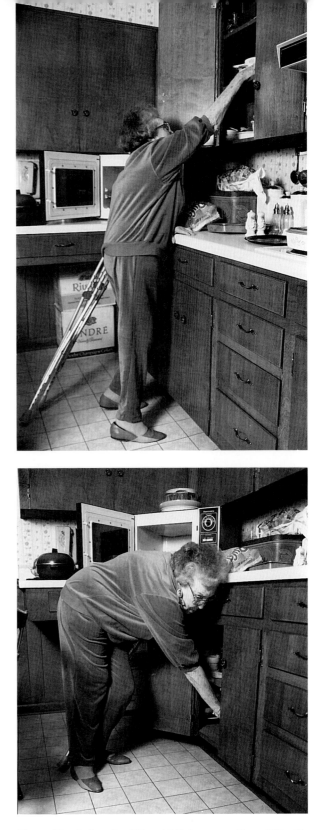

The cabinets in a traditional kitchen are often difficult to reach.

Vertical storage space with dividers spaced 3 in. to 4 in. apart and 18 in. to 24 in. high will hold cake and broiler pans, cookie sheets, large lids, a cutting-board and other objects without stacking. (Vertical storage can be seen to the right of the cooktop in the top photo on p. 154.) Putting an object into or taking it out of a stack is usually a two-handed activity. Many people who need the counter for support or who have the use of only one hand will be accommodated by this convenient built-in feature.

Lowering the upper cabinets makes them more accessible. Most can easily be lowered to a height 15 in. above the counter, and some should be 12 in. above the counter. If the wall cabinets are placed at a height of 12 in. above the countertop (at a height of 32 in.), the lowest shelf will be 44 in. high, a second shelf could be at 54 in. and a third at 64 in.

The traditional counter height is 36 in., with wall cabinets installed 18 in. above the counter, for a lowest-shelf height of 54 in. The NKBA recommends this arrangement, but we don't. We have built kitchens with the above-counter cabinets mounted only 12 in. above the countertop and not noticed any loss of use of the countertop for storage. The only perceptible difference is that our cabinets are easier to reach. When the cabinets are lower and have height-adjustable shelving, many kitchen users can customize their storage areas so they will rarely need to resort to a stepstool.

The space between the above-counter cabinets and the countertop can accommodate an additional shelf or storage unit, or a series of hooks for hanging frequently used utensils and pots and pans. Storage space for small appliances should be at the same height as the counter on which the appliances are likely to be used. Some folks are unable to lift the breadmaker, food processor and other small appliances that weigh more than a few pounds. If traditional cabinet design is used and deep corners are present, this space may be used for an appliance garage. The appliances are stored at the height they are to be used, but are neatly parked in the garage when idle.

Another solution is to build a narrow (18 in. to 20 in. deep) counter along one wall that will serve as a small appliance work and storage center. There the small appliance can be stored in its position of use.

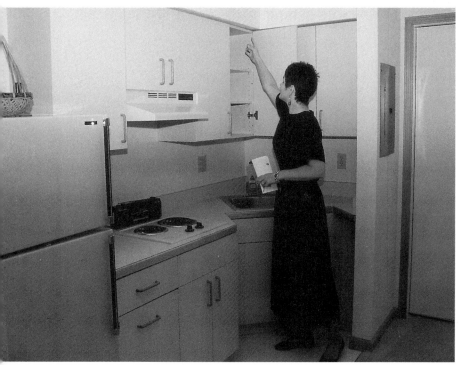

Access to kitchen cabinets can be significantly improved by lowering the upper cabinets to a height of 12 in. to 15 in. above the counter and using adjustable shelving. A 5-ft. tall woman can reach the top shelf of this LIFESPEC cabinet. Except for the unit over the cooktop, the cabinets in this photo are 15 in. above the counter.

Accessibility and flexibility are the hallmarks of good kitchen storage. At left is a conventional corner cabinet with a lazy Susan and above-counter cabinets. All of the goods stored in the cabinets and on the countertop fit neatly and much more accessibly into the recessed corner pantry with shallow-depth, adjustable shelves (above left). The pantry shelving (above right) is recessed behind nicely paneled doors that, when open, allow for easy access to a large quantity of goods. (Photos left and above left: Institute for Technology Development.)

The NKBA rules begin to address the need for storage space, but the rules fall short in ensuring that the storage space will be usable throughout a person's lifespan. The NKBA implies that as long as cabinets are not above the vent hood, oven or refrigerator they are not difficult to reach. However, wall cabinets are hard to get to because you have to reach over a countertop and up to heights that are frequently beyond the range of many people.

The NKBA guidelines state that at least five storage items must be included in the kitchen to improve the accessibility and functionality of the plan. These include (but are not limited to) wall cabinets with adjustable shelves, interior vertical dividers, pull-out drawers, swing-out pantries or drawer/roll-out space greater than the minimum. A plan for a lifespan house, built for the convenience of the occupants,

would rewrite this guideline as follows: "All storage items included in the kitchen should be accessible and functional."

Pantry   Although many kitchen designs today don't include a pantry, we have found that a small pantry in the corner of a kitchen provides easy-to-access storage space. Height-adjustable shelving in the pantry (or closet) allows the user to tailor the kitchen to his or her own size and to the size of the objects that are to be stored on the shelves. If shelving is fixed, the lowest shelf should be mounted 10 in. above the floor; the highest shelf should be no more than 70 in. above the floor.

Shallow-depth (12-in.) shelves offer better access and visibility, which improve organization, efficient use and speedy location of the stored items. If the space is planned for storage of specific items such

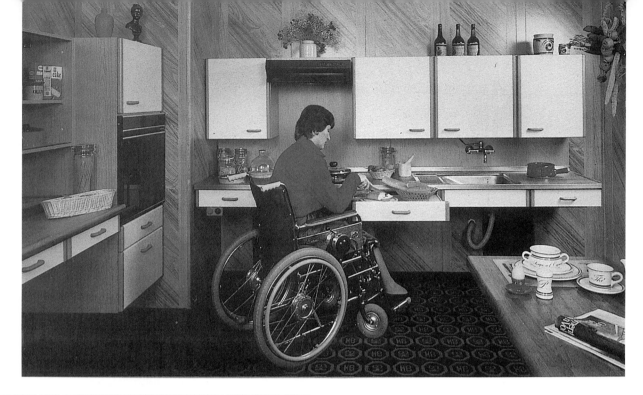

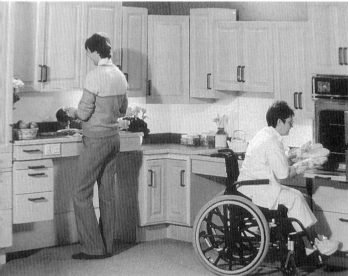

Electronically adjustable kitchen systems. The Granberg Superior Systems kitchen shown in these photos has a height-adjustable countertop, cooktop, sink and cabinets; adjustments are made using a hand crank or an electrical motor. (Photos: Granberg Superior Systems.)

as canned goods, you may wish to use 9 in. as a minimum depth, but 12 in. will allow more flexibility in the items that may be stored. Pots, pans, dinner plates, appliances and mixing bowls usually exceed 9 in. in diameter.

As of yet, easily adjustable kitchen counter and cabinet systems are not marketed as conventional cabinet products. Some foreign-made kitchen systems provide electrically adjusted kitchen units (see Resources on p. 161). These systems (see the photos above and at left) usually have the sink, cooktop, base cabinets, work surface and above-counter cabinets mounted on a frame that moves up and down 11 in. to 13 in. The motorized system incorporates infrared lights under the front edge of the countertop that sense the presence of an object or an individual's legs. If an object breaks the beam of the infrared lights (about 1 in. to 2 in. from the bottom of the counter) the system automatically stops moving. This keeps the countertop from moving to the point where it pinches someone sitting underneath.

Although adjustable counter and cabinet systems have certain advantages, they do not solve all of the problems because they are standard depth and some people may need greater flexibility than these systems offer. Also, they are expensive.

ELECTRICAL DETAILS

Electrical outlets should be located systematically throughout the kitchen so that small appliances can be used at each work surface. One double outlet should be located at each work surface. Outlets are typically placed on the wall above the countertop, but many people have difficulty reaching over the counter. One alternative is to put the outlets at the front of the base cabinets under the countertop. This makes the outlet accessible, but the risk of inadvertently dragging an item off the countertop is greater.

A second alternative is to locate outlets on the bottom of the above-counter cabinets, where they are easy to get to, yet the cords won't get tangled and are out of reach of young children. Extra care may be needed to obtain a neat wiring job that prevents the outlet boxes from interfering with cabinet space.

A third alternative, which we recommend, is to do all of the above, providing outlets in various locations as shown in the drawing below. The small amount of added expense for a few extra feet of wir-

ing and outlets is insignificant compared to the flexibility gained. Specify ground-fault circuit interrupters (see p. 84) for all receptacles within 6 ft. of a water source.

Lighting A kitchen needs strong overhead lighting to provide uniform illumination throughout the room. Fixtures that direct the light upward to reflect off a white or light-colored ceiling will distribute the light evenly.

If incandescent ceiling fixtures are planned, consider using a fixture on a retractable cord. If placed in an area where more lighting may be desired at times, the fixture may be pulled closer to increase the lighting levels. Additionally, it will be easier for a short person to change the light bulb, perhaps with the aid of a reacher (a 30-in. long-handled clamp with a squeeze trigger).

A kitchen also needs task lighting at the sink, range or cooktop and work areas. A good location for the fixtures is under the upper cabinets, but the light source must be shielded so that it doesn't shine

Locating Electrical Outlets

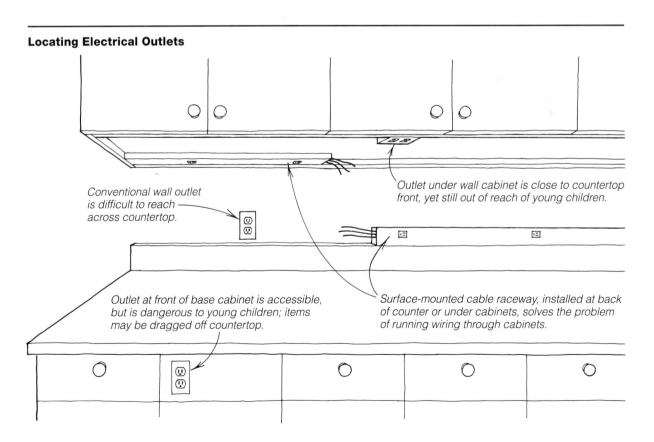

Conventional wall outlet is difficult to reach across countertop.

Outlet under wall cabinet is close to countertop front, yet still out of reach of young children.

Outlet at front of base cabinet is accessible, but is dangerous to young children; items may be dragged off countertop.

Surface-mounted cable raceway, installed at back of counter or under cabinets, solves the problem of running wiring through cabinets.

This kitchen is blessed with abundant natural light combined with task lighting at specific work centers.

directly into the eyes of someone seated, as shown in the drawing below.

Incandescent light fixtures should have multiple bulbs to provide light in the event that one of the bulbs burns out. Low-voltage high-intensity (halogen) lighting is an excellent light source and is often directional. Some halogen lighting systems generate considerable heat, so their installation requirements should be checked carefully.

Daylight is an excellent source of light in the kitchen. The National Kitchen and Bath Association suggests that the square footage of windows and/or skylights should equal or exceed 10% of the square footage of a kitchen. A window located above the kitchen sink or anywhere else in the kitchen will improve visibility. If windows are located above the counter or behind the sink, be sure that the lock for the window and the controls for the window treatment are located at the bottom of the window. Reaching across the 24-in. deep space to access these controls is difficult or impossible for many people. The window should be treated so that direct sunlight

Lighting the Kitchen

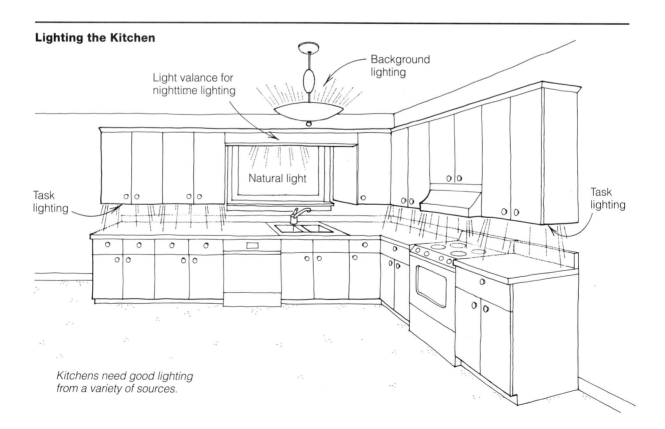

Background lighting

Light valance for nighttime lighting

Natural light

Task lighting

Task lighting

Kitchens need good lighting from a variety of sources.

does not shine into the eyes of the worker, either by shading the windows on the exterior or by diffusing the sunlight with window coverings inside.

VENTILATION

The kitchen should have both natural and mechanical ventilation. All cooking appliances should have a ventilation system that exhausts to the building's exterior, equipped with a fan rated at 150 cfm minimum. Cross ventilation with doors and windows is also desirable.

The range hood should have radiused corners and should be high enough so that the cook doesn't bump into it, yet low enough so the controls may be reached by individuals of short stature. The hood should extend 18 in. or less from the back wall and should be mounted a minimum of 54 in. above the floor. Ideally, controls should be within the optimal reach zone (20 in. to 44 in. above the floor), but because most range hoods are mounted above the stove and because the controls are located on the upper side of the cooktop, they are often located at heights above 44 in. It may be necessary to wire the controls to a second switch located at counter height. The controls for both the light source and the exhaust fan should be located at the front of the unit and should be push button.

The range hood should have a washable filter that fits into the dishwasher. The light should be easy to replace without the use of special tools.

In some kitchen designs a conventional hood would be too large and obtrusive. A simple wall-mounted fan or a smaller custom hood mounted higher up and out of the way may be a good substitute. These venting systems are likely to require a remote switch mounted within the optimal reach zone. They also require high-power fans to pull the fumes from the greater distance. Such powerful fans can be noisy as well as expensive. Some types have extra sound dampening in the housing. A better solution is fans that mount outdoors, like restaurant fans.

Downdraft venting systems are used for cooktops, and often their controls are mounted at counter height. These systems pull the fumes downward through openings at the center or rear of the cooktop. Because they work against the natural draft of the hot air, powerful fans are needed.

Windows placed behind or above a cooktop or range will impossible for most people to reach and operate safely. We recommend that windows not be placed in this location. Windows used for ventilation in the kitchen should be placed so that their controls are between 36 in. and 44 in. above the floor. The windows should have clear space in front of them (for more on windows, see pp. 112-118).

SINK

Much of the time spent in the kitchen is spent working at the kitchen sink. Because the kitchen sink is a primary work area, many users appreciate the opportunity to sit, particularly when performing tasks that take a long time. A counter height that permits standing or seated access can serve wheelchair users, people of different heights and those who simply want to rest their legs.

Sinks are usually mounted at a counter height of 36 in. This height is comfortable for someone who is standing, but too high for someone seated in a wheelchair. In our L.E.A.D. 2010 study of 71 people with disabilities (see pp. 3-6), we found that a 32-in. sink height was preferred by a majority of the wheelchair users, by about 42% of those who use other assistive devices, and by 25% of those who have physical limitations but who do not use an assistive device. ANSI allows a 28-in. minimum height for the sink, because presumably a person seated in a wheelchair will be able to roll under this height. We found this height too low for all but a few of our research subjects who use a wheelchair and for everyone else who doesn't.

Sinks should be built into a kitchen so that they can be adjusted when necessary to suit someone who prefers a lower sink height. Sinks need 6 in. of adjustability at most, extending from a height of 32 in. to 38 in. This range can be achieved by using flexible water feeds and removable segments for the drain. A minimum width of 32 in. will accommodate most wheelchairs and will allow the person on the kitchen stool to be situated in front of the sink at either side.

An Adjustable Sink

Sink Before Adjustment

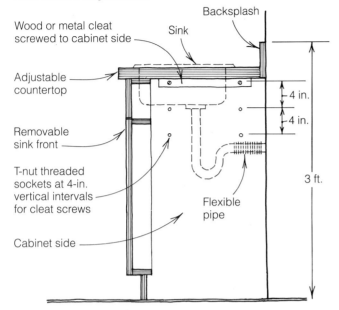

Wood or metal cleat screwed to cabinet side

Backsplash

Sink

Adjustable countertop

Removable sink front

T-nut threaded sockets at 4-in. vertical intervals for cleat screws

Cabinet side

Flexible pipe

4 in.

4 in.

3 ft.

Sink Lowered 4 in.

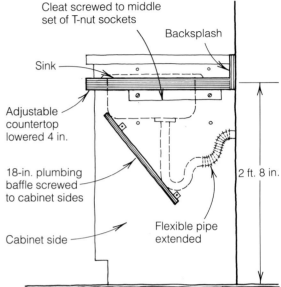

Cleat screwed to middle set of T-nut sockets

Backsplash

Sink

Adjustable countertop lowered 4 in.

18-in. plumbing baffle screwed to cabinet sides

Cabinet side

Flexible pipe extended

2 ft. 8 in.

To lower the sink 4 in., the sink front is removed, the cleats on which the sink rests are attached 4 in. lower, and a plumbing baffle is installed to protect the legs of a person seated at the sink.

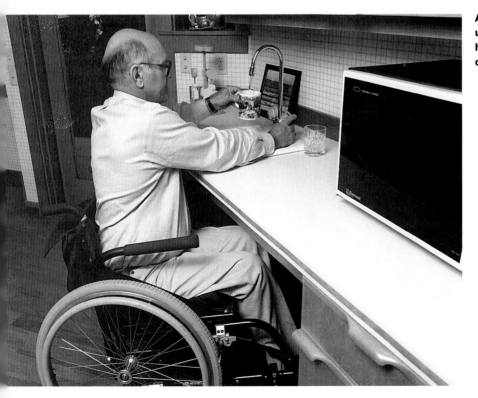

A wheelchair user can comfortably use a sink that's installed at a 32-in. height with the area underneath left open. (Photo: Jay O'Neil.)

For seated users, the sink should be mounted in a counter with knee space below. This space can be open or have retractable doors or a removable door panel. Some companies sell wall brackets to support an adjustable counter, but it is simpler to support the counter on cleats screwed to the adjacent cabinet or wall, as shown in the drawing on the facing page. The cleats can be easily repositioned.

Placing the sink in a corner makes good use of space that is often wasted. The sink with a drain at the back can be recessed into the corner using the deepest part of the corner for the plumbing. The added depth makes it easier to create space for the legs of a person seated at the sink. In a two-cook kitchen where both cooks may want to use the sink at the same time, a sink area less than 36 in. wide may cause problems.

The sink should be made of materials that are slow to transfer heat, or else it should be insulated. Stainless-steel sinks last longer and are easier to clean, but solid surface materials such as Corian provide less heat transfer. They are also more expensive.

The depth of the sink should be between 5 in. and 6½ in. This is shallower than the traditional kitchen sink, which ranges in depth from 7 in. to 8 in. deep. The shallow sink is easier to reach into and will provide greater clearance for legs underneath. The sink controls should be located no farther back than 21 in. from the front edge of the counter. The drains and garbage disposal should be located at the back so they won't interfere with the legs of a seated person The drain control should be situated outside of the sink.

It is probably wisest to select a double sink, rather than a single sink bowl. Although many people like the extra-large capacity of a single sink, the double sink allows two different activities to occur simultaneously. Another thing to consider is adding a second sink for the second cook. Two sinks make sense because specific chores can be segregated to each one. For example, the sink that houses the garbage disposal can be used only for "dirty" work.

Plumbing The sink should have a single lever faucet that controls both the temperature and flow of the water. These permit one-handed use and allow the user to adjust the temperature before turning on the water. A retractable hose spray is a convenient item that allows pots to be filled outside of the sink, eliminating the need to lift them up when they are full of water. A long hose may even let you fill a big pot at the location it is going to be used.

The pipes and plumbing under the sink should be insulated to shield the individual seated at the sink from burns. This can be accomplished by using a piece of plywood that matches the cabinets. A baffle is created by constructing an angled partition to separate the pipes from the knees (see the drawing on the facing page). Another, less attractive method is to wrap the pipes with insulating material. The underside of the counter should not have sink screws that could come in contact with the user's legs, and sharp surfaces should be covered.

APPLIANCES

Careful selection of modern labor-saving products will improve efficiency, safety, ease of use, maintenance and satisfaction. (Product-design and selection criteria are discussed in detail on pp. 25-29.) Although many kitchen gadgets on the market today represent a design world gone berserk, some, particularly a select group of cooktops and microwave ovens, have excellent design features. Rather than being encumbered with unnecessary bells, whistles and impossible-to-use programming features, these improved products are simple, smooth and self-evident. That is, the features and controls are placed logically and operate in the manner and direction that one would expect. The surfaces are smooth and are free from ornamentation that will capture dirt. You do not need an instruction booklet and videotape tutorial to figure out how to use them, because their functions are obvious from their appearance.

Cooktop Although cooktops are usually installed at a height of 36 in., a cooktop installed at 32 in. would enable the seated worker to see into the pots at the back of the stove. A 32-in. height is convenient for standing workers as well, especially when cooking in large pots. For some, this height will still be too high, in which case an angled mirror can be mounted at the back of the stove to reflect the contents of the pots and pans.

A few small adjustments can make a cooktop easier to use. Here, an angled mirror above the cooktop allows a seated cook to see into all pots and pans. Also note that a control switch for the vent hood has been installed along the front edge of the cooktop counter. (Photo: courtesy Whirlpool Corp.)

A good cooktop has staggered burners so that the cook does not have to reach directly across one burner to get to another. The controls on this unit also correlate well with the burners they control.

The ideal cooktop has a smooth glass surface that lights up when the burner is turned on. Smooth-surface cooktops may not have a lip that will catch hot liquids that boil over or spill. This drawback is a potential danger to seated users. Mounting the smooth cooktop in a countertop with a rolled edge may solve the problem.

The burners of the cooktop should be arranged so that the user does not have to reach across one burner to get to another, and it should be obvious which control goes with which burner (see the bottom photo on the facing page). For easy access, the controls should be at the front of the cooktop and should either be a slide control, a touch pad or a large easy-to move dial. The touch pad is advantageous because it is easy to keep clean. Unfortunately, some people can't tell if they have actuated the touch pad unless there are visual clues. Knob or dial controls present problems because they require grasping and turning of the wrist; also, it is hard to clean between and underneath them.

Front controls, however, can be a problem with toddlers, small children and adults with cognitive disorders. Some companies are in the process of developing electronic controls that can be programmed to deactivate the burner and oven controls.

Oven Ovens built into the wall should be mounted with the base of the oven about 30 in. to 34 in. above the floor. Counter space should be available adjacent to the oven, preferably on both sides, and underneath (see the photo below).

A built-in oven with a side-hinged door is better than a freestanding oven with a bottom-hinged door; you can get closer to the oven and you don't need to maneuver around the door. The wall-mounted oven with a side-hinged door would be even better if it had a pull-out shelf just below it that provided a place to set a hot pan and protected the cook from spills.

Traditional stoves with bottom ovens are not recommended because the oven racks are too low for many wheelchair users, and people without feeling

A wall-mounted oven with a side-hinged door allows for easy maneuverability. The convenient pull-out shelf located under this oven adds a measure of safety. (Photo: Independent Living Center, South Carolina Vocational Rehabilitation Department.)

The woman in the photo at left is barely able to reach the controls on the microwave oven, which has been installed at a traditional height for a wall-hung unit. She is taking a risk every time she tries to lift a hot dish out. She would be much better served by a microwave oven installed on the counter. In the photo above, the microwave was installed beneath the counter to make it accessible to a young wheelchair user. Switches on the side of the cabinet unit allow him to control lighting in the area as well. (Photo at left: Institute for Technology Development.)

in their legs may burn themselves without realizing it. The oven door creates a significant obstacle when trying to get something into or out of the oven.

Microwave oven   Microwave ovens cook food quickly in its serving dish, and their side-opening door facilitates access. However, built-in microwaves are often located too high for short people or seated users. Although they are space-efficient, many range-hood/ microwave combinations are inaccessible. The National Kitchen and Bath Association recommends that the shelf on which the microwave is placed be between 36 in. and 54 in. above the finished floor. We prefer a maximum height of 44 in. If the microwave is located higher than this, users will have to lift and lower cookware at levels that may be beyond their range of reach. A microwave at 54 in. would be useless to someone in a wheelchair. We see no reason why a microwave shouldn't be located at a standard table height of 30 in. Like other ovens, a microwave should have a set-down space right next to it.

Refrigerator   Of the many styles on the market, the two-door side-by-side refrigerator/freezer is the most accessible, but it also costs more. The appliance should be frost-free. Slide-out shelving and doors and an automatic ice maker and dispenser are recommended. Many manufacturers supply refrigerators with see-through shelving and drawers, which enhance usability for those with limited abilities. If a single-door refrigerator is required because of space limitations, at least 50% of the freezer space should be within the optimal reach zone. A freezer above the refrigerator section is beyond the reach of many people.

Garbage disposal   Garbage disposals are appreciated by many people because they eliminate a lot of movement getting rid of garbage. The garbage disposal should be located at the back of the sink or off to the side of the knee recess in a separate sink. The electrical wiring and plumbing should be carefully shielded to ensure that the user does not come in contact with either.

Many cooks, but especially those with limited strength or mobility, appreciate the opportunity to complete their kitchen cleanup while seated at the sink. (Photo: Institute for Technology Development.)

Dishwasher The dishwasher is an important labor-saving device and should be routinely included in the lifespan kitchen. As with all appliances, the dishwasher should be placed in a neutrally handed position (see pp. 139-140). Convenience is added if the dishwasher is located so that it can be reached from the side by a person who is seated at the sink (see the photo above).

The dishwasher should have front-mounted controls and a front-opening door. The racks, soap dispenser and silverware holder should be within easy reach. The door lock should require minimum manual dexterity to operate, and the controls should be push button or slide.

The dishwasher should have clearly visible indicators that mark the cycle stage in operation, to prevent inadvertent opening of the door during the cleaning phase, which may cause scalding from the escaping steam.

EVALUATING KITCHEN FLOOR PLANS

Traditional kitchen layouts include the U-shaped kitchen, the L-shaped kitchen, the galley or pullman kitchen and the double L-shaped kitchen. U-shaped and L-shaped kitchens save human energy because they require less movement to complete tasks, they can provide a continuous countertop from one location to another and, if they are large enough, they may accommodate a table in the center. The galley kitchen is located on opposite walls and often has a narrow passage between the counters. The work centers are usually located on both sides of the kitchen. This arrangement dictates that the worker move back and forth from one side to the other.

In this section, sample floor plans of these four typical kitchen layouts are evaluated according to their accessibility, convenience and ease of use, taking into consideration the various factors that were discussed earlier in the chapter.

U-shaped kitchen The U-shaped kitchen in the drawing on p. 158 is designed to open into an adjoining room. One obvious benefit of this layout is that household traffic does not cross a work aisle in the kitchen. Another benefit is that the sink is located between the dishwasher and the range. Cleanup is easy because of the short distance from the sink and garbage disposal to the dishwasher. The range's location near the sink aids the cook because large pots filled with water don't have to be carried far to the burners. (With a spray attachment, a pot could even be filled with water while it is sitting on the burner.) The proximity of sink to range makes spills easy to clean up, too.

The sink is designed so that it may be lowered for seated use or raised to the standard 36-in. height. The drain and water pipes underneath the sink are shielded by a slanted panel that matches the cabinets. The floor under the sink is finished.

The kitchen pantry features shallow-depth adjustable shelving and pull-out shelving in the angular deeper cabinets. The shallow shelves provide easy access, good lighting and efficient organization, and they return floor space to the room that would otherwise be wasted in deep base cabinets.

U-Shaped Kitchen

Elevation 1

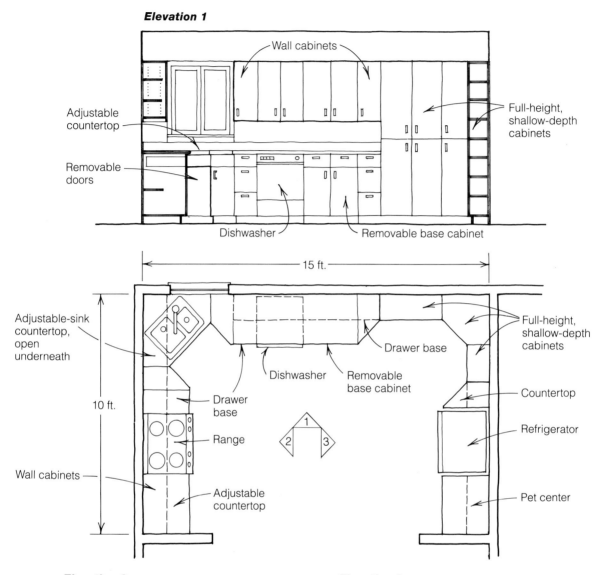

Wall cabinets

Adjustable countertop

Removable doors

Full-height, shallow-depth cabinets

Dishwasher

Removable base cabinet

15 ft.

Adjustable-sink countertop, open underneath

10 ft.

Wall cabinets

Drawer base

Range

Adjustable countertop

Dishwasher

Removable base cabinet

Drawer base

Full-height, shallow-depth cabinets

Countertop

Refrigerator

Pet center

Elevation 2

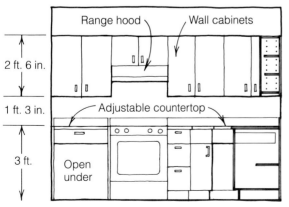

Range hood

Wall cabinets

2 ft. 6 in.

1 ft. 3 in.

3 ft.

Adjustable countertop

Open under

Elevation 3

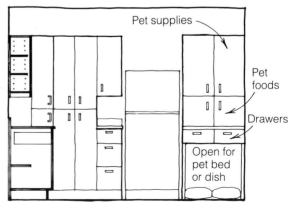

Pet supplies

Pet foods

Drawers

Open for pet bed or dish

L-Shaped Kitchen

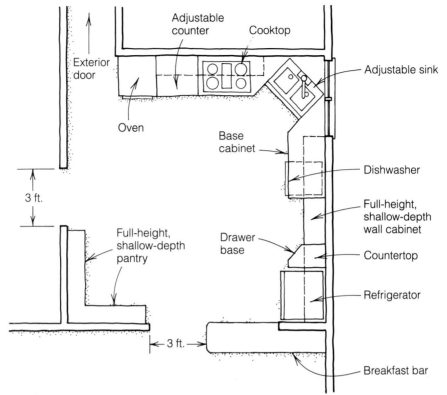

The adjustable height-counter adjacent to the range may be lowered for use as a desk or seated work area. The range can be reached by someone who is seated at the adjustable countertop. The countertop space next to the refrigerator provides a useful set-down area for items that are being taken out of or put into the refrigerator.

This kitchen includes a pet center, actually just a small "cabinet" next to the refrigerator. As shown in Elevation 3, the cabinet incorporates a small open area for the pet's bed and storage for grooming items, food and other supplies.

L-shaped kitchen The L-shaped kitchen in the drawing above makes good use of its corner. Placing the sink in the corner offers three advantages. First, it makes use of an area that is often wasted and inaccessible. Second, it creates the opportunity to have three work centers close together. Third, it provides a work station out of the flow of traffic.

Like the U-shaped kitchen in the drawing on the facing page, this kitchen offers easy access between the sink and dishwasher and between the sink and cooktop. The sink would be more accessible with an adjustable-height unit, a panel to cover the plumbing and a removable front on the cabinet below.

The design of this kitchen permits access to the dishwasher from either side, although its intended use is from the left side. (You could easily stand on the right side of the dishwasher and work at the countertop, or place or remove dishes.) The shallow-depth storage shelves next to the dishwasher and the cabinets immediately above would be ideal locations for the dinnerware.

This kitchen also has an adjustable counter, from which a seated worker can reach both the oven and the cooktop. This counter could serve as a seated work area or as a kitchen desk, although the placement between the stove and cooktop limits its utility as a desk because of the need to use this surface for setting down hot pans.

Pullman Kitchen

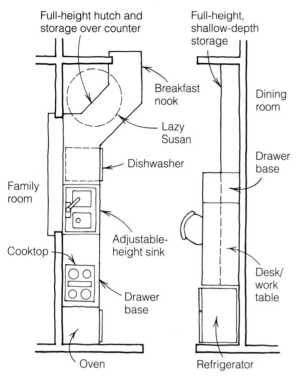

Full-height hutch and storage over counter

Full-height, shallow-depth storage

Breakfast nook

Dining room

Lazy Susan

Drawer base

Dishwasher

Family room

Adjustable-height sink

Cooktop

Desk/work table

Drawer base

Oven

Refrigerator

Double L-Shaped Kitchen

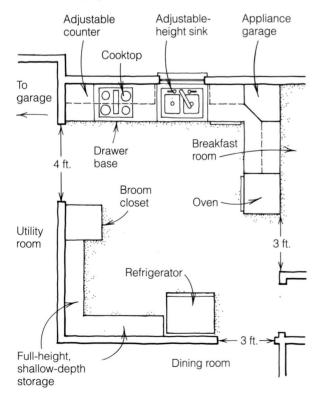

Adjustable counter

Adjustable-height sink

Appliance garage

Cooktop

To garage

Drawer base

Breakfast room

4 ft.

Broom closet

Oven

Utility room

3 ft.

Refrigerator

Full-height, shallow-depth storage

3 ft.

Dining room

The 12-in. drawer-base cabinet to the left of the refrigerator serves as a small set-down area, as does the breakfast bar on the right. The breakfast bar, which separates the kitchen from the family room, is a convenient snack area and an auxiliary work surface. The shallow-depth pantry in the corner of the kitchen adds readily accessible storage for heavy, bulky items.

Galley kitchen The galley kitchen in the drawing at left was adapted from a house plan that shows the kitchen between the family room and dining room, with a breakfast nook at one end of the kitchen. Although this kitchen is crowded and lacks counter space, it has several positive aspects. All the major appliances but the refrigerator are located on the same side of the kitchen, and all of the work centers are connected by a continuous countertop (if the sink is kept at the 36-in. height).

The pass-through above the sink connects the kitchen to the family room. The angled corner adds countertop but blocks accessibility to the dishwasher from the right side. The deep corner cabinets dictate the need for a lazy Susan. Shallow-depth storage above the angled countertop make use of space that might otherwise be wasted. Many people, however, will have difficulty reaching this corner hutch, particularly the upper shelves.

Shallow-depth storage on the opposite wall is fairly accessible, and it returns floor space to a relatively small kitchen. The desk next to the refrigerator can serve as a set-down surface, an alternative-height work counter and a seated work area.

Double L-shaped kitchen The double L-shaped floor plan in the drawing at left has an open counter separating the kitchen from the breakfast room. This low counter area (30 in. to 32 in.) can serve as a space for a quick snack or as a seated work space.

Another work surface is located next to the cooktop. This adjustable counter may serve as a kitchen desk, and it allows the cook to reach the cooktop from a seated position. The oven, located in a neutral position, can be accessed from either the right or the left side. The proximity of the cooktop to the sink means pots can be filled on the stove using a hose. This arrangement also saves steps during cleanup.

RESOURCES

Most of the major appliance manufacturers offer products with some accessible features, so the manufacturers of refrigerators, cooktops, ovens, dishwashers and other general kitchen appliances have not been included in this list. For guidance use the criteria described in Chapter 2 and select products that have controls and space within the optimal reach zone. See also the list of comprehensive catalog companies on p. 221.

Auton Company
Box 10756
Honolulu, HI 96816
(808) 734-1260
Above-counter shelving system that moves up and down.

Clairson International
Closet Maid
720 SW 17th Street
Ocala, FL 32674
(800) 874-0008
Freestanding modular storage systems, cabinet organizers and electronic revolving closet systems.

Delta Faucet Company
Eastern Zone
1425 West Main Street
Greensburg, IN 47240
(812) 663-4433
Single-handed kitchen Eurostyle faucets.

Dwyer Products
Calumet Avenue
Michigan City, IN 46360-5019
(800) 348-8508
(219) 874-5236
Wheelchair-accessible compact efficiency kitchens that include an oven, microwave, refrigerator, sink and cabinetry.

Granberg Superior Systems
2502 Thayer Avenue
Saskatoon, Saskatchewan
Canada S7L 5Y2
(306) 314-9440
Motorized kitchen-cabinet system; height-adjustable counters, cooktops, sinks and cabinets.

Grohe America
900 Lively Boulevard
Wood Dale, IL 60191
(708) 350-2600
Single-handed kitchen faucet with pull-out spray head (faucet and spray head are the same unit); easy push-button operation, interchangeable spray heads.

Hafele America
3901 Cheyenne Drive
P.O. Box 4000
Archdale, NC 27263
(800) 821-5423
(800) 672-4853 (In North Carolina)
(800) 334-1873 (In Eastern U.S.)
(800) 421-0663 (In California)
(919) 889-2322
Hardware accessories for saving space and organizing closets.

Homat Medi
Muidenweg 5
P.O. Box 1090
2800 BB Gouda
The Netherlands
(01820)27144
Electrically or mechanically adjustable kitchen. The "Jack-Up" kitchen uses a crank handle to adjust the height of the counter (including sink and cooktop) from 29 in. to 37 in. off the floor.

LIFESPEC Cabinet Systems
428 North Lamar
Oxford, MS 38655
(601) 234-0330
Adaptable and accessible kitchen cabinet systems in frameless (32mm) or face-frame styles.

LUWA Corporation
Builder Products Division
P.O. Box 16348
Charlotte, NC 28297-6348
(704) 394-8341
Facilitator Handicap sink with sloped side and drain board. Drain in the rear of the sink. One-handed kitchen faucet with integral spray head.

Nicobond Limited
International Division
Niclar House
3/10 Shoreditch High Street
London E1 6PE
01-247 8838/9
Accessible kitchen cabinets, showers, toilets, bathroom accessories.

Owens Design
2295 County Road 292
Bellevue, OH 44811
(419) 483-4872
An above-counter storage cabinet that lowers the shelves down to countertop level. Electronically operated with 110V AC heavy-duty motor. Push-button control.

Penguin Products
47 N. E. 11th Way
Deerfield Beach, Florida 33441
(305) 428-6130
A horizontal refrigerator and freezer.

Rubbermaid
1147 Akron Road
Wooster, OH 44691-6000
(216) 264-6464
Rubber and plastic kitchen and storage accessories.

Ultraflo
P.O. Box 2294
Sandusky, OH 44870
(419) 626-8182
A water distribution system that uses a single line of distribution. Water is operated through preset temperature, push-button selection. Reduces water consumption and avoids hot-water scald through preset temperature.

Vortex Industries
P.O. Box 1133
Fremont, OH 43420
(419) 332-8999
An electrically powered shelf unit that lowers the shelf from an above-counter cabinet to the countertop height. Constructed of solid aluminum arms with particleboard shelves. Supports up to 25 lb. per unit.

White Home Products
2401 Lake Park Drive
Atlanta, GA 30080
(404) 431-0900
An electronic rotating kitchen storage unit that brings the shelves in the storage system to the small sliding glass door opening.

CHAPTER TEN
BATHROOMS

Bathrooms, despite the world of evidence to support the need for new products and plans, haven't changed. Tubs, toilets, vanities and layouts continue to accommodate manufacturers, plumbing conventions and "average" humans rather than users of all sizes and abilities. While there are many new assistive bathing products on the market, they continue to be considered "special," which usually means that they are more expensive. And they still often carry the label "handicapped."

Traditional designs and products say to the user: Do it my way or go without. Go without a bath, go without the ability to use the toilet by yourself, go without your privacy. Standard toilets provide no handholds

Minimal Requirements for an Accessible Bathroom

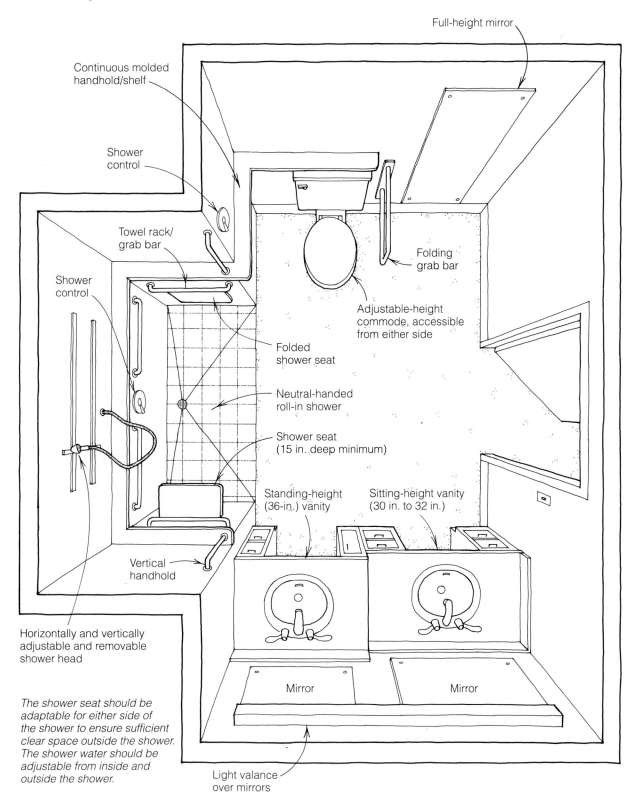

Full-height mirror

Continuous molded handhold/shelf

Shower control

Towel rack/ grab bar

Shower control

Folding grab bar

Adjustable-height commode, accessible from either side

Folded shower seat

Neutral-handed roll-in shower

Shower seat (15 in. deep minimum)

Standing-height (36-in.) vanity

Sitting-height vanity (30 in. to 32 in.)

Vertical handhold

Mirror

Mirror

Horizontally and vertically adjustable and removable shower head

The shower seat should be adaptable for either side of the shower to ensure sufficient clear space outside the shower. The shower water should be adjustable from inside and outside the shower.

Light valance over mirrors

to aid people in sitting down or getting up. Yet many people don't have the strength to lower themselves to or raise themselves up from a seated position. Chairs have armrests, why don't toilets?

Likewise, the conventional bathtub isn't designed to help people get in or out. It demands good balance and agile knees to lower yourself to a seated position in the tub and substantial strength to stand up and step over the side to get out. Many people decide to move out of their homes simply because they have trouble using the bathtub or toilet. Many people feel ashamed and embarrassed to have grab bars in their bathrooms.

Bathrooms that are hard to use are also dangerous. The U.S. Consumer Product Safety Commission has reported that there are more than 110,000 bathtub and shower accidents every year. The report describes the following types of accidents in bathrooms:
• The user experiences a dizzy spell, mobility problems or is simply in a hurry and falls against the bathtub or shower enclosure.
• The bather slips while entering, rising, leaving or maneuvering over the tub edge. The bather may be injured by the hard surface of the tub or may break the shower or tub enclosure.
• Young children and old adults suffer scalds and burns. Serious burns occur because the bather is unable to react quickly enough to get out of the hot water. Young children and frail adults may fall into the tub and be trapped there.
• Young children are left unattended and drown.
• Young children playing near or in the tub slip and fall or break through the tub or shower enclosure.
• Bathers injure themselves against protruding objects such as inappropriately placed grab bars, soap dishes, faucets or towel bars.
• The towel bar or other fixture being used as a handhold fails to support the individual.

A study commissioned by the National Institute on Aging revealed that 9% of adults 65 and older need assistance from another person or special equipment to bathe. (Unfortunately the research study didn't identify what specific problems the survey respondents encountered.) That translates to a total of over 2.5 million people in the U.S. The percentage increases to 31% of those over the age of 85. About 3.5% of the population (or 1 million people) over the age of 65 cannot use the toilet without help.

In 1992 the National Kitchen and Bath Association published a revised set of 27 "rules of bathroom design" (their new rules on kitchen design are discussed in Chapter 9). Unfortunately, some of these rules do little to promote universal design and do not even approach minimally acceptable dimensions for accommodating people of differing abilities. The recommendations in this chapter meet, and in most instances well exceed, the NKBA's rules.

BATHROOM BASICS

There are various of types of bathrooms, often categorized by their location, size and function. Bathrooms range from fancy to functional, spacious to sparse and from multiple to single uses. The primary uses of bathrooms are toileting, bathing and grooming. Secondary uses are linen storage and laundry. The larger the bathroom, the easier it is to make it accessible. Bigger is almost always better. At the same time, there is no reason why reasonably compact bathrooms can't be built to suit everyone's needs.

The master bath is usually connected to the bedroom of the heads of the household. This is often the largest and fanciest bathroom in the house. A children's bath often serves the other bedrooms. It may be smaller than the master bath and have fewer frills. The guest bath is intended for more public use. It will be located on the first floor of a multi-story house and often contains only a toilet and sink. Finally, many houses contain what can be called a utility bathroom, with spartan features and bare-bones fixtures, perhaps containing the laundry facilities.

When you are planning the bathrooms for a new house, it is important to consider how each will be used and where best to locate them. What bathrooms will serve members of the household or visitors who are older or physically challenged? At the very least, take steps now to plan for a future accessible bathroom. If the budget is tight, it still may be wise to do the rough plumbing when the house is built, capping off the pipes and using the room for a closet for the time being.

There should be one full bathroom on each accessible floor of the house. A full bath on the second floor of a two-story house won't help a member of the household who cannot climb the stairs to the second floor. The alternatives for those who build the full bath on the second floor are to install another bathroom on the first floor, provide accessible transportation to the second floor or move.

Unless finances are so tight or the house is going to be so small that two baths are out of the question, plan for a minimum of two. Having two bathrooms solves several problems. First, one may be public and the other private. A public bath should be placed so that it can be reached by guests without their having to walk through bedrooms or other private spaces within the house. A private bath should be located in the bedroom area of the house. Two bathrooms allow for two different bathing systems. Two bathrooms keep the peace in a family trying to prepare for work, school or play at the same time. Each floor of the house should have at least a half-bath. In larger houses, there should be a bathroom in each section of the house.

The lifespan house will have bathrooms that can be reached quickly and easily from the bedrooms at night, via the shortest, most obstacle-free route possible. Bathrooms should be located so that family members can reach them from the bedrooms without exposure to guests. Finally, bathrooms should be located to maximize their primary purpose (for example, bathrooms intended for regular bathing should be near the bedrooms).

Bathroom size is generally between 35 sq. ft. and 100 sq. ft. Space is a problem solver in the bathroom, but unfortunately, it often isn't available. The size of a full bath will be dictated by whether or not the house will have more than one. At least one bathroom should have an accessible bathing system and space to approach the toilet from either side. As throughout the house, all doorways and passageways should have at least 32 in. of clear space. Minimal requirements for an accessible bathroom are shown in the drawing on p. 163.

The size of the full bath will depend on the number and type of fixtures and features it will include. The smallest size bathroom that can accommodate someone in a wheelchair and provide access to a toilet, a traditional-size bathtub (30 in. by 60 in.) and a lavatory is 37½ sq. ft. (5 ft. by 7½ ft.). This size, however, is too small for many people who use wheelchairs because it means that the toilet has to be sandwiched between a wall and the lavatory, which in turn means that the toilet can be approached only from the front for a transfer from the wheelchair. Not all wheelchair users can make this transfer.

Bathrooms need to be planned so that they have sufficient clear floor space (i.e., at least 30 in. by 48 in.) in front of and/or adjacent to each fixture and for moving about the room. People who use wheelchairs and other assistive products (walkers, canes, crutches) need more floor space at the points of interaction with the bathroom fixtures than people who do not use assistive devices. On a bathtub, the points of interaction include operating the faucets and drain and entering and exiting. Although you might assume that the center of the tub would provide plenty of clear floor space, this area may not be usable because there are no handholds.

Clear floor space is important at each end of the bathtub, the areas where grab bars and support surfaces are likely to be located. You will also need open areas around the toilet and the lavatory, near the mirror and in front of the linen closets.

The National Kitchen and Bath Association wisely recommends a 32-in. entrance to bathrooms. But many of their other suggestions are not compatible with the lifespan bathroom. For example, they stipulate at least 21 in. of clear space in front of the sink, toilet, bidet and tub or shower. They also call for a minimum of 6 in. between fixtures and 15 in. from the centerline of the toilet or bidet. These dimensions would render most bathrooms useless to anyone who requires any form of mobility assistance (wheelchair, walker or another person). They also create a cramped bathroom that would be difficult for more than one person to use at a time.

Planning a bathroom layout can help ensure that you have enough space to maximize its use. Before deciding on the size, determine what is going to be included. Will there be one or more bathing centers in the bathroom? Separate tubs and showers accommodate differences in bathing preferences and abilities and allow two people to bathe simultaneously, even in a one-bath house. Will there be one sink or two? Busy households really appreciate separate sink and vanity areas.

How many doorways and what types of doors will be used? Doors are great for privacy and controlling drafts, but beyond that they just get in the way. When studying floor plans, people often visualize the door but overlook the door swing. Poorly designed door swings can really make small bathrooms hard to deal with. People who use assistive devices often find themselves at war with doors in bathrooms.

Pocket doors are very desirable for bathrooms (see pp. 105-107). They don't take up any floor space in the bathroom itself or in the adjacent area. If hinged doors are used, they should swing out from the bathroom, not into it. That will provide more clear space in the bathroom, which is usually smaller than the adjacent room, but it may block a hallway. Also, if the door swings out, someone will always be able to get into the bathroom to assist a person if necessary. Common sense will have to prevail in determining which direction of door swing will be better, but the best solution is not to use a hinged door at all. Using a pocket door solves the problem.

Bathrooms with two doors offer some advantages. A bathroom situated between a bedroom (private space) and the living area (public space) could have doors opening into both areas. The privacy in the bedroom could be preserved because the bedroom door may be closed when guests are in the home, and privacy for the person moving from the bedroom to the bathroom is preserved because there is no need to enter public areas. In a bathroom with two doors, be sure that they don't interfere with each other, as shown in the drawing below.

Handedness   Handedness (see pp. 139-140) plays an important role in the bathroom. The size of the bathroom dictates the number of options available for arranging the fixtures so that there is clear space on both sides and in front of the toilet, at both ends of the bathing system and at the lavatory. People who use wheelchairs must transfer from their chair to the toilet. Ideally, each toilet would be neutrally handed. That is, it would be located so an individual could perform a lateral transfer from the right or the left or approach the toilet straight on. The bathtub or shower also should provide clear space and good handgrips at both ends so that someone may move into it from a position of strength.

Bathroom with Two Doors

Two doors into a bathroom allow the bathroom to be reached from either a private bedroom area or from a public area. Either hinged or pocket doors may be used.

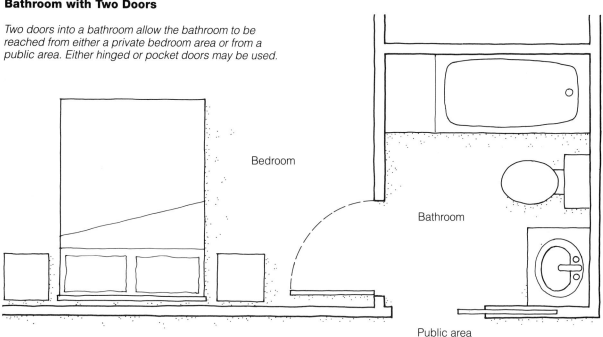

Bedroom

Bathroom

Public area

In our evaluations, we have found time after time that, even in large bathrooms, too little attention is given to proper access and handedness. Toilets are often enclosed in a small walled-in area that dictate that the users must be able to get to and on the toilet without assistance because there's no room for a helper to stand.

Some people need to approach the toilet from the right side and will need a strong, sturdy handhold or surface on that side to assist them in transferring or in lowering themselves to the toilet seat. Other people may do best approaching the toilet from the front or the left. You can't predict which approach will be the best, as people change. You can't predict who will eventually live in the house. You can't predict the abilities of guests. You do know that people are diverse and that neutral handedness will serve everyone. If you have the space, the wisest approach would be to position the fixtures so that they are neutrally handed.

Handholds All bathrooms should have a generous supply of handholds. By "handholds," we mean more than simple grab bars. All of us like to have something to hang onto when we bend, stoop, kneel, squat or climb, especially if we're standing on wet floors. A handhold can be a bar, rail, shelf, armrest, countertop or ledge that has been designed to help support the weight of an individual while getting up or sitting down, or to provide a steadying prop. Handholds can be a ledge built around the bathtub, grab bars that double as towel racks, pull-down grab bars or vanities. Handholds should be capable of supporting up to 300 lb. They should not have any sharp edges, and they should not protrude into areas that are passages or that someone is likely to use for arm movement. Finally, they should be attractive.

Many people despise the institutional look of conventional stainless-steel grab bars. Resources on pp. 189-191 mentions some companies that make entire lines of bathroom furnishings that add beauty and continuity to the bathroom decor. The photos above and on the following pages offer some idea of the products available.

Too often, grab bars are used as quick fixes to cover up poor bathroom and fixture design. Many people who study the ANSI standards come away with the idea that they can make a bathroom accessible by merely throwing in a couple of grab bars. But this is only a minimally acceptable solution.

Grab bars should be used liberally in the bathroom. They should be put anywhere the bather,

Pressalit's Multi System allows users to adjust the position and height of each product to their individual needs. This versatile system, from Denmark, is available from American Standard. (Photo: American Standard.)

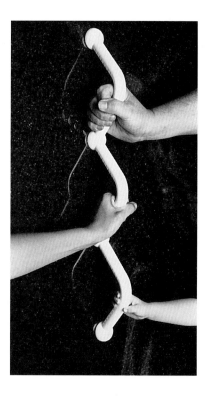

A bathtub with seat and grab bars installed according to ANSI 117.1. This bathtub was used in the authors' research to evaluate the usability of an ANSI bathtub. (Photo: Institute for Technology Development.)

The Ableware multi-level handgrip (right) mounts vertically in the shower, over the tub or next to the toilet. (Photo: courtesy Bel-Art Products.)

Blocking and Backing for Secure Grab Bars

Conventional Method

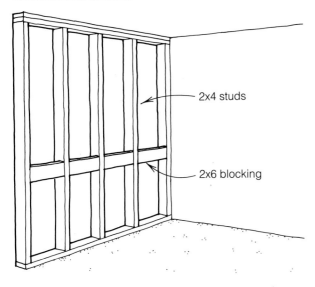

2x4 studs

2x6 blocking

2x6 blocking installed horizontally between wall studs at an appropriate height can serve as backing for grab bars. This method is relatively inexpensive, but the grab bar must be secured directly to the blocks, so the location of the grab bar is limited. The location of the blocking should be recorded so that it can be found later.

This grab bar can help a person who needs some support to use the toilet. It's attractive, available in various colors and folds easily out of the way. (Photo: courtesy HEWI.)

Better Method

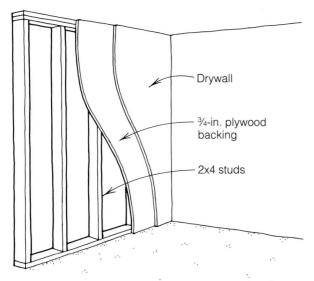

Drywall

¾-in. plywood backing

2x4 studs

Another way to provide grab-bar backing is to sheathe the entire wall in ¾-in. plywood. This approach costs more, but has the advantage of allowing grab bars to be installed later at any location on the wall.

dresser or groomer is likely to make a change in body position. Use the grab bar as a towel bar and a decorator item.

We believe that grab bars and a full series of handholds should be installed in every new bathroom. It is shortsighted to add blocking to the walls when they are built, only to leave the grab bars out "until they are needed." A good system of handholds makes every bathroom safer. And no one has yet found a way to predict when someone will require extra accessibility. The drawing at left shows the recommended methods for installing blocking and backing for grab bars in and around the bathtub, toilet and shower.

A number of grab-bar systems are designed to be used around the toilet (see the photo above). Some are spring loaded and are pulled down to their use position or pushed back up against the wall by the user. These products look somewhat institutional (though many are available in decorator lines). Although many people will find that leaning on the grab bars while using the toilet or using the support while sitting and rising is convenient and comfortable, most will avoid putting these grab bars in until they are needed.

Grab bars should have a maximum exterior diameter of 1½ in. Incidentally, they don't need to be just a straight cylindrical rod. The grab bar shown in the photo at bottom right on p. 168 provides a handhold for steadying and angles to help people pull themselves up.

FIXTURES

In 1966, Alexander Kira wrote a major treatise on the bathroom, carefully documenting the appropriate dimensions to conform to the human form. His suggestions included changing the shape and location of the sink, toilet and bath fixtures. For example, he redesigned the sink to be shallower and wider in front to catch water from dripping elbows and deeper at the rear for easier hair washing. Few, if any, of Kira's recommendations have been adopted. Kira's study concentrated on the shapes and dimensions of plumbing fixtures that would facilitate personal hygiene and toileting activities. Most of his recommendations for bathing and toileting products, while functionally and physiologically correct, were inconsistent with the fixtures used and accepted in virtually all of the Western world. It is likely that his recommendations have met with resistance because they advocated too great a change.

Basic bathroom fixtures include the bathing system (bathtub, shower or combination), toilet and sink. Although fancy bathrooms may also include a whirlpool tub, a bidet and a sauna or spa, this chapter will focus on bathing systems, toilets and sinks. However, the criteria for safety and usability for the bathing system also apply to the sauna, whirlpool or steam bath.

Bathing systems   Bathtubs and showers need to be usable by people of all ages and abilities. They also need to be safe, fit extremes in body sizes from a small child to a very large adult, and be easy to clean.

In our research, we have found that many people regularly alternate between taking a bath and taking a shower. We have also found that as people's range of motion and mobility becomes impaired, their options become more and more limited. Those who have some form of physical limitation but who don't require the use of an assistive device seem to be able to continue to use either a bathtub or shower. Those who use a walker, cane or crutch have more trouble using a shower, while those who use wheelchairs frequently have the greatest freedom using a shower. It is rare for someone with a disability to have the option of bathing or showering. Usually only one fixture in the home has been adapted for their use. Many relegated to only taking a shower long for the ability to soak in the tub. Some of the new accessible systems provide both accessible showering and bathing.

Most tubs are made of fiberglass (or some other plastic-like material) or enameled cast iron, steel or vitreous china. They have a hard surface that is treated to be nonslip. One or two manufacturers produce a "soft" bathtub. These tubs have a foam base with a heavy, vinyl-like covering.

Traditional bathtubs have a number of problems, and the older one gets the more apparent these problems become. Most oblong bathtubs range in length from 58 in. to 72 in., in width from 30 in. to 32 in. and in depth from 12 in. to 18 in. These dimensions do not seem out of line with the human form, but unfortunately, when coupled with the design of the traditional tub, they create problems for users of all ages. Some people are unable to step over the side of the tub; others cannot sit on the floor of the tub and then pull themselves back up; still others cannot reach the faucet when they are seated at one end of the tub. The traditional bathtub may be too wide for some people to be able to reach a grab bar mounted on the wall.

The tub in the photo at bottom left on p. 168 meets the ANSI standards for bathtubs: a conventional tub equipped with grab bars and an 18-in. seat at one end or an in-tub seat. There are no specifications for the in-tub seat except that it has to be able to bear bending stress, shear force and tensile force of 250 lbf on its seat and mountings. The seat at one end of the tub has to be at least 15 in. wide.

ANSI Requirements for Clear Floor Space at Bathtubs

A. With Seat in Tub

B. With Seat at Head of Tub

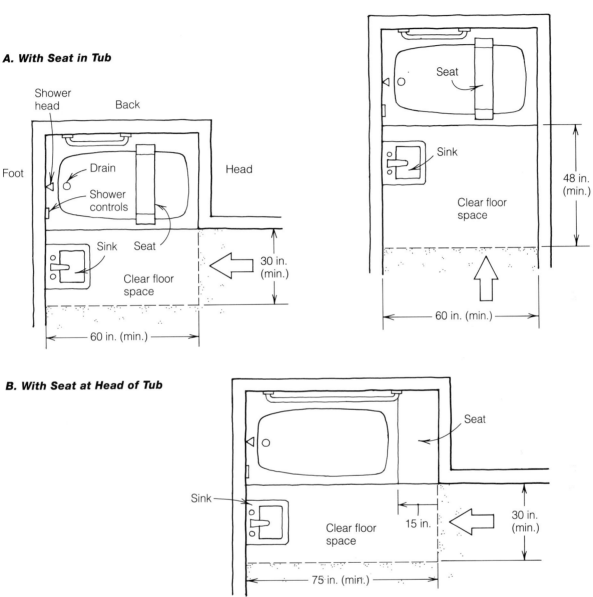

The bathtubs and room configurations shown in the ANSI standards should not be considered as the recommended system, but the bare minimum. The arrangements shown in the drawing above have many problems for ambulatory as well as wheelchair users, although the sinks, which are open underneath, would allow someone in a wheelchair to maneuver near the controls. There is insufficient space and a requirement for contorting the body that will make these bathrooms more difficult for ambulatory people, particularly those who use other assistive products or who may have back problems.

In our research study (see pp. 3-6), we compared three different bathing systems: a tub installed according to ANSI standards with a seat and full complement of grab bars, the Comfort Care system and a 36-in. by 36-in. shower. The ANSI tub, the most difficult to use, was a terrifying test of courage and strength for some of our research subjects. Although the tub, with the 18-in. seat and the grab bars encircling it at two heights, appears to be user friendly, the depth and length of the tub created some significant problems. On several occasions our research assistants had to help lift a participant out of the tub who was unable to get out independently. Several other subjects who were unable to use their legs were able to maneuver onto the 18-in. seat, but when they tried to slide down into the tub, their legs just got in the way and crumpled or gathered in front of them.

Most of the new accessible bathing systems on the market today seem to offer better help to people with physical limitations than the tub meeting ANSI standards, but we have not tested all of them and thus can not come to definitive conclusions. To our way of thinking, these specially marketed "accessible" or "handicap" tubs that are built to accommodate varying needs and a larger number of people should be marketed as "general family" tubs. It is the traditional bathtub that should be labeled "special" because it demands the most strength and agility to use.

Locating Handholds around the Bathtub

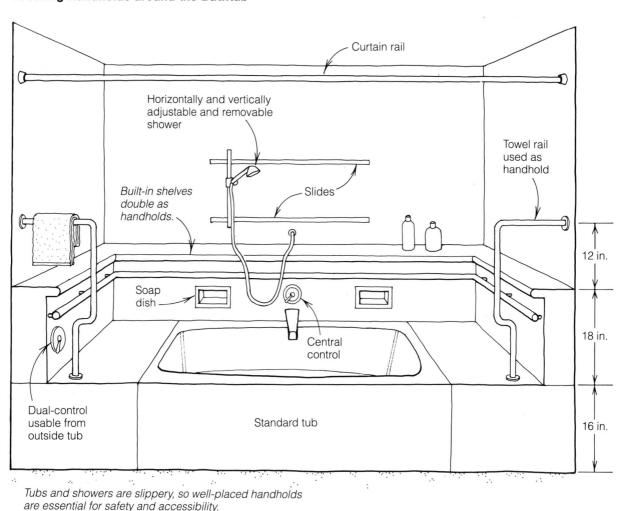

Tubs and showers are slippery, so well-placed handholds are essential for safety and accessibility.

The Precedence tub (above) and the BathEase (right) allow the bather to open a door to enter, thereby eliminating the troublesome need to step over the side. Both of these tubs are equipped with seats. (Photo above: © 1991 by Kohler Co., reprinted by permission of Kohler Co., Kohler, Wisconsin; photo at right: courtesy BathEase.)

The ideal bathtub may not yet exist, but here are some of the criteria that a good accessible tub should meet:

• Minimal risk of falling. The tub should be designed so that the bather never has to stand up in it.

• Safe and easy entry and exit. Handholds and support should be available at every turn.

• Access and control of the water temperature, flow and drain within the optimal reach zone from outside of the bathing system. Everything should be easy to reach from whatever seated position a bather would take in the tub.

• Recessed faucets, faucet handles, soap receptacles and shelving in and around the tub. Nothing should protrude into areas where elbows, heads, knees or other parts of the body would come into contact with them.

The photos above and on the following pages show a sampling of the accessible bathing products available today. The Precedence, produced by Kohler, looks almost like the traditional shower/tub combination except for the door in its side and the seat. This tub enables the user to walk into it, shut the door and then begin filling it. This tub has the advantage of not requiring you to step over the side, but you still will either stand or sit on the seat molded into the tub. Additionally, the doorway and dimensions of the tub are not large enough for a wheelchair user to maneuver in and transfer.

Like the Precedence, another product, BathEase, has a door in its side and a seat molded at one end. This product is designed for people able to walk into and out of the tub.

Many other tubs have doors to facilitate entry. A recent introduction to the market by Silcraft has a door in the side and a molded seat that is tilted to help the bather sit back. The Freedom Bath from Grand Traverse Technologies has a door that rolls away into the frame (manually or automatically). The bather opens the door and gets onto the seat, swings or pulls in the legs, then closes the door. This product eliminates the problem of stepping into the tub, but some users may have difficulty with it because it may not have enough handholds. (It is wise to test a product like this before buying it.)

Other tubs with doors are shown in the photos on the facing page. Like the Silcraft tub, they have a molded seat and a door that seals with the water pres-sure. Unlike the Silcraft tub, they are fairly deep. Two bathing systems available in the domestic American market have a tub that rotate around the user. The Comfort Care System from Ferno Washington, has the user sit on a tray that is mounted at a height of about 19 in. After lifting the legs onto the tray, the user turns a small lever that releases the bathing tube that rotates up and around the body. The user gently pushes on the inside edge to lock the tube into place.

Many people who have seen the Comfort Care System are thrilled with it. They quickly surmise that it will help them get in and out of the tub safely. We tested this tub in one of our research studies and were surprised. First, a number of subjects were able to use this tub and not the ANSI standards tub. But we also

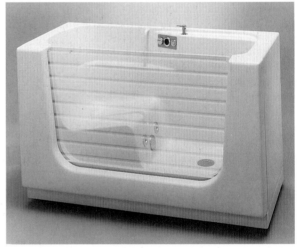

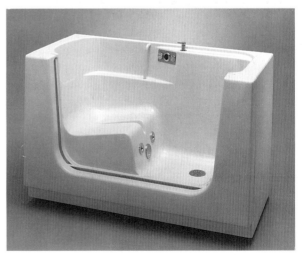

The Silcraft Access 3700 (above) has a seat height that may facilitate transfer from a wheelchair. The Freedom Bath (above right and right) has a door that rolls out of the way when open. (Photo above: Silcraft; photos above right and right: Grand Traverse Technologies.)

found a sizable number who could still not use this bathing system at all, or who found the 36-in. sq. shower easier. Wheelchair users especially objected to the lack of handholds on the system, which made transferring difficult.

The final tub in the assistive tub series is the Dignity Bath. The seat of the Dignity Bath swivels out so the person outside the tub may transfer easily to the seat. The seat swivels in and lowers the bather into the tub.

Tubs with floors elevated to a height of 18 in. to 20 in. (such as the Comfort Care below and the Safe-T-Bath) have several advantages. First, they make it much easier to bathe young children. You don't have to get down on your hands and knees, but you can sit comfortably next to the tub in a chair. Raised tubs are much easier to clean. And you are less likely to fall because because you do not step into these products, but sit down and slide into them.

Faucets and drain controls on bathtubs should be located so they can be reached easily from outside as well as inside the tub. The drain control is usually centered at the end of the tub, under the faucets. Depending on the amount of clear space outside of the tub, operating this control may require only a 15-in. to 16-in. reach. If, as in many homes, the bathtub is right next to the sink or toilet, the reach is greater because the user can't squeeze between the fixtures to reach the faucet or drain. An ideal location for controls is on the wall near the outer edge of the tub.

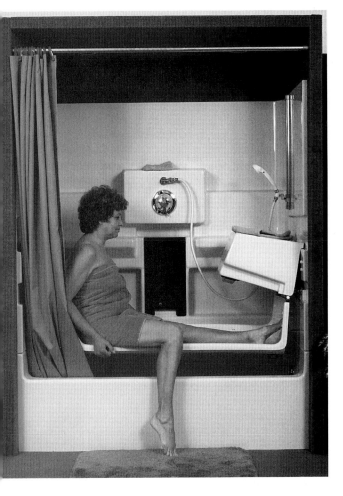

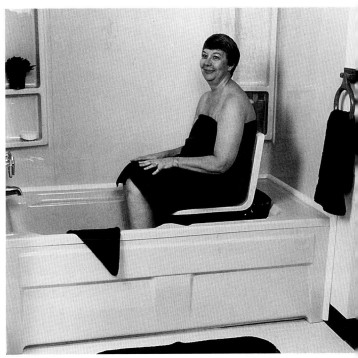

The Comfort Care System (left) fits into a traditional bathtub footprint. It combines a seat tray and a rotating bathing tube. The user sits on the tray, then the tube rotates under the bather to put the bather into the tub. The Dignity Bath (above) has a seat that swivels into and out of the tub. (Photo left: Ferno Washington; photo above: Electric Mobility.)

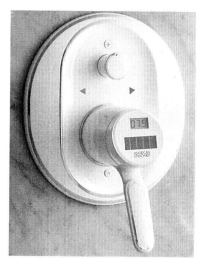

Antiscald faucets are available from several manufacturers, including American Standard (far left) and Delta Faucet (left). Both faucets feature a maximum temperature setting (a screw that limits the travel of the temperature handle) and a pressure-balance system that equalizes the hot and cold water at the faucet if usage elsewhere in the plumbing system (toilet flush) unbalances the flow. (Photo far left: American Standard; photo left: Delta Faucet.)

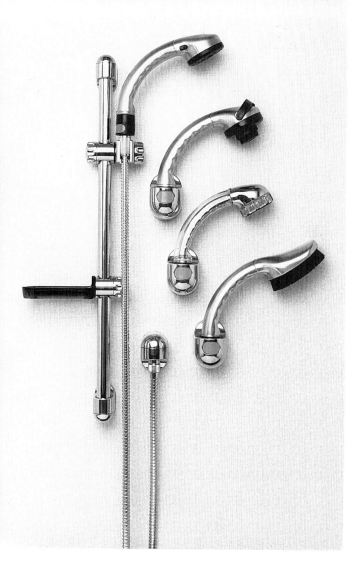

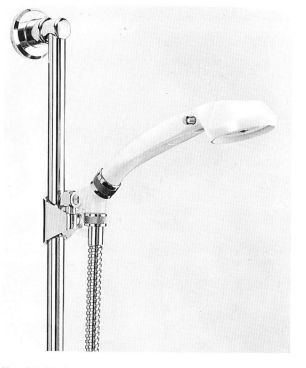

Hand-held showers by Grohe, shown at left, come with various spray nozzles and a large handle for easy gripping. The shower head is mounted on the connection bar and can be adjusted to a convenient height. Above is a hand-held adjustable personal shower (Alsons 1521PB) with push-button volume control. Several spray-handle models are available. (Photo at left: Grohe; photo above: Alsons Corporation.)

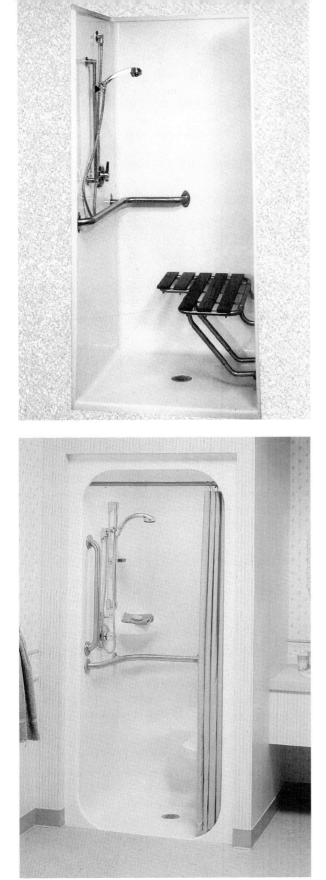

We recommend the use of an antiscald water-control system (see the top photos on the facing page). This system mixes and regulates the water so that it meets a preset temperature; some other products also provide a color-coded indicator of the water temperature. Another feature that prevents scalding is a screw that can be adjusted to limit the travel of the faucet handle, thereby setting a maximum temperature position. Antiscald systems also have a pressure-balance system: a piston in the faucet changes the size of the openings for the hot or cold water in response to changes in pressure. For example if someone flushes the toilet while the shower is in use, the cold-water pressure drops; the higher pressure on the hot-water side pushes the piston toward the cold-water side of the faucet, reducing the size of the inlet holes on the hot-water side and increasing them on the cold-water side.

Faucets should be easy to understand. Some, unfortunately, have separate and confusing controls for the temperature and the water shut-off. Lever-handled faucets are much easier to use than round, cylindrical or knurled knobs.

Hand-held shower heads for the bathtub are delightful plumbing accessories, and they double as standard shower heads as well (see the bottom photos on the facing page). Look for units that attach and detach easily, glide up and down the post and offer a variable spray. Avoid systems with difficult-to-use knobs or small dials and controls.

All kinds of showers are available. In our study we found that a standard 36-in. by 36-in. shower with a 4-in. threshold, an 18-in. seat and abundant handholds (grab bars all away around the interior, grab bar/towel bar on the outside and a sturdy seat) was accessible to more of our research subjects than the ANSI bathtub or the Comfort Care System. The bathers in our research study found support for their

Two 36-in. by 36-in. shower units. The Summit 36 SM one-piece shower stall by Universal-Rundle (above left) has a sturdy bench mounted at a height of 19 in. The Aqua Glass Model SC 4186 (left) includes an 18-in. deep molded seat (barely visible on the right) and a Grohe thermostatic and pressure-balanced valve with a Grohe hand-held shower. (Photo above left: Universal-Rundle; photo left: courtesy Aqua Glass.)

A 36-in. by 60-in. one-piece fiberglass shower (Summit 60SM) is large enough to accommodate a person sitting in a wheelchair. The drain is located out of the way, near the rear wall. (Photo: Universal-Rundle.)

This Silcraft shower has a molded seat with a depth of 14 in. and a width of 28 in. Interior shower dimensions are 36 in. by 43 in. These showers are available in knock-down models, so all pieces can fit through a 30-in. wide doorway. (Photo: Silcraft Corporation.)

movements everywhere they turned and always had some form of handhold within reach.

A 30-in. by 60-in. shower mounted flush with the floor lets someone in a wheelchair wheel right into it. This is also a good size for bathing the dog or a couple of kids simultaneously. See Resources on pp. 189-191 for a comprehensive listing of accessible shower manufacturers and their products.

Some showers with molded-in shower seats and grab bars are not very functional. A shower seat should be at least 15 in. deep, a depth that allows the user to sit on it without having to brace with the legs to keep from sliding out. This depth is about the average depth for many seats and chairs we use much of the time, although it may be a little deep for young children (five-year-olds are best served by a depth of

10 in.). Seats that fold up can be a good choice, provided they are easy to raise and lower.

The controls on a shower unit should be reached easily from outside of the shower enclosure. The shower door shouldn't prohibit the user from getting within 18 in. of the controls.

Perhaps the most accessible bathing area of all is the "wet room" (a room with a built-in shower area). Because it is not itself a bathing system, it doesn't possess any of the problems of accessibility encountered in bath and shower systems. The wet room is a great equalizer and a truly multi-purpose room. The sidebar on pp. 179-180 describes the wet room in greater detail. We recommend that a wet room be included in all new home designs.

The Wet Room

The wet room is an alternative to a manufactured bathing system. The built-in shower area could be in one corner or behind a partition wall, but whatever its location, the only thing that distinguishes the shower area from the rest of the room is that there is a drain and the floor has a slight slope to it to keep the water flowing toward the drain.

The wet room should be tiled (or have some other surface treatment) with a waterproof surface. A number of tiles and floor coverings designed for wet areas claim nonslip properties (see Resources on p. 97), although soap build-up on the floor can sometimes negate the nonslip properties.

The wet room has no barriers to overcome. The shower area can be outfitted with an attractive built-in seat. Soap holders can be recessed into the wall so no one will bump into them.

The open floor area allows a wheelchair or walker user to walk into the bathing area and to use a sturdy shower chair, stand or shower wheelchair. The wet room, because the shower area is larger, may provide shower space for more than one person. It is also a great place for washing the dog.

The best method for enclosing the wet room is to construct it in a corner using two room walls and a third wall to keep the shower spray and water confined. The least expensive method would be to use a shower curtain to keep the splash from spreading too far. While the curtain helps, it does not contain the spray as well as the more enclosed structure, and the curtain doesn't offer the bather any

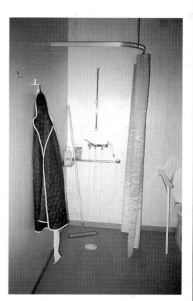

This simple, and somewhat sterile looking, wet room offers the fundamental concept without any frills. A toilet is located next to the shower.

Interior decorator Susan Behar designed this wet room for her daughter. The toilet is located around the corner from the shower. (Photo: Dan Forer.)

support. The drawing below shows suggested features for a fully accessible wet room.

The floors and the walls of the bathroom adjacent to the wet areas need to be impervious to water. The floors and walls should be designed and build by someone experienced in building floors and walls that will be subjected to water.

The floor needs to slope gently toward the drain, enough so that the water will run off but not so much that it will be hazardous or difficult to negotiate. A slope of about 1:50 should be adequate.

With so much water in the air, wet rooms need a good ventilation system and careful planning. The shower area needs to be separated and protected. Soggy toilet paper isn't much use, and a wet toilet seat isn't anyone's idea of comfort.

Electrical outlets must be located away from the shower area, and ground-fault circuit interrupters (see p. 84) are absolutely essential. In planning the location of outlets, be sure to take into account the splash and spray of the shower.

Planning the Wet Room

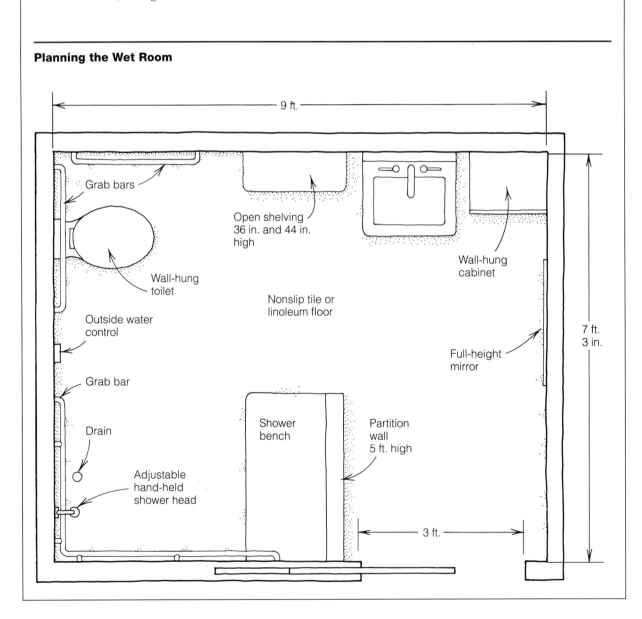

9 ft.

Grab bars

Open shelving 36 in. and 44 in. high

Wall-hung cabinet

Wall-hung toilet

Nonslip tile or linoleum floor

Outside water control

Full-height mirror

7 ft. 3 in.

Grab bar

Drain

Shower bench

Partition wall 5 ft. high

Adjustable hand-held shower head

3 ft.

Sinks The sink (lavatory) and its immediate surroundings can work for or against a good bathroom. It is difficult to manage one's daily preparations when there is little or no space around the sink, yet a lavish vanity and countertop can eat up valuable space that may be needed for maneuverability.

There are four basic types of bathroom sinks: wall-hung, pedestal, legged and drop-in. The wall-hung and pedestal sinks are usually freestanding. The wall-hung does not take up any floor space, while the pedestal usually requires only a few square inches. Although these sinks don't reduce maneuverability, they don't provide any storage areas and they won't hold much paraphernalia. Storage on a shelf above the sink may be beyond the reach of many people.

On sinks that are open underneath, the drain and hot-water pipes should be covered or insulated to prevent a person from being burned. Many people cover the pipes with a foam insulation sleeve, which is effective, but not too attractive. A better choice might be to build a baffle, as shown in the drawing on p. 152.

One compromise that allows for maneuverability, storage and work space is to build vanities that have an open space under the sink and drawer storage on at least one side, as shown in the drawing at right. Drawers provide significantly greater usable space than fixed shelves and are much easier to use.

A wheelchair-accessible lavatory needs to have about 29 in. of clearance from the floor to the bottom of the front of the sink. A sink with a depth of 4 in. is adequate, but, as Alexander Kira demonstrated in his work, a bowl with a depth of 3 in. at the front sloping to a depth of 6 in. to 7 in. at the rear provides adequate space for cleansing the face, washing hands and washing hair.

Large bathrooms offer greater opportunities for flexible design. Rather than mounting two sinks on the counter at the same height, one could be mounted for seated use and the other could be mounted for a more comfortable standing use, as shown in the drawing on p. 182.

Kira demonstrated that many ambulatory people do not wish to have the counter at the frequently used height of 30 in. to 31 in. This height requires many individuals to bend over considerably to get their face close to the water source (which could be slightly lower than the counter height). Many would be better served by a height of 36 in. to 38 in., which would allow them to stand more erect and in a more relaxed position.

Individuals seated in a wheelchair, as well as people who would like to use the sink and grooming area while seated, are best served by 32-in. high counters, with a sink-bowl depth that slopes from 3 in. to about 5 in. to 7 in. to accommodate the user's legs. A height of 32 in. is a good compromise for tall, short and seated persons.

Just as we recommend multiple work-surface heights in the kitchen, we also recommend this consideration for the bathroom. Villeroy and Boch produces an adjustable lavatory that combines beauty, flexibility and accessibility. Unfortunately, this product is expensive.

An Accessible Vanity

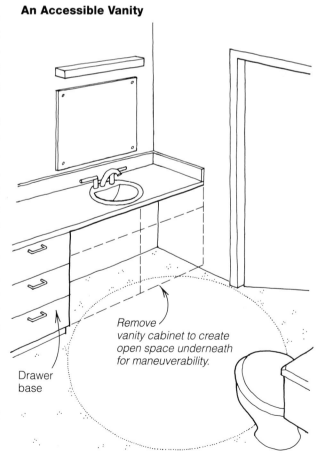

Remove vanity cabinet to create open space underneath for maneuverability.

Drawer base

Two Sinks

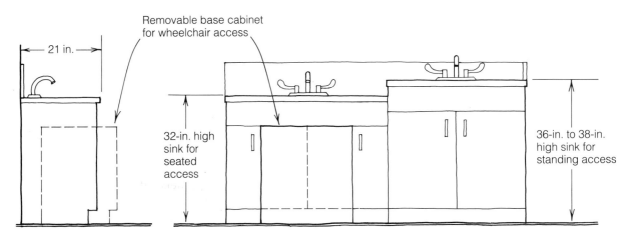

21 in.

Removable base cabinet for wheelchair access

32-in. high sink for seated access

36-in. to 38-in. high sink for standing access

If space allows for two sinks, make one of them suitable for use while standing and the other for sitting.

This typical sink faucet (above) provides great accessibility for water and temperature control, but users with limited finger dexterity have trouble operating the drain control at the back of the fixture. The detachable faucet at right, although sold for use in kitchen sinks, is equally useful in the bathroom. (Photo above: Delta Faucet.)

If a single sink is to be used, then the most practical solution is to build a counter and sink or vanity and sink arrangement at a height that would accommodate seated use. If an open area under the sink is unappealing, removable vanity cabinets can be installed. The few extra feet of flooring material installed under the vanity will be negligible in the overall cost of the project and will save a lot of trouble should the need or desire ever arise for a seated vanity area.

Some so-called accessible faucet and drain sets can be very frustrating. Faucets are outfitted with easy-to-use levers, but the drain control is a tiny plunger located behind the spout. You have to have extremely nimble fingers to be able to reach and manipulate this control. An old-fashioned rubber drain plug on a chain would be much easier to use.

Faucet sets should be within reach. Beware of elongated "handicap" faucets that must be mounted almost entirely beyond the reach of many seated users. An easy seated forward reach for women ranges from 18 in. to 21 in. and for men from 20 in. to 22 in. If the sink or counter is particularly deep, the controls could be moved to one side of the sink to make them easier to reach. Another unconventional recommendation is to consider installing one of the new decorator kitchen faucets with a pull-out hand-held spray in the bathroom sink. These are very handy for washing hair.

Toilets The toilet is a simple, yet elegant contraption. Most continue to operate year after year with only minor attention, and when repair is needed the solution is usually obvious and inexpensive. Yet despite its mechanical simplicity, using a toilet requires strength and agility. The standard flush toilet has changed very little in design in over a century. But the standard flush toilet isn't built to accommodate everyone. The height of a standard chair is 17½ in. to 18½ in., while the seat height of a standard toilet is 15 in. to 15½ in. The lower height is almost impossible for some people to use.

Many manufacturers offer "handicap" toilets with an 18-in. seat height. This is a good height for wheelchair users, since the seats on most wheelchairs are 18 in. to 19 in. high. But 18 in. is too high for a frail, 5-ft. tall woman, whose feet wouldn't even touch the ground once she was seated. Toilets aren't

manufactured with handholds on them, compounding the difficulty for many in using them.

A few entrepreneurs have developed toilets with seats that can lower and raise the user to and from a sitting position. Hydra-Commode offers a relatively simple mechanism with two hydraulic pistons, connectors and tubing to the toilet water supply. The small Hydra-Commode frame fits onto the toilet, to which the regular toilet seat is attached. The hydraulic system lifts the seat up and forward. An electrically operated version, shown in the photo below, is offered by Med/West.

Wall-mounted toilets offer some advantages over floor-mounted toilets. They provide additional clear floor space and they are easy to clean under (see the drawing on p. 184). The University of Wisconsin-

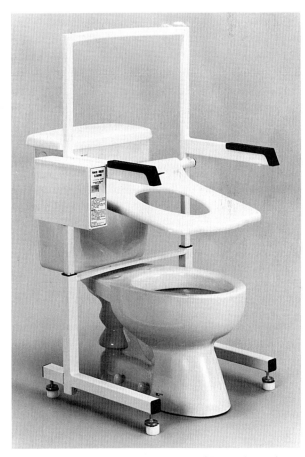

The power elevating toilet from Med/West lifts and tilts the seat to gently lower and raise the user. (Photo: courtesy Med/West.)

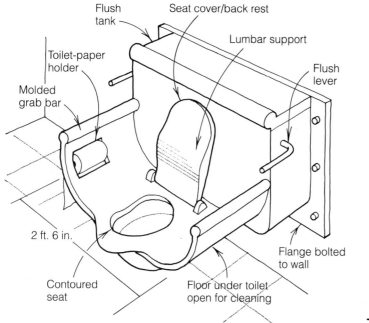

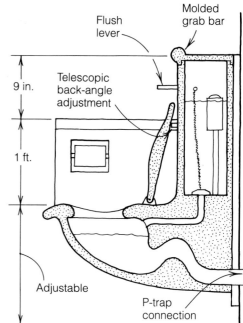

Stout has developed a model commode that is built into a surround with armrests. It has built-in handholds and is reminiscent of a molded whirlpool bath. Although this commode system lacks the ability to lift or lower the user, it does provide built-in surfaces as handholds and could be an "attractive" fixture. A smaller version of this concept that is perhaps less conspicuously different from the "normal" toilet may be more acceptable to the marketplace.

NONSLIP FLOORING

Slippery flooring is a hazard in the bathroom and should be avoided. One important term for selecting suitable bathroom flooring, which is used by most flooring manufacturers, is the coefficient of friction (COF). Simply put, this is the amount of grip or resistance to slipping of a surface; the higher the number, the less slippery the surface. There is no standard method of measuring the coefficient of friction; consequently, information available from manufacturers on the coefficient of friction for their flooring products may be difficult to interpret.

A 1988 study by the Pennsylvania Transportation Institute at Pennsylvania State University measured the changes in slip resistance when several flooring materials were wetted with water with a small amount of detergent in it. Metal-troweled concrete changed from a COF of .55 when dry to a low COF of .16 when wetted with detergent water. Ceramic tile changed from a COF of .7 when dry to .59 when wetted with detergent water, and terrazzo varied from a dry COF of .49 to a detergent-water COF of .42. Three types of resilient tiles were also tested. Their COFs varied from a high of .89, .86 and .70 when dry to lows of .52, .62 and .45 respectively when wetted with detergent water.

People vary in their demand for nonslip surfaces. People without mobility impairments can get by with coefficients of friction as low as .3, while people with mobility impairments, particularly those using assistive devices such as crutches, canes, walkers and artificial limbs, need coefficients of friction ranging from .7 to 1.0. The researchers at Penn State estimated that 88% of the population would be "protected" by a coefficient of friction of .6 for flat surfaces and .8 for ramps (1:12 grade).

Many new ceramic tiles, vinyl and rubber-base linoleum have significantly improved slip resistance. Some nonglazed ceramic tiles have coefficients of friction as high as .8 and .9. These tiles are designed for use in wet areas, thus they are likely to maintain fairly good grip even when wet. (Soap build-up, however, is another story.)

Linoleum products have a greater degree of resiliency than tiles and may help prevent injury in the event of a slip or fall in the bathroom. Some, such as Tarkett (manufactured in Sweden), have been designed for both their cushioning and their slip resistance. For a list of manufacturers and distributors of nonslip flooring, see Resources on p. 97.

BATHROOM STORAGE

Linen closets in bathrooms often seem to be afterthoughts, with doors so narrow that they are difficult for everyone to use to their fullest. The accessible bathroom allows all users to gain access to the storage spaces. Access means that there should be clear space in front of the storage area. If the storage area is deep-er than 18 in., the opening should be at least 32 in. wide. The door or covering should be operable with one hand and should not require fine fingering.

Be generous with bathroom storage space — people rarely complain of having too much. People with physical limitations and chronic health problems often use several assistive products in the bathroom that they may wish to store out of sight, yet have readily at hand.

LIGHTING, VENTILATION AND HEATING

A bathroom needs both natural and artificial light. Mold and mildew are less likely to grow in a sunny bathroom. Lighting is needed at the sink, the grooming mirror and the bathing areas (see the drawing below). At the sink, lighting should be directed downward toward the bowl. As in the other parts of the house, be sure that the lighting is positioned or diffused so that it doesn't shine directly into the eyes of a seated or short person.

Bathroom Lighting and Ventilation

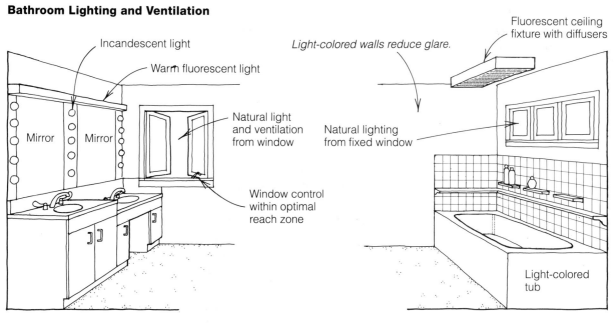

Lighting at Sink

Lighting at Tub

At the grooming mirror, lighting should be positioned on both sides and above. Be generous with lighting in this area. Incandescent or a warm fluorescent light is best at the mirror because it is closest to the spectrum of sunlight and will enhance the warm tones.

Windows in the bathroom are important for ventilation as well as lighting. Bathroom windows are often installed at a higher level than usual to ensure privacy. If this is the case, be sure that they can be opened from a height within the optimal reach zone (20 in. to 44 in. off the floor). You might also consider keeping the windows at a normal height and providing privacy by means of a visual barrier on the outside of the house, such as bushes or a small fenced-in garden.

Don't overlook the lighting in the bathing area. Scrutinize the built-in lighting in the enclosed shower. Will it provide adequate light for the aging eye when the shower is full of steam? Is the lighting over and around the bathtub equally distributed, nonglaring and adequate so that the bather will not be confused by shadows or blinded by glare? Can the bather see to get into the tub?

All outlets in the bathroom should contain ground-fault circuit interrupters (see p. 84). Locate plenty of outlets around the grooming mirror. One double-socket outlet just isn't enough anymore. A strip of electric outlets or an electrical outlet track may be better. Keep electrical outlets away from the bathing system.

Exhaust fans and in-room heaters are important accessories in bathrooms. An exhaust fan in climates prone to mold and mildew is an investment in the war against grime. A good exhaust system is a necessity for interior bathrooms without a window and for bathrooms in cold climates .

In-room heating systems (infrared heat lamps or wall-mounted units) are important for people who have difficulty regulating their body temperature, particularly in cold climates. For many people, a slight chill when getting out of the tub or shower is a minor inconvenience, but for others, a chill can ruin the positive effects of a soak in the tub. Some people start to ache when they get cold, and the aching may not stop for hours.

Be careful with coil wall-heater units. Don't put a towel bar near the units, and locate them where the bather is unlikely to fall or brush up against them. Remember, some people have no feeling in parts of their body and may not realize that they are burning themselves.

Mirrors   Bathrooms often have a single, fixed mirror over the sink. Consider installing a tilting mirror instead, to allow children and seated people the opportunity to adjust the mirror to their liking. Also, put a full-length mirror in the grooming or dressing area. A full-length mirror accommodates everyone, regardless of size, age or abilities.

You might want to consider a lighted magnifying mirror, which is mounted on a swinging or telescoping arm. These mirrors are helpful to people with vision problems, and they can be easily adjusted to suit the individual.

EVALUATING BATHROOM FLOOR PLANS

Given enough space, it is fairly easy to design an accessible bathroom. In this section we will examine three typical floor plans that illustrate the basic design issues of a barrier-free bathroom, especially handedness and movement within the space.

A small wheelchair-accessible bathroom   The drawing at left on the facing page shows a small bathroom that is just barely wheelchair accessible. It is unlikely that all wheelchair riders could use this bathroom, however, because the spaces between the fixtures are fairly minimal.

The doorway is 3 ft. wide and enters into an area that has a clear diameter of 5 ft. This clear floor space is possible because of the open space under the vanity and the use of a wall-hung toilet.

The location of the toilet is not ideal, although it may be approached from either side by a wheelchair user capable of transferring to the toilet from a front angle. One disadvantage of this bathroom is that the person on the toilet has no privacy if the door isn't closed. Also, if the door of the bathroom is left open, the view would be of the toilet. Most people don't find toilets aesthetically pleasing.

Note the bathtub in this drawing. Although the approach at the end adjacent to the toilet would be difficult for someone in a wheelchair, this bathtub does offer seating at both ends. A seated entry to the bathtub may in fact be safer than a standing entry, although we are unaware of any research supporting the claim.

The bathtub has an 18-in. wide bench at each end. The user would sit on the bench, swing his or her legs over the side into the tub, and then slide down. In our research we found that some people have problems sliding into the tub. Because of the nonslip surfaces, the feet and legs do not necessarily slide smoothly along the bottom surface of the tub. People with weak or paralyzed legs may find that the weight of their body carries them down into the tub,

but their legs are caught underneath them. When people move into the tub from a seated entry they do not necessarily slide in. The legs and feet are used to brace themselves as they lower themselves from one level to the other.

We also found that the seated entry did not work for a number of people who are not strong enough to pull themselves back out of the tub. Although they could lower themselves into the tub, they couldn't get out.

A less accessible bathroom The drawing below shows another small bathroom. Note in this particular layout that people using a wheelchair could get to the toilet from the front or the right side (facing the toilet). (On the right side they could back alongside the toilet or pull up facing it.) The area could be open under the sink and storage located on the right side.

A Small Wheelchair-Accessible Bathroom

A Less Accessible Bathroom

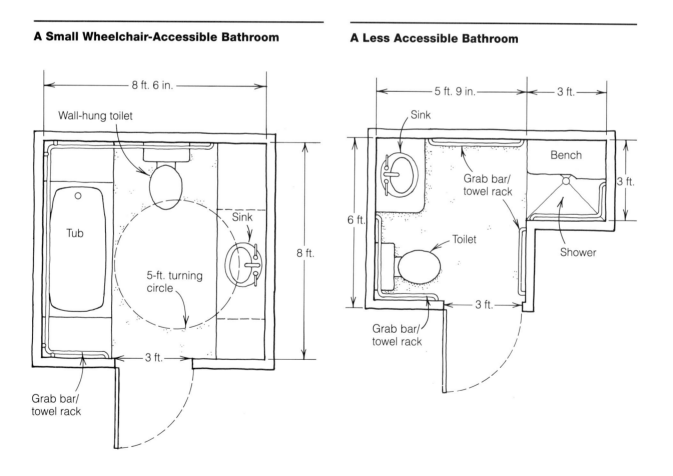

Although this particular bathroom doesn't have a 5-ft. diameter area for maneuvering a wheelchair, it does provide just enough space for some maneuverability. However, both the shower and toilet are accessible only from the front and one side.

One nice feature of a small bathroom is that it may provide enough handholds to people who are unsteady or need some support for walking that they may travel around the bathroom without having to use their walker, cane or crutches. In this bathroom, grab/towel bar beginning at the edge of the shower could extend to the area by the sink. The edge of the sink/lavatory would serve as a support surface to the other wall, which also has a grab/towel bar surrounding the toilet.

A large bathroom   The drawing at right shows a large bathroom (about 100 sq. ft.) that has both a shower and a tub. You can approach the toilet from either side (though there is more space to the left of the toilet), the bathtub has clear space at both ends and the shower alcove provides some privacy for the toilet user if the bathroom door is open.

This bathroom gives the family a number of alternatives. Two could bathe at once. Someone who has difficulty using the tub has an accessible shower. And someone who prefers a seated-entry tub has that option. As this floor plan shows, space solves many accessibility problems.

A Large Bathroom

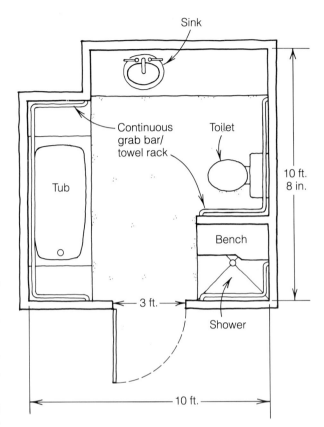

RESOURCES

The comprehensive catalog companies on p. 221 also supply items for the bathroom.

Alsons Corporation
525 East Edna Place
Covina, CA 91723
(818) 966-1668
Hand-held shower heads, vitreous china bathroom fixtures.

American Specialities
441 Saw Mill River Road
Yonkers, NY 10701
(914) 476-9000
Stainless-steel grab-bar systems for showers, tubs and toilets; bath and shower seats, hotel and commercial washroom accessories.

American Stair-Glide Corporation
4001 East 138th Street
Grandview, MO 64030
(800) 821-2041
(816) 763-3100
Company offers a bath lift in addition to full line of stair and platform lifts.

American Standard
Eastern Region (10410 North Kensington Parkway, Suite 101, Kensington, MD 20895)
Southern Region (9755 Dogwood Road, Suite 120, Roswell, GA 30075)
Central Region (III Crossroads of Commerce, 3501 Algonquin Road, Suite 100, Rolling Meadows, IL 60008)
Western Region (P.O. Box 2045, 812 West Union Street, Montebello, CA 90640)
(800) 821-7700, ext. 4023
Pedestal sinks, 18-in. high toilet; distributor of Pressalit's Multi System, a fully adjustable system of bathroom products including sinks, toilets, seating and grab bars.

Aqua Glass Corporation
P.O. Box 412
Adamsville, TN 38310
(800) 238-3940
(901) 632-0911
Acrylic accessible showers, traditional bathtubs with grab bars and bath seats.

Aquatec Health Care Products
ICM Building
1003 International Drive
Oakdale, PA 15071-9223
(412) 695-2122
Full-length and seat-length hydraulic bath lifts (products are made in West Germany).

Arjo-Century
6380 West Oakton Street
Morton Grove, IL 60053
(800) 323-1245
(708) 967-0360
Accessible bathing system, The Spa. Bather sits in seat and egg-shaped tub rotates around bather.

BASCO
P.O. Box 237
Bohemia, NY 11716
(516) 567-4404
Grab-bar systems.

BathCraft
1610 James P. Rodgers Drive
Valdosta, Georgia 31601
(912) 333-0805
Barrier-free showers without sills, with bench seats; bathtubs with grab bars.

BathEase
2537 Frisco Drive
Clearwater, FL 34621
(813) 791-6656
An acrylic bathtub/shower combination that has a door in the side for easy access.

Bel-Art Products
Maddock, Inc.
6 Industrial Road
Pequannock, NJ 07440-1993
(201) 694-0550
Grab-bar systems.

BPS Architectural Products
10816 Fallstone Road
Suite 505
Houston, TX 77099
(800) 255-9513
(713) 568-9945
Accessible modular vanity and wardrobe systems.

Bradley Corporation
P.O. Box 309
1901 Fountain Blvd.
Menomonee Falls, WI 53051
(414) 251-6000
Grab-bar systems, roll-in showers, partial bath seats.

E.F. Brewer Company
13901 Main Street
P.O. Box 159
Menomonee Falls, WI 53051-0159
(800) 558-8777
(414) 251-9530
Stainless-steel grab bars systems, portable and armchair commodes.

Braun Corporation
1014 South Monticello
P.O. Box 310
Winamac, IN 46996
(800) 843-5438
Fiberglass roll-in shower made of four pieces, with a reinforced mid-section for grab bars and a transfer seat.

Brickhouse Design Group Ltd.
8 Joan Lane
Massapequa Park, NY 11762
(516) 795-6962
Acrylic grab bars.

Briggs Plumbingware
4350 West Cypress Street
Suite 800
Tampa, FL 33607
(813) 873-3610
Pedestal sinks, 18-in. high toilet.

Carters (J&A) Ltd.
Aintree Avenue
Whitehouse Business Park
Trowbridge, Wiltshire
England BA14 OXB
(033) 575-1901
Seat benches, shower chairs and grab bars.

Chiltern Medical Developmnets
6 Wedgewood Road
Bicester, Oxfordshire
England OX6 7UL
(086) 924-670
Bath lifts, grab bars and accessible showers.

Clarke Medical Products
5510 Amber Drive, Unit 10
Mississauga, Ontario
Canada L4W 2V1
(416) 238-6163
Bath lifts, grab bars.

Concept Fiberglass Homes
U.S. Army Ammo Plant
P.O. Box 1633
Grand Isle, NE 68802
(800) 262-3559
(308) 381-1965
Fiberglass shower bases and grab bars.

Crane Plumbing
Fiat Products
1235 Hartrey Avenue
Evanston, IL 60202
(312) 864-9777
Accessible shower modules, wheelchair-accessible shower receptors, tub/shower module with grab bars and bath seats, 18-in. high toilets.

CWECO
P.O. Box 2456
Gardena, CA 90247
(800) 292-9236
(213) 538-9440
Metal grab bars.

Delta Faucet Company
Eastern Zone (State Road 46 West, Greensburg, IN 47240)
Western Zone (Highway 62, Chickasha, OK 73018)
(800) 345-3358
Delta Scald Guard Bath mixing valves and lever handle faucets.

Dignified Products Corporation
P.O. Box 337
Mantua, NJ 08051
(800) 548-7905
(609) 468-0316
Hydraulic bath lift, bathtub with hydraulic bath seat, Dignity sink that moves up and down hydraulically.

Diversified Fiberglass Fabricators
P.O. Box 670
Cherryville, NC 28021-0670
(704) 435-9586
Bathtub transfer bench.

Dryad Jebron
249 Ayer Road
P.O. Box 347
Harvard, MA 01451
(800) 445-5388
(508) 772-6005
Nylon-coated aluminum-alloy grab bars and accessories, flip-up grab bars, door closers.

Elcoma Metal Fabricating Ltd.
878 Williams Street
Midland, Ontario
Canada L4R 4P4
(800) 421-3375
(705) 526-5944
Stainless-steel, brass and painted grab bars, flip-up grab bars.

Electric Mobility
#1 Mobility Plaza
Sewell, NJ 08080
(800) 662-4548
Hydraulic bath lift.

Everest & Jennings
Advantage Patient Care Products
3233 East Mission Oaks Boulevard
Camarillo, CA 93010
(805) 987-6911
Grab bars, toilet safety rails, toilet transfer aid, bath bench, tub rails and raised toilet seat.

Ferno Healthcare
Ferno Washington
70 Weil Way
Wilmington, OH 45177-9371
(512) 382-1451
The Comfort Care System, a bathing system that may be used in new construction or remodeling; it includes a bath tray and bathing tube that rotates around the bather.

Florestone Products
2851 Falcon Drive
Madera, CA 93637
(209) 661-4171
Terrazzo accessible shower receptacle; wheelchair-accessible shower stalls with bath seats and grab bars; shower/bath with grab bars.

Franklin Brass Manufacturing Company
P.O. Box 5226
Culver City, CA 90231
(800) 421-3375
(213) 306-5944
Stainless-steel, brass and baked-enamel finish grab bars, retractable shower seat.

Frohock-Stewart
455 Whitney Avenue
P.O. Box 330
Northboro, MA 01532
(800) 343-6059
(617) 393-2543
Bath and shower seats, tub rails and stainless-steel grab bars.

GAMCO
(General Accessory Manufacturing Company)
One Gamco Place
Durant, OK 74701
(800) 451-5766
Stainless-steel grab bar systems, shower seats.Gendron

Gendron
Lugbill Road
Archbold, OH 43502
(419) 445-6060
(800) 537-2521
Bathtub rails, safety bench, safety seat, toilet handrail, raised toilet seat.

Grand Traverse Technologies
223 Lake Avenue
Traverse City, MI 49684
(616) 961-2041
Bathing system with door that rolls into the frame of the tub so that bather is not encumbered by maneuvering around the door. Integral seat in bathing system.

Grant Water X Corporation
21846 River Oaks Drive
Rocky River, OH 44116
(800) 243-5237
(216) 331-3050
Hydraulic bath lift.

Grohe America
900 Lively Boulevard
Wood Dale, IL 60191
(708) 350-2600
Hand-heldd showers with interchangeable shower heads.

Guardian Products/Sunrise Medical
12800 Wentworth Street
Box C-4522
Arleta, CA 91331
(800) 423-8034
(818) 504-2820
Complete line of bath lifts, grab bars and other bathing aids.

Hansgrohe
2840 Research Park Drive
Soquel, CA 95073
(408) 479-0515
Decorative faucet mixers, hand-held shower sprayers grab bars and matching bathroom accessories.

HCG North America
3740 Prospect Avenue
Yorba Linda, CA 92686
(714) 524-2997
Wall-mounted and pedestal lavatories made of vitreous china.

HEWI
2851 Old Tree Drive
Lancaster, PA 17603
(717) 293-1313
Complete decorative line of nylon-coated steel-core bathroom and door hardware products, including grab-bar systems, accessories, shower rods, shower and tub seats and adjustable mirrors.

High Seas
4861 24th Avenue
Port Huron, MI 48060
(313) 385-4411
Marine-quality stainless-steel grab-bar systems.

HRD/MCS
26211 Grosbeck Highway
Warren, MI 48089
(313) 777-7060
Accessible shower.

Invacare
899 Cleveland Street
Elyria, OH 44036
(800) 333-6900
Bath seats, tub transfer chairs, raised toilet seats, tub safety bars, grab bars, commodes and shower chairs.

Kimstock
2200 South Yale Street
Santa Ana, CA 92704
(800) 366-2268
(714) 546-6850
Barrier-free showers.

Kohler Company
44 Highland Drive
Kohler, WI 53044
(800) 772-1814
(414) 457-4441
Barrier-free bathtub (the Precedence), barrier-free tub/shower (the Freewill), pedestal and overhang sinks, 18-in. toilets.

Lumex
100 Spence Street
Bay Shore, NY 11706-2290
(800) 645-5272
Grab bars, safety rails, bath seats, transfer benches, raised toilet seat, shower chairs, shower hoses and other aids to daily living.

Mansfield Plumbing Products
150 First Street
Perrysville, OH 44864
(419) 938-5211
Vitreous china sink, 18-in. high toilets and wheelchair.

Medline Industries
One Medline Place
Mundelein, IL 60060-4486
(708) 949-3150
Bathroom safety and assistive products: transfer benches, bath benches, knurled chrome grab bars, bathtub safety rails, toilet safety rails.

Med/West
P.O. Box 130
Marshalltown, IA 50158
(515) 752-5446
Electrically powered elevating toilet seat.

National Fiber Glass Products
5 Greenwood Avenue
Romeoville, IL 60441-1398
(815) 886-5900
(708) 257-3300
Accessible shower stalls.

Nicobond Limited
International Division
Niclar House
3/10 Shoreditch High Street
London, England E1 6PE
(01) 247 8838/9
Accessible showers, toilets, bathroom accessories, kitchen cabinets; Multi Bathroom System, which has a track around the perimeter of the room that allows both horizontal and vertical adjustment of grab and support bars, shower seating and sink.

Normbau
P.O. Box 548
Shepherdsville, KY 40165
(800) 358-2920
(502) 538-7388
Grab bars, railing systems, bath hardware and accessories, handles and cabinet hardware. Grab bars and other products are nylon coated and available in many different colors.

NEACO
Norton Engineering Alloys
Company, Ltd.
Norton Grove Industrial
Estate, Norton
Malton, N. Yorkshire
England YO17 9HQ
*Comprehensive line of grab bars,
railing systems, bath hardware
and accessories, handles and
cabinet hardware. Grab bars and
other products are nylon coated
and available in many different
colors.*

PCP-Champion
300 Congress Street
Ripley, OH 45167
(800) 888-0867
(513) 392-4301
*Bathtub safety rails, grab bars,
bath/shower benches, bath
transfer benches, raised toilet
seats, commode seats with safety
grips and commode chairs.*

Perfect Patient Care
144 East Kingsbridge Road
Mount Vernon, NY 10550
(800) 634-9317
*Grab bars, shower and bath
benches and toilet safety rails.*

Porta Shower of America
134D, Route 111
Hampstead, NH 03841
(800) 422-0098
*Portable shower unit that can be
set up in areas where access to
plumbing may be difficult.*

Pressalit Rehab
1259 Route 46, Building 2
Parsippany, NJ 07054
(800) 346-2380
(201) 263-8533
*Raised toilet seats, toilet support
arms, vertical or horizontal
adjustable wash basin, grab-bar
systems, shower benches.*

Safe-T-Bath of New England
185 Millbury Avenue
Millbury, MA 01527
(617) 865-2361
Barrier-free bathtub.

SafeTek International
P.O. Box 23
Melbourne, FL 32902
(800) 526-0374
(407) 952-3664
*Safety support bars, grab-bar
systems made of thermo-plastic
and available in a variety of
colors.*

Silcraft Corporation
528 Hughes Drive
Traverse City, MI 49684
(800) 678-7100
(616) 946-4221
*Barrier-free showers, accessible
bathing systems with door in
side and integral seat.*

STEP
7075 Silver Shoals Road
Gainesville, GA 30506
(800) 892-5755
(404) 887-9557
*Barrier-free roll-in showers,
bath seats and bathtub inserts.*

Tuffcare
1501-A S. W. 2nd St
Pompano Beach, FL 33069
(800) 548-6596
*Bath seats and benches, bathtub
safety reails and grab bars.*

Ultraflo Corporation
P.O. Box 2294
Sandusky, OH 44870
(419) 626-8182
*A water-distribution system that
uses a single line of distribution.
Water is operated through preset
temperature, push-button
selection, which reduces water
consumption and avoids hot-
water scald.*

Universal-Rundle Corporation
Bathing Systems Division
303 North Street
P.O. Box 29
New Castle, PA 16103-0029
(412) 658-6631
*Wheelchair-accessible showers,
accessible sinks, pedestal sinks,
18-in. high toilets, wall-mounted
toilets.*

Villeroy & Boch (USA)
Interstate 80 at New Maple
Avenue
P.O. Box 103
Pine Brook, NJ 07058
(201) 575-0550
*Ceramic pedestal sinks, wall-
mounted sinks with trap covers,
height-adjustable lift sinks,
17-in. high toilet.*

CHAPTER ELEVEN
BEDROOMS

A person who is ill or disabled may spend considerable time in the bedroom, so the bedroom needs to be planned with care. Bedrooms need to be in a location that affords privacy, yet is near a bathroom. They also need an emergency escape route and well-designed windows that bring in a plentiful supply of light and air. There must be sufficient clear space for maneuvering around furniture and accessible closets for storing clothing, linen and bedding. Adequate wiring for lights, communication devices and medical equipment is essential. Because the bedroom may not always remain a bedroom, it should be able to be converted to other uses, such as a home office or an in-law apartment.

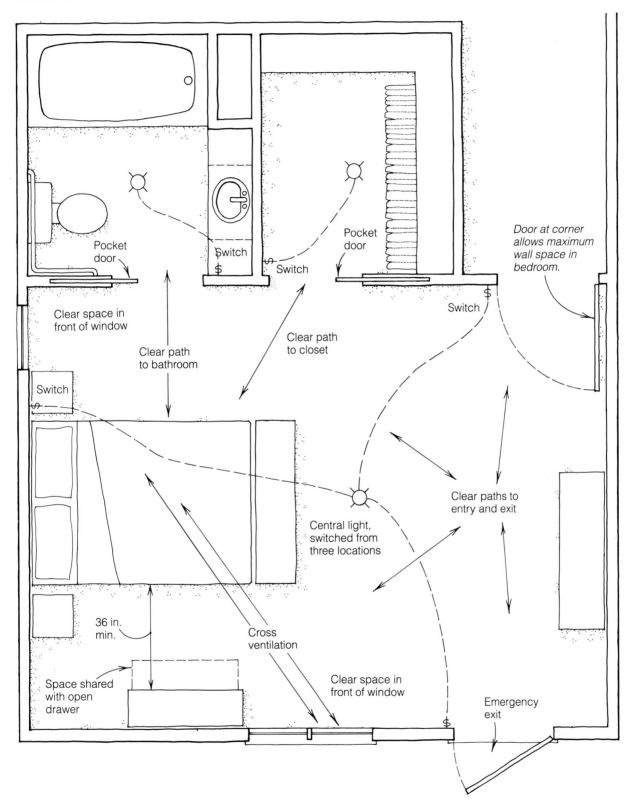

Pocket door

Switch
$

Switch

Pocket door

Clear space in front of window

Clear path to bathroom

Clear path to closet

Door at corner allows maximum wall space in bedroom.

Switch
$

Switch

Clear paths to entry and exit

Central light, switched from three locations

36 in. min.

Space shared with open drawer

Cross ventilation

Clear space in front of window

Emergency exit

ADJACENCIES AND PRIVACY

Bedrooms should be located so that a bathroom is only a few steps away from the bed. The route to the bathroom should be free of obstacles and easily negotiable in the dark (having to get up at night to go to the bathroom is one of the most bothersome aspects of getting older). For people using wheelchairs or other assistive devices, every corner, every piece of furniture and every door can be a hurdle in trying to get to the bathroom.

Bedrooms should be located where they afford privacy within the household as well as privacy from visitors. (People who have difficulty hearing may not even be aware that guests are in the house.) Bedroom/bathroom suites provide the greatest sense of privacy. Although many believe that privacy within a home isn't a big issue, for people whose movements are restricted, donning a bathrobe can take several minutes, and the task may require the help of another person.

DOORS AND WINDOWS

Bedrooms should be located along exterior walls. This allows for natural light and ventilation and for a direct emergency escape route.

Bedrooms should have a minimum of two windows, ideally on adjacent walls, to allow for cross ventilation when the door is shut. The location and number of doors and windows will affect the usable wall space for placement of furnishings and the privacy of the room. If windows are located on one wall of the room, the door on a second and closets on a third, there may be only one wall left for placement of the bed. Windows above the head of the bed can be difficult for some people to reach and operate.

The authors of *A Pattern Language* point out that the door to a small room, such as a bedroom, should be located at a corner so that the entire wall will be available for placement of furnishings. A door in the corner of the room allows for greater flexibility in furniture placement and more privacy. The bed and dressing area can be situated so that the occupant is not in full view, even with the door open. General guidelines for bedroom design are shown in the drawing on p. 193.

Ideally windows should be located with plenty of clear floor space around them (30 in. by 48 in.), and window hardware should be located within the optimal reach zone (20 in. to 44 in. above the floor). Many people are unable to crawl onto a bed or reach over furnishings to access window hardware. If furniture has to be placed in front of windows, as is often the case in small rooms, automatic window openers and automatic drapery openers may need to be installed. If this seems extravagant, consider the frustrations of someone with physical limitations who must rely upon another person to open and close the drapes or the window.

Emergency egress All bedrooms should have a window or door that allows an emergency escape to the outside of the house. An escape window should be big enough to allow people to get through it and out. First, the sill needs to be at a height that is accessible to all. The preferred height is 18 in. to 20 in., since the height of most wheelchair seats is 18 in. to 20 in., and sill heights at this level provide an easier transition from chair to window. Many home owners, however, do not want windows with low sills for reasons of privacy and because they are hazardous in children's play areas. A height of 30 in., the maximum we would allow, would be difficult for many people, but perhaps not insurmountable.

On windows used as an escape route, the sill needs to support the weight of a person, and it must not have sharp edges or protrusions. Also, the window opening should be wide enough to accommodate a large person trying to get out who may not be able to crawl through the space head first. Codes often stipulate a width of 24 in., which is in fact wide enough for a large man — as long as he has full use of his extremities. But someone who can't bend the knees or who has limited use of the legs may be unable to get through the window. A 24-in. space is not large enough to allow someone to sit in the window and lift the legs up to and through a window opening. We recommend that emergency escape windows be at least 30 in. wide (see the drawing on the facing page). Upper-story bedrooms need an exterior escape route to the ground below. You need a balcony or platform, ladder, or exterior stairs built into the house or available so that everyone on the second floor may evacuate safely.

Escape Windows — General Guidelines

Windows for emergency egress should be low enough and wide enough so that a person who uses a wheelchair can escape through them. Sills should support a person's weight and be smooth; windows should be easy to open.

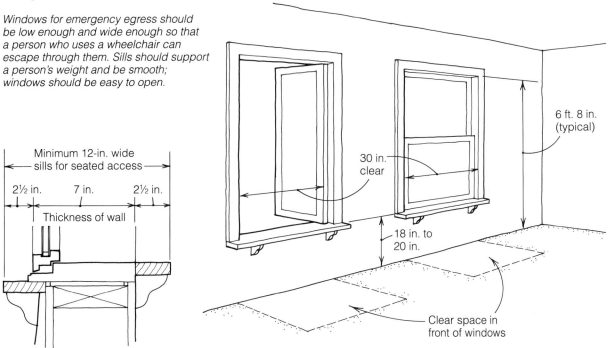

Minimum 12-in. wide sills for seated access

2½ in.   7 in.   2½ in.

Thickness of wall

6 ft. 8 in. (typical)

30 in. clear

18 in. to 20 in.

Clear space in front of windows

PATHWAYS AND CLEAR SPACE

Pathways and clear space are determined by the location of the doors, closets and furnishings. Beds and other furnishings come in a variety of sizes. Allow 36 in. of clear space on both sides of the bed. This is enough room for bed making and for someone using a wheelchair or another assistive device. (Many people who use wheelchairs can approach the bed from only one side.) The room should be large enough and should have windows, doors and closets positioned so that there is more than one option for placing a bed in the room. The clear space around the bed can be shared with (i.e., overlap) the clear space in front of a chest of drawers and other furnishings.

In homes with more children than bedrooms, it may be important to create the appearance of two rooms in the one. Furniture (such as bookcases) can often be used as a divider. Bunk beds can be placed in the center of the room, with one child being "assigned" to each side. Another solution is to install a large pocket door between the two sections of a bedroom, as shown in the photo at right.

A large pocket door separates the two small wings of this bedroom. When closed it creates the sense of two rooms, yet because of the wide doorway the space feels roomy and natural when the door is open.

CLOSETS

It makes no sense to design an inaccessible closet for an otherwise accessible bedroom. For full access, walk-in (or roll-in) closets are the best bet, provided that they are equipped with an accessible entrance.

As with every other door in the house, a closet door-way should be at least 32 in. wide. The center aisle should be at least 36 in. wide.

Common wall closets should be designed so that they don't have blind, inaccessible corners. This can be accomplished by building all closets with a

A Walk-In/Roll-In Closet

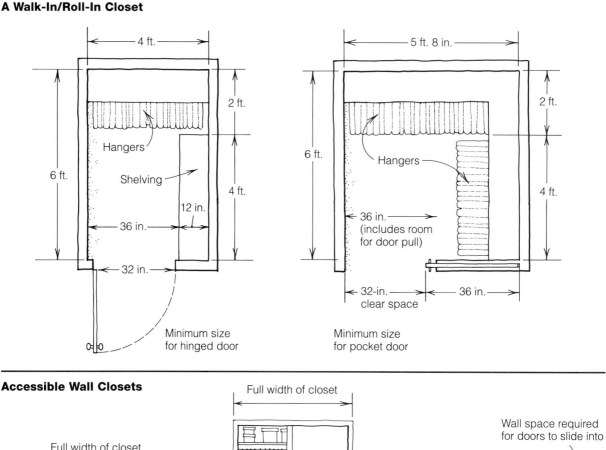

Hangers

Shelving

Minimum size for hinged door

Hangers

Minimum size for pocket door

Accessible Wall Closets

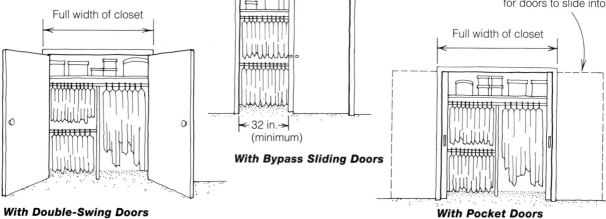

Full width of closet

Full width of closet

Wall space required for doors to slide into

Full width of closet

With Double-Swing Doors

With Bypass Sliding Doors

With Pocket Doors

full-length opening. Either hinged doors or pocket doors may be used. (For more on pocket doors, see pp. 105-107.) When using traditional sliding closet doors, select those with hardware that is suspended from above; avoid sliding doors that require tracks on the floor.

Walk-in closets can be easily equipped with commercially available storage systems and built-in shelves. Clothes rods can be set at various heights to suit a wide range of users. The photos below show some of the closet storage systems that are available commercially. These easy-to-assemble systems, which

An open basket storage system is useful because the clothes are easy to see and can be stored within the optimal reach zone. (Photo: Clairson International.)

This closet hardware system from Hafele (far left) features a clothes rod that pulls down and out, so clothes on the upper rod are within easy reach of nearly anyone. (Photo: Institute for Technology Development.) The carousel closet system from White Home Products (left) combines good organization and use of space with accessibility. (Photo: courtesy White Home Products.)

Homemade Closet-Rod Supports: Two Details

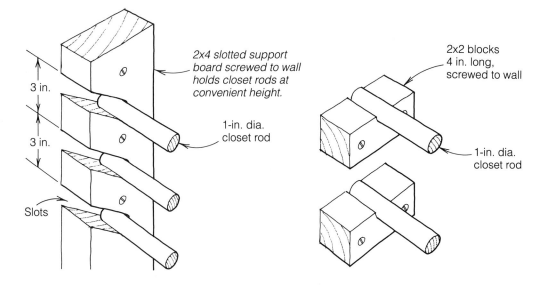

2x4 slotted support board screwed to wall holds closet rods at convenient height.

3 in.

3 in.

Slots

1-in. dia. closet rod

2x2 blocks 4 in. long, screwed to wall

1-in. dia. closet rod

Planning Ahead

Today's bedroom may be an efficiency apartment or home office tomorrow. Careful planning can make the transition in functions smooth.

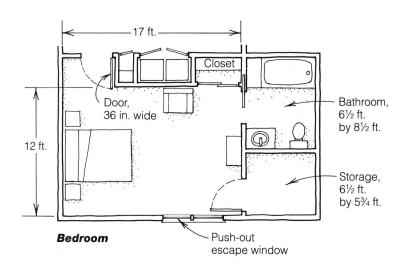

17 ft.

Closet

12 ft.

Door, 36 in. wide

Bathroom, 6½ ft. by 8½ ft.

Storage, 6½ ft. by 5¾ ft.

Bedroom

Push-out escape window

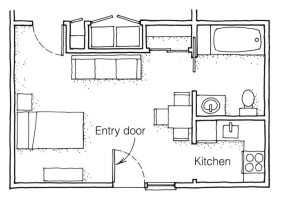

Entry door

Kitchen

Efficiency Apartment

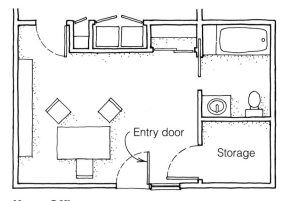

Entry door

Storage

Home Office

are often made of plastic-coated wire, feature efficient use of space and full visibility, in a wide range of sizes, configurations and color combinations.

If you want to make an existing closet more accessible, it's fairly easy to devise your own closet-rod system. Two designs (one of them adjustable) are shown in the top drawing on the facing page.

ELECTRICITY AND COMMUNICATIONS

Bedrooms should be wired to accommodate a full array of medical equipment, should the need arise. Oxygen regulators, humidifiers, personal emergency-response systems and home dialysis units need electricity. They shouldn't have to compete for outlets with the lamps, radios, televisions and computers in the room.

Walls that are likely to have a bed along them should be wired for at least four outlets, and ideally four outlets on each side of the bed. A switched outlet should be installed with a switch at the entrance and another at bedside. Some people appreciate having a switch in their bedroom that controls exterior floodlights. Telephone jacks and cable television cables should be wired into each bedroom. For more on wiring the bedroom, see pp. 82-83.

PLANNING FOR THE FUTURE

Bedrooms can go through many changes over the years. As children grow from infant to toddler to teen to young adult, the room changes with them. When the child leaves the home, the room may be converted to a completely different purpose. Good planning allows for greater options in responding to the changing needs of the household.

Designs that incorporate two separate bedroom areas in the house are ideally suited for future alterations to an efficiency apartment or a home office. This approach allows the children's bedrooms and bath to be separate from the master bedroom and bath. They may be on opposite sides of a single-story house or on separate floors. Bedrooms located on each story of a multi-story house ensure that there will be a bedroom available for the family member unable to climb the stairs. Bedrooms located at opposite ends of the house allow the creation of a separate apartment that can house a relative, an office, a teenager wanting some independence or a family member with physical limitations.

An exterior door from a bedroom creates the opportunity for multiple uses in the future. The door can serve as an entrance to an office for a home business (see the bottom drawing on the facing page). The door may also make it easier to convert the room to a rental or an apartment for a relative. Although installing a door is not a difficult undertaking, the room design and relationship of the bedroom to the other rooms in the house will make a difference in the smoothness of the transition.

A sliding glass door that opens onto a small patio or balcony off the bedroom is a perfect solution to emergency egress and a delightful feature as well. For more on sliding glass doors, see pp. 101-103.

RESOURCES

Clairson International
Closet Maid
720 SW 17th Street
Ocala, FL 32674
(800) 874-0008
Freestanding modular storage systems, cabinet organizers and electronic revolving closet systems.

Hafele America Co.
3901 Cheyenne Drive
P.O. Box 4000
Archdale, NC 27263
(800) 821-5423
(800) 672-4853 (In North Carolina)
(800) 334-1873 (In Eastern U.S.)
(800) 421-0663 (In California)
(919) 889-2322
A variety of hardware accessories for saving space and organizing closets.

Lee/Rowan
6333 Etzel Avenue
St. Louis, MO 63133
(800) 325-6150
Flexible storage and organization products made from epoxy-coated steel.

Scan-Plast Industries
1 Industrial Drive
Rutherford, NJ 07070
(800) 366-ELFA
(201) 933-7330
Wire-basket and frame storage system of epoxy-coated steel.

White Home Products
2401 Lake Park Drive
Atlanta, GA 30080
(404) 431-0900
Space-saving movable storage systems, including a revolving Closet Carousel.

CHAPTER TWELVE
SERVICE AND MAINTENANCE CENTERS

Every house needs some room in the rough, spaces for the less glamorous yet necessary functions and activities of the household. Whether the various service and maintenance centers are concentrated in one room or scattered throughout the house, it is important that they be carefully designed for efficiency and accessibility. This chapter will discuss planning centers for laundry, utilities, cleanup, repair, indoor gardening, recycling and general storage. It will conclude with a suggestion for combining these various centers into a single nerve center — the ugly room.

The Ugly Room

The ugly room combines most of the maintenance, service and utility centers.

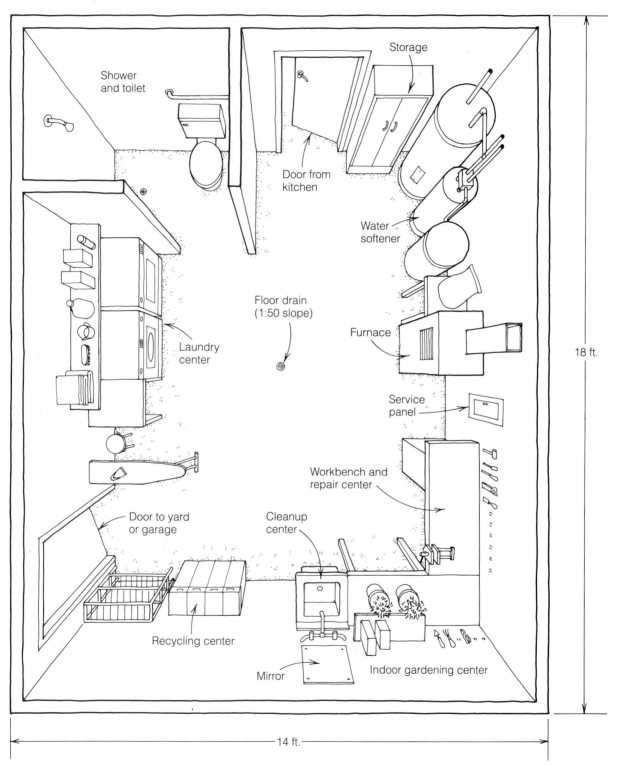

Shower and toilet

Storage

Door from kitchen

Water softener

Floor drain (1:50 slope)

Furnace

Laundry center

Service panel

Workbench and repair center

Door to yard or garage

Cleanup center

Recycling center

Mirror

Indoor gardening center

18 ft.

14 ft.

LAUNDRY CENTER

When you consider how much time is spent keeping a family in clean clothes, you have to wonder why so little time is spent designing the laundry center. A little planning can go a long way toward reducing the effort it takes to accomplish this basic household chore.

A fully equipped laundry center should contain a washer, dryer, utility sink, ironing area, table for folding laundry, drying rack and storage shelf (see the drawing below). The actual design of the center may depend on the type of washer and dryer. Stacked units (washer on bottom, dryer on top) save floor space, but unless the unit is designed with the controls in the center at the front and with the doors and bins at accessible locations, many people will have difficulty using them. Some of the models are simply two standard units with controls in standard locations, which makes them difficult to use.

In our research, we found that virtually everyone using a wheelchair and many others who were ambulatory had difficulty reaching the controls located at the back of the washer and dryer, couldn't reach the laundry located in the bottom of the washing machine and had considerable difficulty getting the clothes out of the dryer. The laundry detergent kept on a shelf above and to the right of the washing machine was out of reach for many.

Front-loading washers and dryers solve many of these problems, particularly if they are placed on an 8-in. by 10-in. platform so that the door and bottom of the washer and dryer bins are within the optimal reach zone. Several companies make front-loading domestic washers, including Akea, Miele, Whirlpool and White Westinghouse (see Resources on p. 207). The controls of the Whirlpool washer and dryer are located on the front of the equipment. They have good high-contrast graphics and a simple organization. The doors are in the optimal reach zone and at the same height. Transferring wet laundry to the dryer is a short, simple movement. The clothes in either the washer or dryer are within reach of a seated person, and getting at them does not require a standing person to bend very much. The front-loading washer and dryer can be arranged with a countertop above them, which makes them even more desirable as space-savers.

The laundry center needs a good work surface for sorting, folding or flat drying clothes. A work surface that permits seated work is desirable. The room

Laundry Center

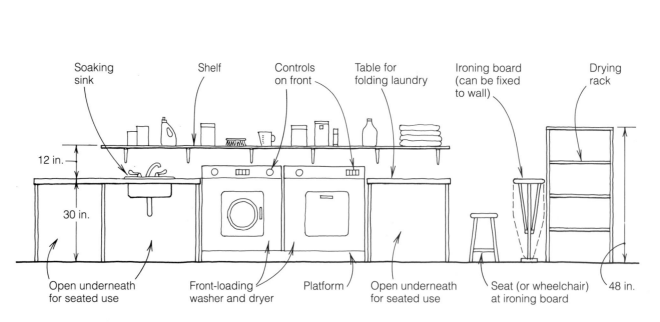

This built-in ironing center from NuTone contains a light and a small amount of storage. It can be installed to accommodate seated use, and when it's not being used it folds up neatly into the wall. (Photo: courtesy NuTone.)

should either have a built-in countertop or space for a work table. If a table is located in the room, be sure there is plenty of clear space around it.

The storage space for detergents and other cleaning chemicals should be convenient to the washer. The launderer should be able to scoop detergent out of the box without having to move the box closer to the washer first.

The ironing board and iron may be located in the laundry center. There are some excellent built-in products that provide the ironing board, a light source and storage for the iron in a small closet space. These products can be used by a seated person without having the legs of a standard ironing board in the way. A clothes rod and hangers can be included in the laundry center. The rod height should be ad-

justable so it can be used by people who are seated or of different heights.

Plan too for an indoor clothesline or drying rack. One simple solution is to install a retractable clothesline often sold for use over bathtubs.

Doing the laundry is a major household labor, yet laundry centers are often located in basements, garages, back porches and remote utility rooms, far from where the clothes are removed and stored. If the laundry center is going to be located in an area separate from other maintenance centers in the house, it makes sense to put it in or near the bedrooms and bathrooms. That way, the dirty clothes can be removed, dropped into a hamper, washed, dried and put away all in the same part of the house. A drawback to having a laundry center close to the bedroom and bathroom is that it may be a bit messy and noisy.

UTILITIES CENTER

The utilities center may contain the functional units for the heating, ventilation and cooling systems, the water-treatment equipment, the water heater and the electrical service panel. All of these systems should be located so that they are accessible, and they should be arranged according to the frequency they are likely to be accessed.

Water softeners require regular attention. It is not unusual for 50 lb. of salt to be added once a month. Although there are services available that will deliver the salt to the home on a regular basis, many home owners prefer to manage this activity themselves. The water softener should be located near the entry, where the sacks of salt will be brought into the house. The water softener should have a 30-in. by 48-in. clear space in front of it. A set-down space immediately adjacent to the water softener at a height equal to or slightly above the softener bin would allow a person to rest the bag while pouring the salt into the bin.

Some homes, particularly those with their own wells, are equipped with water filters. These filters require changing monthly or even more frequently if the water is hard or has high amounts of chemicals in it. Put this filter in a position where it can be reached and near a trash receptacle.

Utilities Center

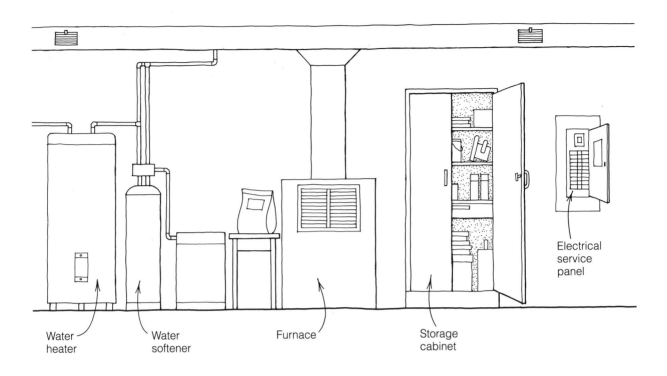

Water heater

Water softener

Furnace

Storage cabinet

Electrical service panel

Cleanup Center

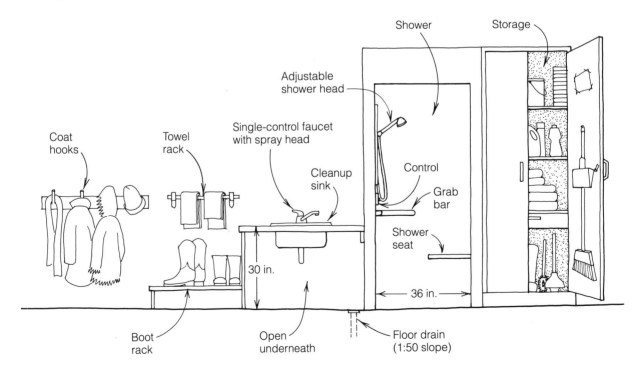

Shower

Storage

Adjustable shower head

Single-control faucet with spray head

Cleanup sink

Control

Grab bar

Shower seat

Coat hooks

Towel rack

30 in.

36 in.

Boot rack

Open underneath

Floor drain (1:50 slope)

Generally little maintenance is required of the heating, ventilation and cooling systems. Oil, gas and wood burners require at least annual maintenance. The filters in forced-air systems need to be changed regularly. And natural gas, propane and oil systems should be situated so that the pilot light can be reached from a clear space.

Electric service panels in houses range in size from 24 in. to 40 in. long and 14 in. to 16 in. wide. A 38-in. long panel should have the base mounted 16 in. above the floor. On a standard 16-in. by 38-in. panel, the fuse switches are located 6 in. above the base of the box. Thus, a unit mounted with the base of the box at 16 in. has the fuse switches extending from the lowest height of 22 in. to a maximum height of 48 in. A window to provide natural light in this room will help in the event of a power failure.

MUDROOM AND CLEANUP CENTER

The traditional farmhouse mudroom has an exterior entrance, a floor that is easy to clean and an area where dirty boots, shoes and coats can be stored. Useful additions to the traditional mudroom would be a sink and perhaps even a utility shower and toilet.

A large utility sink comes in handy for many projects, such as indoor gardening, washing oversized roaster pans used only once or twice a year, scrubbing dirty sneakers and rinsing heavily soiled clothes. But utility sinks are usually 8 in. to 14 in. deep and thus pose a problem for users who are seated because they cannot pull their chair under the sink. An alternative to providing an open space directly beneath the sink is to provide an open counter area on either side of it. Although this arrangement is not as convenient, a seated user could access the sink from the side.

WORKBENCH AND REPAIR CENTER

Every home needs a place for hobbies, projects and repair work, and for these activities a workbench is ideal. The workbench will need a sturdy surface that won't be ruined by a major hammering job or a solvent spill. Hardwood is the traditional choice.

Workbench and Repair Center

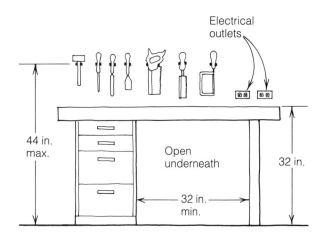

A workbench with 4x4 legs (or two 2x4s glued together) on one end and a 12-in. to 18-in. wide cabinet drawer base on the other end is simple to construct. A 32-in. height will be comfortable for a variety of people, standing or seated, and convenient for projects. One good location for the bench is against a wall with electrical outlets; tools can be stored on the wall above the bench.

INDOOR GARDENING CENTER

Research has shown that growing plants is therapeutic. Also, a researcher at NASA has shown that certain types of indoor plants, such as spider plants and philodendron, are able to remove formaldehyde, smoke and other unhealthy substances from the indoor air. So planning a house full of beneficial plants can result in cleaner air to breathe. Providing a space for some gardening indoors is also helpful to those who are unable to get outdoors or otherwise do much outdoor gardening.

Indoor gardening requires only enough space for a utility sink, a work surface and storage for potting soil, pots, plant food and tools. One nice arrangement is a counter adjacent to a sink that allows someone to sit and work. A retractable sprayer at the sink will facilitate indoor gardening for people of all ages and abilities.

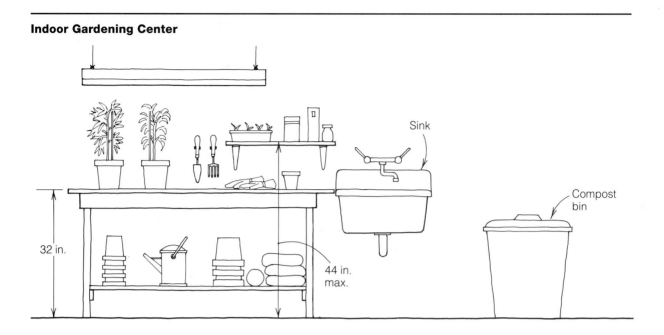

Indoor gardeners need a place to throw plant debris. A small garbage bin nearby with a lid and some dirt in it could be the start of an indoor composting station for the household vegetable refuse.

The indoor gardening center can share space with the workbench and repair center, or it could be part of a greenhouse or sun room.

RECYCLING AND STORAGE CENTERS

Many people are finding that their recycling needs far surpass a couple of boxes or bags in the kitchen. If space permits, a larger recycling center can make the chore much easier. A sink comes in handy for rinsing out containers and removing labels. Separate bins for aluminum cans, glass jars, plastic containers and recyclable paper might be necessary. The bins could be nothing more elaborate than plastic garbage containers that slide under a counter or work table.

The kitchen often serves as the storage center for a wide variety of cleaning solutions and chemical products. A separate storage area is better. The storage center could consist of pegboard hangers for brooms, mops and miscellaneous tools. The vacuum cleaner and attachments should have a convenient niche. And a generous supply of narrow shelving could serve various needs, such as keeping poisonous substances out of the reach of children and holding sports equipment and endless other goods.

THE UGLY ROOM

In most houses, the various service and maintenance centers are in different parts of the house. The laundry room is in one area, the water heater in another, the electrical service panel and heating system somewhere else. We think it makes a lot of sense to concentrate these centers in one single, accessible room, which we call "the ugly room."

A full-scale ugly room would include all of the centers discussed above and would allow for doubling up on such items as the utility sink and storage. The ugly room should be designed so that tasks can be done quickly and efficiently. Changing the filter on the furnace should be as easy as putting a new roll of toilet paper on the holder; finding the tripped circuit breaker or replacing a fuse should be no more onerous than replacing a light bulb in a lamp; doing the laundry should be as simple as possible.

The ugly room should have a wide door to the outside — a 36-in. door would make it easy to transport large items in and out. The floor should be flush or with minimal thresholds. A cement or heavy-duty linoleum floor will take the likely abuse and will facilitate cleanup. A drain in the floor adds to the flexibility of the room.

All the room's components should be located and oriented so that they are easily accessible with the least amount of bending, stooping and kneeling. Each component should have clear space (30 in. by 48 in.) in front of it, and the controls or sections that require maintenance should be put within the optimal reach zone (20 in. to 44 in. above the floor).

A good location for an ugly room would be adjacent to the kitchen and garage area. The kitchen should be on a direct line with the exterior entrance so that groceries and garbage can be toted the shortest possible distance. The ugly room could be located behind the garage or carport, although this wouldn't necessarily be a convenient location for the laundry center. The drawing on p. 201 offers one idea for an ugly-room layout.

The Closet Maid ventilated storage system is convenient and adaptable for use in a maintenance room. (Photo: courtesy Clairson International.)

RESOURCES

See also p. 199 for companies that make modular storage systems.

Andi-Co Appliances
65 Campus Plaza
Raritan Center
Edison, NJ 08837
(201) 225-8837
Front-loading washers and dryers manufactured by AEG (Advanced Engineering from Germany).

Asko Asea
903 N. Bowser, #170
Richardson, TX 75081
(214) 644-8595
Scandinavian washers and dryers. Washer is front loading, but the outer door of the washer, which is hinged at the bottom, may create a barrier for someone having to reach over it to the contents inside.

General Electric Company
Building 6, Room 106
Louisville, KY 40225
(502) 452-4311
Spacemaker washer and dryer. These small stacked units have the control panel within reach (about 50 in. from the floor). The dryer is on top and may be difficult to reach for some.

Gibson
6000 Perimeter Drive
Dublin, OH 43017
(800-458-1445
SpaceMaster washer and dryer. These small stacked units have the control panel within reach (about 50 in. from the floor). The dryer is on top and may be difficult to reach for some.

Hotpoint
Appliance Park
Louisville, KY 40225
(800) 626-2000
Individual space-saving models can be stacked or separate.

Kelvinator
13211 Northend Avenue
Oak Park, MI 40237
(313) 542-4820
Front-loading washer and dryer. Washer has large, side-hinged door.

KitchenAid
701 Main Street
St. Joseph, MI 49085
(616) 982-4500
A 24-in. wide stacked LaundryCenter. Controls for the dryer are just within reach, but the dryer will be difficult for many to reach.

Miele Appliances
22 D Worlds Fair Drive
Somerset, NJ 08873
(201) 560-0899
Front-loading washer and dryer. Made in Germany.

NuTone
Madison and Red Bank Roads
Cincinnati, OH 45227-1599
(800) 543-8687
Built-in ironing center.

Whirlpool Corporation
2000 U.S. 33 North
Benton Harbor, MI 49022
(800) 253-1301
(616) 926-3164
Stacked Thin Twin Laundry System with the controls within reach. The dryer may be difficult for many to reach. Whirlpool also makes separate compact washer and dryer models; the dryer can be mounted on the wall at a convenient height.

White Westinghouse
Appliance
116 Corporate Boulevard #E
South Plainfield, NJ 07080
(908) 753-7105
Front-loading washer and dryer.

PART FOUR

REMODELING AND RETROFITTING

The time to repair the roof is when the sun is shining.
— *John F. Kennedy*

CHAPTER THIRTEEN
REMODELING FOR A LIFETIME

To live is to change. Unfortunately, our houses aren't always designed to change with us. Changes in the physical structure of a home are necessary for a variety of reasons. Some people buy a small house thinking that they will move to a larger house when the family starts to grow, only to find that when the need to move arises they can't afford to or no longer want to. In this case, the house may need an additional bathroom, bedroom or family room. Changes are needed when features or fixtures become worn out and need replacing. Changes are made when the house is sold and the new owners want to make it suit their needs. Changes are made on the whim or wish of the owner. Changes are made when an

Creating an Accessible Entrance through the Garage

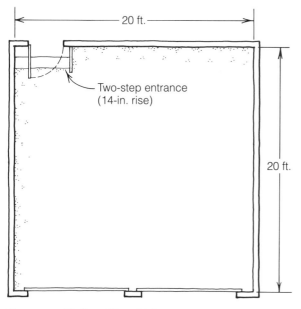

Garage with Two-Step Entrance

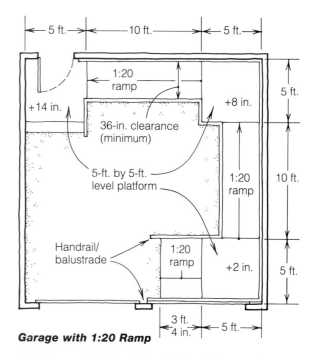

Garage with 1:20 Ramp

A 1:20 ramp that rises 14 in. is 23 ft. 4 in. long and takes up floor space on three sides of the garage.

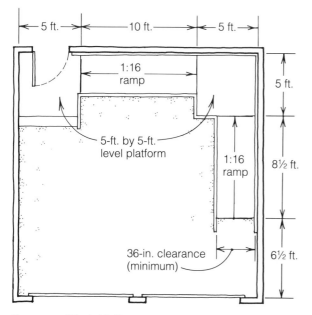

Garage with 1:16 Ramp

A 1:16 ramp is 18½ ft. long and takes up floor space on two sides of the garage.

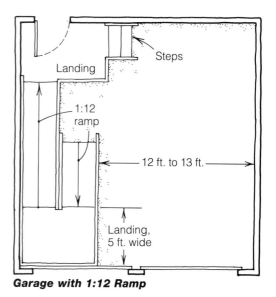

Garage with 1:12 Ramp

A 1:12 switchback ramp is 14 ft. long and leaves half of the garage open.

elderly relative starts visiting more often, and staying longer. Changes are made when we become older, experience an illness or suffer an injury. Each of these reasons for change provides an opportunity for improving the quality of the living environment.

A recent report from the National Center for Health Statistics states that 5.3% of Americans use some type of assistive device and 2.9% live in a home with accessibility features (LaPlante, 1992). Among people over the age of 75, however, those figures rise to 34.9% and 14.3%, respectively. The report also shows that 77.5% of home modifications are paid for by the home owner without third-party (insurance or government) assistance. There would probably be more accessibility features in homes if financial assistance were available to help pay for them. This point is particularly important in light of the fact that the number of people who use and need assistive devices and home accessibility modifications is growing faster than the population as a whole. The total population increased about 13% between 1980 and 1990, while the use of anatomical braces more than doubled and the use of walkers and wheelchairs nearly doubled.

Too often, a renovation to create an accessible living space arises out of desperation and results in changes that degrade the structure. Remodeling and renovation, regardless of the reason, should enhance the quality of the structure and should fit in with the style of the house. Each change on a home is an opportunity to make it right. If an appliance needs to be replaced, it should be replaced with a product that meets the design criteria outlined on pp. 25-26. If the bathroom fixtures need to be replaced because the porcelain has become stained or chipped or the fixture itself has worn out, it's the perfect time to install fixtures that will provide longer service to a changing household.

The essentials of remodeling a home environment to accommodate changes in human abilities are really bare minimums. These essentials do not necessarily mean that the individual who has mobility difficulties will be integrated into the entire living environment. More could and should be done within the house to improve accessibility, but the changes described in this chapter are the most important for basic accessibility.

The goal of remodeling should be to make the structure entirely accessible so that all members of the household will be equally able to enjoy all the spaces of the house. However, many families spend all of their funds to build a new addition for the person who has a mobility limitation and run out of money before they are able to make changes in the remainder of the house. But it is the remainder of the house where the family will be. The person with mobility problems is still cut off from everyone else, is still denied entrance to the family gatherings, formal and informal.

REMODELING ESSENTIALS FOR PEOPLE WITH PHYSICAL LIMITATIONS

A few basics must be changed if someone with physical limitations is going to be able to use a living environment. The first is to ensure that the individual is able to approach, enter and leave the house, get to and use a place of rest, get to and use bathroom facilities and get to and use the kitchen. Remodeling and creating adaptable kitchens and bathrooms are discussed in the chapters 14 and 15, respectively.

Exterior pathways   A pathway that is uneven (flagstone, brick or loose stone) or that has spaces between smooth surfaces larger than ½ in. is a problem. Many people as they age are less steady on their feet, and a small difference in a surface can cause them to lose their balance and fall. Injuries from falls can be prevented if smooth, clean and well-lit surfaces are provided on external walkways. In persons older than 75, more than half of the deaths from injury are due to falls; persons 65 and older account for more than 70% of the deaths due to falls (Hogue, 1982).

There are several ways to make existing pathways safer. Refurbish concrete or asphalt sidewalks that have become cracked. In brick sidewalks, replace loose bricks and replenish mortar that has loosened over the years. Prune or remove bushes that overhang sidewalks, blocking the light from the floodlight that once illuminated the pathway. Remove or prune bushes and trees that drop leaves, fruit or other debris onto the sidewalk or that provide too much shade and keep ice and snow from melting.

Lighting should be available from the point where the individual disembarks from the vehicle into the house. Adding light to a walkway, driveway and entryway is relatively inexpensive. Lighting on walkways should reflect downward onto the path and should not glare into the eyes of the walker. For more on exterior pathways, see pp. 47-51.

Entrances Houses differ, but a few criteria remain constant when accommodating someone with physical limitations. Whether the person uses public transportation, drives a car or is a passenger in an automobile, the entrance path begins at the point of disembarkation. If accessibility is defined only as placing a ramp over the stairs so that a wheelchair can be hauled up and down, little has been done to enhance the mobility of the person. The remodeling results should provide the individual an effortless opportunity to get in and out of the house. If it is a struggle to get from the end of the ramp to the automobile, little has been done to extend the environment of this individual.

The pathway from the vehicle area into the house should be smooth and as short as possible. If the house has an attached garage or carport, the person entering will be protected from the elements while moving into the house. The problem likely needing a solution with a house that has a garage or carport is to provide a level entry into the house.

There are three ways to provide a stepless entry: building a ramp, installing a platform lift and raising the elevation of the vehicle staging area to a level consistent with the foundation so that a ramp will be unnecessary and so that the vehicle will be used to climb the elevation. Building a ramp is likely to be the least expensive option. Sometimes, however, there isn't enough room in the garage to accommodate a ramp with a negotiable slope. Thus, a combination

A simple covered pathway can provide protection from the elements between a detached garage and the house.

of building up the driveway and installation of a ramp may be the best alternative. For more on entrances, see pp. 43-46.

If a ramp is used it may be built in segments so that the slope may be kept as low as possible. First, the ramp can switch back on itself with a small landing (minimum of 5 ft. by 5 ft.). Or the ramp could accomplish part of the rise along one side of the garage and the other part on another side. If the height to be bridged is the equivalent of two steps into the house (about 14 in.), a 1:20 grade ramp would need to be 23⅓ ft. long. A typical two-car garage is 20 ft. to 24 ft. square. Obviously a straight ramp would not be of much help.

The drawing on p. 211 shows a 20-ft. by 20-ft. garage with a two-step (14-in.) transition into the house, and three ways to make it accessible: a 1:20 ramp, a 1:16 ramp and a 1:12 ramp. Much of the parking area in the garage is taken up by the 1:20 ramp and the transitional 5-ft. by 5-ft. platforms at the turns. A 1:16 ramp requires 18½ ft. of ramp. A 1:12 ramp (14 ft. long) with an intermediate landing keeps half of the garage open.

A garage too small for a ramp would mean either raising the floor of the garage and overlaying the driveway to accomplish the gain in elevation or installing a platform lift. A platform lift may be the best solution in terms of preserving open floor space. Platform lifts are available that lift a wheelchair from to a maximum height of from 2 ft. to 12 ft. A platform lift requires little space in the garage (only about 4 ft. by 4 ft. 3 in.), and would not be likely to detract from the aesthetics. A lift would leave enough space for the garage to hold two vehicles, provided one of them was a compact.

Some homes in warm climates may not have an attached garage or carport and may not have close entries from the car park area. One immediately apparent solution is to extend or reroute the driveway so that the automobile can get closer to the house or closer to a more accessible entry. The driveway should be built to accomplish the climb up to a level equal with the floor of the house (see pp. 47-50).

The person entering the house should be protected from the weather. The best entry to remodel for accessibility would be the entry through the garage or carport because the protection from the elements is already in place. If the house doesn't have a garage or carport, the entrance selected for adding a protected entryway should be the one closest to the parking area. In some instances, it may be less expensive to make a new entryway than to attempt to add a ramp or reroute the driveway. In other situations, an unprotected entry could be protected by extending the existing entryway, adding a porch or a porte cochère (see the drawing and discussion on p. 59). On pp. 54-60 are numerous suggestions for creating accessible entrances, many of which are equally applicable for remodeling.

Interior pathways   The most common obstacle to accessible pathways inside the house is the width of the doorways. There are three possibilities for making doors wider. First, if the door is unnecessary it can be removed. Without the door in the frame, the opening may be wide enough (minimum 32 in.) to allow an easy passage. Second, if the door frame is wide enough but the door in the frame takes too much space, offset hinges, which are often available at hardware stores, may be used to allow the door to swing out of the frame and provide a clear opening (see the drawing below). Third, the door frame and door may need to be replaced.

Many homes are built with hallways, walls and doorways more out of convention than of necessity. The more hallways, walls and doorways, the more ob-

Offset Door Hinges

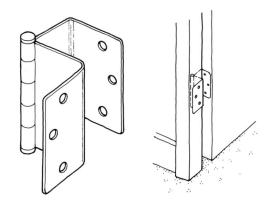

Offset door hinges allow a door to pivot completely out of the doorway, leaving an extra 2 in. of clearance, which may be all that is needed for wheelchair accessibility.

stacles for maneuvering about. If mobility becomes a problem for someone in the household, look about the house and determine if removing a non-load bearing wall would provide wider and straighter pathways and increase the usable space. Many homes have formal dining rooms, formal living rooms and even playrooms that go unused because when the less mobile family member is in this room, he or she is cut off from the rest of the brood.

Remodeling a sunken living room is not too difficult if there is only a one-step difference, since you can build a ramp to replace the step. Design the ramp to have as shallow a slope as possible, and integrate the ramp into the other features of the room (see p. 127). Ramps in the house can be integrated with bookshelves, countertops, indoor garden areas lined with natural rock, half-walls, seating and storage cabinets. The ramps should have a standard (1½-in. diameter) handrail on both sides so the person traveling on it has a handhold that can be grasped.

Multi-level homes Multi-level homes that have all of the facilities needed for independence on an accessible floor are not as critical a candidate for remodeling as the many homes that have all of the sleeping and bathing facilities on the second floor. Although it's not ideal to cut off the person with mobility limitations from the inaccessible floor, the individual at least will be able to function within the house that has bathing, toileting, sleeping and dining facilities on an accessible floor.

Two alternative solutions to homes that do not contain all of the necessary components on one floor are to install the missing features on the accessible floor, or to make all levels accessible through the addition of an elevator (or stairway lift).

Doing both may be best. Installing an elevator makes the entire house accessible, while adding toilets if they are not available on each floor will undoubtedly make living easier. It is not as important to duplicate bedroom, dining and bathing facilities if other levels of the house may be reached. Toilets, however, are visited more frequently and urgently, and having to travel to another floor by elevator or stairway lift may create significant discomfort.

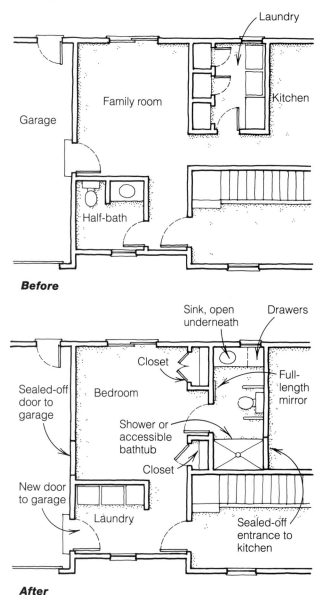

Family Room/Bedroom Conversion

Before

After

Adding a bedroom and full bath Sometimes it's easy to decide which room to convert to a first-floor bedroom and full bath. In the drawing above, a family room has been converted to a bedroom by removing the door to the garage and sealing the wall. A new entrance passes through the former half-bath, and this area has been converted into a small laundry room. The former laundry room has been enlarged

Dining Room/Bedroom Conversion

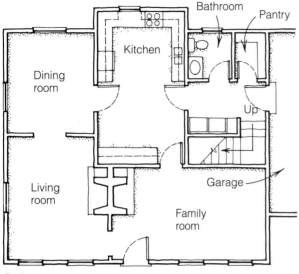

Before

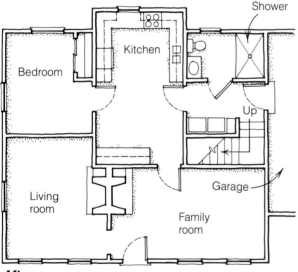

After

(by sealing off the entrance to the kitchen) and converted into a full bath that accommodates an accessible shower or bathing system.

Often there's no easy choice for a first-floor bedroom conversion, as in the floor plan in the drawing at left. Although either the dining room, living room or family room could be converted to a bedroom, none of them is close to an area that could be easily converted to a bathroom. On this floor plan, the best room to convert would be the dining room because it has no fireplace and it is the smallest of the three. Sealing the doorway between the living room and the dining room creates the bedroom, and the pantry/half-bath space can be converted to a bathroom with a small shower. The transition is not ideal, however, because of the exterior entrance from the garage at this location and the stairs leading to the basement.

The floor plan in the top drawing on the facing page presents few options for adding a bedroom and accessible bathroom to the first floor. We would recommend converting the dining room and bathroom to a small bedroom suite. An angled wall seals off the kitchen from the new bathroom area. The door to the new bedroom would be left intact, and a pocket door would be put where the new entry to the bathroom would be. The existing closet area would be removed to enlarge the area in the bathroom so that a walk-in shower could be added, or the shower could be omitted and a door could be installed to provide a direct entry from the bedroom. The sink would be moved to the opposite wall.

The home in the bottom drawing on the facing page provides an easier, though not ideal, conversion. The library can be converted into a bedroom without interfering with entrance pathways and without sacrificing dining, living-room or family-room space. The dinette, though a convenient place for the family to have a quick meal, can be incorporated into the bathroom area; the additional space would allow for the installation of a fully accessible bathing system as well as sufficient clear space around the toilet.

Installing an elevator or stairway lift In order to allow a family member with physical limitations to reach all the areas of the house, perhaps to enjoy the bedroom he or she has occupied for many years (and

Dining Room/Bedroom Suite Conversion

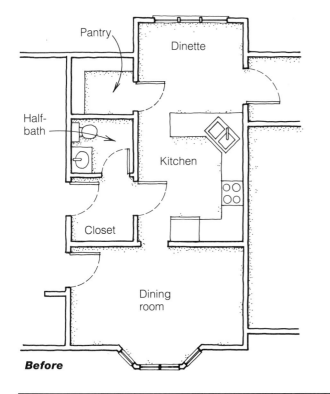

Pantry

Dinette

Half-bath

Kitchen

Closet

Dining room

Before

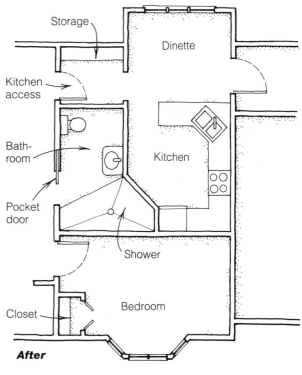

Storage

Dinette

Kitchen access

Bathroom

Kitchen

Pocket door

Shower

Closet

Bedroom

After

Library/Bedroom Conversion

Before

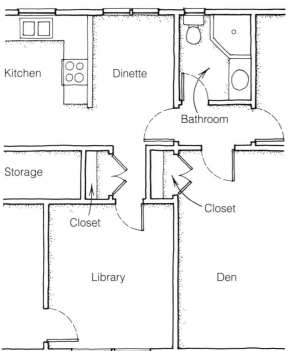

Kitchen

Dinette

Bathroom

Storage

Closet

Closet

Library

Den

After

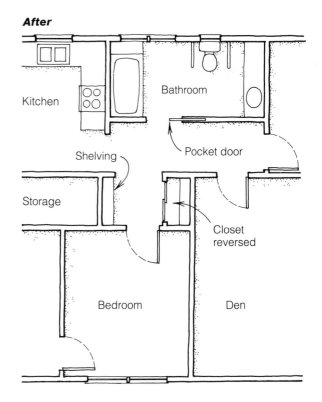

Kitchen

Bathroom

Pocket door

Shelving

Storage

Closet reversed

Bedroom

Den

perhaps because it is the most cost-effective solution), an elevator or stairway lift may be installed. The advantages and disadvantages of elevators and stairway lifts are described on pp. 128-133.

The decision whether to install an elevator or a stairway lift should be based on the dimensions of the stairs, the availability of space for installation of an elevator and the abilities of the individual or individuals who will be using the assistive system. Tracks for stairway lifts occupy about 12 in. If the stairways in the house are narrow (30 in. or less), the lift may present a hazard to people walking up and down the stairs. Someone else in the household who uses an assistive device such as a cane or walker instead of the stairway lift would be hampered by a clear stair width of less than 30 in. Also, some people cannot use a stairway lift because they cannot transfer from their wheelchair to the seat on the lift.

Find space for an elevator if the stairs in the house are too narrow. The ideal location for an elevator is where it can be accessed from public areas on both the first and second floors. Many two-story homes, however, were not planned to accommodate the installation of an elevator in the future, and consequently they don't have public spaces lined up one above the other. See the drawing on p. 132 for a house plan that would accommodate an elevator.

Putting things within reach   The essential elements of the environment (excluding the kitchen and bathroom) that are often out of reach for people with physical limitations include light switches and outlets, doors and windows, telephones, thermostats and storage areas. The goal is to make each room accessible, and this means bringing as many of the operable components of these devices into the optimal reach zone (20 in. to 44 in. off the floor, and 20 in. deep). If a wall containing any of these elements is part of the remodeling plans, keep in mind the criteria for wiring and switches specified on pp. 81-85.

There are five methods for changing the location of electrical components:
• using surface-mounted adapters
• running surface-mounted wiring to new locations

• fishing cable through the walls and installing new light switches and electrical boxes
• integrating the electrical components into a remote-control system that can be operated from any position within the home.

The least expensive (and least attractive) solution is to put an adapter at each of the light switches. The adapter connects mechanically to the existing switch by a small rod that extends to within reach of the user. This device, however, has two problems. First, it assumes that the light switch is in a location that can be approached. Second, because it is unattractive, it sends the message that something is wrong with the person who uses it (rather than with the placement of the switch itself).

Outlets will probably also need to be moved. Most people use an extension cord instead because it is the least expensive and the quickest fix. This solution generates the potential for danger. Extension cords are apt to be overloaded or to become entangled or crushed under furniture, setting up an opportunity for a fire. Extension cords trip people and get caught around furnishings. The best solution is to move the outlet.

The second solution involves adding a surface-mounted wiring system. Delaware Industries (Baseway Products, 8987 Route 14, Streetsboro, OH 44241) manufactures a surface-mounted housing for the wiring system of homes. This border channel, which outlines the room like a baseboard, carries all of the wiring of the house. Once it is installed, tapping into it to change the location of a light switch or outlet is a simple matter of removing the cover.

The third solution is to rewire for new locations. Usually this requires opening the wall at the new location and fishing wires to the opening from the old switch or outlet boxes. The old positions can be concealed with blank cover plates or patched to match the finish wall. Eliminating the old holes in this way will probably cost a good deal more than using cover plates, but it is more attractive. One method would be to tear out the bottom half of the walls, rewire, then install wainscoting over the area that have been torn out. Installing wainscoting may eliminate the need for complete refinishing of the entire wall.

The fourth solution is to install a home control system and to connect the components that would have been operated through the switches and outlets to this system. Home control systems, described on pp. 90-92, are mainstream products that are likely to build value in the environment for all users. Systems that use plug-in modules are relatively easy to install because they do not require rewiring the present system. With these systems, the outlet is not made accessible, but the device that would be plugged into it is operable through remote control.

Telephone jack and television cable boxes can be relocated to more accessible locations. Cordless telephones are a great solution to an inaccessible communication systems. Remote telephones are often carried in a holster mounted on a wheelchair. Voice-actuated phones are another solution that closes the gap between physical barriers and people's needs. Companies that make remote-control systems are listed on pp. 95-96.

REMODELING ESSENTIALS FOR PEOPLE WITH VISUAL LIMITATIONS

The changes in vision that accompany the aging process occur so gradually that people continually make adjustments in their activities to compensate for their decreased abilities. Many don't even realize how much they have changed their lifestyle until someone else points it out to them. Very gradually people reduce the scope of their activities to keep the level of the demands of the activity consistent with their capabilities.

Following are suggested changes that should be made in residential environments to accommodate individuals who are blind, have low-vision difficulties or who are simply getting older.

Exterior pathways   People who have visual limitations are aided by many of the accommodations made for people with physical limitations. All exterior pathways should be smooth and even. Any abrupt or unexpected change in the surface of the pathway creates a hazard for an individual who is blind or partially sighted. If the pathway is flagstone, loose gravel or soft material it should be replaced with a solid surface such as concrete or asphalt.

Places in the pathway where there are level changes, such as curb cuts, should be identified for the person with visual limitations in one of three ways: a change in surface texture, a protective wall or an increase in visual contrast.

Surface texture can be changed by brushing the concrete or putting in a surface with a different resilience from that of the rest of the walkway. Many people with visual impairments are able to detect changes in the smoothness or resilience of a surface and are alerted to an upcoming change in the level of the pathway. The U.S. Architectural and Transportation Board (1983) suggested that changes in pavement could serve as landmarks and indicators of hazards such as stairs and other changes in elevation. Unfortunately, surfaces may be covered by snow and ice or fallen debris that would camouflage the difference in texture. Thus, surface texture changes need to be accompanied by other measures.

A protective wall, seat or planter can prevent someone from stepping off an unexpected level change. One way to construct a protective barrier around a curb cut that "cuts" into a walkway is shown in the bottom photo on p. 258.

The walkway should have high visual contrast with the surrounding areas, and any level changes in the pathway should be marked by borders of visual contrast. A level change, such as a curb cut that intersects a walkway, can be identified by painting the sloping areas in red or by painting alternating stripes of black and yellow. While neither painted solution is particularly attractive, we are unaware of other methods to help identify the level change on the surface of an existing walkway.

Get rid of protruding objects (branches, windows, etc.) that overhang the pathway. A blind person will not detect them with a cane, and a person with low vision who is concentrating on footing may not see the object before colliding with it.

People with visual limitations are at significant risk if there is ice or slippery debris on the walkway. Pathways should be easily cleared during inclement weather so that the individual will not encounter puddles, icy patches and snow. Someone with low vision may not be able to discern the presence of ice on a walkway and may not take precautions when walking.

Lighting directed onto the pathway should provide an even level of illumination across the area. Shadows often look like changes in the surface and may cause any individual to trip, not only people with low vision.

Level changes (ramps and stairs) Add handrails to ramps and stairways that don't have them, even short runs. The handrails not only assist in steadying oneself when ascending or descending the steps, but also serve as a marker for the edge of the steps. The handrails will prevent the individual with visual limitations from tripping over or walking into the open stairs. Just as with level changes on walkways, people with visual limitations should be forewarned of the approaching level change in a stairwell by the change of surface texture.

Put protective barriers around open stairwells. All should be enclosed, but those on a route into and within a house especially need to offer protection for someone who may be unaware of their presence. In some homes, you enter the front door, walk a few paces and encounter one set of stairs leading to the second floor and a second set leading to the basement. Someone with a visual impairment may be unable to identify the stairs or may be unable to determine which leads up and which goes down.

Some homes have stairs that start immediately behind a door without a landing. These are more dangerous than the open stairs because guests who are unfamiliar with the environment or even a confused family member may open the door thinking that they are entering a room, only to find themselves halfway down the stairs (see the drawing on p. 126). There are a few remedies for this problem. The first is to build a small (4-ft. long) landing at the top of the stairs. The second is to use a decorative gate rather than a solid door. The gate keeps people from walking onto the stairs unexpectedly, and provided there is sufficient lighting, lets them identify where they are before they have taken the fateful step.

Add lighting to steps and stairwells. These are ideal locations to install lighting that comes on automatically when the door is opened or that is activated by sound or light. Light fixtures should be added near and on stairwells to provide even lighting at the top, bottom and on the steps. Falls often occur at the first step because the individual failed to see the step or misjudged its height or depth.

The visual environment One of the simplest yet most effective improvements to existing homes is to add lighting. Few living environments have sufficient lighting, particularly for older eyes, which require almost three times as much light as younger eyes. This is because older eyes often have corneal clouding, thickened or opaque lenses and weaker musculature on the iris that limits dilation of the pupil.

Interior lighting should be increased, should have good shades or valances so that the light does not shine directly into people's eyes and should be directed onto work areas. If the work surface is glossy or reflects light (such as a glass tabletop), cover it with a light-colored tablecloth that will absorb rather than reflect the light.

It's a good idea to increase the amount of natural light in the house. However, if the sun shines directly through a window at eye level, it can make it impossible to see because everything else will appear to be in a shadow. Glare in a house may be reduced by improving the window treatments. This can be accomplished by adding awnings on the outside, replacing glazing with tinted glass or adding sheer window curtains inside.

Add an intercom system at the entrance to the dwelling. Someone with a visual deficit, unable to identify the caller by looking through the side lite or a peephole, will be able to talk with the visitor before opening the door. (Companies that make intercom systems are listed on p. 96.) Listen to the quality and be sure the system has a volume control before purchasing it. Many people with visual impairments might also have a hearing deficit.

REMODELING ESSENTIALS FOR PEOPLE WITH HEARING IMPAIRMENTS

Everyone has heard stories of someone who is assumed to be critically injured or dead by his friends or family because he did not answer the door or the telephone. The person in question would be taking a bath or ironing when who should appear but his concerned son, an ambulance and all of the neighbors. After repeated attempts to get the attention of the person were unsuccessful, the son (in desperation) called for reinforcements.

A few simple additions to the living environment can help ease the tension on both the hearing-impaired person and visitors or guests. Begin by improving visibility and opportunities for surveillance. Increase exterior lighting and remove overgrown bushes and tree limbs that obstruct views from windows. Add a peephole, or better yet a side lite, to solid exterior doors. Video intercoms like the Aiphone (described on p. 90) are expensive but effective devices for people with hearing impairments.

Add visual indicators to sound signalling systems. Put a flashing-light adapter on the telephone and doorbell so that the occupant will know that these have been actuated (see pp. 96-97 for a list of companies that make these products). Install smoke and gas detectors that have an acoustic and a visual alarm (such as a strobe light).

Decrease background noise levels in the house by adding sound-absorbent materials (carpeting, drapes and upholstered/cushioned furnishings) or by installing acoustical tiling or acoustical baffles. Noise levels may also be reduced by tracing the sources of the noise and damping them.

Much of the noise created by products is not caused so much by the product but by the surrounding products set into vibration when the furnace, dishwasher or refrigerator are running. Many people have become so accustomed to the thump and grind of an air conditioner that they don't realize the noise is caused by the casing vibrating against an adjacent wall. A piece of sponge or a simple sheet-metal screw eliminates the noise in minutes.

With the exception of the modifications to accomplish level changes in the residence, all of the recommendations in this chapter should enhance the living environment for all of the household members, even those recommendations designated for people with visual or hearing limitations.

RESOURCES

Comprehensive Catalog Companies

Access with Ease
P.O. Box 1150
Chino Valley, AZ 86323
(602) 636-9469
Full line of self-help aids.

Alimed
297 High Street
Dedham, MA 02026
(800) 225-2610
(617) 329-2900
Full line of self-help aids.

Care Catalog Services
1877 N.E. Seventh Avenue
Portland, OR 97212
(800) 443-7091
(503) 288-8174
Full line of self-help aids.

Comfortably Yours
61 West Hunter Avenue
Maywood, NJ 07607
(201) 368-3499
Full line of self-help aids.

Fred Sammons
P.O. Box 32
Brookfield, IL 60513-0032
(800) 323-5547
(708) 323-1700
Bathing and home health-care equipment.

Llewellyn-SML
1 Regent Road
Liverpool
England L3 7BX
051-236-5311
Bathing and home health-care equipment.

Maddak
Pequannock, NJ 07440-1993
(201) 694-0500
Independent living line of products (Ableware) includes bathing, toileting, dressing, food preparation and eating aids.

Sears, Roebuck and Company
P.O. Box 804203
Chicago, IL 60680-4203
(800) 326-1750
Comprehensive catalog of home health-care equipment.

Smith & Nephew Rolyan
N93 W14475 Whitaker Way
Menomonee Falls, WI 53051
(800) 558-8633
Bathing, grooming and other assistive devices.

United Medical
1210 Madison
Memphis, TN 38104
(800) 348-2273
(901) 725-1353
Bathing and home health-care equipment.

CHAPTER FOURTEEN

REMODELING THE KITCHEN

Whether you are considering a modest facelift, a replacement project or a full-scale renovation, you have the opportunity to establish a kitchen that will be accessible, efficient and safe for everyone in the household. A facelift may involve upgrading the surfaces (new floors, wall treatments, cabinet and counter finishes). Careful selection of the new finishes, and perhaps some rearrangement of interiors of the cabinets, can improve visibility and usability of storage areas. A replacement project may call for new appliances and new cabinets, which can offer the chance for significant improvement of the usability of the kitchen. On a major overhaul, the entire kitchen may be changed, allowing for the creation of a true

Creating a Sit-Down Sink

An attractive and functional sit-down sink can be created by removing the cabinet below the sink and making a few changes.

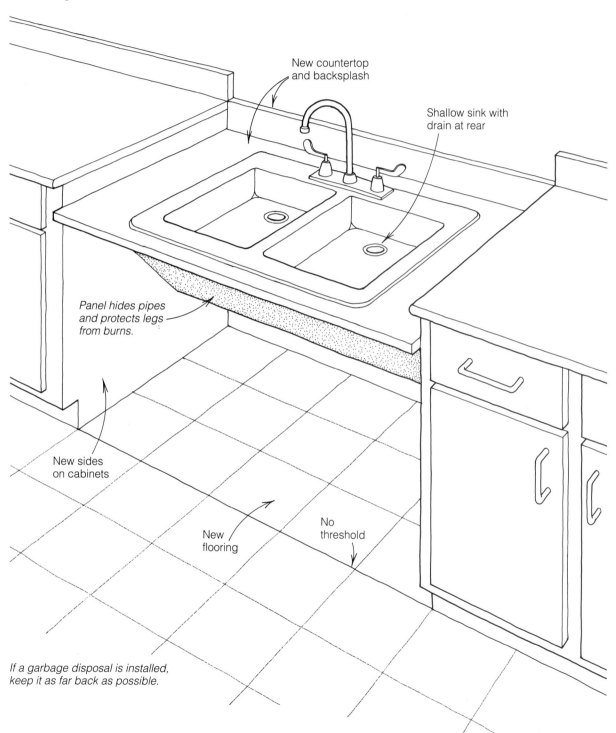

New countertop and backsplash

Shallow sink with drain at rear

Panel hides pipes and protects legs from burns.

New sides on cabinets

New flooring

No threshold

If a garbage disposal is installed, keep it as far back as possible.

lifespan kitchen as described on pp. 134-161. A review of the discussion on product design (pp. 25-29) will also be helpful if you are thinking about remodeling your kitchen.

Before beginning the project, evaluate your kitchen from three perspectives. First, look at the kitchen relative to the needs of your household today. Second, envision the function and performance of the kitchen as the people age or the household grows. Third, consider the effects of any remodeling projects on the long-term or resale value of the house. The important point is to look beyond immediate needs. Don't simply evaluate the current shortcomings of the kitchen, but rather consider the future shortcomings of any specific plans that you make. Obviously, the budget for the project will impose its own set of constraints and considerations.

Begin the planning process by completing a careful inventory of the existing kitchen, including the cooking habits of the household. Identify the primary work centers of the cook or cooks and apply the principles of the work triangle to each of the work centers and their relationship to each other. Many cooks won't use all three components of the traditional work triangle (the refrigerator, sink and the cooktop or range) for every meal. Some may use the refrigerator and microwave for one meal; the refrigerator, sink preparation area, microwave oven and grill for the next; and the refrigerator, sink preparation area and cooktop for the next. The cook may be very tall or very short. The cook may use a three-wheel scooter, a wheelchair, a cane or a walker, or have difficulty using one arm.

Cooking patterns and food consumption habits have changed and are continuing to change. The kitchen designed a decade or more ago may not reflect the current needs of the household. As the Maytag survey cited on p. 139 showed, the kitchen has become one of the primary family gathering areas in the home. This chapter will focus on the principal concerns of a kitchen remodel: work centers, storage, appliances, lighting, and improving movement (pathways and clear space).

WORK CENTERS

The kitchen work centers include the sink and adjacent countertop area used for preparing foods and cleaning up; a work surface, mix or food preparation area where foods are chopped, sliced, combined in blenders or mixers or stirred in a bowl; and cooking areas, which may include cooktops, a microwave, ovens and the adjacent set-down spaces or countertops. Chapter 9 describes the design of work centers in greater depth. This section will describe methods for creating new work centers or modifying existing work centers without having to replace the cabinets in the kitchen.

The sit-down sink   One goal of any kitchen remodel should be to allow for sitting down while working at the sink. There are several ways to accomplish this. One method is to remove the cabinet housing the plumbing and wrap the pipes with insulation. This is often not an attractive or effective option, however, as the insulated pipes are now visible and may interfere with the legs of a seated user. Also, the sink may remain at an uncomfortable height.

A more aesthetically pleasing solution will take a little more time and money. After removing the cabinet housing the sink and plumbing, it may be possible to lower the existing sink as much as 4 in. by adjusting the length and fittings of the drain and supply pipes (see the drawing on p. 223). No major plumbing work is required. That 4-in. drop will usually be sufficient for comfortable seated work. Additional work that could be done includes installing a new sink with a shallow (5-in.) depth. The existing countertop may have to be cut or replaced, and new, matching sides added to the cabinets. A baffle can be added as shown in the drawing on p. 152 to cover the plumbing. Finally, new flooring may be needed.

Although more expensive, it may be worthwhile to install a new solid-surface sink/countertop unit (such as one of Corian) that won't conduct heat as readily as stainless steel or porcelain. A sink with a white surface may be easier to use because items in a sink full of water will be easier to see.

Countertops Countertops can be improved significantly by providing at least two different work surface heights, ideally 32 in. and 36 in. Countertops are traditionally installed at 36 in. This is fine for tall people and for short-term tasks. But it is too high for short people who are completing tasks that take time (shelling shrimp) or exerting downward force (kneading bread or filling canning jars).

If the kitchen has only stand-up work centers, add spaces where someone may work while seated. Countertops 32 in. high will accommodate someone who is seated on a small stool, a chair with casters or a wheelchair. This lower countertop can serve as a kitchen desk, an eating area or a comfortable work area. If space permits, a small work table can be added onto the end of an island, as shown in the bottom photo on p. 226.

If the kitchen is not large enough to allow additional countertop space and moving the walls is out of the question, there are other ways to create work surfaces. Pull-out work surfaces may be mounted under existing countertops, and fold-down work surfaces may be mounted on the ends of cabinets or on the wall. Another solution is to build a cart with a countertop surface matching that of the kitchen. The cart may be moved into a convenient position for the work at hand. The cart may be left open on one side so that a seated individual may pull up underneath.

Creating Work Surfaces at Different Heights

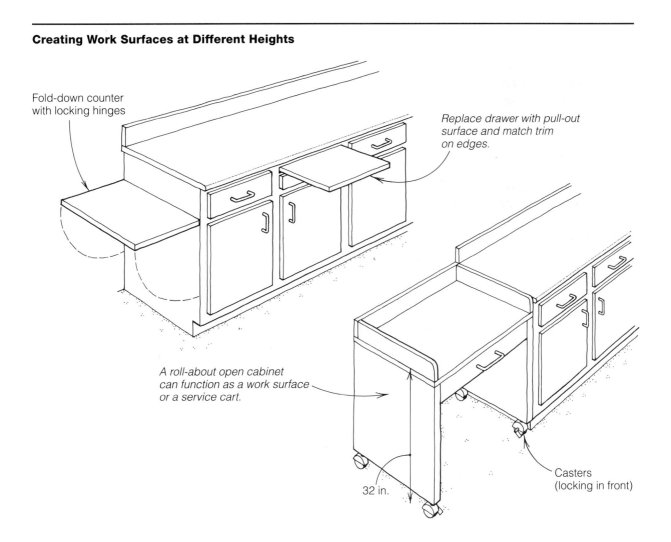

Fold-down counter with locking hinges

Replace drawer with pull-out surface and match trim on edges.

A roll-about open cabinet can function as a work surface or a service cart.

32 in.

Casters (locking in front)

A lower work surface can be created simply by adding a small work table where space permits, as in the photo above. Here, the proximity of electrical outlets makes the location particularly useful for seated work. In the top photo, open space under the low countertop allows for seated use from either side. (Photo at top: The Design Coalition, Madison, Wisconsin.)

STORAGE

As we age, we are most likely to encounter difficulty in maintaining energy levels and in bending, stooping and kneeling. Storage that isn't located conveniently to the work or use areas means extra steps. Low cabinets with fixed shelving and above-counter cabinets that are out of reach pose difficulties and risks to kitchen workers.

If the appearance, location and amount of storage of the present kitchen cabinets are acceptable but reaching and bending are problems, the remodeling should involve lowering the above-counter cabinets and installing roll-out cabinet accessories. Above-counter cabinets can be lowered 6 in. without compromising the work space on the typical 24-in. deep countertop mounted at a height of 36 in. The lowered height is likely to bring the entire second shelf within the reach of most women, and may allow many short individuals to reach even the top shelf without using a stepstool.

If insufficient or poorly organized storage is the problem, then more significant remodeling may be required. Some kitchen storage problems may be

Face-Frame vs. Frameless Cabinets

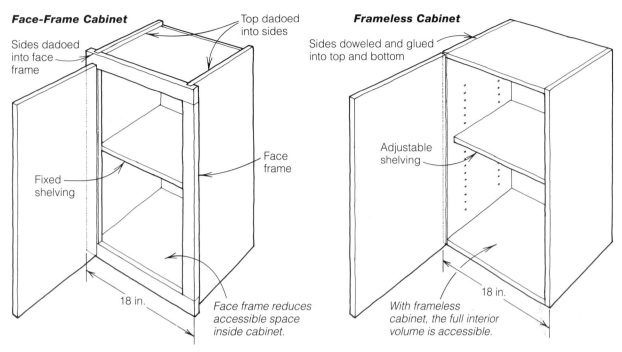

Face-Frame Cabinet

Sides dadoed into face frame

Top dadoed into sides

Fixed shelving

Face frame

18 in.

Face frame reduces accessible space inside cabinet.

Frameless Cabinet

Sides doweled and glued into top and bottom

Adjustable shelving

18 in.

With frameless cabinet, the full interior volume is accessible.

solved by the addition of cabinets; others will require removing old cabinets and changing their location or replacing them altogether.

When selecting replacement cabinets, it is important to look at the flexibility of the system. European-style cabinets (also called Eurostyle, frameless or 32mm cabinets) are customarily constructed with adjustable shelves, which can be spaced and arranged for maximum efficiency to hold various-sized cans, boxes, appliances and cookware (see the drawing above). Drawers are easier to use and organize than traditional cabinet shelves and bring the contents of the storage area into the light. The goal should be to locate as much shelving as possible within the optimal reach zone (20 to 44 in. off the floor).

Rubbermaid and Clairson International (Closet Maid) produce a complete line of roll-out bins, shelving and storage boxes that can be mounted in existing cabinet spaces (see Resources on p. 161). Although these accessories may reduce the overall amount of storage space, they will make many of the areas within the kitchen more accessible to those unable to reach low areas.

The Closet Maid storage system is ideal for transforming standard, inaccessible kitchen cabinets into usable units. (Photo: Clairson International.)

Often, kitchen cabinets can be improved substantially simply by refinishing the surfaces and replacing the hardware. Paint the inside of wood cabinets an off-white or almond color with a flat latex enamel. Lighter surfaces reflect light and make kitchens appear brighter and larger. Large D-shaped door and drawer pulls (5-in. opening) are easier to grasp than small knobs or J-pulls. D-pulls are ideal because they can be used without being grasped.

If more storage space is needed but space or budget preclude adding more cabinets, the countertop may offer a solution. As shown in the drawing below, appliance garages can be built into the corners, and small shelves (about 8 in. deep) can be installed along the backs of countertops. The shelves can be left open or be enclosed by small sliding doors.

A simple, although not too attractive, way to increase storage area is to install pegboard on the wall and hang cooking utensils on it. The pegboard can be installed at any height. A more attractive choice might be to install a rustic piece of wood containing wrought-iron hooks or a piece of laminated board with hooks of a contrasting color.

These "hang-up" storage spaces should be near the places where the utensils will be used. Hang cooking utensils on either side of the range and cooktop, but not directly above or behind them. The user shouldn't have to reach across a hot burner to retrieve an item, risking a burn. Also, utensils hanging over the cooktop become dirty faster because of spattering grease and the steam rising from cooking pots.

REPLACING APPLIANCES

When selecting new products, look beyond the gimmicks and fancy features and evaluate their ease of use, energy efficiency and environmental impact. Over the life of the appliances, these factors will become increasingly important.

To summarize the detailed discussion of product selection in Chapter 2, look for controls located

Adding Storage without Adding Cabinets

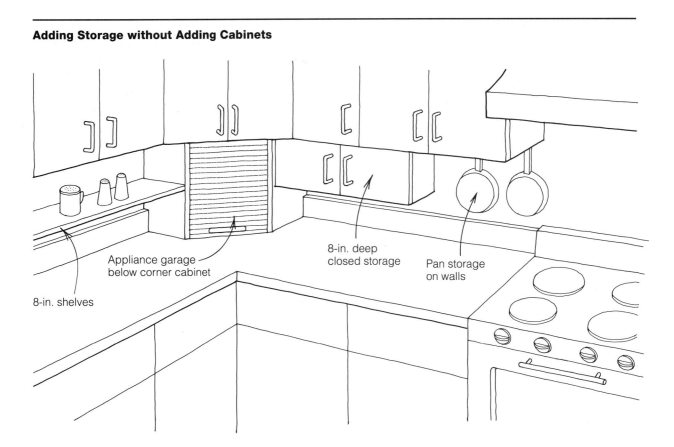

Appliance garage
below corner cabinet

8-in. deep
closed storage

Pan storage
on walls

8-in. shelves

The D-pull handles on this dishwasher are easier to use than the thin grip that comes with the machine.

within the optimal reach zone (20 in. to 44 in. high, 20 in. deep) and controls that can be operated with a closed fist. The arrangement and operation of the appliance should be obvious, and the visual displays necessary for operation should be in large print (¼-in. type) and high contrast (black on a light background or white on a dark background).

Some appliances can themselves be remodeled. Standard handles on dishwashers and refrigerators, for example, are not easy to use by people with arthritis or other hand strength and dexterity limitations. An enlarged D-pull (8 in. to 10 in. long and 2 in. deep) can easily be added. If the D-pull is selected to match other hardware or color schemes in the kitchen, it will not stand out as an add-on. It can also double as a towel bar.

Refrigerators without pull-out shelving demand a deep reach to get to their contents. Inexpensive lazy Susans and storage and stacking bins may help bring more of the storage space within reach. A canned-drink dispenser is available that rolls the next can into place at the front.

LIGHTING

Lighting in the kitchen can be tricky. Good natural lighting from an east or west window can become an eye-fatiguing glare when the sun is low in the sky. Consider adding a window to allow more natural light into the kitchen. An awning on an existing window might eliminate a glare problem and eliminate the need for curtains.

Adding lights under above-counter cabinets or putting in a row of track lighting that can be aimed toward the darkest corners of the kitchen may quickly solve the annoying lighting problems that you have endured for years. A dark kitchen can be made considerably lighter by changing the colors of the surfaces (for example, from dark wood paneling to white walls and cabinets). Brightening the surfaces helps a lot in small kitchens that do not have good natural or indoor lighting.

U-Shaped Kitchen Remodel

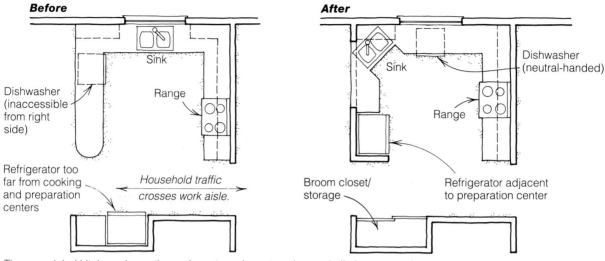

The remodeled kitchen places the work centers closer together and eliminates a major pathway crossing a work aisle. The dishwasher has been relocated to a neutral-handed position.

IMPROVING MOVEMENT

Movement problems can be caused by bad floor plans, poorly placed appliances or even a drawer located in the wrong spot. Try to analyze the nature and source of your current problems. Are two cooks constantly running into each other? Are drawers opening into frequently used pathways? Are cabinet doors interfering with appliance use? Also, evaluate movement in the kitchen with an eye toward the future, when a member of the household may have difficulty getting about. Remodel with the goal of ensuring that someone in a wheelchair will be able to participate in all kitchen activities. Make all traffic aisles at least 36 in. wide, and allow for clear floor space in front of all appliances. Try to see that the new kitchen is neutrally handed, that is, that all areas and appliances can be approached from front, left and right. Try to select products that are neutrally handed.

Some problems in the kitchen can be solved by simple means, such as by moving the contents of a drawer or cabinet. Other problems require a completely new design.

In the sections that follow, three kitchens are shown before and after remodeling. The goal of each remodel was to streamline traffic flow and to group work centers together in accessible arrangements.

U-shaped kitchen remodel   Although the U-shaped-kitchen shown in the drawing above had the sink directly under the window and a convenient counter space, there were some problems. The dishwasher's location near the corner limited access to the front and the left side. The refrigerator was separated from the rest of the kitchen by a major pathway, and a set-down space on the right side of the refrigerator was in this traffic pathway. The remodel puts the refrigerator in the kitchen area proper with a set-down space to its right; each of the major appliances is accessible from the front or from either side.

Galley kitchen remodel   The galley kitchen shown in the top drawing on the facing page required the cook to lift and carry items across the corridor from sink to stove, oven and refrigerator. None of the appliances were connected with a continuous countertop, and all were bisected by a pathway. Remodeling the kitchen into a U shape connects all of the appliances with a continuous countertop. The cooktop counter extends to form a breakfast bar, and the pass-through at the opposite end of the kitchen is convenient for transferring items from the storage area into the kitchen.

Galley Kitchen Remodel

Before

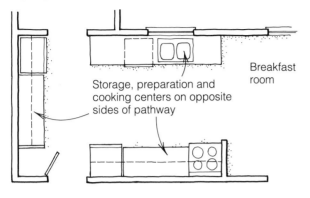

Storage, preparation and cooking centers on opposite sides of pathway

Breakfast room

After

Dishwasher

Breakfast bar

Storage, preparation and cooking centers connected

Set-down area

Downdraft-range

Storage

In the remodeled kitchen, the work centers are grouped in one area. The work aisle is no longer crossed by the pathway to the breakfast room.

L-Shaped Kitchen Remodel

Before

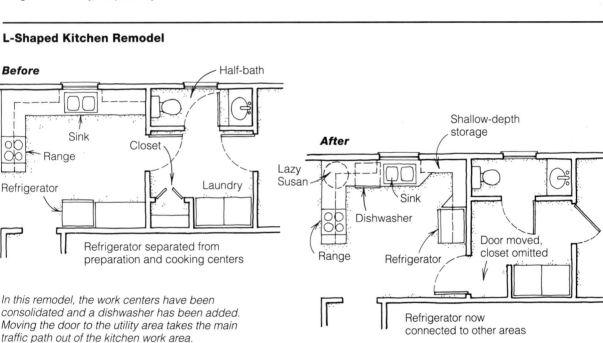

Half-bath

Sink

Closet

Laundry

Range

Refrigerator

Refrigerator separated from preparation and cooking centers

After

Shallow-depth storage

Lazy Susan

Sink

Dishwasher

Range

Refrigerator

Door moved, closet omitted

Refrigerator now connected to other areas

In this remodel, the work centers have been consolidated and a dishwasher has been added. Moving the door to the utility area takes the main traffic path out of the kitchen work area.

L-shaped kitchen remodel Most of the small L-shaped kitchen shown in the drawing above was occupied by a pathway into a half-bath and laundry area. As with the previous kitchens, the refrigerator was separated from the remainder of the kitchen. In the remodel, a lazy Susan is tucked into one corner; a shallow-depth storage area in the other corner of the room reduces the amount of dead space. The refrigerator has been moved to the same side of the pathway as the other appliances, and a dishwasher has been added. The remodeled kitchen is not interrupted by the pathway to the half-bath and laundry, and the use of space has been maximized.

CHAPTER FIFTEEN
REMODELING THE BATHROOM

Many people find themselves in houses that don't allow them to use their bathrooms without assistance. The traditional tub and toilet are not synonymous with ease of use. Some people are forced to improvise by keeping a commode near them. Some houses have a bathroom only on the second floor, which can be a great inconvenience for a person who has difficulty climbing stairs. Some problems can be solved by modifying existing bathrooms, others by adding new bathrooms. This chapter will explore both options, expanding on the more extensive discussion of bathroom design in Chapter 10, with an emphasis on changing bathroom design in existing homes.

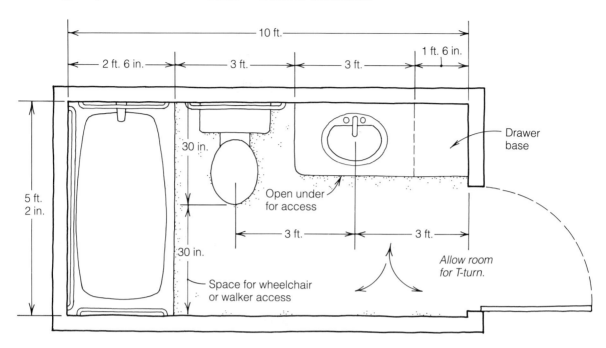

10 ft.

2 ft. 6 in.   3 ft.   3 ft.   1 ft. 6 in.

5 ft. 2 in.

30 in.

Open under for access

30 in.

Drawer base

3 ft.   3 ft.

Allow room for T-turn.

Space for wheelchair or walker access

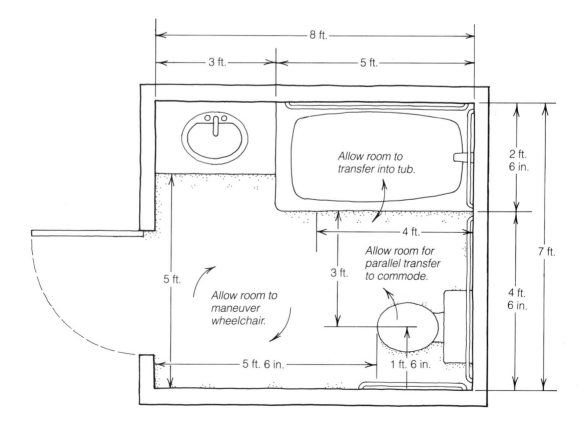

8 ft.

3 ft.   5 ft.

Allow room to transfer into tub.

2 ft. 6 in.

4 ft.

Allow room for parallel transfer to commode.

7 ft.

4 ft. 6 in.

5 ft.

Allow room to maneuver wheelchair.

3 ft.

5 ft. 6 in.   1 ft. 6 in.

Bathrooms are remodeled for many of the same reasons kitchens are recast. Many bathrooms need a facelift after 10 or 20 years of service. The floors and walls may need replacing or refinishing. The fixtures may need replacement. Many bathrooms need change because they simply can no longer be used by a member of the household. Any bathroom remodel, from simple to complex, offers the opportunity to create a room that is accessible and convenient for everyone.

EVALUATING PROBLEMS AND NEEDS

Before beginning a remodeling job, the bathroom should be evaluated from the standpoint of its current and future needs in providing for the members of an evolving household. Any changes that are considered should also be assessed for their effect on the value of the house. A bathroom that has been remodeled wisely should make the house more appealing to a wider group of people when it comes time to sell it.

Bathing   Few people have a problem bathing. Most can wash their body without too much effort, although some people have difficulty reaching their feet and back. The problem for most people is not washing itself but rather getting into and out of the bathtub. If a bathroom is to be modified, the most important feature that should be changed is the tub.

There are several questions that should be asked regarding the bathing system: Should the existing system be completely replaced? Will a new product fit into the space occupied by the previous bathing system or will a different space be required? Is there a product that will provide transgenerational use and yet fit in the required space? Is there a product that will fit directly over the existing bathing system without having to remove it? If the bathing system isn't going to be replaced, are there assistive products available to allow all household members safe and independent use? How will these assistive devices affect the other members of the household? Will they be in the way? Will they have to be installed and removed with each use? Is there sufficient storage space within the bathroom for the assistive products?

Using the toilet   Many people have difficulty sitting down on and rising from the toilet. Several options for making the toilet more accessible are offered on pp. 183-184. Whenever possible, locate the toilet so that it can be used independently by someone in a wheelchair or someone who uses a walker or other assistive device. If a toilet is located too close to or too far from an adjacent wall, the usefulness of wall-mounted grab bars is limited. In this case, pull-down grab-bar systems should be installed (see p. 169).

People of different sizes prefer different toilet-seat heights. Many have difficulty transferring to or using a low commode. Others find the 18-in. high "handicapped" toilet much too high. The product choice is limited to either a high seater, low seater or a wall-mounted product. There are toilet-seat height adapters that clamp onto the toilet bowl and raise the seat, but they have some drawbacks. First, each adapter raises the seat height to one level, which may be too high for some members of the household, particularly if more than one generation resides in the dwelling. Second, they are lightweight but bulky, and take some time and effort to install and remove. Third, they are likely to need frequent cleaning because the flush water does not reach the height of the adapter. The few alternatives to this less than perfect solution are described on pp. 183-184.

Grooming   Grooming usually occurs at the sink and in front of a mirror. Many grooming aids need electricity. Most bathrooms have been constructed for grooming to be accomplished while standing, and it is difficult if not impossible to do while seated. Electrical outlets are often placed above the sink on the light fixture or alongside the medicine cabinet, locations that are out of reach for many people.

CREATING NEW BATHROOMS

It can be less costly to add a new bathroom than to remodel an existing one. It may be wise to look at the opportunities within the house for adding another bath. The best place to look is along a wet wall (a wall with plumbing in it). It is also generally easier to add plumbing to houses built over crawl spaces and basements than to those built on slabs.

A half-bath It isn't necessary to have a full bath in every location. If the problem is that a toilet isn't close enough to a bedroom, a half-bath (toilet and sink only) could be added in the corner of a bedroom. To ensure that this room will meet the mobility patterns of just about everyone, a space of 5 ft. by 5 ft. should be allotted for full access by a wheelchair user, and the fixtures must be placed to maximize the space available.

Bathrooms may be created out of existing closets. Walk-in closets that are at least 4 ft. by 6 ft. or 5 ft. by 5 ft. provide enough space for the half-bath (see the drawing at right). The loss of closet space can be rectified by creating a series of small storage areas in underused areas in adjacent rooms (a platform bed with built-in storage drawers underneath creates a lot of extra storage room).

A 5-ft. by 5-ft. space will not provide a turning diameter of 5 ft., which is recommended for a wheelchair-accessible room. Someone in a wheelchair, however, can move about in less space if there is sufficient room to pull up and back up for a T-turn. We think this kind of compromise between space and mobility is acceptable given the limited function of a half-bath. In a kitchen or full bath, where more activities are conducted, space should be provided for quick and efficient movement.

A half-bath may have to be designed to accommodate the specific needs of a person with a disability. If it is going to be used by someone in a wheelchair, the toilet should be located so that the person can transfer from his or her strong side by whatever method the person prefers. Some people back the chair alongside the toilet and move laterally. Others pull up front to back alongside the toilet and rotate their body as they transfer from their wheelchair seat to the toilet seat. Others pull up to the front end of the toilet, pull themselves to a standing position and turn before lowering onto the toilet seat.

A full bath It is difficult to create a full bathroom (toilet, sink and bathing system) that is wheelchair accessible in a space of 5 ft. by 8 ft., which is the size of a standard small bathroom. Moving up to 5 ft. 2 in. by 10 ft. or 7 ft. by 8 ft. will provide ample room to create an accessible full bath. General guidelines for an accessible full bath are shown in the drawing on p. 233.

Creating a Half-Bath

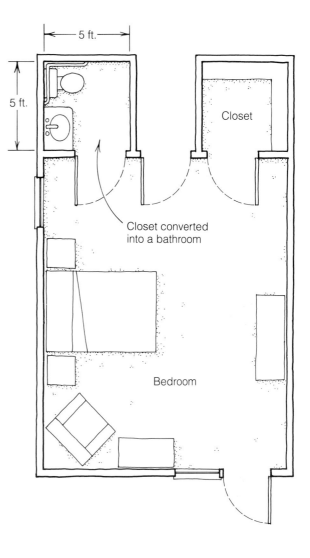

5 ft.

5 ft.

Closet

Closet converted into a bathroom

Bedroom

An accessible bathroom doesn't have to, and shouldn't, look like a hospital room. The institutional look can be avoided by using colors (coordinating grab bars and fixtures, for example), built-in storage areas that frame the fixtures and a motif. An institutional ("handicapped") bathroom may detract from the value of a home, while an attractive bathroom that happens to be accessible will add value.

One of the keys to ensuring that the bathroom added to a bedroom enhances rather than detracts from the value of the house is to select fixtures that help use the existing space efficiently, such as a wall-mounted toilet, wall-mounted sink and vanity and

Converting a Closet to a Bathroom (not Fully Accessible)

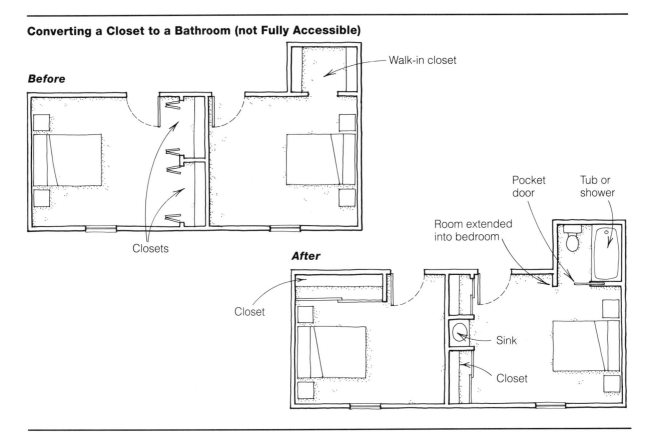

Before

Walk-in closet

Closets

After

Closet

Room extended into bedroom

Pocket door

Tub or shower

Sink

Closet

Converting a Bathroom and Closet to an Accessible Full Bath

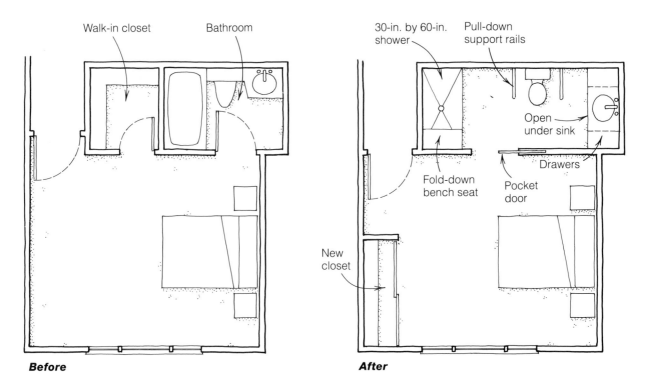

Walk-in closet

Bathroom

30-in. by 60-in. shower

Pull-down support rails

Open under sink

Drawers

Fold-down bench seat

Pocket door

New closet

Before

After

pull-down grab bars. Most wheelchair footrests are less than 8 in. high, so a wall-mounted toilet or vanity cabinet 8 in. above the floor will provide enough room for someone turning in a wheelchair.

Bathrooms can also be added to laundry or utility rooms. This may not be a glamorous solution, but if these rooms are large enough they can be ideally suited for such a change because they already are plumbed with hot and cold water supply and waste drain pipes. If the laundry room has a door, then the only changes that may be required are to locate the necessary fixtures in the available space.

Many people who cannot use the bathtub may find that a 3-ft. by 3-ft. shower installed in the laundry room solves their problem. If the laundry room is already equipped as a wet room with a drain in the floor (see pp. 179-180), it may only be necessary to install the water supply and a shower-curtain surround for an area near the drain.

ENLARGING EXISTING BATHROOMS

One of the greatest problems with bathrooms is the lack of space for maneuvering. The standard 5-ft. by 8-ft. bathroom with a toilet, tub, sink and vanity doesn't provide enough room for someone using an assistive device. In bathrooms where space is a problem, there are ways to enhance mobility without moving walls. First, consider the door. If it swings into the bathroom and creates a barrier to movement in the bathroom, reverse the swing so that it swings out, or install a pocket door (see p. 166). If the doorway opening isn't large enough, offset hinges may solve the problem without actually widening the door opening (see the drawing on p. 214). The doorway can also be widened.

If bathroom closets or storage cabinets are limiting maneuverability, they can be removed. A closet or shelving can be created in another part of the bathroom, or elsewhere. The vanity cabinet uses a lot of maneuvering space. By removing all or part of it, a roll-under counter can be created. If one section of the vanity is kept, it should have drawers that extend the full depth of the counter.

The drawings on the facing page offer before and after depictions of two typical bedroom/bathroom sections of single-family homes. The "after" drawings show how remodeling can improve maneuverability, safety and storage efficiency.

A few companies offer small, modular showers (not necessarily wheelchair accessible) that are assembled when installed. These showers are a good alternative to one-piece units, which don't fit through most doorways. These showers can also provide an independent bathing opportunity for someone who has difficulty with the standard bathtub. Although small, many can fit where the linen closet used to be.

REPLACING BATHROOM FIXTURES

Space isn't always the problem in a bathroom. It may be that the room is big enough to maneuver in, but that the fixtures are old or can't be used easily by a member of the household. Grab bars and a seat bench can be added at one end of the tub, but this solution has limited utility because many people will still be unable to use the tub independently. Also, it's not an attractive solution. When fixtures are replaced, use the opportunity to make them accessible.

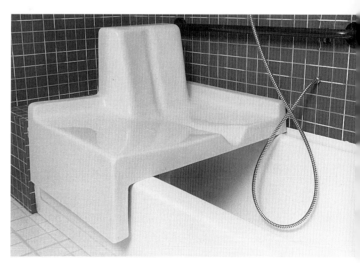

This bathtub transfer bench with seat insert provides a stable surface for someone who has difficulty using a standard tub. (Photo: courtesy Diversified Fiberglass Fabricators.)

Replacing a bathtub A bathtub may be replaced with another conventional bathtub, a shower enclosure that fits into the existing space, an accessible bathtub or a wet-room area. The least expensive, simplest alternative is to replace the bathtub with another conventional bathtub, but this solution will not help those with differing or changing abilities.

Shower enclosures (either one-piece or modular) are available that fit into the space of a bathtub, so a 30-in. by 60-in. inaccessible bathtub can be replaced by a 30-in. by 60-in. shower. Installing a roll-in shower with no threshold will usually require opening the floor to provide new drains and to build a waterproof floor that includes the areas around the shower, as shown in the drawing below.

Showers, particularly those without a threshold, offer access to bathing to just about everyone. They don't offer a seated tub soak, but most people can get into them. The primary difficulty is finding a shower enclosure that will fit through the doors of the house. A few companies offer modular showers that are assembled on site, that can be gotten through doorways (see Resources on pp. 189-191).

A number of companies offer various forms of accessible bathtubs. These are listed in Resources on pp. 189-191, but those that have models that will fit

Converting a Typical Bathtub Enclosure to a Shower

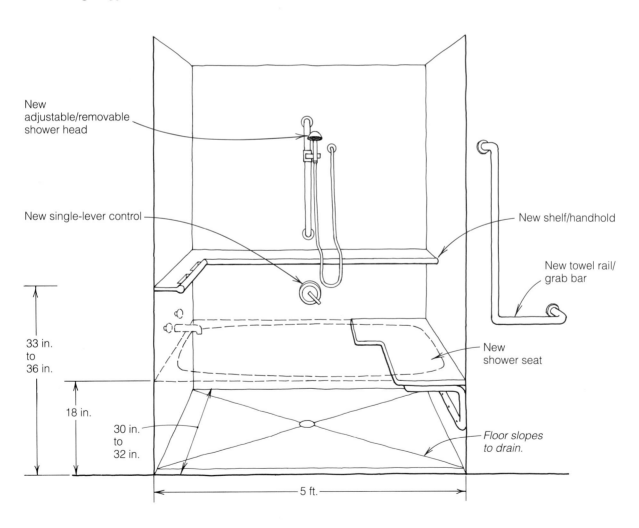

New adjustable/removable shower head

New single-lever control

New shelf/handhold

New towel rail/ grab bar

New shower seat

33 in. to 36 in.

18 in.

30 in. to 32 in.

Floor slopes to drain.

5 ft.

directly into the space vacated by a conventional bathtub deserve a second mention here. These include the Comfort Care System by Ferno Washington, the Precedence Series by Kohler, Safe-T-Bath of New England and BathEase. All of these bathing systems are high priced. The Comfort Care System has several options for the bather in getting into and out of the tub. The other three systems have doors in their sides. In both the BathEase and Kohler products the bather walks into the tub. In the Safe-T-Bath product, the bather sits in the doorway of the tub, then scoots in. For photos of these products see pp.173-175.

Removing the bathtub and replacing it with a tiled, wet-room area may require considerable labor, but could be one of the most attractive and useful solutions. In this instance the tub is taken out, the plumbing is replaced in the wall to convert to a shower (hand-held and/or wall-mounted) and the walls and floor are covered with ceramic tile that isn't too slippery. As shown in the drawing at right, it is best to extend the tiles beyond the boundaries of the old 30-in. by 60-in. bathing area because of increased splash from the shower. While the walls are open for the plumbing work, blocking should be added for grab bars. A recessed soap and shampoo shelf can easily be added at this time as well. (For more on wet rooms, see pp. 179-180.)

Many grab bars are placed too high in shower areas. They should be installed horizontally, at a height of 34 in. to 36 in. The bather should be able to put weight directly on the bar and hang on at a height about the same as the height of a cane or walker. Grab bars at this height also won't interfere with the elbows of people washing their hair.

Replacing a toilet   If the toilet seat is too low for a member of the household, a seat adapter could be added (see the discussion on. p. 234), but this is not an attractive option. A better long-term solution may be to replace the floor-mounted toilet with a wall-mounted toilet (see the drawing on p. 240), which allows someone in a wheelchair to maneuver closer to the toilet because there is no pedestal base. The wall-mounted toilet can be installed at whatever height is most convenient, which is often 17 in. to 19 in. for those who are physically challenged.

Converting a Bathroom to a Small Wet Room

Before

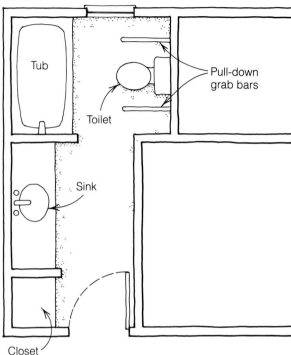

After

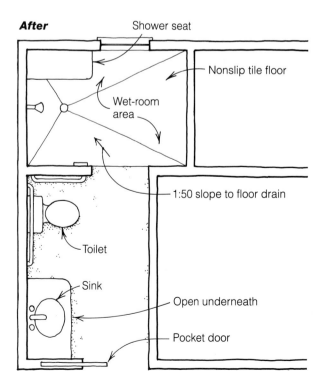

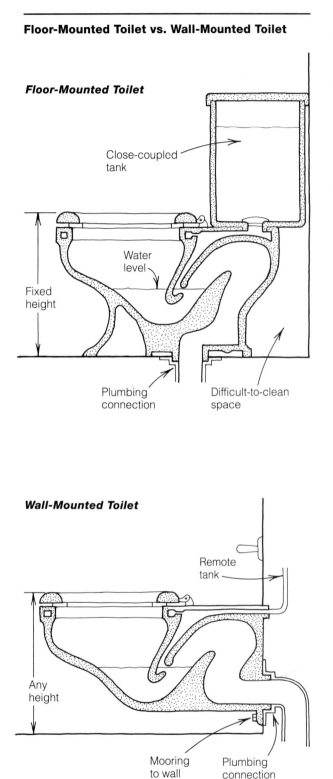

Floor-Mounted Toilet vs. Wall-Mounted Toilet

Floor-Mounted Toilet

Close-coupled tank

Water level

Fixed height

Plumbing connection

Difficult-to-clean space

Wall-Mounted Toilet

Remote tank

Any height

Mooring to wall

Plumbing connection

A wall mounted toilet can be installed at whatever height is most suitable for the person or persons using it.

A wall-mounted toilet can be expensive, however. The toilet itself costs more than a conventional floor-mounted fixture, a substantial amount of new plumbing may be required and a new floor treatment will be needed. A wall-mounted toilet requires a 6-in. thick wall to allow for the waste pipe, which must be rerouted from the floor.

ADDING GRAB BARS

All bathrooms should be built with grab bars, and grab bars should be added as part of any bathroom remodel. The idea that grab bars can be added "when they're needed," doesn't make much sense. When people become disabled, whether temporarily or permanently, the last thing they need to face is a round of remodeling in the house. Furthermore, few people realize just how much use grab bars will receive in any bathroom.

Adding grab bars to walls that have been prepared for them with the appropriate blocking is a simple matter of mounting the bars to the reinforced wall section. Grab bars may be located on walls that do not have blocking provided the grab bars are mounted on solid structural materials such as wall studs. Positioning the grab bar over studs, however, may not situate the bar in the most ideal location for the user.

Grab bars don't have to be attached to walls to be effective. Shower stalls are available with integral grab bars (make sure they meet ANSI standards for strength). A floor-mounted grab-bar system works well around toilets and the bathing area, but the bars do not extend into the bathtub. On the other hand, a floor-mounted system around the toilet may interfere with someone's ability to get close to the toilet. These systems are helpful for people who need support for sitting and rising, but not for people who will be transferring from a wheelchair.

Support rails are available that mount directly on the toilet (see the photos on the facing page). These provide some help when sitting and rising, but they may be too low and may not give the sense of security that is needed. One of the most versatile grab bar systems around the toilet mounts on the wall and

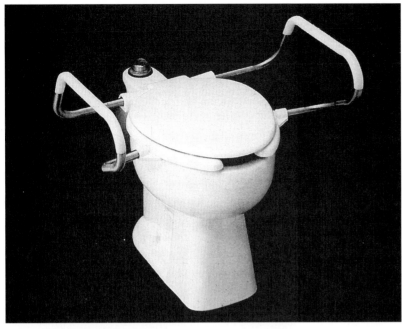

These toilet support rails by various manufacturers are representative of the different styles and systems available (companies that make accessible products for the bathroom are listed on pp. 188-191). When selecting a system, consider the needs of the user, the space available and the structural support of the walls near the toilet. (Photos: Institute for Technology Development.)

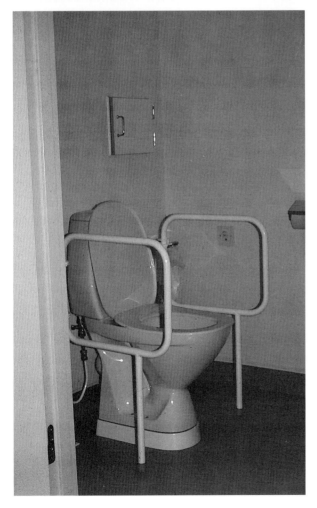

can be pulled down as needed. There are also clamp-on grab bars for the bathtub, which may be more convenient for the bather than a fixed grab bar on the wall.

ASSISTIVE BATHROOM ACCESSORIES

There are many other assistive products that may be incorporated into the bathroom. Some people opt for these accessories because they need a quick and cheap fix for a problem. Needless to say, if all bathrooms were built to the standards we propose for the lifespan house, such piecemeal fixes wouldn't be necessary. Outfitting a bathroom with these devices is something like always driving your car with the cheap replacement tire found in the trunk. You can't really get the car up to speed, you don't have the same level of control and it looks funny.

Products for bathing Assistive products for using the bathtub include bath seats and chairs, bench seats, lifts, nonslip surface treatments and hand-held shower heads. Bath seats come in various forms. Some are simply water-resistant chairs that are placed in the bathtub. These do not help the bather get into and out of the tub, but merely provide a seat so that the bather doesn't need to sit on the bathtub floor. This solution is limited in its ability to help the unsteady bather and in providing a satisfying bath. The bather is always out of the water and must have one hand free to hold the hand-held shower unit.

Other transfer benches allow the bather to sit on them outside the tub and swivel into the tub. These devices eliminate the problem of having to step over the bathtub wall. A third type of bath seats lowers the bather to the bottom of the tub. These products allow the bather to have a nearly typical bath. Some of these seats also swivel to pick the bather up from the outside of the tub. Others require bathers to maneuver themselves around so their torso is situated on the chair correctly and their legs are in the tub. These products operate on hydraulic pressure. Some attach over the faucet of the tub and others are attached with an adapter. The Dignity Bath (see p. 175) is a complete bathtub with the hydraulic chair as an integral component.

The bath bench is similar to the bath seat in that the bather is not lowered to the bathtub floor but sits out of the water. The bath bench extends from one side of the bathtub to the other (see the photo on p. 237). Some have an additional extension outside of the bathtub to help someone transfer from a wheelchair.

One problem with bath seats, benches and chairs is that they get in the way of other bathers. Given the option, most bathers will opt to sit in the water rather than above it. Thus, the fixed benches and seats would be removed by others capable of using the tub. Some of the products are relatively light-weight and may be removed without too much difficulty. Others are heavier and difficult to remove and store. Seats that raise and lower the bather may be used by other bathers without too much complaint.

Shower seats make a lot of sense for the wet room or large shower. They are not used as a means of getting into or out of the shower, but merely as a place to sit while showering. For some people with limited stamina, these are ideal bathing aids.

Shower benches, which mount on the wall, are available as fixed or folding units. The latter can be folded up out of the way when not in use, although the hinge mechanism on some units makes them difficult to raise and lower. Shower benches should be at least 12 in. deep, and they should be constructed so that water drains off them. They should also be comfortable to sit on.

Lifts or hoists are available for transporting someone from the bed to the bathroom or from a wheelchair onto the toilet or into the bathtub. These systems are mounted on the ceiling, in the floor or are on wheels. Some require an attendant to operate them; others may be operated by the individual being transported. They are a significant aid for someone unable to get into a tub without assistance because the caregiver doesn't have to lift the individual.

Floor-mounted lifts require less floor space than those on wheels, but they are less versatile. Lifts on wheels, however, need about 24 in. by 24 in. of clear space adjacent to, and ideally under, the bathtub or toilet to which the individual is being transferred.

Nonslip surface treatments are available as one-use chemical sprays, stick-on appliqués and mats. In our tests of chemical sprays, our evaluators were un-

The Lubidet attaches to any toilet. It provides a warm-water wash and warm-air dry. (Photo: courtesy Lubidet.)

specifically designed to assist people who have had hip surgery, to help keep them from getting into a position that would be too much strain on their healing joints.

Hydraulic toilet-seat lifts exist, although they seem to be only sporadically available in the United States. They are ingenious devices because they can be ignored by those who don't wish to use them, yet they are readily available for those who do. Most hydraulic lifts fit directly onto the existing toilet and use the traditional toilet seat. They eliminate the difficulty of lowering down or rising from the commode because the hydraulic lift slowly moves the person into position.

The toilet-mounted sitz bath or bidet mounts behind the toilet seat and provides a warm water spray for cleansing and warm air for drying (see the photo at left). These products offer many people who have difficulty with personal hygiene a tremendous opportunity for self-care.

able to determine which side of a bathtub surface had been treated with the spray. They were also concerned about a gummy build-up of the product over time and how frequently the tub would need cleaning to remove the product.

Appliqués have been around for a long time. These products add texture to the surface of the tub, but they also catch dirt around their edges. After some time they generally become worn and unsightly. Some of the bath mats available today have exceptionally good suction grips to hold them on the surface of the tub. These mats need to be removed frequently so that they and the surface underneath may be cleaned.

Products for toileting Toilet-seat adapters, discussed on p. 234, raise the height of the standard toilet seat to 18 in. to 20 in. They are usually clamped in place and replace the existing seat. Some of these seats are

PART FIVE

MULTI-FAMILY HOUSING

Give to every other human being every right that you claim for yourself.
— *Thomas Paine*

CHAPTER SIXTEEN
REGULATIONS AND STANDARDS

Virtually every recommendation outlined in this book applies equally to single-family and multi-family housing. In many cases, accessibility is a more critical issue in multi-family housing because multi-family houses often have more turnover and therefore are more likely to house multiple generations and people with a broader range of abilities than the average single-family dwelling. The apartment that houses a couple with young children may one day have to be suitable for a single, elderly empty-nester.

The purpose of this section of the book is to extend design suggestions from the single-family home to multi-family housing, including recommendations for creating accessible multi-family housing sites and

Regulations Defining Minimum Accessibility and the Building Standards that Apply to Them

Regulation	Standard
Architectural Barriers Act of 1968 (ABA)	Uniform Federal Accessibility Standard (UFAS)
Section 504 of the Rehabilitation Act of 1973 (504)	Uniform Federal Accessibility Standard (UFAS)
Fair Housing Amendments Act of 1988 (FHAA)	Fair Housing Accessibility Guidelines, including some components of ANSI 117.1
Americans with Disabilities Act of 1990 (ADA)	Americans with Disabilities Act Accessibility Guidelines, including components of ANSI 117.1

Building Types and Accessibility Laws that Govern Their Design and Construction

Type of Building	Laws		
	Dwelling Unit	Site	Common Areas
Private, single-family detached (site or factory built)	zoning, building codes	zoning	
Private, single-family detached, manufactured	zoning, building codes HUD	zoning	
Rental, single-family, detached	zoning, building codes	zoning	
Private funds, rental, townhouse or multi-family of four units or less	zoning, building codes	zoning	ADA
Federal funds, townhouse or multi-family of four units or less	zoning, building codes ABA, 504	zoning, ABA, 504	ADA
Private funds, multi-family of more than four units	zoning, building codes, FHAA	zoning, FHAA	FHAA, ADA
Federal funds, multi-family of more than four units	zoning, building codes, ABA, 504, FHAA	zoning, ABA, 504, FHAA 504, FHAA	FHAA, ADA

design considerations for making common spaces easy-to-use environments for people of all ages, sizes and abilities.

In this chapter we will review the regulations and standards concerning accessibility and present their basic intent, scope and jurisdiction. It is not our intention to provide complete details, merely to explain what the regulations do and do not provide. The federal regulations and standards are available from the agencies listed on p. 253.

Many people have spent much of their lives fighting to help make the built environment more accessible, and without their efforts we would not have the minimum standards and regulations that we have today. However, much remains to be done. The existing regulations and standards are not always easy to understand and use, nor is it always clear where jurisdictions begin and end. Further, current regulations are overwhelmingly oriented toward the problems of wheelchair users, a distinct minority of people with disabilities. Often the proposed solutions aren't even the best ones for this targeted audience.

One big problem with the standards is that architects, builders and developers treat them as ideal solutions rather than as the minimal standards they are. There is a world of difference between these approaches. Minimum standards represent the least acceptable solution, not the best or most creative solution. Existing regulations and standards should be treated as a starting point for designing a more accessible world, not as a blueprint for that world.

Standards are minimum guidelines providing specifications for barrier-free design. They are not laws or rules, but rather a set of voluntary criteria. Regulations, on the other hand, are the laws that set the standards as the minimum criteria for construction. The top chart on p. 247 lists current accessibility standards and the regulations that enforce them.

Accessibility standards and the various agencies that promulgate and enforce them involve a potentially confusing array of jurisdictions. Anyone who is involved in accessible building should obtain the specific standards and regulations applicable to the facility being built, remodeled or managed.

Detailed standards may seem to stifle creativity, but creative architects, builders and developers should welcome the challenges and opportunities to improve the built environment. For example, build-

ings can be connected with pathways that invite the inhabitants to use them, and accessible and well-designed passageways connecting dwelling units to community spaces can help establish comforting communities. A community is formed when the environment helps form bonds among the occupants. Bonds are formed when residents are encouraged to meet and to linger with their neighbors.

The regulations or laws that affect single-family and/or multi-family housing are summarized in the bottom chart on p. 247. These include building codes, zoning ordinances, the Architectural Barriers Act (1968), Section 504 of the Rehabilitation Act (1973) as amended, the Fair Housing Amendments Act (1988), and the Americans with Disabilities Act (1990). Additionally, manufactured housing (sometimes called mobile homes) is regulated by national standards under the Department of Housing and Urban Development (HUD).

Building codes and zoning ordinances usually affect all types of construction within the state, locality or municipality. It is often possible, however, to obtain waivers from the codes or petition to have the zoning changed for a particular site. North Carolina and California are two states with building codes that have progressive accessibility requirements.

Any building constructed or altered using federal funds must comply with the Architectural Barriers Act of 1968. All types of construction funded with federal funds or that house programs receiving federal funds are governed by Section 504 of the Rehabilitation Act of 1973. Virtually all multi-family housing projects, regardless of whether they were built with federal funds, are regulated by the Fair Housing Amendments Act of 1988. Finally, the Americans with Disabilities Act of 1990 affects all areas of public accommodation and all employment opportunities and locations.

THE ARCHITECTURAL BARRIERS ACT OF 1968

The Architectural Barriers Act (ABA) requires that federally funded construction, including alterations, and buildings leased with federal funds be made accessible to individuals with disabilities. The act directs the various federal agencies, such as the General Services

Administration, the Department of Housing and Urban Development, the Postal Service and the Department of Defense, to create standards for accessibility. The ABA relies upon the Uniform Federal Accessibility Standards (UFAS) and is enforced by the Architectural and Transportation Barriers Compliance Board (ATBCB).

SECTION 504 OF THE REHABILITATION ACT OF 1973

The Rehabilitation Act was passed in 1973, but authorizing regulations were not issued until April 28, 1977. The Rehabilitation Act was modeled on the antidiscrimination language of the Civil Rights Act of 1964. It prohibits discrimination on the basis of disability in buildings and programs funded by the federal government.

The Reagan administration adopted a narrow definition of the scope of the act, arguing that the regulations applied only to specific programs receiving federal funds. It is now applied to all programs and all aspects of agencies that receive federal funds. Thus, a building constructed on a private college campus funded by monies from a private benefactor would have to be accessible to individuals with disabilities if any part of a federally funded project was to be housed in the building. The Uniform Accessibility Standards (UFAS) apply to buildings under the jurisdiction of Section 504.

THE FAIR HOUSING AMENDMENTS ACT OF 1988

The Fair Housing Amendments Act (FHAA) of 1988 expanded coverage of Title VIII of the Civil Rights Act of 1968, which prohibits discrimination in the sale, rental or financing of dwellings based on race, color, religion, sex or national origin. The FHAA prohibits discriminatory housing practices based on handicap and familial status. It specifically states that unlawful discrimination includes a failure to design and construct covered multi-family dwellings available for first occupancy after March 13, 1991, in accordance with certain accessibility requirements. Guidelines providing technical assistance in defining the ac-

ceptable minimums for meeting the FHAA were published March 6, 1991, and technical corrections were published in the Federal Register on July 26, 1991.

The "acceptable minimums" described in the guidelines are not mandatory, nor do they prescribe specific requirements that must be met. They are simply minimum recommendations. Builders and developers may choose to depart from the guidelines and use alternative methods to demonstrate that they have met the requirements of the FHAA. The guidelines clearly state that if federal funds are involved, the FHAA does not interfere with the application of the ABA and Section 504.

The Fair Housing Accessibility Guidelines generally rely upon ANSI A117.1-1986. The FHAA has seven requirements and a number of guidelines that define the scope of the requirements. Other regulations, which are more general, specify to what extent a builder or developer must go to comply with the regulations. Anyone who is involved in multi-family housing development and construction needs to be familiar with the FHAA regulations on accessibility. A brief summary is provided in the chart on p. 250; the full guidelines can be obtained from the address given in Resources on p. 253.

The FHAA regulations are concerned mainly with individuals in wheelchairs and their movements into and through the public areas and dwelling units of a multi-family facility. Without minimizing the special needs of wheelchair users, we believe that the regulations should also consider the large majority of people with disabilities who do not use a wheelchair. For example, Requirement 7 states that space within kitchens and bathrooms be designed so that an individual in a wheelchair can maneuver. What about the problems of someone who is unsteady or weak, or the difficulties encountered by people with low vision? There should be a minimum standard addressing their needs, too.

Furthermore, the FHAA regulations assume that everyone uses a wheelchair of average dimensions. The wheelchair industry has produced an array of new products that have changed the footprint of the chair and the capabilities of the individual using the chair. Some chairs, either because they maneuver the rider into a standing position or because they lift the seat in which the person is sitting, eliminate the problem of access to objects above a height of 54 in.

FHAA Guidelines

REQUIREMENT 1

Accessible building entrance on an accessible route

"Each building on a site shall have at least one building entrance on an accessible route, unless prohibited by the terrain."

REQUIREMENT 2

Accessible and usable public and common use areas

"…each covered multi-family dwelling with a building entrance on an accessible route shall be designed in such a manner that the public and common use areas are readily accessible to and usable by handicapped persons."

REQUIREMENT 3

Usable doors

"…each covered multi-family dwelling with a building entrance on an accessible route shall be designed in such a manner that all the doors designed to allow passage into and within all premises are sufficiently wide to allow passage by handicapped persons in wheelchairs."

REQUIREMENT 4

Accessible route into and through the covered dwelling unit

"…all covered multi-family dwellings with a building entrance on an accessible route shall be designed and constructed in such a manner that all premises within covered multi-family dwelling units contain an accessible route into and through the covered dwelling unit."

REQUIREMENT 5

Light switches, electrical outlets, thermostats and other environmental controls in accessible locations

"…all covered multi-family dwellings with a building entrance on an accessible route shall be designed and constructed in such a manner that all premises within covered multi-family dwelling units contain light switches, electrical outlets, thermostats, and other environmental controls in accessible locations."

REQUIREMENT 6

Reinforced walls for grab bars

"…covered multi-family dwellings with a building entrance on an accessible route shall be designed and constructed in such a manner that all premises within covered multi-family dwelling units contain reinforcements in bathroom walls to allow later installation of grab bars around toilet, tub, shower stall and shower seat, where such facilities are provided."

REQUIREMENT 7

Usable kitchens and bathrooms

"…covered multi-family dwellings with a building entrance on an accessible route shall be designed and constructed in such a manner that all premises within covered multi-family dwelling units contain usable kitchens and bathrooms such that an individual in a wheelchair can maneuver about the space."

The FHAA is a significant step forward, but a small one. Unfortunately, however, it reinforces the belief that design guidelines are needed only for people in wheelchairs.

THE AMERICANS WITH DISABILITIES ACT OF 1990

The Americans with Disabilities Act (ADA) extends the protections of the Rehabilitation Act to all segments of society and commerce, not just those receiving federal assistance. The ADA recognizes that the 43 million or more Americans who have a disability are part of a discrete and insular minority that has been subjected to unequal treatment based on characteristics beyond their control. The ADA text states that the goal of the nation relative to people with disabilities should be to ensure "equality of opportunity, full participation, independent living, and economic self-sufficiency."

The ADA has five sections, which are referred to as titles. The chart below summarizes their main

ADA Subchapters Summarized

TITLE I

Employment

The ADA regulations state that "no covered entity shall discriminate against a qualified individual with a disability because of the disability of such individual in regard to job application procedures, the hiring, advancement, or discharge of employees, employee compensation, job training, and other terms, conditions, and privileges of employment."

TITLE II

Public services

The ADA states that "no qualified individual with a disability shall, by reason of such a disability, be excluded from participation in or be denied the benefits of the services, programs, or activities of a public entity, or be subjected to discrimination by any such entity."

TITLE III

Public accommodations and services operated by private entities

This section of the ADA appears to apply to multi-family housing. The law states that, "no individual shall be discriminated against on the basis of disability in the full and equal enjoyment of the goods, services, facilities, privileges, advantages, or accommodations of any place of public accommodation by any person who owns, leases (or leases to), or operates a place of public accommodation."

TITLE IV

Telecommunications relay services

This section mandates telecommunications services for individuals who are hearing impaired and speech impaired.

TITLE V

Miscellaneous provisions

This section provides a description of the relationship of the ADA to other laws and basically states that it does not diminish any other laws that are equal to it or provide greater protection. It also describes technical assistance requirements to be provided by various federal agencies and their roles and responsibilities in the implementation of the Act.

points. Only Title III concerns public accommodations, but for the sake of providing a complete introduction, we will discuss the other titles briefly too.

Title I affects everything related to employing personnel — defining the essential functions of a job, the employment application, requirements and pre-employment tests as well as the manner in which a particular employee is accommodated or assisted so he or she is able to complete a job.

The "public entities" section of Title II broadens the scope of the act to include state or local government, or any department or subdivision thereof, and the National Railroad Passenger Corporation or any commuter authority. This section encompasses all public entities operating fixed-route systems such as bus or rail systems (excluding aircraft and public-school systems). The essence is that public buildings and transportation systems must provide equal access and opportunity for transportation for all people.

Title III relates most directly to multi-family housing. The list of places of public accommodation covers virtually every commercial, professional, retail and recreational entity in existence. However, the extent of jurisdiction of the ADA relative to multi-family housing is unclear and has yet to be decided through case law. Some builders and developers believe that the ADA does not apply to multi-family housing facilities. This may in fact be true only if there are no rental offices, manager's offices, laundromats or any public (common) buildings on the site of the multi-family facility. Thus an apartment building that contains only apartments, corridors and entrances may not be subject to the ADA.

The individual residences of a multi-family housing facility would not fall within the "public accommodations" jurisdiction of the ADA (they are covered by FHAA), but "public" areas within these facilities are likely to fall under the jurisdiction of the ADA. "Public" areas would include any restaurant, bar, auditorium, sales or rental office, laundromat, barber or beauty shop, professional office, library or gallery, and exercise or recreation sites.

Title IV mandates that companies offering telecommunications systems for the general public offer access to individuals with communications disabilities. This may be accomplished through telephone relay services for persons who use telecommunications devices for deaf persons (TDDs) or similar devices.

Title V describes the relationship of the ADA to other laws and technical assistance requirements to be provided by various government agencies.

Thus, although the FHAA concentrates on the movement of people with disabilities throughout the multi-family complex, buildings and residences, the ADA provides residents with disabilities the right to enjoy all the privileges of living in the multi-family housing facility that all other residents enjoy. That is, the FHAA states there needs to be an accessible route to the public and common areas, such as a laundry, swimming pool or exercise room. The ADA states that you not only need to get people into the laundry room and pool, but they also need to be able to wash their clothes and swim.

The ADA requires that architectural and communication barriers be removed unless doing so causes an undue hardship or materially alters the service provided. It adds that any alterations, additions or renovations that are made must be in compliance with the ADA accessibility guidelines. The effective dates for barrier removal and alterations was January 26, 1992. The law made exceptions for businesses with 25 or fewer employees and gross receipts of $1 million or less, stating that the first date for civil action to be brought against businesses of this size for a violation was July 26, 1992; and not before January 26, 1993 against businesses with 10 or fewer employees and gross receipts of $500,000 or less. The ADA accessibility requirements apply to new construction for first occupancy after January 26, 1993, stating that they must be readily accessible and usable by individuals with disabilities.

The ADA Accessibility Guidelines (ADAAG) essentially encompass the technical specifications of sections 4.2 through 4.35 of the American National Standard Institute's document A117.1-1986. Sections 4.1.1 through 4.1.7 and sections 5 through 10 are different from ANSI 117.1 in their entirety.

Unlike previous laws, the ADA spells out provisions for enforcement. The regulations allow for injunctive relief to make facilities readily accessible or to provide an auxiliary aid or service, the award of monetary damages to persons aggrieved, assessment of a civil penalty in the amount of $50,000 for a first violation and a civil penalty not exceeding $100,000 for any subsequent violation.

RESOURCES

The Access Board
Architectural and
Transportation Barriers
Compliance Board
1331 F Street NW
Suite 1000
Washington, DC 20004
(800) 872-2253
(202) 653-7848
Information, complaints and resources on the Architectural Barriers Act of 1968 and the Americans with Disabilities Act.

American National Standards
Institute
Sales Department
1430 Broadway
New York, NY 10018
(212) 642-10018
American National Standard for Buildings and Facilities Providing Accessibility and Usability for Physically Handicapped People, ANSI A117.1-1986.

Coordination and Review
Section
Civil Rights Division
U.S. Department of Justice
Washington, DC 20530
(202) 307-2222
Section 504 and Fair Housing resources.

Department of Justice,
Nondiscrimination on the
Basis of Disability by Public
Accommodations and in
Commercial Facilities, Final
Rule. *Federal Register,* Vol. 56,
No. 144, Friday, July 26, 1991
/ Rules and Regulations.

Department of Justice
Office of the Americans with
Disabilities Act
Civil Rights Division
P.O. Box 66118
Washington, DC 20530
(202) 514-0381
Americans with Disabilities Act.

Fair Housing Accessibility
Guidelines: Design Guidelines
for Accessible/Adaptable
Buildings. *Federal Register,* Vol.
56, No. 44, Wednesday, March
6, 1991 / Rules and
Regulations.

Office of Fair Housing and
Equal Opportunity
Room 5116
Department of Housing and
Urban Development
451 Seventh Street SW
Washington, DC 20410-2000
(202) 708-2878
Copy of the Fair Housing Amendment Act law or regulations. Contact the HUD regional office nearest you or the address above. HUD should also have information on Section 504 and Fair Housing Act.

Superintendent of Documents
U.S. Government Printing
Office
Washington, DC 20402
(202) 783-3238
Uniform Federal Accessibility Standards, Fed-STO, 795, April 1, 1988; U.S. Government Printing Office, 1990:704-034/30206

CHAPTER SEVENTEEN
THE MULTI-FAMILY HOUSING SITE

Multi-family housing comes in all shapes and sizes, from spacious complexes to compact high-rises. Sites vary from flat to hillside or rolling terrain. But all multi-family housing sites have similar features, and their residents have similar needs. In the coming years, the most successful and appreciated multi-family housing sites will be those that meet the broadest range of basic human needs. Apartment complexes that provide a sense of social interconnectedness, a sense of belonging to a community, will attract and retain residents more successfully than those that ignore or minimize these needs.

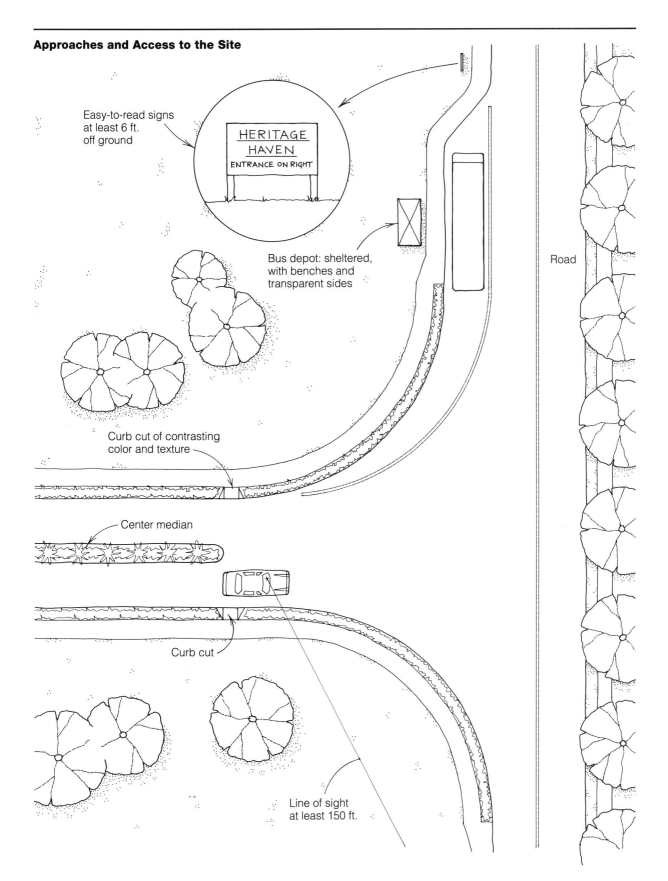

Approaches and Access to the Site

Easy-to-read signs at least 6 ft. off ground

HERITAGE HAVEN
ENTRANCE ON RIGHT

Bus depot: sheltered, with benches and transparent sides

Road

Curb cut of contrasting color and texture

Center median

Curb cut

Line of sight at least 150 ft.

This chapter is divided into three sections. The first section discusses ways to improve the approach and access to the site; the second section deals with the control of vehicles and vehicular travel; the third section offers some advice on improving access to the buildings. As is true of the rest of this book, this discussion of multi-family housing is not intended to apply only to facilities that are to be used by individuals with disabilities. Our design suggestions are intended to serve people in their many shapes, sizes and varying abilities throughout their lifespan.

The recommendations in this chapter are consistent with both the Fair Housing Amendments Act of 1988 and the Americans With Disabilities Act of 1990. However, there is much more to creative universal design than is contained in the standards underlying these regulations and the ideas presented in this chapter. The developer and designer are challenged to venture beyond methods to circumvent the regulations and to create housing for the people who will be using it.

APPROACH AND ACCESS TO THE SITE

People will approach or enter the site either in private or public vehicles or by walking. Many of the principles of dealing with single-family sites described in Chapter 4 apply here as well. Perhaps most important, if vehicular traffic is allowed on the site and the site is hilly, let the vehicle do the climbing. Bring the drive up or down to the building entrances so that people don't have to do any excess climbing on their own.

A friendly complex is one in which all directions and locations are easily marked and identified. An attractive sign that can be read and understood easily from a distance will allow drivers to get where they want to get with minimal confusion. The sign should clearly identify the facility and indicate the location of the entrance. The line of a sight of a driver easily extends from about 4 ft. to about 15 ft. above the ground. Signs that are under or above this range may be blocked or otherwise not seen. The ideal height for a sign is at least 6 ft. off the ground. Local ordinances often restrict the use of advertising displays and signs, but most will allow some form of

identification for a building or property. The drawing on p. 255 gives general guidelines for approaches.

Multi-family building sites need signs that identify clearly the path the driver must take and can be seen quickly and easily from an auto at night in a rainstorm. Each decision point (intersection) on the site needs a sign. The signs can certainly be decorative and should maintain the "theme" of the site, but they should also be visible. High contrast between the background and the letters is essential. The best is white on black or yellow on black. Other color combinations may be used if they have a strong contrast and good lighting is provided.

Signs should be visible under low-light conditions. This can be accomplished by providing a light source or by ensuring that they will be illuminated by the low beam of headlights. Signs should be within an unobstructed view from all possible directions.

The vehicular entrance should be designed so that exiting traffic does not interfere with entering traffic. If the entrance is located on a busy street, traffic should be controlled with a wide driveway that is equipped with a median. The driver's vision should not be obstructed by landscaping, pedestrians, signs or structures. Other options are to work with the city to get a traffic light installed at the intersection, to add an entrance on a less congested side street or to add merge and turn-off lanes along the edge of the property. All drivers should feel competent pulling in or out.

Pedestrians should be provided with ample sidewalks. While that may seem like a rather obvious observation, the fact is that too many places today don't provide for safe and efficient pedestrian traffic. This neglect is often the result of shortsighted thinking. On a site on the outskirts of town, the developers may argue that residents won't be walking to any destinations and therefore don't need sidewalks. But people like to walk for exercise and relaxation. Sidewalks connect interiors with exteriors, inviting people to extend their environment out of doors. Sidewalks should be constructed to provide pedestrians with a safe walking area distinct from traffic lanes.

The multi-family facility must have good walkways from the edge of the property to the entrance and connecting all of the entrances. The walkways should be at least 5 ft. wide to allow ample room for

Multi-family housing structures should be connected by wide pedestrian pathways.

traffic in both directions. A 4-ft. sidewalk is sufficient only for a single-family residence.

Walkways should be as level as possible. The maximum slope in the direction of travel should be 1:20, with a level rest area every 40 ft. If this isn't possible on a hilly site, do not exceed a slope of 1:12, and provide level rest areas approximately every 30 ft. The maximum cross slope should be 1:50. Cross slopes make steering wheeled devices difficult and walking uncomfortable for many people.

Smooth, solid surfaces with a slight texture to improve traction are best for walkways. Use concrete or asphalt and make sure that the surface does not trap water, especially in cold climates. Bricks, flagstone and other landscaping stones should be reserved for low traffic areas. They should not have any gaps between them greater than ½ in. We recommend using the decorative stones as the "shoulder" to the walkway, not as the walkway itself, which should be kept smooth.

Water drainage from the walkways is important, and drainage grates may be required. These should not be put in the walkway, but must be placed to one side, preferably in a median area so that pedestrians do not have to walk on them. The space between the bars on the grates should be ½ in. or less.

Keep in mind that the surface of the walkway is also affected by what grows above it. A smooth sidewalk can be turned into a fairly challenging obstacle course by the pods from a locust tree or the wet, slippery leaves from a maple tree.

If public transportation is provided to the edge of the property or if people are likely to walk to the site, the sidewalk should begin at the edge of the site and continue uninterrupted to each entrance of the building or buildings. If the residents use public transportation, there should be a well-lit, weather-protected waiting depot, oriented so that people are protected from inclement weather and splashes from passing traffic. The depot should be equipped with

benches (preferably with backs) and a space to keep personal belongings off the ground. People should be able to monitor their surroundings and see approaching buses without having to leave the shelter.

The transition from shelter to transportation should be short and free of obstacles. Although many public buses will have lifts that can be lowered onto the sidewalk, there must be curb cuts and smooth transitions for people using wheeled devices. Curb

The curb cut at left has good and bad points. What's good is that the curb edges are painted red and are easy to see and the curb-cut section has a different texture from the sidewalk. What's bad is that the curb cut is sunk into the walkway and poses a tripping hazard for the unaware pedestrian.

A well-designed curb cut (below) does not interfere with the walkway. The sloped area is of a different texture, and the curb edges are painted a contrasting color. A border of planters keeps the pedestrian from stumbling.

cuts or ramps should be continuous with the walkway and should be provided at multiple locations along a block, not just at the corners. People often need a curb cut in the middle of the block. If, for example, a vehicle is blocking a curb cut at one corner, someone in a wheelchair may have to travel another full block to reach another curb cut.

Curb cuts that are part of the foot-traffic pathway cause problems for pedestrians not paying attention or unable to see the change in ground level. Curb cuts are best if they are located off of the main pathway and protected by a median or a planting area. If the curb cut is designed as part of the walkway, there should be at least 4 ft. of walkway that is not intersected by the curb ramp. The photos on the facing page show examples of curb-cut design.

The curb-cut area should be as wide as the sidewalk and wider in areas of high pedestrian traffic. It is better for everyone if the person using the wheeled device does not have to cross through 20 ft. of pedestrian traffic in order to get to the 3-ft. curb cut. Curb ramps should not be extended into the street, where they create obstacles for pedestrians, dams to collect water and debris and hidden obstructions for snow plows. Pedestrians should be aware of the presence of curb ramps. One way to accomplish this is consistency — build all curb ramps in the same manner, in the same locations on every street.

Curb ramps can be made more noticeable for those without visual difficulties by the use of a contrasting colored surface in the sidewalk. Visually impaired individuals may be alerted to upcoming curb ramps by a change in the walkway's surface texture (from smooth to small aggregate surface or ribbed).

VEHICLES ON THE PROPERTY

Once a vehicle has entered the property, it should be directed as efficiently as possible to the building entrance or a parking space. This task is all the easier with good signage (see p. 256). The speed of vehicle traffic must be controlled. Speed bumps at pedestrian crossings, clearly demarcated by signs and paint, will alert drivers and comfort pedestrians.

Walking paths should be clearly separated from vehicular paths. Cars and pedestrians can coexist bet-

ter if they are provided separate but equal paths. Fences, decorative walls and decorative bushes work well to keep cars and people separate, but they should not obstruct the vision of either drivers or pedestrians. The "barrier" should be between 15 in. and 24 in. high. The barrier should keep children off the street, but should be low enough that a toddler on a scooter could be seen by a driver. We advise against using a single chain slung between posts as a barrier in any location because it usually hangs relatively low to the ground and can be difficult to see. A person who is blind and uses a cane would not detect a chain.

Fences and decorative walls that double as seating areas are an attractive way to provide a place for rest and relaxation and invite residents to venture into the outdoor common spaces.

Multi-family housing structures should provide the occupants options for entering their unit. A porte cochère at the main entrance of the building should be large enough to accommodate and protect cars, drivers and pedestrians. Passenger loading zones should be well-marked and should be set off out of the main driveway so that those not stopping for passengers may continue unimpeded, and those picking up passengers don't need to hurry. The pathway to the loading area should be unobstructed and continuous with the entrance to the building so that a curb ramp will be unnecessary. The access aisle at the passenger loading area should be at least 48 in. wide (ANSI); this width will allow someone using a wheelchair to maneuver onto the ramp of a van or to disembark from the wheelchair and pull it into the car. The 4-ft. clearance also allows the door of a car to be opened and for someone to get around it. The ADA states that the passenger loading area must be 60 in. wide and 20 ft. long with 114 in. of vertical clearance.

The passenger loading area should be level. People using wheelchairs or who have difficulty maintaining their balance will have trouble with any area with a cross slope greater than 1:50. A level loading area is convenient for everyone because it is difficult to open doors when the car is sloped so that the door has to be pushed open uphill.

Mammoth parking lots lend a transient, used-car-lot atmosphere to even the most attractive of multi-family housing complexes. Smaller lots that are situated near the entrances likely to be used by the residents are a better solution. With small, dispersed

Entrances vary in accessibility and convenience. The porte cochère in the photo at left is large enough to cover an automobile and protect disembarking passengers from the elements. The entrance in the photo above provides a covered walkway, but the passenger must travel farther and will not be sheltered while getting out of the car.

lots, residents stand a better chance of being able to park near their home. A small lot buffered by landscaping can almost completely conceal the presence of the vehicles.

Many people will need accessible parking spaces as close as possible to the entrance; the size and number of these spaces are specified by various standards and regulations. As shown in the drawing on the facing page, cars require a space at least 96 in. wide

(ANSI) with an access aisle of 60 in; vans require a space 96 in. wide with an access aisle of 96 in. ANSI suggests that the same access aisle may be shared by two adjacent accessible parking spaces.

As shown in the drawing on the facing page, parking spaces with universal dimensions are 132 in. wide with a 60-in. access aisle between. This allows individuals using wheelchairs to access either side of the automobile and to maneuver about, and it is

Accessible Parking Spaces

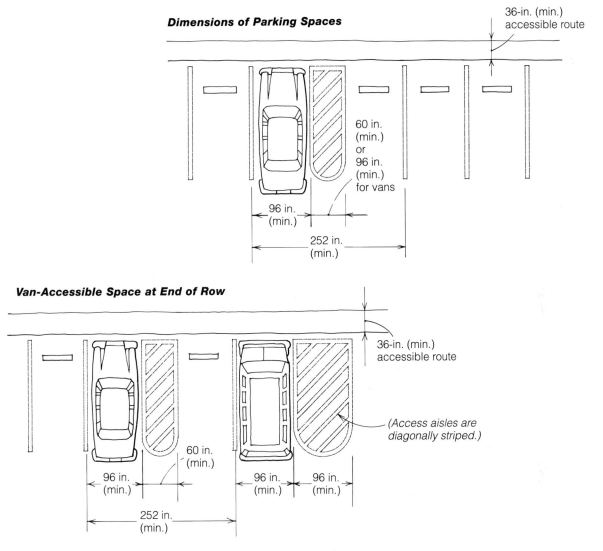

Dimensions of Parking Spaces

36-in. (min.) accessible route

60 in. (min.) or 96 in. (min.) for vans

96 in. (min.)

252 in. (min.)

Van-Accessible Space at End of Row

36-in. (min.) accessible route

(Access aisles are diagonally striped.)

60 in. (min.)

96 in. (min.)

96 in. (min.)

96 in. (min.)

252 in. (min.)

Universal Parking Space

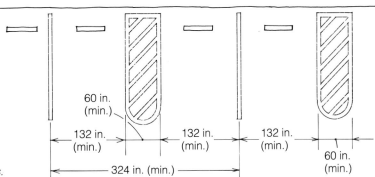

60 in. (min.)

132 in. (min.)

132 in. (min.)

132 in. (min.)

60 in. (min.)

324 in. (min.)

Universal parking spaces are designed to accommodate any type of vehicle, but their use reduces the number of available spaces.

Ask a wheelchair user to describe what's wrong with most 'handicapped' parking spaces and you are likely to get a longer answer than you bargained for. This fairly typical parking bay at a motel has several flaws. It does not have enough room for disembarking and transferring into a wheelchair, it has no 60-in. access aisle to the side of the parked vehicle, it is on a cross slope and it lacks a vertical sign.

large enough for someone using a van with a ramp. Some parking lots may not be large enough to have all universal parking spaces, so some will have to be the minimally acceptable width of 96 in. with a 60-in. access aisle and some will need to be designated for van use. A parking space large enough to accommodate a van with a ramp needs to be 96 in. wide and have an access aisle of 96 in. The ramp has to have a dimension long enough to hold the wheelchair, and the wheelchair rider has to be lined up with the van ramp to wheel onto it.

The ADA specifies the minimum number of accessible spaces per total parking spaces (see the chart at left). These recommendations, however, should be treated as minimally acceptable. The optimum number of accessible spaces may well be higher. Accessible spaces (not reserved for an individual) must be designated with a vertical sign displaying a universal accessibility symbol. The sign cannot be obscured by a parked vehicle and is best if it can be seen from the driver's seat of an automobile.

Minimum Number of Accessible Parking Spaces* Mandated by ADA

Total Parking Spaces in Lot	Minimum Number of Accessible Spaces
1-25	1
26-50	2
51-75	3
76-100	4
101-150	5
151-200	6
201-300	7
301-400	8
401-500	9
501-1000	2% of total
1001 and over	20 plus 1 for every 100 over 1000

*96 in. wide minimum with 60-in. access aisle, except 1 in every 8 or not less than 1 must be van accessible (96 in. wide with 96-in. access aisle).

ACCESS TO BUILDINGS ON THE SITE

We are strong advocates of connections. Doorways should invite passage in and out and help the transition from inside to outside. An accessible entrance has the following attributes:

• easy-to-open or automatic doors, preferably double doors with an airlock

• lighting that helps adjust from the bright glare of sunshine to the shaded recesses within or from the dark of night to the brightly lit interior

• outdoor lighting so people can survey the area around the entrance before leaving the building

• large observational windows so that people may be seen both within and outside the building and on each side of the doors
• recessed floor mats for wiping feet and trapping water from tires on baby carriages, wheelchairs and children's riding toys
• a temporary set-down shelf or surface for packages
• ample space off to the side of the entranceway. People need to "ready" themselves for the entrance and exit, and they need a spot to stop and chat without feeling as if they are blocking traffic.

The primary entrances to multi-family housing should be equipped with automatic opening doors. Automatic doors ease the entrance and exit of everyone, but especially of those who have their arms full of packages or who are pushing a stroller or using a walker or wheelchair. Resources on p. 265 lists companies that make automatic doors. Ideally doors should be completely automatic, slide horizontally and be separated by an airlock.

Revolving doors certainly help to control air flow, but most are difficult to use. Many people have trouble initiating the movement of the door and are afraid to enter the doorway area when someone else is pushing the door because it is moving faster than their comfort level. Individuals using assistive devices are significantly disadvantaged by the revolving door. If a revolving door is used, it should be next to a conventional door, preferably automatic.

Conventional doors in series separated by an airlock need to be arranged so that either both sets of doors open in the same direction or both sets open away from each other. If both sets of doors swing away from the airlock (space between the doors), the minimum amount of clear space required is 48 in. If one swings into the airlock, then the minimum amount of space is 48 in. plus the space for the swing of the door.

Entrances should be equipped with good floor mats, which help keep the interior floor surfaces clean and dry. We prefer recessed mats because they are easy to maneuver on and they do not create a tripping hazard. Loose or freestanding floor mats can move, buckle or wrinkle. Institutional carpeting may be the best surface for use at entrances. A good grade of carpeting with an exceptionally short pile reduces noise, soaks up moisture and presents a nonslip sur-

face. The tight, short pile will not significantly impede the wheelchair user.

Unfortunately, many multi-family facilities use marble or other hard-surface flooring materials at their entrances because of their long life and ease of cleaning. These surfaces can be extremely hazardous, particularly when wet.

Access between buildings Multi-family facilities that entice occupants into common spaces and interconnecting pathways are more likely to foster a sense of community among the residents. People will interact with each other if they are given the opportunity. Multi-family housing should be designed to encourage and facilitate casual interaction among residents, which is the least intimidating form of social intercourse. The local climate is often a big factor in determining whether buildings are connected by internal circulation corridors or exterior pathways. Either can be successful if planned to be logical, usable and accessible.

The Fair Housing Amendments Act and ANSI suggest that the minimum width for accessible routes (pathways, corridors and hallways) is 36 in. with a 60-in. space for passing every 200 ft. We consider these dimensions to be only minimally acceptable.

Routes between and within buildings should be at least 60 in. wide, but we prefer 8-ft. corridors if space and finances permit. Anything less than 60 in. may feel cramped. People will not feel they have the option to stop and talk with someone because they will need to keep moving or block traffic.

Every route in a multi-family building should be accessible, which means that it has the following attributes:
• a smooth, nonslip surface
• no steps or level changes greater than ½ in.
• elevators within a reasonable distance of the most direct route
• a grade change no steeper than 1:20
• enough width (60 in.) for people to pass without difficulty
• widened areas where people may stop and talk without impeding the flow of traffic
• places to set down packages and to sit
• no more than 200 ft. between resting points
• protection from inclement weather
• good lighting.

Security systems   A sense of security contributes to the residents' confidence in venturing from their apartments and joining activities within and outside the multi-family community. Many people are trapped by their fear and will not venture out alone after dark. Many multi-family facilities rely upon electronic surveillance systems to monitor several entrances, parking lots and the perimeter of the property. Stopping at the front desk is almost like dropping by the main guard house of a penitentiary because the black and white video terminals under the stark surveillance lights ruin the aesthetic appearance of the most glamorous facilities.

Many communities have implemented a neighborhood watch program instead of hiring a 24-hour or night-watch security force. The neighborhood watch system has several advantages. It may help neighbors become more neighborly, the responsibility for the security of the area is shouldered by the residents and the management/owners (and ultimately the residents) do not have to pay for the security service. The success of some neighborhood watch activities may be thwarted by the design of the community. Many apartment complexes have windowless corridors that can be surveyed only through fish-eye peepholes on a resident's door or by opening the door and looking up and down the hallway. Neighborhood watch activities are much easier when a window in one unit has within its view an entrance to another unit. Thus, when Mrs. Jones happens to look out her window and sees someone outside Mrs. Smith's door, she can observe the interaction for a few seconds to ascertain if the visitor appears to be friend or foe.

Some multi-family housing facilities employ security personnel that monitor the gate and grounds 24 hours a day. Some places enlist volunteers from among the residents, others use their regular staff. Still other facilities employ a paid professional security firm. While all of these extraneous measures assist the resident in feeling more secure, each facility should provide:
• ample lighting for all parking areas and walkways
• apartment units that have good surveillance opportunities
• entrances to the apartment complex that are easily monitored by residents before leaving their car in the parking lot
• casual opportunities for residents to get to know each other so that neighbor will know neighbor.

RESOURCES

Signage Systems

Allenite
1522 Holmes Street
Kansas City, MO 64108
(800) 825-0150
(816) 842-0963
Signage systems that include accessibility symbols and braille plates.

Andco Industries Corporation
P.O. Box 7366
4019 Viewmont Drive
Greensboro, NC 27406-9522
(800) 476-8900
(919) 299-4511
Signage systems with tactile and braille characters.

APCO
388 Grant Street, SE
Atlanta, GA 30312-2227
(404) 688-9000
Signage systems with tactile and braille characters.

ASI Sign Systems
555 West 25th Street
New York, NY 10001
(800) ASI-SPEC
(212) 675-8686
Signage systems with tactile and braille characters.

Best Manufacturing Sign Systems
1202 North Park Avenue
Montrose, CO 81401-3170
(800) 235-BEST
(303) 249-2378
Signage systems with tactile and braille characters.

Charleston Industries
955 Estes Avenue
Elk Grove Village, IL 60007
(800) 722-0209
Signage systems with tactile and braille characters.

Increte Systems
INCO Chemical Supply Co.
8509 Sunstate Street
Tampa, FL 33634-1311
(800) 752-INCO
(813) 886-8811
Tactile warning systems for permanent concrete surfaces.

Massillon Plaque Company
5757 Mayfair Road
P.O. Box 2539
North Canton, OH 44720
(800) 854-8404
(216) 494-4199
Signage systems with tactile and braille characters.

Mohawk Sign Systems
P.O. Box 966
Schenectady, NY 12301-0966
(518) 370-3433
Signage systems with tactile and braille characters.

OMC Industries
P.O. Box 3188
Bryan, TX 77804
(800) 488-4662
(409) 779-1400
Cast bronze signage systems that include international accessibility symbols and braille characters.

Premier Sign Systems
4850 West Belmont Avenue
Chicago, IL 60641
(800) ADA-0304
(312) 283-1181
Signage systems with tactile and braille characters.

REHAU
P.O. Box 1706
Leesburg, VA 22075
(800) 247-9445
(703) 777-5255
Tactile warning systems incorporated in polyurethane tiles.

Scott Sign Systems
P.O. Box 1047
Tallevast, FL 34270
(800) 237-9447
(813) 355-5171
Signage systems with tactile and braille characters.

The Southwell Company
Box 299
928 No. Alamo
San Antonio, TX 78291
(210) 223-1831
Signage systems with tactile and braille characters.

The Supersine Company
6000 East Davison Avenue
Detroit, MI 48212
(313) 892-6200
Signage systems with tactile and braille characters.

Automatic Door Systems

Besam
171 Twin Rivers Drive
Hightstown, NJ 08520
(609) 443-5800
Automatic door systems.

Dor-O-Matic
7350 West Wilson Avenue
Harwood Heights, IL 60656-4786
(708) 867-7400
Automatic door systems.

Dorma Door Controls
Dorma Drive
Reamstown, PA 17567
(800) 523-8483
Door closers for easy-to-open doors.

Keane Monroe Corporation
P.O. Box 5016
Monroe, NC 28111-5016
(800) 438-1937
(704) 289-5581
Automatic door systems.

LCN Closers
121 West Railroad Avenue
Princeton, IL 61356
(800) 526-2400
Power-assist door openers and closers.

Norton Door Controls
P.O. Box 25288
Charlotte, NC 28229-8010
(800) 438-1951
Power door openers and closers.

Stanley Magic-Door
Route 6 & Hyde Road
Farmington, CT 06032
(800) 232-3663
(203) 677-2861
Automatic door systems.

CHAPTER EIGHTEEN
COMMON AREAS

Multi-family housing buildings and complexes can foster the sense of community through careful and thoughtful design of the common areas. Common spaces vary considerably in their size and function, but each can contribute to the quality of life for the residents. Common areas inside the building might include the entrances, lobbies, restrooms, laundry room, community kitchen and mailroom, as well as rooms dedicated to recreation (TV room, pool, health club, fitness room). Common areas outside the building might include a pool, tennis court, barbecue area and garden or park. The drawing on the facing page shows some typical common areas in a multi-family housing setting.

Fully Accessible Common Areas

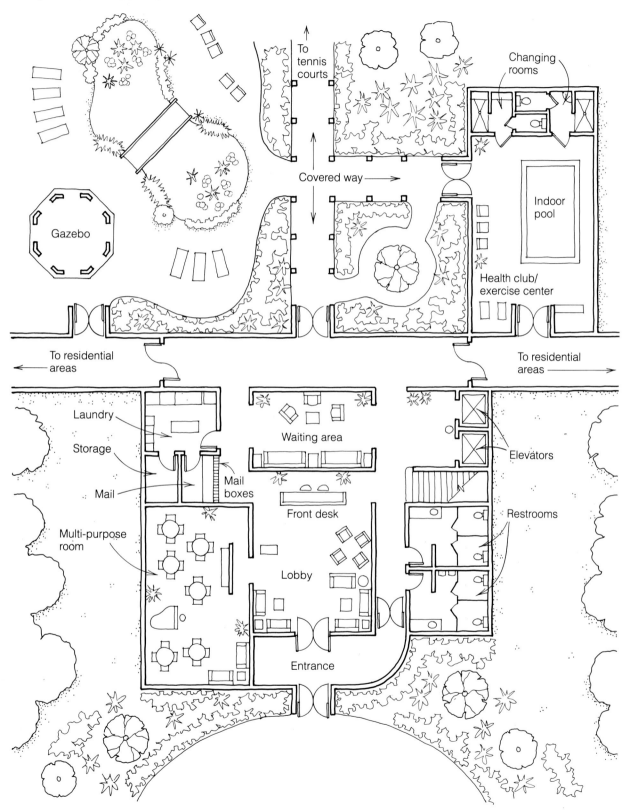

To tennis courts

Changing rooms

Covered way

Gazebo

Indoor pool

Health club/ exercise center

To residential areas

To residential areas

Laundry

Storage

Mail

Multi-purpose room

Mail boxes

Waiting area

Front desk

Lobby

Entrance

Elevators

Restrooms

FUNDAMENTALS OF BUILDING DESIGN

Multi-family housing design should address the functional quality of the building and its inhabitants. Common spaces should provide a sense of privacy, create the sense of belonging, enhance the sense of control and ensure the sense of safety and security. These are the same goals that we advocate relative to single-family residences as well (see pp. 22-23). In multi-family housing, the common spaces are an extension of the residence, so these quality-of-life basics must extend to the common spaces of the structure.

Privacy Privacy in multi-family housing is particularly important. Obviously, privacy within one's apartment is a given. Residents should be afforded a view from their windows without being on display, and they should be able to carry on conversations within their residence without fear that their neighbors will hear every word.

Privacy extends beyond the individual unit. While the common spaces should be designed so that they support casual interaction, they should also be designed so that the residents don't have an audience for everything they do. Main gathering areas (lobbies, lounges) should not be placed at the front or primary entrance. Lobbies should be placed off to one side, where they are visible to passers-by but not on the main traffic path.

Belonging In a multi-family community, a sense of belonging comes from creating the opportunities for the residents to get to know each other. As the authors of *A Pattern Language* say, "A building cannot be a human building unless it is a complex of still smaller buildings or smaller parts which manifest its own internal social facts."

These social facts of a building are the elements that create a community. A monolithic front entrance needs alcoves or small spaces that invite people to stop and spend a few minutes together or allow the solitary person to take a moment to watch the weather outdoors or a small bird in a bush.

The social fabric of a multi-family complex brings people into contact with each other, allowing them to interact with other residents or to avoid interaction. These options are created by accessible thoroughfares through the buildings and resting, lounge, activity and recreational areas just off these main routes.

The complex that has a healthy community atmosphere will bring people together in casual interaction. Two key areas are the pathways leading from the primary entrance to the residences and the pathways and areas adjacent to the mailboxes. Residents should have the option of walking through a communal area to leave and enter the complex. This option provides them the opportunity to exchange greetings with other residents. Similarly, community mailboxes should be located in an area where there is room for people to congregate while waiting for and retrieving the mail.

Spaces for casual interaction should be interspersed throughout a multi-family building or complex of buildings. Pathways should have small resting or gathering areas; a lobby or lounge should be available outside the front entrance, the mail room, the laundry and recreational areas. People should have the choice of public and private paths to and from their residence.

Control A sense of self-worth comes from knowing that you are in control and are competent in your environment. Being in control of your environment means being able to get about and manipulate every aspect without having to rely upon someone else for assistance. Being able to open the door, cross the threshold, get to the room you want to get to, use the telephone, use the restroom or talk to someone at the front desk without the assistance of anyone else is being in control.

Being in control is being able to determine where you are, where you want to go and how you will get there. Architecture is often based on a repetition of a theme, that is, symmetry. Some multi-family housing units are large, and each wing of the building in a complex of buildings looks alike. It is easy to become disoriented and lost when everything looks the same and there are no signs to provide directions.

Some people lose confidence in their ability to find their way around a large complex. They know the way to their apartment — they go there and they stay there. They are uncomfortable venturing out to enjoy the offerings of the community because they are afraid they won't be able to find their way home.

A Minimally Accessible Common Area (not recommended)

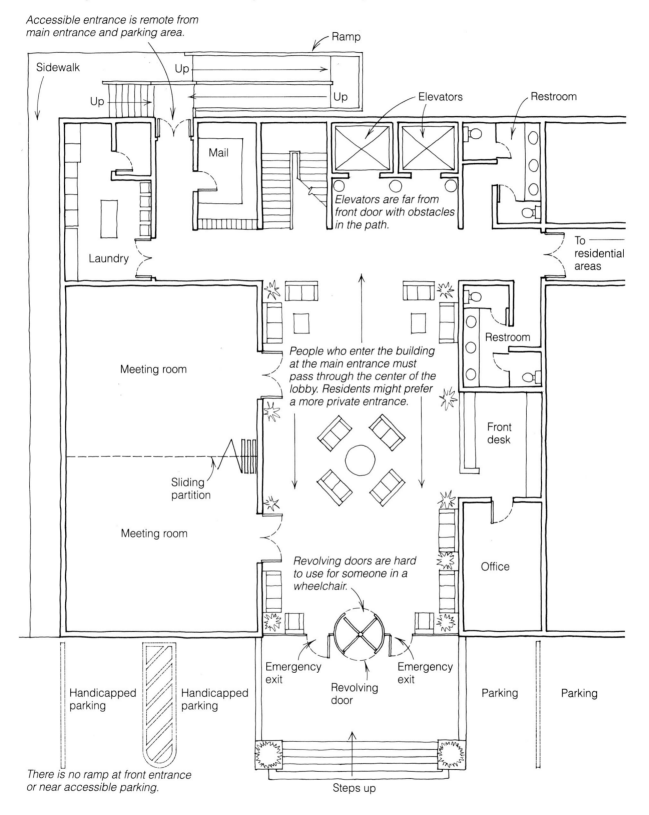

Accessible entrance is remote from main entrance and parking area.

Ramp

Sidewalk

Up

Up

Up

Up

Elevators

Restroom

Mail

Elevators are far from front door with obstacles in the path.

Laundry

To residential areas

Restroom

Meeting room

People who enter the building at the main entrance must pass through the center of the lobby. Residents might prefer a more private entrance.

Front desk

Sliding partition

Meeting room

Revolving doors are hard to use for someone in a wheelchair.

Office

Emergency exit

Revolving door

Emergency exit

Handicapped parking

Handicapped parking

Parking

Parking

There is no ramp at front entrance or near accessible parking.

Steps up

Safety and security   Safety is the feeling that nothing harmful will befall you while in an area. People feel safe in an environment if they are competent in it. They are safe if they are not afraid of falling, of being trapped on the elevator, of being surprised by someone in the hallway or of having difficulty getting from their car to their apartment.

Security is the freedom from fear. Security comes from having a sense of trust in the neighborhood, from believing that the community is safe. People are secure when the spaces within the perimeter are safe.

In some neighborhoods this sense of security may come from having a guard house, security staff and a fenced perimeter. Some places, too, may install personal emergency response systems connected directly to the management office. Individuals with disabilities, children and older adults may gain a sense of security knowing that help can be summoned at the push of a button. (For more on personal emergency response systems, see p. 93.)

ESSENTIAL ELEMENTS OF COMMON SPACES

All public areas should have the following essential components:
• nonglare uniform lighting and accessible communications devices
• an accessible, easily identified entrance and exit
• accessible pathways of circulation
• readily identified emergency pathways and exits.

Unfortunately, many common areas are not well designed. A typical minimally accessible common area is shown in the drawing on p. 269; a fully accessible common area is shown in the drawing on p. 267.

Lighting   Although the Americans with Disabilities Act doesn't deal with lighting, light plays an important role in providing people with confidence when moving about an area. Glare and transition lighting are aspects to consider near entrances, particularly entrances where there is a level change in the floor. People moving from the bright outdoors to an interior room will have difficulty seeing changes in the floor just after entering, and people moving toward a bright outdoors facing a row of windows as they exit may be blinded by the glare.

The great expanse of glass overlooking a beautiful view is an architectural feature that should not be given up, but the designer must be sure to provide adequate interior lighting to ensure that the person entering the room may travel safely through it. The addition of an overhang on the outside may help by blocking the sun from shining directly into the room. Subdued lighting is always attractive and is associated with rest and relaxation.

The slightest change in the level of the floor, even ½ in. or less, must be lit. Small electrical strips with the light embedded in them will work fine to designate where the level change occurs (rise, step or ramp). People do not always see "Watch Your Step" signs, and when they do they don't always understand what it is they are supposed to watch for. Lights directed onto the area that presents a danger draw attention to it.

Telephones   Multi-family housing common areas may not offer much in the way of public telephones because the residents, for whom this service would be required, would be expected to return to their residences to make their telephone calls. Some places, particularly those that have large complexes and multiple public-use areas, do offer public telephones for the convenience of their residents and guests.

The ADA states that no individual with a disability may be "excluded, denied services, segregated or otherwise treated differently than other individuals because of the absence of auxiliary aids and services." Individuals who have difficulty using the telephone include people who have hearing and/or speech and voice disorders. The law does not require the multi-family housing facility to provide the individual with a hearing impairment with a means of receiving incoming calls (in the area of public accommodation) because the telephone in the area of public accommodation would not generally be used as a phone for incoming calls for the residents of the facility. The law does suggest, however, that if the residents are provided access to the telephones for outgoing calls on more than an incidental convenience basis, then the individual who is hearing impaired must be afforded this same communications opportunity and a TDD should be available for use.

A TDD (telephonic device for the deaf) is a telephone communications system that sends text messages typed into them through a typewriter keyboard. It is a text telephone. A TDD is capable of communicating only with other TDDs, or TDD-compatible devices such as a computer with a modem and TDD-compatible software.

The ADA specifies that if one or more telephones are available on a floor, then at least one telephone per floor must be accessible. In addition to the standard clear floor space and range-of-reach requirements, the ADA specifies that all accessible telephones are to be equipped with a volume control. If there are two or more banks of telephones on a floor, at least one telephone per bank must be accessible.

The ADA also requires that if there are four or more interior and exterior public pay telephones at one location, and at least one of the phones is an interior phone, then at least one interior text telephone must be provided. (A text telephone is a telephone that is compatible with telecommunications devices for people who are deaf.) The law also states where there is an interior bank of telephones with three or more public pay telephones, then at least one must be equipped with a shelf and an outlet to accommodate a portable text telephone, a TDD.

Few multi-family housing facilities provide a bank of public pay telephones in common areas because the residents have their own phones available for use. The ADA suggests that if multiple pay phones are made available in the common areas, then at least one needs to have an accessible reach, a volume control and (if four or more phones are available) must accommodate a public text telephone.

Doors and doorways   An accessible primary entrance is not the only area of concern. Even though the Fair Housing Amendments Act concentrates on getting the residents through the door and into their individual units, accessible routes should be provided to all areas.

The Americans with Disabilities Act states that at least 50% of all public entrances must be accessible. This is the minimum requirement. In a well-designed building, all entrances are accessible. The cost of building an accessible doorway need not be any greater than the cost of building an inaccessible doorway.

A Doorless Doorway

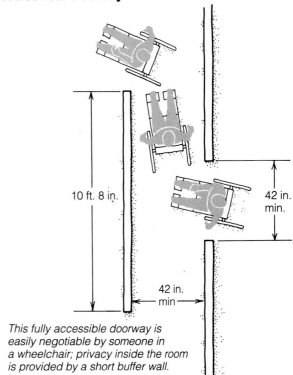

10 ft. 8 in.

42 in. min.

42 in. min.

This fully accessible doorway is easily negotiable by someone in a wheelchair; privacy inside the room is provided by a short buffer wall.

As stated in Chapter 17, automatic doors to the common areas are ideal, but where the expense or placement of these conveniences isn't feasible, as few doors as possible should be used. Obviously if the doors are required for fire retention or child retention in an area, the removal of a door is not an alternative. If a door is not needed, however, an alternative entrance enclosure should be considered. The one shown in the drawing above provides full privacy for a meeting, activity or dining room, but does not require people to have to negotiate their way through a door. If the walls are adequately spaced (minimum of 42 in. apart), an individual in a wheelchair should have absolutely no difficulty entering the room.

Avoid door hardware that requires the use of a tight grip or grasp, such as door knobs and thumb latches. There are so many types and styles of easy-to-use door hardware available today that there is no excuse for using a product that isn't accessible (see pp. 108-111 for more on door hardware). Horizontal push bars, large D-handles, lever handles and push

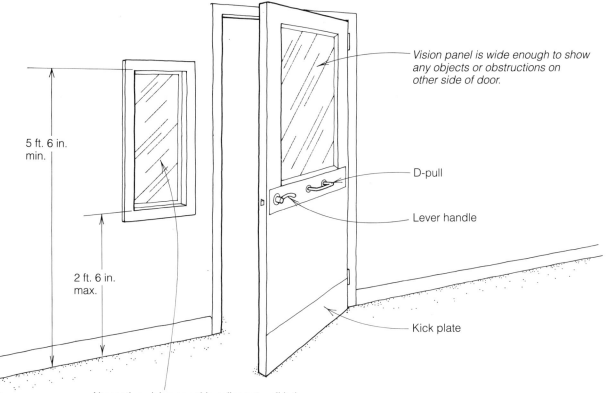

Vision panel is wide enough to show any objects or obstructions on other side of door.

5 ft. 6 in. min.

2 ft. 6 in. max.

D-pull

Lever handle

Kick plate

Alternative vision panel in adjacent wall is large enough to show obstructions on other side of door.

plates will accommodate all door hardware requirements and everyone's needs.

Be sure that there is clear visibility from both sides of doors that are likely to have people entering and exiting at the same time. As shown in the drawing above, these doors should have windows in them, or there should be windows on both sides that allow full visibility of the area adjacent to the door.

Emergency exits People react in widely different ways to emergencies — some remain detached and cool while others lose control. Emergency exits need to be designed for those who panic. Emergency signals and lighting need to tell them what to do and draw them into the appropriate action.

Few designers have time to engage in "what if" scenarios related to the spaces they create. Although it will be many years before we see all the benefits from the changes enforced by the Americans with Disabilities Act, we look forward to them. We know too, however, that we are going to learn some new lessons about emergency egress the hard way.

For example, the ADA states that 50% of the entrances/exits need to be accessible. How do we know that this 50% will be accessible in the event of a fire or after an earthquake? As each space is designed, the emergency egress from each corner of that space should also be designed. What if the person is visually impaired or deaf? Are the egress pathways wide enough to allow the person in a wheelchair an equal chance of escape? Is the room designed with adequate spaces for furnishings so the occupants won't be tempted to block off an escape route to gain extra space within the room?

Ideally, emergency warning systems should have both auditory and visual signals. Resources on

Emergency Exits

Good Escape Routes

Escape route is clear and can be visually established without reliance on signage.

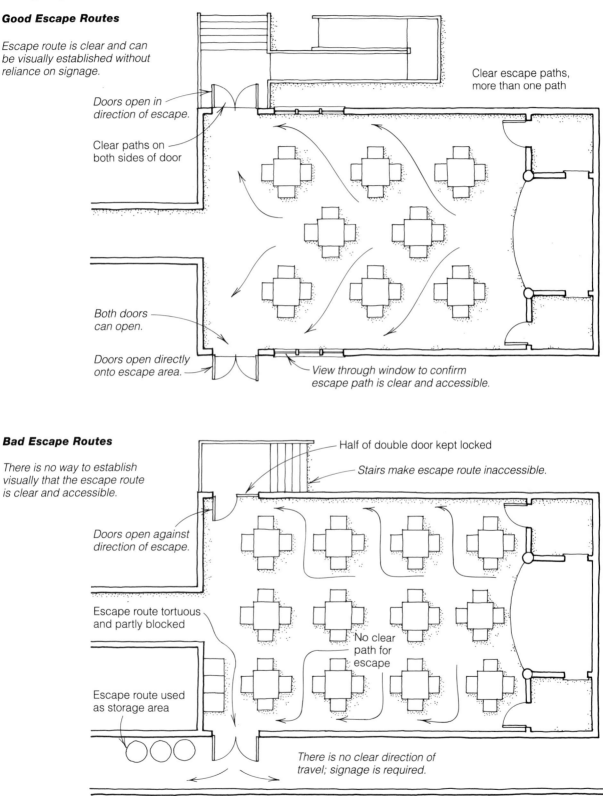

Doors open in direction of escape.

Clear paths on both sides of door

Clear escape paths, more than one path

Both doors can open.

Doors open directly onto escape area.

View through window to confirm escape path is clear and accessible.

Bad Escape Routes

There is no way to establish visually that the escape route is clear and accessible.

Half of double door kept locked

Stairs make escape route inaccessible.

Doors open against direction of escape.

Escape route tortuous and partly blocked

No clear path for escape

Escape route used as storage area

There is no clear direction of travel; signage is required.

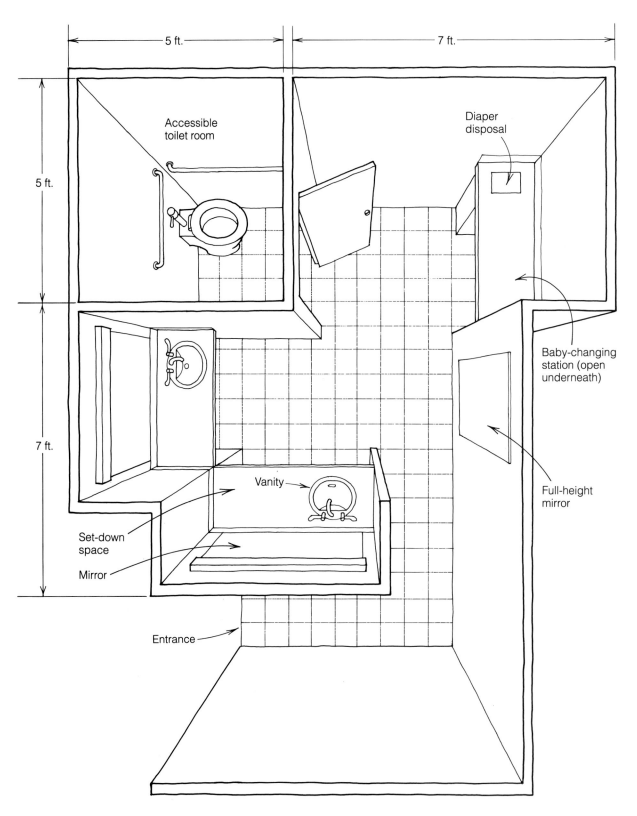

5 ft.

7 ft.

5 ft.

7 ft.

Accessible toilet room

Diaper disposal

Baby-changing station (open underneath)

Full-height mirror

Vanity

Set-down space

Mirror

Entrance

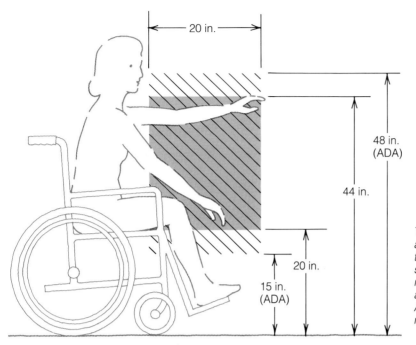

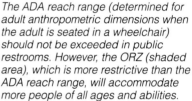

The ADA reach range (determined for adult anthropometric dimensions when the adult is seated in a wheelchair) should not be exceeded in public restrooms. However, the ORZ (shaded area), which is more restrictive than the ADA reach range, will accommodate more people of all ages and abilities.

p. 281 lists companies that make exit signs equipped with a flashing light, an audible signal and lighting to show the escape route. Signs with multiple cues are highly recommended.

GUIDELINES FOR COMMON AREAS

The lobby and corridors are not the only public spaces in multi-family housing. Other common areas include restrooms, elevators, water fountains, laundry rooms and recreational areas. Federal regulations govern the design of these spaces, but the mandated standards are in many cases only minimally acceptable and should be considered as starting points, not goals.

Restrooms Although multi-family housing residences each have their restroom facilities, it is important to provide restrooms in the common areas of the building or buildings. While some people may prefer to retreat to the privacy of their residence, others may not have that option.

Each restroom provided for public use should be accessible (see the drawing on the facing page). Obviously this means that the restroom must be on an accessible path and have an accessible door and accessible fixtures and furnishings. The standards call for at least one toilet stall in each public restroom to be accessible; if more than six stalls are present, then an additional stall 36 in. wide with parallel grab bars on either side of the stall must be provided for non-ambulatory individuals.

The standards (ADAAG and ANSI) relative to toilets and restrooms are rather detailed and specific and cannot be reproduced in their entirety here. (The interested reader can obtain a copy of these standards from the addresses listed on p. 253.) The standards provide several alternatives for stall width, depth and placement of grab rails.

Similar to the optimal reach zone (ORZ) that we defined for use throughout the house, the ADA defines a reach range that should not be exceeded in public restrooms (see the drawing above). The reach ranges defined in the ADA are for adult anthropometric dimensions when the adult is seated in a

Elevator Cars: Minimum Dimensions

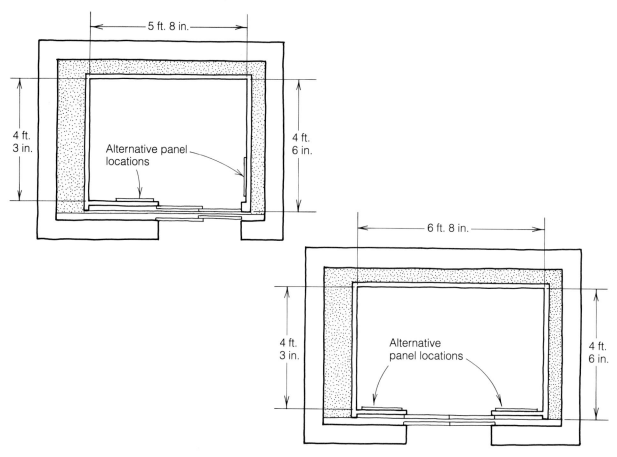

wheelchair. The ORZ is more restrictive (covers a smaller area) than the ADA reach range. We recommend that designers follow the ORZ guidelines rather than the minimal ADA requirements because the ORZ accommodates people of all ages and abilities.

The ADA also calls for controls, dispensers and receptacles to be within the reach range and specifies that electrical and communication systems should be no less than 15 in. above the floor. The toilet-paper dispenser should be no less than 19 in. above the floor and should have a continuous flow of paper, not a sheet or two at a time.

The well-designed public restroom provides a well-lit full-length mirror, so people of all sizes and shapes can make use of it.

The well-designed public restroom provides space for placing a handbag or briefcase in an area

away from the wet sink area, but within reach. Some people cannot reach to the floors and thus may not have any place to set belongings. Besides, it's unpleasant to have to put your things on the floor, but in some places without shelving you have no choice.

The well-designed public restroom recognizes that babies need to be attended to. Baby-changing stations, located in both the male and female restrooms, are conveniences that help parents keep everyone happy. A baby-changing station should be located out of the public eye, with diaper-disposal and cleanup facilities provided.

Elevators   Elevators that serve each level, including mezzanines, are required in new multi-story buildings that are open to the public. Elevators are not required in buildings that do not have public-use areas

Control-Panel Specifications

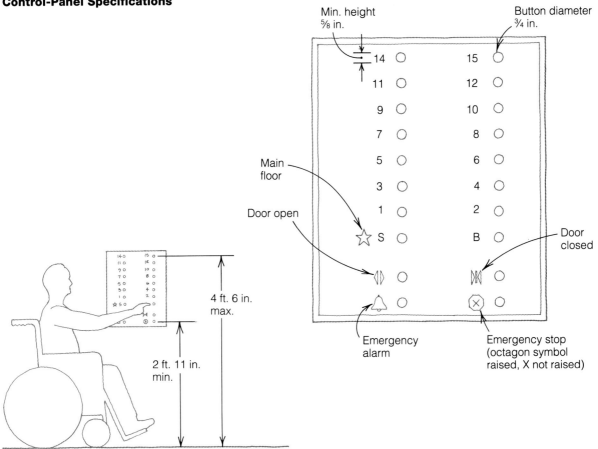

Min. height ⅝ in.

Button diameter ¾ in.

14 ○   15 ○
11 ○   12 ○
9 ○   10 ○
7 ○   8 ○
5 ○   6 ○
3 ○   4 ○
1 ○   2 ○
☆ S ○   B ○

Main floor

Door open

◁▷ ○   ▷◁ ○
🔔 ○   ⊗ ○

Door closed

Emergency alarm

Emergency stop (octagon symbol raised, X not raised)

4 ft. 6 in. max.

2 ft. 11 in. min.

because the Americans with Disabilities Act only covers nonresidential areas and the Fair Housing Amendments Act does not specifically state that multi-storied, multi-family housing must have elevators. It is unusual, though, for apartment buildings with more than two floors not to have elevators.

As the population ages, greater numbers of people will encounter difficulties climbing stairs. A research survey completed in 1983 by the Gallup Organization for Martech, Inc., showed that 17% of people between the ages of 55 and 64 have more difficulty climbing stairs today than they did when they were younger. The percentage increases to 27% for people over the age of 75.

Elevators need to be accessible to people who use wheelchairs, who move slowly, or who have visual or hearing impairments. It will be more convenient for all of us as new elevators are installed that provide control panels with a greater degree of uniformity from elevator to elevator as well as redundant audible and visual cues designating the location of the elevator and doors that close slowly.

Elevator manufacturers should provide a product in compliance with the ADA. The architect or specifier, however, should be certain that the product selected meets the minimums that are specified in the regulations.

Water fountains Drinking fountains need to be located where people can get to them, on an accessible route, with clear floor space (30 in. by 48 in.) and on the same level as the floor (not on a platform).

The ADA suggests that at least half of the drinking fountains should be "accessible," but this is somewhat difficult to define. Some people have difficulty bending over, so an accessible fountain for them is one at a height allowing them to stay erect.

Alternatives to having both high and low drinking fountains (some new models incorporate two heights) include providing a water cooler at an accessible height and paper cups or providing one drinking fountain at a reachable height (36 in.) with easy-to-operate one-handed controls (no gripping or grasping) with a supply of paper cups within reach, as shown in the drawing below.

The ADA has specific guidelines defining the height of the spout (36 in.), the placement of the spout (at the front) and the height of the flow of water (4 in. above the spout) to allow the placement of a cup or glass under the stream. The ADA also asks that wall-mounted units provide at least 27 in. of clear space between the bottom of the apron of the fountain and the floor. There should be at least a 30-in. wide opening 17 in. to 19 in. deep. Manufacturers of drinking fountains that meet the ADA standards are listed in Resources on p. 281.

Personal territory   Clear demarcation of personal territory is critical at the boundary between public and private areas. The sense of control is also supported by having a sense of personal territory. This personal territory may only be a few feet of grass in front of the window of one's apartment, or a few feet in the hallway or a small patio, a parking place or storage area. Wherever the residents stack their claims to space should be clearly demarcated and respected by the other residents and visitors. Many multi-family facilities have outdoor patios and balconies. These spaces need to be clearly differentiated from the pathways provided for community use.

Water Fountains

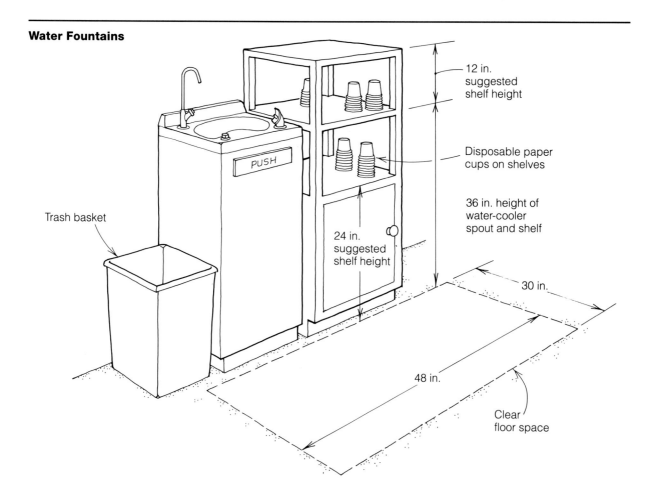

12 in. suggested shelf height

Disposable paper cups on shelves

36 in. height of water-cooler spout and shelf

30 in.

48 in.

Clear floor space

24 in. suggested shelf height

PUSH

Trash basket

Minimum ADA Requirements for Laundry Room

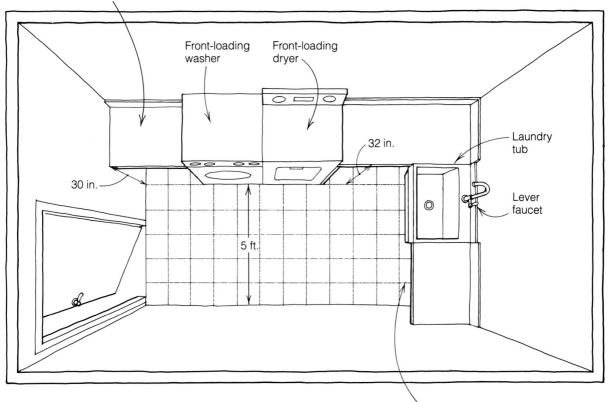

Work surface open
underneath for seated use

Front-loading
washer

Front-loading
dryer

32 in.

Laundry
tub

Lever
faucet

30 in.

5 ft.

*This laundry room meets or
exceeds minimum ADA standards.*

Work surface open underneath
for parallel access to sink

Care should be taken in designing multi-family residences to recognize that the residents will consider the territory just outside of their unit as theirs — whether it is a common pathway or their private balcony. These spaces need to be designed so that there is sufficient territory for others to pass without violating the privacy of the resident. If resting areas or public-use areas are to be part of the pathways, these need to be positioned so that they are clearly separate from the private areas.

Laundry room The laundry room needs a few basics (see the drawing above). There should be ample work space that will allow someone to be seated while working. A countertop or table height of 30 in., with at least 30 in. of open space, will accommodate some-

one in a wheelchair or someone sitting in a conventional chair. At least one front-loading washer should be provided. If the dryers are separated from the washers, a space for setting a basket for collecting the wet clothes to be transferred to the dryer should be provided near the washing machine. A front-loading washer provides an adequate work surface on top.

Adequate clear space (30 in. by 48 in.) needs to be provided in front of the laundry equipment. If the clear space is also a traffic aisle, then a minimum of a 60-in. aisle should be available. A laundry tub or sink may serve a broader range of people if it is installed at a height of 32 in., rather than 36 in. Tall people will have less difficulty using a 32-in. sink than short people or people seated in a wheelchair would have using a 36-in. sink.

Ramped Entrance to Swimming Pool

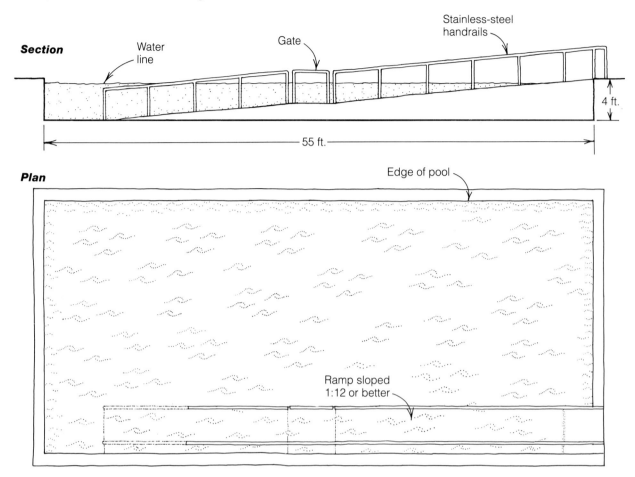

Section

Water line

Gate

Stainless-steel handrails

4 ft.

55 ft.

Plan

Edge of pool

Ramp sloped 1:12 or better

Recreation areas Exercise rooms, game rooms, hot tubs, swimming pools, whirlpools and sauna rooms should be designed to accommodate everyone. Solutions to making these public areas accessible are no more difficult or different than the solutions for making the private areas accessible. The designer should integrate accessibility into decorative features. Accessible entrances, spaces for wheelchairs and other assistive equipment within furnished rooms, electrical outlets and lighting controls, door and cabinet hardware, work surfaces at more than one height, neutrally handed approaches to equipment and clear space are design criteria that should be applied routinely to these public areas.

A hot tub or whirlpool can be designed so that a person in a wheelchair can use it, particularly if there is an accessible path and a convenient "transfer" bench located adjacent to the tub. The transfer bench should be an attractive addition to the decor of the room.

A swimming pool may be equipped with a ramped entrance rather than or in addition to a ladder or steps (see the drawing above). A ramped entrance makes getting into or out of the water easier for a person with mobility problems and for everyone else, too. The opportunities for creative solutions like this are endless. All it takes are designers who understand that differences in human ability are the norm, not the exception.

RESOURCES

Ebco Manufacturing Company
265 North Hamilton Road
P.O. Box 13150
Columbus, OH 43213
(616) 861-1350
Accessible drinking fountains.

Don Gilbert Industries
5611 Krueger Drive
Jonesboro, AR 72401
(800) 825-9041
(501) 932-5622
*Emergency-exit and lighting
systems with light-emitting
diodes, audible emergency beeper
and flashing emergency mode.*

Halsey Taylor
Route 75
Freeport, IL 61032
(815) 235-0066
Accessible drinking fountains.

Herrco Enterprises
1219-B Greenwood Road
Baltimore, MD 21208
(800) 522-3678
(301) 486-7274
*Infrared sensor activated
automatic faucets.*

Hydrotek, USA
927 N. Pennsylvania Avenue
Winter Park, FL 32789
(800) 922-9883
(407) 647-0400
*Infrared sensor activated
automatic faucets.*

Murdock
2488 River Road
Cincinnati, OH 45204
(513) 471-7700
Accessible drinking fountains.

Pawling Corporation
Standard Products Division
One Borden Lane
P.O. Box 200
Wassaic, NY 12592
(914) 373-8181
Recessed floor mats.

Reliable Fire Equipment
Company
12845 South Cicero Avenue
Alsip, IL 60658
(708) 597-4600
*Smoke detectors with strobe
alarm and 85 dB horn.*

Sunroc Corporation
Route 452
Glen Riddle, PA 19037
(215) 459-1000
Accessible drinking fountains.

World Dryer
5700 McDermott Drive
Berkeley, IL 60163
(800) 323-0701
(312) 449-6950
*No-touch warm-air hand dryer
that operates when people put
their hands in front of the dryer.
Sensamatic faucet that dispenses
water when hands are located
under the faucet.*

BIBLIOGRAPHY

INTRODUCTION

American National Standards Institute. 1986. *American national standard for buildings and facilities providing accessibility and usability for physically handicapped people.* New York: ANSI.

Elkind, J. 1990. Incidence of disabilities in the United States. *Human Factors* 32(4): 397-406.

LaPlante M.P., G.E. Hendershot, and A.J. Moss. 1992. Assistive technology devices and home accessibility features: prevalence, payment, need, and trends. Advance data, No. 217, September 16, 1992 from *Vital and Health Statistics of the Centers for Disease Control,* National Center for Health Statistics, U.S. Department of Health and Human Services.

Pynoos, J., Cohen, E., Davis, L., and S. Bernhardt. 1987. "Home modifications: improvements that extend independence." In *Housing the aged: design directives and policy considerations.* New York: Elsevier Science Publishing Company. 277-303.

U.S. Bureau of the Census. 1989. *Projections of the population of the United States, by age, sex, and race: 1988 to 2080.* By G. Spencer. Current Population Reports Series P-25m No. 1018 (January).

U.S. Senate Special Committee on Aging. 1991. *Aging America: trends and projections.* Washington, D.C.

Vanderheiden, G.C. 1990. Thirty-something million: should they be exceptions? *Human Factors* 32:383-396.

Wylde, M.A. 1990. Final report: development of design criteria and performance standards for barrier-free environments. Washington, D.C.: National Institute for Disability Rehabilitation and Research, Research and Demonstration Program Grant No. G008635202-88.

CHAPTER 1

Baker, G.T., B.C. Griffith, F. Carmone, and C.K. Krauser. 1982. *Report on products and services to enhance the independence of the elderly.* Philadelphia: The Commonwealth of Pennsylvania, Department of Aging.

Cornoni-Huntley, J., D.B. Brock, A.M. Ostfeld, J.O. Taylor, and R.B. Wallace. 1986. *Established populations for epidemiologic studies of the elderly.* NIH Pub. No. 86-2443. Washington, D.C.: National Institute on Aging.

The Disability Rag. Box 145, Louisville, KY 40201. A valuable bimonthly magazine on disability issues published by activists. $16/yr.

Evans, D.A., et al. 1989. Prevalence of Alzheimer's disease in a community population of older persons. *Journal of the American Medical Association* 262, No. 18.

Kellor, M., R. Kondrasuk, I. Iverson, J. Frost, N. Silberberg, and M. Hoglund. 1971. Technical manual: *Hand strength and dexterity tests.* Pub. No. 721. Minneapolis: Sister Kenny Institute.

LaPlante M.P., G.E. Hendershot, and A.J. Moss. 1992. Assistive technology devices and home accessibility features: prevalence, payment, need, and trends. Advance data, No. 217, September 16, 1992 from *Vital and Health Statistics of the Centers for Disease Control,* National Center for Health Statistics, U.S. Department of Health and Human Services.

MarkeTrak Survey. 1993. Hearing healthcare in the media. *The Marketing Edge* Vol. V, No. 1. Alexandria, Va.: Hearing Industries Association.

National Aeronautics and Space Administration. 1978. *Anthropometric source book. Vol. I: Anthropometry for designers.* Pub. 1024. Washington, D.C.: NASA.

—————. 1978. *Anthropometric source book. Vol. II: A handbook of anthropometric data.* Pub. 1024. Washington, D.C.: NASA.

—————. 1978. *Anthropometric source book. Vol. III: Annotated bibliography of anthropometry.* Pub. 1024. Washington, D.C.: NASA.

National Center for Health Statistics. 1990. Current estimates from the National Health Interview Survey, 1989. *Vital and Health Statistics of the Centers for Disease Control,* Series 10. No. 176.

Pheasant, S. 1986. *Bodyspace: anthropometry, ergonomics and design.* Philadelphia: Taylor & Francis.

Woodson, Wesley E. 1981. *Human factors design handbook.* New York: McGraw-Hill.

CHAPTER 2

Buttery, H. 1988. The cost of independence. *Design* 471:30-31.

Calkins, M.P. 1988. *Design for dementia: planning environments for the elderly and the confused.* Owing Mills, Md.: National Health Publishing.

Cary, J.R. 1978. *How to create interiors for the disabled.* New York: Pantheon.

Casper, D.E. 1987. *Interiorscapes of houses: design and construction, 1983-1987*. Monticello, Ill.: Vance Bibliographies.

Chasin, J. *Home in a wheelchair: house design ideas for easier wheelchair living*. Washington, D.C.: Paralyzed Veterans of America.

Code bodies nix universal design amendments. 1992. *Journal of Light Construction* December 1992.

Cotler, S. 1974. *Making facilities accessible to the physically handicapped*. Albany, N.Y.: State University Construction Fund.

Dunning, G. 1989. *Architecture of accessibility: planning for the disabled — a partially annotated bibliography*. Monticello, Ill.: Vance Bibliographies.

Faletti, M.V. 1984. "Human factors research and functional environments for the aged" in *Elderly people and the environment*. Altman, I., M.P. Lawton, and J.F. Wohlwill, eds. New York: Plenum Press.

Health and Welfare Canada. 1985. *Independent living aids*. Ottawa: Health Service and Promotion Branch.

Liebrock, S., and S. Behar. 1993. *Beautiful barrier-free: a visual guide to accessibility*. New York: Van Nostrand Reinhold.

NAHB Research Center. 2nd ed. 1992. *The directory of accessible building products*. Upper Marlboro, Md.: NAHB Research Center.

National Library Service for the Blind and Physically Handicapped. 1983. *Accessibility: designing buildings for the needs of handicapped persons*. Washington, D.C.: Library of Congress.

Olson, S.C., and D.K. Meredith. 1973. *Wheelchair interiors*. Chicago: National Easter Seal Society for Crippled Children and Adults.

Pastalan, L.A., and M.E. Cowart, eds. 1989. *Lifestyles and housing of older adults: the Florida experience*. New York: The Haworth Press.

Raschko, B.B. 1991. *Housing interiors for the disabled and elderly*. New York: Van Nostrand Reinhold.

Silvey, T.F. 1955. Technology and cultural lag. *Adult Leadership* November, 1955.

Sorensen, R.J. 1979. *Design for accessibility*. New York: McGraw-Hill.

Struyk, R.J. and H.M. Katsura. 1988. *Aging at home: how the elderly adjust their housing without moving*. New York: The Haworth Press.

U.S. Veterans Administration. 1978. *Handbook for design: specially adapted housing*. Washington, D.C.: USVA.

CHAPTER 3

The Accessible Housing Design File. 1991. Produced by Barrier Free Environments Inc., with support from the National Institute for Disability Rehabilitation and Research. New York: Van Nostrand Reinhold.

CHAPTER 4

Alexander, C., S. Ishikawa, and M. Silverstein. 1977. *A Pattern Language*. New York: Oxford University Press.

American Association of Retired Persons. 1990. *Understanding senior housing for the 1990s: an American Association of Retired Persons survey of consumer preferences, concerns and needs*. Washington, D.C.: AARP.

Corlett, E., C. Hutcheson, M. Delugan, and J. Rogozenski. 1972. Ramps or stairs? *Applied Ergonomics* 3(4) 195-201.

Reschovsky, J.D., and S.J. Newman. 1991. Home upkeep and housing quality of older homeowners. *Journal of Gerontology: Social Sciences* Vol 46 (5): 288-297.

Southern Building Code Congress International. 1985. *Standard Building Code*. Birmingham, Ala.: SBCCI.

CHAPTER 5

Alexander, C., S. Ishikawa, and M. Silverstein. 1977. *A Pattern Language*. New York: Oxford University Press.

American Association of Retired Persons. 1990. *Understanding senior housing for the 1990s: an American Association of Retired Persons survey of consumer preferences, concerns and needs*. Washington, D.C.: AARP.

Brock, H., and G. Mefford. 1990. *Gardening for all*. Lansing, Mich.: I PAM Assistance Centre.

Corlett, E., C. Hutcheson, M. Delugan, and J. Rogozenski. 1972. Ramps or stairs? *Applied Ergonomics* 3(4) 195-201.

Cox, J., and M. Cox. 1987. *Flowers for all seasons: a guide to colorful trees, shrubs, and vines*. Emmaus, Pa.: Rodale Press.

Dirr, M.A. 1983. *A manual of woody landscape plants*. 3rd ed. Champaign, Ill.: Stipes Publishing.

Hudak, J. 1980. *Trees for every purpose*. New York: McGraw-Hill.

Kramer, J. 1973. *Gardening without stress and strain*. New York: Charles Scribner's Sons.

Little, E.L. 1980. *The Audubon Society field guide to North American trees, eastern region*. New York: Alfred A. Knopf.

——— . 1980. *The Audubon Society field guide to North American trees, western region*. New York: Alfred A. Knopf.

Nickels, Karen. Out of print. *An accessible entrance ramp.* Madison, Wis.: The Design Coalition.

Reschovsky, J.D., and S.J. Newman. 1991. Home upkeep and housing quality of older homeowners. *Journal of Gerontology: Social Sciences* Vol. 46(5): 288-297.

Smith, E. 1991. *Entryways: creating attractive, inexpensive no-step entrances to houses.* Atlanta: Concrete Change.

Steinfeld, E. 1979. *Access to the built environment: a review of literature.* Washington: D.C.: U.S. Department of Housing and Urban Development.

————. 1979. Designing entrances and internal circulation to meet barrier-free goals. *Architectural Record* 166:65-67.

————. 1979. Designing the site to meet barrier-free goals. *Architectural Record* 165:69-71.

————. 1980. *Accessible buildings for people with walking and reaching limitations.* Washington: D.C.: U.S. Department of Housing and Urban Development.

Union Carbide Agricultural Products Company. 1985. *A guide to gardening for people with special needs.* Research Triangle Park, N.C.: Union Carbide Agricultural Products Company.

Wyman, D. 1969. *Trees for American gardens.* New York: Macmillan.

CHAPTER 6

American Association of Retired Persons. 1990. *Report of a study of the use of wheelchairs by adults 55 years and older* technical report. Washington, D.C.: AARP.

————. 1990. *Understanding senior housing for the 1990s: an American Association of Retired Persons survey of consumer preferences, concerns and needs.* Washington, D.C.: AARP.

————. 1992. *Personal emergency response systems* technical report. Washington, D.C.: AARP.

Architectural and Transportation Barriers Compliance Board. 1988. *Toward an accessible environment: effective research.* Washington, D.C.: Architectural and Transportation Barriers Compliance Board.

————. 1990. *Slip resistant surfaces advisory guidelines.* Washington, D.C.: Architectural and Transportation Barriers Compliance Board.

————. 1990. *Visual alarms.* Washington, D.C.: Architectural and Transportation Barriers Compliance Board.

Ballast, D.K. 1987. *Carpet use in architecture: technical and design considerations.* Monticello, Ill.: Vance Bibliographies.

Bender, M.B. 1975. "The incidence and type of perceptual deficiencies in the aged." In *Neurological and sensory disorders in the elderly.* Fields, W.S., ed. New York, Stratton Intercontinental Medical Book Corp.

Bigazzi, P.E. 1988. Autoimmunity induced by chemicals. *Journal of Toxicology and Clinical Toxicology* 26: 125-126.

Bowe, F. 1984. *Alarms.* Washington, D.C.: Architectural and Transportation Barriers Compliance Board.

Boyce, P. 1981. *Human factors in lighting.* New York: Macmillan.

Buffalo Organization for Social and Technological Innovation (BOSTI). 1982. *Accidents and aging.* PB84-158849. Springfield, Va.: U.S. Department of Commerce, National Technical Information Service.

Dadd D.L. 1986. *The nontoxic home.* Los Angeles: Jeremy P. Tarcher.

Dickey, R., and S.H. Shealey. 1987. Using technology to control the environment. *American Journal of Occupational Therapy* 41(11).

Environmental Defense Fund. 1987. *Radon: the citizens' guide.* New York: Environmental Defense Fund.

Garland, J.D. 1977. *National electrical code reference book.* Englewood Cliffs, N.J.: Prentice-Hall.

Greenberg, S., ed. 1991. *The healthy house catalog.* Cleveland: The Healthy House.

Henry, C.J., L. Fishbein, W. Meggs, N. Ashford, P. Schulte, H. Anderson, J. Osborne, and D. Sepkovic. 1991. Approaches for assessing health risks from complex mixtures in indoor air: a panel overview. *Environmental Health Perspectives* 95:135-143.

Hiatt, L.G. 1986. *Smart houses for older people: general considerations. Washington, D.C.:* U.S. Administration on Aging.

Home Ventilating Institute. 1986. *Home Ventilating Guide.* Pub. 12. Arlington Heights, Ill.: Home Ventilating Institute.

Hughes, P.C., and R. Neer. 1981. Lighting for the elderly: a psychobiological approach to lighting. *Human Factors* 23(1):65-85.

Institute of Electrical and Electronics Engineers. 1977. *National electrical safety code.* New York: IEEE.

Jackson, R., M.R. Sears, R. Beaglehole, and H.H. Rea. 1988. International trends in asthma mortality. *Chest* 94:914-918.

Kane, D.N. 1985. *Environmental hazards to young children.* Phoenix: The Oryx Press.

Klerman, G.L., and M.M. Weissman. 1989. Increasing rates of depression. *Journal of the American Medical Association* 261:2229-2235.

Lynn, B.S. 1980. Age differences in the severity and outcome of burns. *Journal of the American Geriatrics Society* 28:118-122.

MacEachern, D. 1990. *Save our planet: 750 everyday ways you can help clean up the earth.* New York: Dell.

Merz, B. 1982. Lighting in homes: a study of quality and quantity. *Lighting in Australia* 2(4):26-28.

National Center for Health Statistics. 1990. Current estimates from the National Health Statistics, 1989. *Vital and Health Statistics of the Centers for Disease Control,* Series 10, No. 176.

National Library Service for the Blind and Physically Handicapped. 1981. *Gardening for handicapped and elderly persons.* Washington, D.C.: Library of Congress.

Palmquist, R.E. 1984. *Guide to the 1984 national electrical code.* Boston: G.K. Hall.

Small Homes Council-Building Research Council. 1983. *Noise control.* Vol. 5, No. 4. Champaign, Ill.: University of Illinois.

Templer, J., D. Lewis, and J. Sanford. 1983. *Ground and floor surface treatments.* Washington, D.C.: Architectural and Transportation Barriers Compliance Board.

U.S. Environmental Protection Agency, Office of Air and Radiation. 1988. *The inside story: a guide to indoor air quality.* Washington, D.C.: EPA.

Vaughan, T.L. C. Strader, S. Davis, and J.R. Daling. 1986. Formaldehyde and cancers of the pharynx, sinus and nasal cavity: II. residential exposures. *International Journal of Cancer* 38: 695-688.

Weale, R.A. 1961. Retinal illumination and age. *Transactions of the Illuminating Engineering Society* 26:95.

Wing, C. 1990. *Visual handbook of building and remodeling.* Emmaus, Pa.: Rodale Press.

Wurtman, R.J. 1975. The effects of light on man and other animals. *Annual Review of Physiology* 37:467-483.

CHAPTER 7

Barrier free environments. 1981. *Doors & Entrances.* Washington, D.C.: Access Information.

Howell, S. 1976. *Windows.* Cambridge, Mass.: Department of Architecture, Massachusetts Institute of Technology.

Ireton, K. 1989. Pocket doors: should you buy a kit or build your own? *Fine Homebuilding* 54:63-67.

Pearson, R.G., and M.G. Joost. 1983. *Egress behavior response times of handicapped and elderly subjects to simulated residential fire situations.* Washington, D.C.: U.S. Department of Commerce.

Smith, A.C. 1985. Poor building designs hinder safe emergency escape by handicapped. *Occupational Health & Safety* October 1985: 63-65.

Steinfeld, E. 1979. Designing entrances and internal circulation to meet barrier-free goals. *Architectural Record* 166:65-67.

Watrous, L. 1975. Talking fire protection systems: protecting living units for handicapped. *Fire Journal.* May 1975: 80-81.

Woods, W. 1984. *Windows.* Washington, D.C.: Architectural and Transportation Barriers Compliance Board.

CHAPTER 8

American Association of Retired Persons. 1992. *Cane technical report.* Washington, D.C.: AARP.

Buffalo Organization for Social and Technological Innovation (BOSTI). 1982. *Accidents and aging.* Washington, D.C.: U.S. Department of Commerce, National Technical Information Service.

Corlett, E., C. Hutcheson, M. Delugan, and J. Rogozenski. 1972. Ramps or stairs? *Applied Ergonomics* 3(4) 195-201.

Cornoni-Huntley, J., D.B. Brock, A.M. Ostfeld, J.O. Taylor, and R.B. Wallace. 1986. *Established populations for epidemiologic studies of the elderly.* NIH Pub. No. 86-2443. Washington, D.C.: National Institute on Aging.

Cotler, S. 1981. *Elevators and lifts.* Access Information Bulletin. Washington, D.C.: National Center for a Barrier Free Environment, Paralyzed Veterans of America.

Czaja, S. 1983. *Hand anthropometrics.* Washington, D.C.: Architectural and Transportation Compliance Board.

Donoghue, E.A. 1986. Elevators for the handicapped. *Building Standards* September-October 1986:18-22.

Johnson, D.A. 1991. Factors to consider when investigating accidents on stairs. *Safety News* August: 1,3,17.

Kiewel, H.D. 1981. *Ramps, stairs, and floor treatments.* Access Information Bulletin. Washington, D.C.: National Center for a Barrier Free Environment, Paralyzed Veterans of America.

NEISS Data Highlights. 1981. Injuries associated with selected consumer products treated in hospital emergency departments. *National Injury Information Clearinghouse* Vol. 15, Jan.-Dec. 1991. Washington, DC.: National Electronic Injury Surveillance System, U.S. Consumer Product Safety Commission. Directorate for Epidemiology.

Shepherd, J. 1982. Floor to floor service (elevators and stairlifts). *Royal Institute of British Architects Journal (RIBAJ)* 1982.

U.S. Bureau of the Census. 1990. *U.S. population estimates by age, sex, race and Hispanic origin: 1989.* By Frederick W. Hollman. Current Population Reports Series P-25, No. 1057 (March 1990).

U.S. Consumer Product Safety Commission. 1975. *The elderly and stairway accidents.* Washington, D.C.: U.S. Consumer Product Safety Commission.

Wild, D., U.S.L. Nayak, and B. Isaacs. 1981. Description, classification and prevention of falls in old people at home. *Rheumatology and Rehabilitation* 20:153-159.

CHAPTER 9

Aids to independent living. 1983. Benton Harbor, Mich.: Whirlpool Corporation Appliance Information Service.

Clark, Sam. 1983. *The motion-minded kitchen: step by step procedures for designing and building the kitchen you want with the space and money you have.* Boston: Houghton Mifflin.

Designs for independent living. 1991. Benton Harbor, Mich.: Whirlpool Corporation Appliance Information Service.

Domestic kitchen design feedback. 1984. *Architect's Journal (AJ).* 180:61-66.

Gilbreth, L., O.M. Thomas, and E. Clymer. 1954, 1960. *Management in the home: happier living through saving time and energy.* New York: Dodd, Mead.

Grandjean, E. 1973. *Ergonomics of the home.* New York: John Wiley & Sons.

Howie, P.M. 1968. *A pilot study of disabled housewives in their kitchens.* London: Disabled Living Foundation.

Maytag Company kitchen design survey of 100 certified kitchen designers. New York: Gabrielle Bamberger Public Relations.

National Kitchen and Bath Association. 1992. New kitchen guidelines. *Kitchen and Bath Business.* June 1992: 48-51.

Orleans, P. 1981. *Kitchens.* Access Information Bulletin. Washington, D.C.: National Center for a Barrier Free Environment.

Paralyzed Veterans of America. 1973. *The wheelchair in the kitchen.* Washington, D.C.: Paralyzed Veterans of America.

Perchuk, F., and E. Rand. 1990. Kitchens for the '90s. *Interior Design* 61:170-174.

U.S. Bureau of the Census. 1990. *Marital status and living arrangements: March, 1989.* Current Population Reports Series P-20, No. 445 (June 1990).

Vance, M. 1989. *Kitchens: recent journal articles.* Monticello, Ill.: Vance Bibliographies.

Ward, J.S., and N.S. Kirk. 1970. The relationship between some anthropometric dimensions and preferred working surface heights in the kitchen. *Ergonomics* 13(6) 783-797.

Yuen, M. September 1991. *American kitchen life survey conducted for the Palmolive liquid gel automatic dishwasher detergent product group.* New York: Market Response.

CHAPTER 10

American National Standards Institute. 1986. *American national standard for buildings and facilities providing accessibility and usability for physically handicapped people.* New York: ANSI.

Barrier Free Environments. 1985. *Adaptable housing.* Access Information Bulletin. Washington, D.C.: Paralyzed Veterans of America.

Bathroom Basics. August 1991. *Which?.* London: Consumer's Association Ltd.

Bobrick. 1978. *Planning guide for designing washroom facilities for the physically handicapped.* Corte Madera, Calif.: Bobrick Washroom Equipment.

Casper, D.E. 1987. *Architecture of the bathroom: projects and remodeling, 1977-1987.* Monticello, Ill.: Vance Bibliographies.

Cochran, W. 1981. *Restrooms.* Access Information Bulletin. Washington, D.C.: National Center for a Barrier Free Environment, Paralyzed Veterans of America.

Cornoni-Huntley, J., D.B. Brock, A.M. Ostfeld, J.O. Taylor, and R.B. Wallace. 1986. *Established populations for epidemiologic studies of the elderly.* NIH Pub. No. 86-2443. Washington, D.C.: National Institute on Aging.

Gregg, M. 1988. *Public health surveillance of 1990 injury control objectives for the nation.* Vol. 37/SS-1. Washington, D.C.: U.S. Department of Health and Human Services.

Hogue C.C. 1982. Injury in late life: (part I) epidemiology. *Journal of the American Geriatrics Society* 30:183-190.

_____ . 1982. Injury in late life: (part II) prevention. *Journal of the American Geriatrics Society* 30(4), 276-280.

Host-Jablonski, Lou, and Karen Nickels. 1991. *The Accessible Bathroom*. Madison, Wis.: The Design Coalition

Kira, Alexander. 1976. *The Bathroom*. New York: Penguin Books.

Lee, P.S. 1983. Preventing patient falls. *Nursing* 13:119-120.

Muto, W.H. 1977. Human factors considerations in the design and evaluation of bathroom fixtures for the handicapped. *Proceedings of the Human Factors Society, 21st Annual Meeting.*

National Institutes of Health. 1988. *Urinary incontinence in adults,* Vol. 7, No. 5.

National Kitchen and Bath Association. 1992. New kitchen guidelines. *Kitchen and Bath Business* June 1992: 48-51.

Schletty, A.V. 1984. Home injuries are no accident! *Aging* April-May.

Thornely, G., M.A. Chamberlain and V. Wright. 1977. Evaluation of aids and equipment for the bath and toilet. *British Journal of Occupational Therapy* October 1977, 40:243-246.

U.S. Consumer Product Safety Commission. 1983. *Injury data and related literature pertaining to persons 65 years of age and older.* Washington, D.C.: U.S. Consumer Product Safety Commission.

Wild, D., U.S.L. Nayak, and B. Isaacs. 1981. Description, classification and prevention of falls in old people at home. *Rheumatology and Rehabilitation* 20:153-159.

CHAPTER 11

Parsons, H. 1981. Residential design for the aging (for example, the bedroom). *Human Factors* 23(1), 39-58.

CHAPTER 12

Amola, G. *You can do family laundry — with hand limitations*. Storrs, Conn.: University of Connecticut, School of Home Economics. Copies available from NARIC, 8455 Colesville Rd., Suite 935, Silver Spring, MD 20910-3319.

CHAPTER 13

Blasch, B. and L. Hiatt. 1983. *Orientation and wayfinding*. Washington, D.C.: Architectural and Transportation Barriers Compliance Board.

Graff, J. 1985. *Adapting interiors and furnishings for the disabled*. Madison, Wis.: University of Wisconsin-Extension.

Harvey, M. 1984. *Help yourself! hints from the handicapped*. Ottawa: Health and Welfare Canada, Disabled Persons Unit, Social Service Programs Branch.

Hogue C.C. 1982. Injury in late life: (part I) epidemiology. *Journal of the American Geriatrics Society* 30:183-190.

——— . 1982. Injury in late life: (part II) prevention. *Journal of the American Geriatrics Society* 30(4), 276-280.

Housing Resource Center. 1990. *Remodeling and building for accessibility sourcebook,* 2nd ed. Cleveland: Homewise Housing Resource Center.

LaPlante M.P., G.E. Hendershot, and A.J. Moss. 1992. Assistive technology devices and home accessibility features: prevalence, payment, need, and trends. Advance data, No. 217, September 16, 1992 from *Vital and Health Statistics of the Centers for Disease Control,* National Center for Health Statistics, U.S. Department of Health and Human Services.

Phillips, R.H., and J.P.S. Salmen. February 1983. Building in accessibility: design and product specification. *The Construction Specifier,* February 1983. Reprint available from 61 Madison St., Alexandria, VA 22314.

Pynoos, J., and E. Cohen. 1992. *The perfect fit: creative ideas for a safe & livable home*. Washington, D.C.: American Association of Retired Persons.

Rickman, L. 1991. *A comprehensive approach to retrofitting homes for a lifetime*. Upper Marlboro, Md.: NAHB Research Center.

CHAPTER 16

American National Standards Institute. 1986. *American national standard for buildings and facilities providing accessibility and usability for physically handicapped people*. New York, ANSI.

Federal Register. *Fair housing accessibility guidelines: proposed rule*. Washington, D.C.: Department of Housing and Urban Development, Friday, June 15, 1990.

——— . *Fair housing accessibility guidelines: design guidelines for accessible/ adaptable buildings*. Washington, D.C.: Department of Housing and Urban Development, 56(44), Wednesday, March 6, 1991.

——— . *Fair housing accessibility guidelines: technical corrections*. Washington, D.C.: Department of Housing and Urban Development, 56(121), Monday, June 24, 1991.

——— . *Nondiscrimination on the basis of disability by public accommodations and in commercial facilities: final rule*. Washington, D.C.: Department of Justice, Friday, July 26, 1991.

National Assisted Housing Management Association. 1991. *Fair housing and Section 504: a guidebook for managers of assisted housing.* Alexandria, Va.: National Assisted Management Association.

Southern Building Code Congress International. 1985. *Standard building code.* Birmingham, Ala.: SBCCI.

Wooten, K.L. 1992. *Americans with Disabilities Act, Title III public accommodations compliance manual.* Nashville, Tenn: M. Lee Smith Publishers.

CHAPTER 17

The ADA: access state and local government. 1991. Jackson, Heights, N.Y.: Eastern Paralyzed Veterans Association.

Barrier free design: the law. 1991. Jackson, Heights, N.Y.: Eastern Paralyzed Veterans Association.

Blasch, B., and L. Hiatt. 1983. *Orientation and wayfinding.* Washington, D.C.: Architectural and Transportation Barriers Compliance Board.

Kearney, Deborah. 1992. *The new ADA: compliance and costs.* Kingston, Mass.: RS Means.

People with disabilities explain it all for you: your guide to the public accommodations requirements of the ADA. 1992. Mary Johnson and the editors of *The Disability Rag,* eds. Louisville, Ky.: Avocado Press.

Understanding the Americans with Disabilities Act. 1991. Jackson, Heights, N.Y.: Eastern Paralyzed Veterans Association.

CHAPTER 18

Altman, I., M.P. Lawton, and J.F. Wohlwil, eds. 1984. *Elderly people and the environment.* New York, Plenum Press.

American Institute of Architects. 1985. *Design for aging: an architect's guide.* Washington, DC: The American Institute of Architects Foundation.

Lawton, M.P. 1986. "Environment and aging." In *Classics in aging.* Reprinted, Series I, Vol. I. Albany, N.Y.: Center for the Study of Aging.

Martech Associates. 1984. *Product needs of older Americans.* Portland, Ore.: Martech Associates.

Moos, R.H., and S. Lemke. 1980. Assessing the physical and architectural features of sheltered care settings. *Journal of Gerontology* 35:571-583.

Newcomer, R.J., M.P. Lawton, and T.O. Byerts, eds. 1986. *Housing an aging society: issues, alternatives and policy.* New York: Van Nostrand Reinhold.

Ontario Association of Homes for the Aged. 1984. *Designed for seniors: guidelines in the planning process for enriched housing.* Woodbridge, Ont.: OAHA.

Pynoos, J., and V. Regnier. 1987. *Housing the aged: design directives and policy considerations.* New York: Elsevier Science Publishing Company.

Zeisel, J., G. Epp., and S. Demos. 1978. *Low-rise housing for older people.* No. 023-000-0043408. Washington, D.C.: U.S. Government Printing Office.

INDEX

S

T

EDITOR: **Jeff Beneke**

DESIGNER/LAYOUT ARTIST: **Henry Roth**

ILLUSTRATOR: **Vince Babak**

COPY/PRODUCTION EDITOR: **Ruth Dobsevage**

ART ASSISTANT: **Iliana Koehler**

TYPEFACE: **ITC Stone Serif**

PAPER: **Warren Patina Matte, 70 lb., neutral pH**

PRINTER: **Arcata Graphics/Hawkins, New Canton, Tennessee**